D0560029

INTIMATE STRATEGIES

OF THE

CIVIL WAR

OTHER BOOKS BY THE EDITORS

By Carol K. Bleser

Tokens of Affection: The Letters of a Planter's Daughter in the Old South
In Joy and in Sorrow: Women, Family, and Marriage in the Victorian South
Secret and Sacred: The Diaries of James Henry Hammond, a Southern Slaveholder
The Hammonds of Redcliffe
The Promised Land:
The History of the South Carolina Land Commission, 1869–1890

By Lesley J. Gordon

General George E. Pickett in Life and Legend

INTIMATE STRATEGIES

OF THE

CIVIL WAR

Military Commanders and Their Wives

EDITED BY

CAROL K. BLESER AND LESLEY J. GORDON

OXFORD

UNIVERSITY PRESS

2001

973.780922
I 61

OXFORD
UNIVERSITY PRESS

Oxford New York
Athens Auckland Bangkok Bogotá Buenos Aires
Cape Town Chennai Dar es Salaam Delhi Florence Hong Kong Istanbul
Karachi Kolkata Kuala Lumpur Madrid Melbourne Mexico City Mumbai
Nairobi Paris São Paulo Singapore Taipei Tokyo Toronto Warsaw

and associated companies in

Berlin Ibadan

Copyright © 2001 by Oxford University Press, Inc.

Published by Oxford University Press, Inc.
198 Madison Avenue, New York, NY 10016

Oxford is a registered trademark of Oxford University Press

All rights reserved. No part of this publication may be reproduced, stored
in a retrieval system, or transmitted, in any form or by any means, electronic,
mechanical, photocopying, recording, or otherwise, without the prior
permission of Oxford University Press.

Library of Congress Cataloging-in-Publication Data

Intimate strategies of the Civil War : military commanders and their wives
/ edited by Carol K. Bleser and Lesley J. Gordon
p. cm.
ISBN 0-19-511509-0
1. United States—History—Civil War, 1861–1865—Biography. 2. Generals—United
States—Biography. 3. Generals—Confederate States of America—Biography.
4. Generals' spouses—United States—Biography. 5. Generals' spouses—Confederate
States of America—Biography. 6. Married people—United States—Biography.
7. Married people—Confederate States of America—Biography. 8. United States. Army—
Biography. 9. Confederate States of America. Army—Biography.
I. Bleser, Carol K. Rothrock.   II. Gordon, Lesley J. (Lesley Jill).

E467 .I58 2001 973.7'8'0922—dc21   [B]   2001036064

1 3 5 7 9 8 6 4 2
Printed in the United States of America
on acid-free paper

To Andrew J. Weiland, M.D., with boundless gratitude

CKB

To the memory of Jill E. Hungerford, Ph.D. (1965–1999)

LJG

University Libraries
Carnegie Mellon University
Pittsburgh, PA 15213-3890

CONTENTS

PART TWO: UNION MARRIAGES

Historians have just begun to explore the ties between the home front and the battlefront during the Civil War, especially in the realm of marriage and family. Traditional Civil War narratives emphasize the sacrifices wives made for their husbands, both North and South. Yet, many scholars have begun to question these popular portrayals and wonder whether the trauma caused by civil war did not have a negative effect on the private lives of individuals. War brought excessive violence, death, fear, deprivation, and long separations to individuals as much as to the nation. Did war's trauma also rock the very foundation of family and intimate relationships? In addition, how much effect did personal relationships have on the war's outcome? For instance, how much influence did officers' wives have on their husbands' military decisions? *Intimate Strategies of the Civil War: Military Commanders and Their Wives* seeks answers to these questions.

Some recent Civil War historians have argued that the common soldiers' ideology was closely aligned to their conceptions of home and family, and others have posited that unhappy Confederate wives and mothers helped break the South's will to fight.[1] Still much work remains to be done. As recently as 1998, in James M. McPherson and William J. Cooper, Jr.'s edited collection, *Writing the Civil War: The Quest to Understand*, scholars complained of the continuing gaps in the literature. James L. Roark observed: "Analysis of the impact of the war on southern family relationships and behavior, including marriage patterns, child rearing, economic responsibilities, and the distribution of power within the household remains in its infancy."[2] Philip Shaw Paludan similarly commented: "Four years of slaughter, 620,000 deaths, and half a million wounded, tens of thousands of amputations surely meant something significant about family life." However, he adds, "There is little writing by historians to tell us exactly what."[3] *Intimate Strategies of the Civil War* helps us to understand more deeply "exactly what" the impact of the Civil War was on personal relationships, family, and marriage in mid-nineteenth-century America.

This book is a collection of twelve essays, each written specifically for this book, each focusing on the marriage of a prominent Civil War commander and his wife, and each written by a scholar with a special knowledge of the individuals. Thus, this collection is on the one hand cohesive and tightly focused on its subject, while on the other hand it offers a very wide range of views and interpretations. The marriages considered are those of five Confederate generals, the president of the Confederacy, who was a would-be general, five Union generals, and one Union admiral. They include Jefferson Davis, Robert E. Lee, Thomas (Stonewall) Jackson, George E. Pickett, Richard Ewell, Josiah Gorgas, Ulysses S. Grant, William T. Sherman, Joshua Lawrence Chamberlain, George A. Custer, John C. Frémont, and Samuel Phillips Lee. Although these military commanders are well known, their wives and the lives they led as spouses to these famous men are little known. *Intimate Strategies* tells of their marriages and gives equal footing to the famous husbands and to their wives.

Most essays in the volume center on the war years, although many of the marriages predate the war and others lasted well into Reconstruction and beyond. For some couples the patterns of interaction were well established before the war began; for others it was the war that brought them together. Individually, the articles are dual biographies of these unions addressing the unique inner dynamics and wartime experiences of each husband and wife. Together, the authors discuss the broader issues of war and marriage including the impact of the Civil War on traditional gender roles, private and public identity, and the balance of power within the relationship. There was intense sexual passion in some of these unions, almost siblinglike companionship in others. These famous couples faced problems shared by many lesser-known husbands and wives during wartime, including feelings of loneliness, isolation, frustration, and anxiety. Although the subjects of this book were members of the elite, their emotions were typical of all Civil War couples. The wives of these military commanders pleaded for news from the front and for the opportunity to see their husbands. Their husbands, even in the midst of battle, worried about their families and finances and appealed to their wives for more personal letters from home.

The study bridges the artificial gap separating military history from women and gender studies—a gap that did not exist for the participants. Soldiers' experiences in camp and at the front were not completely disconnected from those of civilians. In fact, individual identities interwove the battlefield experience with that of the family. Soldiers were sons, brothers, husbands, and fathers, who phrased their ideology for fighting in the language of home, family, and fireside. During the heat and chaos of battle, men thought of home and called for their wives and mothers. Far from the front, or within enemy lines, the women waited, prayed, and thought of their men, and many temporarily assumed masculine gender roles in their husbands' absence.

All of the twelve marriages included are of the Victorian era, and for the most part the participants subscribed to the doctrine of separate spheres—an ideology, held by most American nineteenth-century middle-class and upper-class husbands and wives, that nature dictated sharply differentiated roles for each gender. The usual assumption was that the sphere of the man consisted of activities outside the home, such as business, soldiering, politics, and the world in general, whereas the sphere of the woman included the emotional and physical maintenance of the home, the care of the children, the nurturing of the husband, and the ethical and spiritual guardianship of the family. Although in public many of the military luminaries spoke condescendingly of women's place in the male sphere, we discover that in private many of these wives were their principal advisers and confidantes.

The following chapters show that some of these marriages were primarily ones of give and take, some wives eagerly offering advice and directions to their husbands and seeking to share the spotlight. Other wives more quietly provided a strong and steady influence on their spouses to help them perform the daunting tasks they faced as military commanders. Still others chafed at the demands of war and pressures put on their marriages by their husbands' military duty. Not one woman in this collection, however, fits perfectly into the nineteenth-century stereotype of the passive and submissive wife, and some of these husbands crossed the boundary into "her" sphere and actively participated in domestic matters.

This single volume of essays also highlights fresh and exciting work from a wide assortment of writers. Our authors are male and female, new scholars and older, well-established historians. Emory M. Thomas, John F. Marszalek, and John Y. Simon are eminent Civil War military historians, and Carol K. Bleser is a leading scholar on the history of the nineteenth-century southern family and marriage. Shirley A. Leckie, Virginia Jeans Laas, Sarah Woolfolk Wiggins, and Pamela Herr are critically acclaimed editors and biographers. Lesley J. Gordon, Peter S. Carmichael, Sarah Gardner, and Jennifer Lund Smith represent a younger generation of historians (see our biographical directory for more information on each author). The diversity of the contributors' backgrounds, interests, ages, and even gender makes for a broad array of assumptions and interpretations of the past. The authors of this book do not always agree with one another in their assessment of what made successful and unsuccessful marriages, how much impact wives had on their husbands' professional lives, and how much we can know about the private side of history. Nor do we, the editors of this book, always agree with some of our authors' conclusions. Furthermore, the theme of this collection forced biographers to look at both partners united in a marriage—something not always easy to do given the historical evidence available and our authors' own inclinations. Readers will readily see a difference in focus from essay to essay; sometimes an author gives equal time to both; in others, the individual husband or his wife gains greater attention from the writer. However, nowhere do we find much evidence that our Victorian husbands and wives placed less emphasis on their personal relationships than we do today. What makes *Intimate Strategies of the Civil War: Military Commanders and Their Wives* unique, insightful, and important is that it mirrors the rich, changing nature of history itself in the midst of massive upheaval and change.

Part One focuses on the South. Carol K. Bleser opens the collection with a fresh look at the Confederacy's first couple, Jefferson Davis and Varina Howell. Recounting their prewar marriage, Bleser finds the Davises clashing early on in their personal relationship over traditional southern gender roles. Varina, intelligent, outspoken, and spirited, initially balked at playing the obedient, demure wife to her groom, eighteen years her senior. She voiced her discontent directly to her patriarchal husband. Jefferson, extremely unhappy with his young wife, chastised her into becoming a more dutiful wife, although she never entirely lost her streak of independence. The arrival of children and Jefferson's expanding political career in the decade before the war busied both Davises and they seemed to settle into a less-volatile relationship. The Civil War, Bleser maintains, actually brought the couple closer together. Varina spent one-third of the war pregnant, and Jefferson spent much of that time physically ill. They also grieved the loss of their son Joseph, who died tragically in an accidental fall. Nevertheless, Jefferson Davis, the Confederacy's beleaguered and haggard chief executive, found a loyal champion in his wife. Unlike many other couples in this volume, the Davises were rarely separated during the war. Instead, Varina was constantly at his side, and on many occasions, she stepped in to substitute for her husband when he was too ill to perform his duties. Varina learned to duplicate her husband's handwriting so well she later claimed that many official documents of the Confederacy were actually signed by her rather than the president. After the war, the Davis marriage changed yet again. Jefferson's imprisonment at war's end and the notoriety of having been the Confederacy's ex-president put new strains on their relationship. Varina had worked tirelessly to free her husband from prison and had continued to be his most faithful supporter. Yet the Davises, both plagued by poor health, spent a good deal of time apart in the postwar years, which led to another estrangement. When Davis accepted the offer to live on the Mississippi estate of a wealthy widow, Sarah Dorsey, the Davis marriage seemed near the point of extinction. However, shortly before Dorsey's death, Varina and Jefferson reconciled. After Jefferson Davis's death in 1889, Varina left the South to live in New York City—a move that helped free her from the grip of the man, who had so long dominated her, as well as allowing her to pursue a literary career. As the widow of the South's only president, Varina was able to live a comfortable life supported by her writings, extensive southern landholdings, and public appearances. She finally had the independence she had craved as a young bride, although as Bleser concludes,

Varina Howell Davis never had obtained the love she so fervently sought from her husband.

Although Varina Davis's political influence over her husband has been hotly debated by historians, and her role as first lady harshly criticized by many of Jefferson Davis's biographers, the wife of Robert E. Lee has rarely been credited with affecting her husband's military career one way or the other. Yet Emory M. Thomas, in his recent biography of Robert E. Lee, noted that the general's decision to join the Confederacy was largely to avoid uncomfortable questioning from his friends, family, and fellow Southerners, but most especially from Mary Custis Lee, who had become "a fiercely partisan Confederate." Thomas states: "Robert E. Lee would have been most in danger in his own bed."[4] That decision, of course, was an especially significant one for the history of the war and the future of the South. Even today, Lee stands as the sainted hero of the Confederate South. Had his wife not been such a strong advocate of states' rights and Lee so unwilling to avoid her disapproval, perhaps the history of the Civil War would have been dramatically different. In his essay in this volume, Thomas focuses on the relationship between Mary Custis and Robert E. Lee, finding a long if not idyllic marriage. Seemingly opposites in many ways, the Lees apparently complemented one another. In addition, even though Mary was burdened by ill health, especially severe arthritis, she nonetheless provided her husband with significant wealth, respectability, and social prestige in elite southern slaveholding society. Although it is not clear that Mary ever directly counseled her husband on military affairs, Thomas demonstrates that Robert did confide in her and did fill his letters to her from the battlefield with rich detail, sometimes more so than the official correspondence he sent to President Davis.

Another larger-than-life hero of the Confederacy was Thomas Jonathan Jackson. On July 21, 1861, at the battle of Bull Run, Jackson earned his famous nickname "Stonewall" for his stalwart performance in the field. He wrote his wife Mary Anna soon after the fight, assuring her that he was safe. "Whilst great credit is due to the other parts of our gallant army," the pious Jackson told her, "God made my brigade more instrumental than any other in repulsing the main attack." He hastily added: "This is for your information only—say nothing about it. Let others speak praise, not myself."[5] Sarah Gardner's essay on the Jacksons demonstrates that in fact Mary Anna was extremely intent on telling others about her husband's dramatic exploits in battle, while he tried unsuccessfully to discourage her. His devout Christianity tempered his ego, but it did not discourage Mary Anna. The Jacksons, like other married couples in this volume, differed over camp visits and furloughs, and playfully bantered about the frequency and content of correspondence. Additionally, Mary Anna endured frequent inaccurate rumors about her husband's safety. Tom Jackson tried to recreate a homelike setting at the front; the only major ingredient missing was the presence of his wife. However, war engendered particular tensions in the Jackson marriage, and these tensions, Gardner argues, in turn reveal much about Southerners' efforts to construct their own narratives of the Civil War. Mary Anna Jackson had married a hero of the Mexican War, and she endeavored mightily to perpetuate that noble image of her husband. This need became acute during the Civil War, especially since she found his accounts of military exploits lacking. The general's insistent chastisement of her efforts did not quell her need to glorify her husband. After his death in 1863, Jackson's widow assumed a very public role in promoting her husband and adding to his legendary status. After his death and the Confederacy's defeat, Mary Anna spent the rest of her life promoting her image of her fallen husband, sanctioning "worthy" biographies, publishing her own account of her life with him, publicly disputing those versions of her husband's life with which she disagreed, and contributing artifacts of his life to Confederate bazaars and to the museum in Richmond. She was determined, in effect, to maintain proprietary control of the postwar image of Stonewall Jackson.

LaSalle Corbell Pickett, like Mary Anna Jackson, was resolved to present an idealized and romanticized public portrait of her husband, herself, and her marriage. Lesley J. Gordon, in her essay on the Picketts, shows that Mrs. Pickett, like other wives in this volume, tied her identity directly to that of her famed husband. Only George Pickett was no hero: he was an unsuccessful, bitter man whose name happened to become associated with the most famous failed charge in American military history. Sallie Pickett told her readers that her point of beginning was the moment she allegedly first met George on the beaches at Old Point Comfort, Virginia, eleven years before they married. In retrospect, he became her reason for being. Civil war brought George from the western frontier back to the South, back to his family and back to LaSalle. As the war progressed, so did their courtship. In the spring of 1863, George found he could not concentrate on his responsibilities as a division commander. He slipped away from headquarters to see her, with or without permission from his superiors. Fellow officers scorned his behavior, seeming to question George's manliness and competence as an officer. George and Sallie married in the fall of 1863, but their marital happiness was short-lived. His division's famed charge at the Battle of Gettysburg in July 1863 marked a turning point in his life. George grew bitter and disillusioned by war, and he suffered an emotional and physical breakdown in the spring of 1864. By the war's end, traditional white southern gender roles had shifted and he became utterly dependent on his wife. Sallie continued to provide emotional and financial support for both George and their infant son when George faced charges of war crimes and they fled to Canada fearing for their lives. After her husband's death in 1875, LaSalle Corbell Pickett began to write extensively of her marriage, celebrating George as the ideal southern white male and Confederate hero. In her many writings, neither war, defeat, exile, personal loss, nor poverty could dampen their relationship. Gordon

reveals that the heroic soldier-husband, submissive wife, and happy southern marriage were all LaSalle Pickett's postwar and postmarriage creation.

Peter S. Carmichael looks at another wartime couple whose marriage
was far from happy. Lizinka Brown, a wealthy and outspoken widow, refused to conform to a passive role in her second marriage to her cousin,
the hesitant and indecisive Richard Ewell. She immediately and openly
assumed the stronger role in the relationship and he appeared emotionally lost without his wife physically beside him. Richard seemed to comply
with her "unwomanly behavior," even modifying how he carried himself
on the battlefield until their relationship came under intense public scrutiny. The stinging criticism and ridicule from outsiders apparently altered
the dynamics of their relationship, and after the war, Richard reasserted
male hegemony at a tremendous cost. Their marriage emerged from the
war experience scarred, and serious disagreements remained. Tragically,
the Ewells died within a few days of one another, each struck down by the
sudden onset of typhoid fever, their ongoing marital strife never resolved.

Countering these stories of troubled southern marriages is an essay by
Sarah Woolfolk Wiggins on Josiah and Amelia Gorgas. Born into a large,
poor family in Pennsylvania, Josiah Gorgas married into a prominent family in the antebellum South. When he chose the army as his career he
went wherever duty called, and in the summer of 1853, he was stationed
in Alabama. Josiah soon met and fell in love with Amelia Gayle and a
mere six months later, they were married. Amelia, like Mary Lee, and
Lizinka Ewell, came from the South's slaveholding elite, and her marriage
to Josiah certainly provided him with respectability and social status he
probably could not have achieved on his own. As the nation neared dis-
union and civil war, Amelia and her family were undeniably Confederate,
and Josiah accepted his in laws' southern affiliation without hesitation.
Turning his back on his own family and his native Pennsylvania, Josiah
became the Confederacy's chief of ordnance, proving to be one of the
most talented administrators in the South's troubled military bureaucracy.
During the war, the Gorgases managed to be together, and it is not clear
that Amelia directly influenced her husband's military decisions. The Gorgas marriage seemed initially a traditional southern one in which Josiah
acted the patriarch, albeit northern not southern, and Amelia willingly
played the role of submissive wife and mother. However, it was Reconstruction, rather than the Civil War that changed the dynamics of the
Gorgas marriage and brought real hardship to their family life. Southern
defeat and slave emancipation left Josiah Gorgas, like many Confederate
leaders, bewildered and bitter. Josiah no longer had a profession in the
military, and for several months after the war, as he cast about for suitable
employment, he lived apart from his wife and six children. The couple
forged a different partnership and the notion of separate spheres no
longer seemed viable. It began with Josiah sharing his financial concerns
with his wife. Then in 1869 when they endured their second separation

from one another, Amelia learned to sign her husband's name to correspondence, handle bills, and run the farm. Josiah suffered a massive stroke
in 1879 and Amelia stepped in as primary caregiver, attending to her ill
husband, helping to act in his place as a college librarian at the University
of Alabama, and working as a hospital matron. She made enough money
not only to support herself and her husband but also to pay for their son's
medical education. After her husband's death in 1883, Amelia continued
working in the library and the hospital, finally retiring in 1907. In the
end, the Gorgases remained strongly devoted to each other and very much
in love. However, the trials of Reconstruction upset the patriarchy and
with Josiah's death in 1883, Amelia moved permanently and it would appear rather easily out of the traditional southern domestic sphere into the
working world of the late nineteenth century.

Part Two shifts focus northward, beginning with an analysis of the
Grants by John Y. Simon. Simon describes how the marriage of Ulysses
and Julia Grant withstood financial woes, accusations of alcoholism, sectionalism, civil war, and sudden unwanted fame. On the surface, their
marriage seemed quite romantic, matching the son of an abolitionist with
the daughter of a slaveholder. But despite Simon's contention that it was
a happy marriage, there were dark days, particularly during the seven years
preceding the Civil War as Ulysses struggled to support his growing family.
Their devotion to one another, however, is unmistakable. The secession
crisis and outbreak of the war failed to alter Julia's allegiance to her husband, although she owned slaves and regularly brought them with her to
accompany her husband at the front. Simon characterizes their relationship as affectionate and teasing, describing how Julia often relieved her
husband's concern about military problems with a lighthearted quip or
some calculated absurdity. By assuming new responsibilities for their children and family finances, Julia also provided her husband with a stable
domestic relationship that enabled him to function most effectively as a
commander. She frequently joined him at the front and occasionally even
stepped in to try to influence his military decisions. In the fall of 1862,
for example, after the disappointing battles of Iuka and Corinth, several
officers petitioned Julia Grant to try to persuade her husband to censure
the vexatious William S. Rosecrans. Julia herself recalled her husband listening patiently to her pleas but he refused to change his mind. Nonetheless, he apparently did not take offense that officers were using his wife
as a way to reach him rather than seeing him directly.[6] Still, Simon insists
that Julia played no direct role in her husband's military or political affairs, but he does admit that she was better able to manage his sudden
public acclaim than the general was. Julia may have also saved her husband from assassination. Offended by Mary Lincoln's recurrent rudeness,
Julia opted to turn down an invitation to go to the theater with the president and first lady on April 14, 1865, and instead the Grants left Washington, D.C., to visit their children. Had Julia Grant not possessed a mind

of her own and the forcefulness to get her way on that fateful night, Simon speculates, history might have been very different.

The Sherman marriage is perhaps the most unusual in this collection. William T. "Cump" Sherman and Ellen Ewing had grown up as foster siblings before they married in 1850. Their sixty-year relationship, first as brother and sister, then as husband and wife, was complex and turbulent, writes John Marszalek. Ellen's father and Cump's foster father and father-in-law, Thomas Ewing, played an immensely influential role in both their lives. Ewing was a powerful lawyer and politician in his own right. However, in the Sherman household, he cast an especially long shadow. Ellen adored her father and was intensely loyal to him and his desires. Cump, the adopted son and frustrated son-in-law, desperately sought both approval and autonomy from Ewing. Religion also caused problems. The Ewings were Catholic and young Cump had to become a Catholic to become part of the family. Early in his adult life, however, Cump stopped practicing Catholicism while Ellen became even more devout. Their disagreements over religion undermined their marriage and affected their relationship with their children, particularly when their son Tom became a Jesuit priest. Cump refused to have anything else to do with him, blaming his wife for the loss of his son. These unusual dynamics made for a stressful marriage even without a civil war and Sherman's emergence as a famous general. Although the Sherman marriage remained contentious to the end, the general's success in the war did seem to affect his wife's stubborn devotion to her father. When her husband began to emerge as one of the Union's most victorious commanders and increasingly as his own man, Ellen left her father's home for good. The Civil War appeared to break the hold Thomas Ewing had had on both Shermans.

Jennifer Lund Smith's essay on Joshua Lawrence Chamberlain and his wife Fannie narrates another story of two strong-willed individuals and the changing dynamics of their relationship. During their first seven years of marriage, the Chamberlains seemed to have found a happy medium, raising a young family and living modestly on Lawrence's professor salary. However, the war changed everything. Smith hints at problems in the Chamberlain marriage before 1861, but the war and General Chamberlain's newfound celebrity only added to their discord. Fannie Chamberlain refused to be the submissive, dutiful wife despite her husband's quite conventional efforts to be master of the household. Unlike most of the wives discussed in this collection, Fannie Chamberlain had very little interest in her husband's military career. The wife of the hero of Little Roundtop and a Congressional Medal of Honor recipient seemed ambivalent toward the entire war effort. For her, the conflict meant long anxious separations from her husband and his stubborn refusal to follow her wishes and come home. When peace finally came and her husband returned, he was wounded and distracted by his wartime exploits. For him, it was the foremost experience of his life, but for his wife it was something she refused to share with him. In 1868 there were rumors of domestic abuse and a divorce appeared imminent, even in disapproving Victorian America. Late in life and late in their marriage, the Chamberlains apparently reconciled. For this northern couple, the Civil War tried and tested their marriage and almost destroyed it.

George Armstrong Custer, like Joshua Lawrence Chamberlain, emerged from the war a famous Union hero. However, the Custers, unlike the Chamberlains, were newly wed during the war and were only beginning to adjust to their new status and relationship when Custer's star began to rise. Serving as a reliable subaltern for Major General Philip Sheridan, Custer was willing to take extraordinary chances in battle and perpetrate the required destructiveness against the property of a civilian population in the Shenandoah Valley. As the "Boy General," he won the strong affection of his men in both the Michigan Brigade and the Third Division. However, his fame was a double-edged sword, writes Shirley Leckie. On the one hand, it was the crucial element that won him Elizabeth Bacon, daughter of Daniel Bacon, retired judge of Monroe County, Michigan. On the other hand, his continuing exploits in the military sentenced his young bride to intense anxiety and worry. Nonetheless, both Armstrong and Elizabeth worked jointly to achieve fame for the Boy General. While her husband was at the front, Elizabeth stretched the boundaries of ladylike behavior by living alone in Washington, D.C. Charming and deft at socializing, Libbie captivated the attention of important politicians, careful to avoid behavior that would cast doubt on her virtue in any way. The Custer marriage was a passionate one, but privately there were signs of strife. In addition to the extended physical separation from her husband, Libbie endured Armstrong's frequent "silent seasons" when he distanced himself emotionally from his wife and she struggled to gain his approval. Although Armstrong welcomed Libbie's help in charming politicians, he disapproved of his wife's interfering directly with his military affairs. He reprimanded her for giving female advice to his staff members and chastised her for what he deemed inappropriate remarks about professional officers. They had no children, and Elizabeth blamed herself for this failing even though it seems likely that Armstrong's gonorrhea prevented him from fathering children. After the war, Armstrong's ambition was not satiated nor was his love of war fulfilled. He continued his military service in the Seventh Cavalry, fighting Indians in the Far West and the couple's long separations persisted. There were also rumors of Armstrong's extramarital affairs and his penchant for gambling. On June 25, 1876, Libbie's worst fears were realized when her Boy General was killed at the Battle of Little Bighorn. Nevertheless, already well practiced at acting the model wife, Elizabeth Bacon Custer became the model widow with new power to defend her beloved Autie against all critics. She wrote books, gave public lectures, and oversaw commemorations all about her dead husband. In much the same manner as Mary Anna Jackson and

LaSalle Corbell Pickett, Libbie Custer discovered a measure of her own independence and autonomy by promoting a man and creating a myth.

The long and complex marriage of John Charles Frémont and Jessie Benton, which began as a passionate love match between an ambitious adventurer and a senator's rebellious daughter, included periods of intense rapport and partnership, as well as times of psychological and geographical distance. Pamela Herr explores the Frémonts' unusual working partnership during the Civil War, focusing particularly on the chaotic early months when John Frémont served as commander of the Western Department of the Union Army with headquarters in St. Louis, and Jessie became his chief aide and confidante. Their collaboration allowed the intelligent, energetic, and politically savvy Jessie to assume the role extraordinary even in the wartime era when many women acted beyond the boundaries of woman's traditional sphere. During the turbulent one hundred days of John Frémont's St. Louis command, the couple displayed both a genuine antislavery idealism, which made John the titular head of the radical wing of the Republican party, and an eager self-promotion that challenged President Lincoln's political power. At their St. Louis headquarters, "General Jessie," as critics began to call her, wrote her husband's confidential letters, regulated his appointments, adroitly managed the press, virtually ran headquarters when her husband was in the field, and defended his controversial limited emancipation decree in a notorious meeting with Abraham Lincoln, who pronounced her "quite a female politician." After scarcely three months in command, just as John claimed to be on the verge of battlefield victory, Lincoln fired his controversial general. John Frémont's subsequent Civil War career was disappointing: a brief and unsuccessful command in western Virginia and a failed attempt to wrest the Republican presidential nomination from Lincoln in 1864. Despite even his wife's vigorous efforts, which included a book that artfully justified his western command, the war left the Frémonts' politically tarnished and personally embittered.

Virginia Jeans Laas rounds out the collection with a detailed look at the fifty-four-year marriage of Admiral Samuel Phillips Lee and his wife Elizabeth Blair. Phil Lee, like his distant cousin Robert, fervently sought social acceptability and prestige to make up for family tragedy. Marrying into the politically powerful and wealthy Blair family, he strove to keep his financial and personal independence from his meddlesome in-laws with mixed success. Laas contends that Phil wanted and needed a partner, not a subordinate, and Elizabeth, fiery and outspoken, preserved the appearance of patriarchy while exercising significant influence on her husband's career and living arrangements. However, their marriage was not without turbulence, at times displaying painful tensions and strained intimacy. Phil's long tenure in the navy meant he was separated from his wife and family for extended periods, often longer than those faced by army officers. Admiral Lee, like General Sherman, competed with his father-in-law for his wife's loyalty. Laas concludes that the war did not dramatically transform the Lee marriage; their patterns were already well established before the conflict commenced. However, Phil's retirement in 1873 brought an end to his long sea voyages and an end to those well-worn patterns. The Lees clashed over where they would reside, and neither would give in. A sharp disagreement arose over their shared residence, and for more than ten years, Phil lived in the country and Elizabeth alternated between the farm and a city dwelling. Phil's attempt to keep the appearance of a patriarchy was blatantly defied by his wife.

Some of these marriages were clearly happy ones; others were more strained and still others seemed downright dysfunctional. None stayed entirely static, and many of these stories seem to reaffirm the modern notion that a successful marriage takes hard work. Although this collection looks at only a dozen famous couples, taken as a whole they do give us insight into the complexity and variety of nineteenth-century American marriage and family. Romantic companionate marriage was becoming more the norm among Victorian couples, but money and social status still played a role. Men of modest means or besmirched family reputations married women with untarnished family names and better financial standing and vice versa as was the case of Varina Davis, the impoverished daughter of the Howells of Natchez, Mississippi. Multiple pregnancies were common to most of the married couples in this volume; so too were severe illness and death. Parents tragically and repeatedly witnessed the sudden deaths of their young children, and these losses took a toll on marriages, no matter how strong. In addition, among the twenty-four husbands and wives included in this book, several were the products of "blended" or foster families. Death and economic woes caused some Victorian families to break up and children to be doled out to relatives, neighbors, and friends. William T. Sherman, Thomas Jonathan Jackson, and Fannie Adams Chamberlain all grew up in some form of a foster family. Phillips Lee and his four siblings were put under the care of a court-appointed committee when their mother died suddenly and their father suffered a nervous breakdown. John C. Frémont, born illegitimately, was raised by a single mother who struggled to support him and her other children by running a boardinghouse. For each of these men and women, their unstable childhood and untraditional family lives clearly had an impact on their personalities and personal relationships.

Since *Intimate Strategies of the Civil War* examines six southern and six northern couples, one might expect to find some notable differences between the regions. Nevertheless, these couples reveal more similarities than differences. Perhaps this is because all of these couples came from the same class and race and that the males were prominent leaders. However, it is significant that both northern and southern couples displayed estrangement and dysfunction: husbands bristled at intrusive in-laws, wives sought to influence their husbands, and widows sought to promote their husbands' idealized images. Both Confederate and Union wives tried to act as moral agents, seeking to instill religiosity in their husbands.

The Civil War divided families, but in this study, spouses sided with their mates rather than break up a marriage over politics. Mary Lee's ardent Confederate views helped seal her husband's decision to wear gray; Josiah Gorgas married a southern woman and turned his back on his native Pennsylvania to serve the Confederacy; Julia Grant had southern roots and southern sensibilities toward slavery, yet she remained loyal to her husband's northern affiliation. Phillips Lee was born in Virginia, and his wife Elizabeth had family ties to the South, but the Blairs were strongly pro-Union and Phillips followed suit. Had Phillips Lee opted to join the Confederacy, it seems likely that it would have caused a considerable breach in his relationship with his wife. Elizabeth's father was a close adviser to Lincoln; her brother Montgomery served in the president's cabinet and another brother was a Union general.

Most of the wives of military commanders in this collection sought with mixed success to have some influence over their husbands' professional careers. Carol Bleser strongly asserts that Varina Davis's role in running the Confederate government was much larger than many have previously believed. Shirley Leckie depicts Libbie Custer using her considerable charisma and charm to win political support for her husband and promote the "Boy General." Virginia Jeans Laas finds Elizabeth Blair Lee continuously counseling her husband on military affairs and using her powerful family connections to help her husband's naval career. Jessie Frémont was essentially her husband's unofficial "chief of staff," even going so far as to pay a visit to Abraham Lincoln to urge him to intervene on behalf of General Frémont. Jessie Frémont's book, *The Story of the Guard,* written during the war, publicly defended her husband's military record in print. Lizinka Ewell similarly swayed her husband with military advice, pressuring him to keep her son out of harm's way in battle. However, there were limits to these wives' influence. Libbie Custer seemed always careful not to overstep her bounds; Lizinka Ewell, Varina Davis, and Jessie Frémont each received harsh reminders of their limitations as women when they tried to overstep traditional gender roles and intercede on their husbands' behalf. These devoted wives endured severe criticism not only from their contemporaries but also from historians. Husbands too were seen as weak and unmanly for allowing their wives such seemingly strong control over them. Men like Jefferson Davis, Phillips Lee, John Frémont, Armstrong Custer, and Dick Ewell were often themselves dependent on their wives' help, but it was a dependency they did not relish, frequently appeared to resent, and often attempted to hide.

Mary Lee, Amelia Gorgas, Julia Grant, and Ellen Sherman seemed to fit the more traditional female role of nurturing to their husbands privately, but they were important confidantes who provided emotional support necessary to sustain their husbands on the battlefield. Emory Thomas demonstrates that General Lee regularly confided to his wife, Mary, military details from the front; Ellen Sherman and Julia Grant habitually acted as soothing tonics to their husbands during difficult times, especially early in the war when both men were under a good deal of public scrutiny. John Marszalek argues that Sherman regularly ignored his wife's advice. Yet Ellen Sherman, like Jessie Frémont, boldly visited the president herself in hopes of gaining Lincoln's support in countering the harsh accusations hurled at her husband. Amelia Gorgas became the family's primary caregiver and financial support when a stroke incapacitated her husband Josiah. After his death, she continued to work to support herself and their family with her own income. Their son, William Crawford Gorgas, who eliminated yellow fever from the Panama Canal region, attributed much of his success in life to his mother. For other wives, their influence was not as apparent during the war as after—especially after their husbands' deaths. Mary Anna Jackson, LaSalle Corbell Pickett, and Libbie Custer became "professional widows" of military commanders who devoted their long lives after their husbands' deaths to promoting a romanticized image of their husbands, their marriages, and themselves.

Only Fannie Chamberlain seemed to have no direct influence on her husband's military career, although her obvious disapproval of his commitment to the war created serious problems in their marriage. Jennifer Lund Smith states that Fannie Chamberlain was unqualified to counsel her husband; but none of the other wives in this collection were formally "qualified" as political or military advisers. These women, like women of almost any time and place, had spheres of influence, intimate strategies that were outside the formal, exclusively male modes of official military and political communication. General Chamberlain's wife, however, honestly seemed indifferent to her husband's military career, and thus uninterested in offering him advice—except in trying to get him to come home, which of course she was entirely unsuccessful in accomplishing.

Did the marriages of these famous commanders affect the war itself? The Davis marriage appeared to be a steadying influence on the Confederate president, who was in ill health, during his rocky presidency and perhaps even extended the length of the war. So too did the marriages of Grant and Sherman. Without their supportive wives and families, who is to say that these commanders would have politically and militarily survived the war? The marriages of Armstrong Custer and Phillips Lee helped gain both men promotion, attention, and leading roles in the Union war effort, while Frémont's marriage added to Lincoln's political woes early in the war. The marriages of George Pickett and Dick Ewell distracted and undermined their ability to command. Although Robert E. Lee's marriage to Mary Custis, and Josiah Gorgas's marriage to Amelia Gayle determined their decisions to remain true to the Confederacy, it is not clear whether their private lives had any real impact on either their military performance during the war or on the Confederacy's defeat. Nor did the marriages of Stonewall Jackson and Joshua Chamberlain appear to have any direct influence on the war itself: these two men probably would have achieved the same military glory in battle no matter what their marital status was.

Related to the impact of these marriages on the war is whether southern women acted subversively to weaken their husbands' commitment to the Confederacy. Recently some historians have argued that the deep discontent of southern elite white women contributed to the Confederacy's demise. Disheartened and disillusioned with the war's deprivations, they demanded that their husbands return home. However, none of these six studies of southern women support this assertion. Varina Davis, Mary Lee, Mary Anna Jackson, LaSalle Corbell Pickett, Lizinka Ewell, and Amelia Gayle Gorgas were wives who faced varying forms of loneliness, anxiety, illness, and death, but none of them appeared to lose faith in "the Cause" for southern independence. These women, married to some of the Confederacy's best-known leaders, did not plead with their husbands to end the war and come home. Instead, each one, whether happily married or not, remained loyal to her husband and to the new nation.

What was the Civil War's impact on marriage? Perhaps not surprisingly, the answer does not appear to be a simple one. The Civil War brought couples like the Picketts and the Custers together and tore others, like the Jacksons, tragically apart. Joshua Chamberlain's rise in the Union military distanced him from his wife. For the Davises and the Shermans, the four-year conflict marked a time of greater emotional closeness during their otherwise rocky marriages. For Robert and Mary Lee, Josiah and Amelia Gorgas, and Phillips and Elizabeth Lee, the patterns of their relationship seemed well set before the war began and the conflict apparently had little effect on their unions. The postwar period and the end of their husbands' military careers often proved more troubling for couples than the war itself, as evidenced in the marriages of Josiah and Amelia Gorgas, Phillips and Elizabeth Lee, and Lizinka and Richard Ewell.

The inner dynamics of these twelve marriages shed fascinating light not only on the individuals themselves but also on the events surrounding them. We see how the marital relationships of some of the Civil War's most prominent commanders shaped politics, military decisions, and public memory. Marriage and family was not (and is not) disconnected from the world of politics and war.[7]

Bellport, New York
September 2000

Carol K. Bleser

Economy, Pennsylvania
September 2000

Lesley J. Gordon

PART ONE

CONFEDERATE
MARRIAGES

ONE

The Marriage of Varina Howell and Jefferson Davis
A Portrait of the President and the First Lady of the Confederacy

CAROL K. BLESER

B y studying in this book the ties between husbands and wives, we hope to be able to look more closely and personally not only at the impact of their "intimate strategies" on the Civil War, but also at the impact of war on the individual marriages. A different picture becomes apparent also when one shifts the emphasis from the study of specific individuals—as in biographies in which the biographer concentrates on one of the partners in the marriage, the Civil War commander—to that of the couple united in marriage. For example, in the study of the marriage of Varina Howell and Jefferson Davis, I might say that Varina has been considered by many of his biographers as the shrew of the Confederacy. She has been characterized by them as willful, neurotic, aggressive, selfish, and difficult, a constant trial to her ever-patient and understanding husband. For an observer looking at the couple through a broader lens, a much more salutary picture of her appears. Also, studying the partners in this marriage reveals quite a different and unexpected perspective on Jefferson Davis's presidency of the Confederacy. Seeing the dynamics of the Davis marriage sheds light in many ways on the character of the individuals and the events they influenced. By that I mean understanding their private relationship adds much to our understanding of Jefferson Davis's public actions as president of the Confederacy and as a symbol of the Lost Cause.[1]

Although Jefferson Davis was a man of many accomplishments, he has the misfortune of being compared to Abraham Lincoln as a wartime leader and comes off second best, as anyone would. However, this chapter is an exploration of his marriage to Varina Howell. Our understanding of the husband's role in a late-twentieth-century marriage inevitably biases our view of Davis as a husband. He once again comes up short, again perhaps unfairly. What we do find is that Varina Howell was a woman of significant character and ability, a woman easily understood in the late twentieth century, and a woman badly treated by history, which often pictures her as a burden on her husband. We find that she provided important and consistent support for Jefferson Davis despite the inevitable stresses in a marriage between two strong people with differing views on their respective roles.

Many of the Davises' marital problems probably stemmed from Jefferson's insistence on always playing the part of the patriarchal, authoritarian spouse. Varina, however, especially during the early years of their marriage, refused to be the deferential and subordinate wife. Born on May 7, 1826, the second of the eleven children of William Burr Howell and Margaret Kempe Howell and the oldest sister to numerous younger siblings, Varina soon learned to take responsibility for the others. She was something of a tomboy, and according to one family tale, eight-year-old Varina rescued several of her younger brothers and sisters when the family house caught fire and burned. Varina's strengths came neither from her father, who was not a good businessman, nor from her mother, who had inherited money but was only slightly more competent than her husband in financial matters. Indeed, it became increasingly difficult for William Howell to support his growing family. He did, however, find the funds to send his eldest daughter to a private school for two terms when she was about ten. Following her return to the Howell home in Natchez, Mississippi, Judge George Winchester, a family friend, tutored Varina for several years in Latin, French, English literature, and history. He encouraged her to think independently and introduced her to the political debates of the day. Varina Howell grew up confident, well informed, and eager to express her opinions, a strong eldest daughter in a family with many young children whose parents always suffered from a shortage of money.[2]

In late 1843 and early 1844, seventeen-year-old Varina spent a lengthy Christmas holiday season at Hurricane, a plantation home on the Mississippi River between Natchez and Vicksburg. Her host, Joseph Emory Davis, an old friend of her parents and one of the wealthiest planters in Mississippi, apparently hoped that Varina's beauty and accomplishments would enchant his reclusive thirty-five-year-old widowed brother, Jefferson. For years, Joseph had acted as a surrogate father to his younger brother. Joseph, born in 1784, was the eldest child in a family of ten children. Jefferson, born twenty-four years later on June 3, 1808, was the youngest. Although little is known of Jefferson's early years, it is likely that his three oldest sisters and his mother pampered him as the youngest child. In 1823 and 1824, at the age of fifteen, Jefferson Davis attended Transylvania University for one year. Admitted to the United States Military Academy in

1824, he graduated from West Point in 1828 despite numerous demerits, mediocre grades, and twice narrowly avoiding expulsion for misbehavior connected with drinking.[3]

Lieutenant Davis spent the next seven years on usually uneventful duty at small forts and outposts along the upper Mississippi River. In 1832 he fell deeply in love with Sarah Knox Taylor, the daughter of Lieutenant Colonel Zachary Taylor, his commanding officer. Taylor tried to prevent the match because he did not want his daughter to marry an army officer, especially Davis, to whom Taylor also had personal objections, for reasons that are not clear. Taylor never fully assented to their marriage although his opposition declined after Davis resigned from the army. Their wedding took place at the home of the bride's aunt near Louisville on June 17, 1835. The couple settled in Mississippi, where Joseph Davis had determined to establish Jefferson on land adjoining his plantation. However, on September 15, after only three months of marriage, Sarah died of fever.[4]

Davis as a grieving widower spent the next eight years developing his plantation, which he called Brierfield. There he changed from a happy, sociable, yet somewhat irresponsible and immature young man into a somber, brooding, serious, reserved, and demanding planter.

Jefferson Davis was more than twice the age of Varina Howell when he met her at his brother's home in late 1843. Her initial impression of her future husband was remarkably perceptive—more perceptive it seems than the delegates from the six seceded states meeting in Montgomery in February 1861, who chose Davis to be president of the Confederacy. "He impresses me," wrote the teenager to her mother, "as a remarkable kind of man, but of uncertain temper, and has a way of taking for granted that everybody agrees with him when he expresses an opinion, which offends me; yet he is most agreeable and has a peculiarly sweet voice and a winning manner of asserting himself."[5]

Despite her mixed first impression, Varina and Jefferson were soon attracted to one another. She was tall and had thick dark hair and a lovely figure, but her most outstanding features were her large, deep, expressive eyes. Varina's youth was another advantage; Jefferson's brother Joseph had married a sixteen-year-old when he was forty-three. Varina, in turn, thought Jefferson must be old, but she admired his clear-cut profile and gracefulness on horseback and thought him "the strongest and most helpful of men."[6] They talked and walked together, and they fell in love. There was some mild opposition to the marriage from the Howells, probably based on the eighteen-year age difference and on the conflicting political loyalties of the two families—the Howells were Whigs, the Davises Democrats. Their objections, however, soon evaporated in light of the Davises' wealth. As the time for their marriage approached and clearly in response to a question she posed, Jefferson wrote Varina that were it his "will to decide where and how we should live, your preferences and judgement should certainly exercise gr[ea]t influence on that will."[7] This was a promise that Davis failed to keep again and again throughout their long union.

They were married on February 26, 1845, in an Episcopal ceremony in the parlor of the Briers, the Natchez home of the Howells. Varina wore a simple white embroidered Indian muslin dress with touches of lace, a most unostentatious wedding dress. The honeymoon that followed included stops on the Mississippi River below Natchez, at Rosemont Plantation, where Jefferson had grown up and where his mother still lived, and at nearby Locust Grove to see his sister, Anna Smith. There the groom took his bride to visit the grave of his first wife, Sarah Knox Taylor Davis.[8] Shortly before Jefferson Davis's death in 1889, Varina urged a friend to oppose his daughter's engagement to a widower. "I gave the best and all my life to a girdled tree," she wrote. "It was live oak, and was good for any purpose, except for blossom & fruit, and I am not willing for Belle to be content with anything less than the whole of a man's heart."[9] Varina apparently never was convinced that Jefferson loved her as much as he had loved his first wife. She was probably right. In his brief "autobiography," dictated several weeks before his death in 1889, after Varina had nursed him for many years, he recalled his first marriage in 1835, commented most favorably on Sarah Dorsey, on whose plantation he stayed from 1876 to 1878, and only in the final paragraph did he mention his second wife. He does not state her first name and about her he comments only, "she has borne me six children—four sons and two daughters." He incorrectly gives the year of their marriage as 1844, rather than 1845, but one takes particular interest in that Jefferson Davis acknowledges Varina only as the mother of his children.[10]

Less than six months after their wedding, Jefferson successfully ran for election to the House of Representatives. After his victory the couple departed for Washington and arrived shortly after the opening of Congress in December 1845. Nineteen-year-old Varina wrote this lively informative letter to her mother on January 30, 1846.

> Now let me tell you all the news I can think of—about two weeks since, I went to the President's to dine. Mrs. P.[olk]'s entertainments consisting entirely of dinner parties, and levees—she is a strict Presbyterian you know. Well! I wore my black watered silk, and a white polka dress made of bobbinet, and trimmed with my wedding lace—a white japonica in my hair. Mrs. P. came up dressed to death—she is a very handsome woman is too entertaining for my liking—talks too much a la Presidents wife—is anxious to please. Polk is an insignificant looking little man. I don't like his manners or any thing else—we had about fifty courses it seemed to me. I went from there to Mrs. Walker's. . . . I spent an hour very pleasantly with her then came home. Shortly after we gave a little hop here. I invited some sweet looking girls— some intelligent looking young men, and the other ladies did the same—we

had quite a delightful time of it I assure you—at least every body but me had—you will know I did not when I tell you that Jeff had the hottest fever I ever felt in the next room to where it was all going on. I danced twice, and then went to him—but could not persuade myself to leave him again. I don't know which ached worst his dear head or my heart. I don't know Ma how it is that I cannot feel like telling any one but you how I feel towards Jeff. I feel so fearful—so uneasy—he has not been well since we arrived here—he has little fevers—cold constantly—severe earaches he sits up until two or three o'clock at night writing—until his eyes even lose their beauty to *me* they look so red and painful. I feel as if he would not stand it another year. I had fearful enough anticipations of what a public life would be but they were nothing like the reality.[11]

Although there is no evidence that Varina had opposed Jefferson's decision to run for Congress at that time, in her memoir she wrote, "I began to know the bitterness of being a politician's wife." It meant to Varina "long absences, pecuniary depletion from ruinous absenteeism, illness from exposure, misconceptions, defamation of character; everything which darkens the sunlight and contracts the happy sphere of home."[12] When the Mexican War began in 1846, she opposed her husband's decision to serve and thought that he had promised not to volunteer. Davis, however, soon made it clear that he was going to war. After an argument, Varina lamented to her mother, "Though it was carried on in love between us, it is not the less bitter"; she "cried until" she was "stupid." To make matters worse, Jefferson, seldom able to accept or to understand dissent from his views, accused his wife of having "*something* the matter" with her because she had tried to change his mind. "I *know* there is not," she wrote.[13]

A month later Jefferson Davis wrote his sister with great pride in himself and with some concern over Varina. Letters of this sort have probably helped to form history's picture of Varina. However, this letter, written by an older man about his wife, a spirited twenty-year-old girl, is almost chilling.

I am on my way to Vicksburg as Colonel of the Regiment raised in Mississippi for the Mexican War. This movement was unexpected, though I hope not unnecessary, at least it was felt by me as a real compliment to be thus chosen over a field of competitors when absent, and if occasion offers it may be that I will return with a reputation over which you will rejoice as my Mother would have done. . . . Varina [is] far from well. I wished to leave her in the North this summer, but she would not consent. If circumstances warranted it I would send her to you. To you and your family alone of all the world could I entrust her and rest assured that no waywardness would ever lessen kindness. . . .

She will probably stay with her Mother most of the time during which I

will be absent. With Eliza [the wife of Joseph Davis] she could not be contented, nor would their residing together increase their good feeling for each
other. This distresses me as you will readily imagine, but if you ever have an
opportunity to understand Varina's character, you will see the propriety of
the conclusion, and I feel that you will love her too much to take heed of the
weaknesses which spring from a sensitive and generous temper.[14]

Once Jefferson had left for Mexico, Varina and his relatives began to
squabble. The Davis brothers had decided that during Jefferson's absence,
a new home would be built at Brierfield in which their widowed sister,
Amanda Bradford, and her eight children would live with Jefferson and
Varina. With her husband away, Varina tried to alter the plan. Both she
and Amanda objected to sharing a single household and together sabo-
taged the part of the scheme that called for joint occupancy by the two
families. Also, Varina and Joseph Davis, who considered himself in charge
of his sister-in-law during her husband's military duty, clashed over her
attempts to give the carpenters instructions without first consulting her
brother-in-law.[15]

Davis, informed in Mexico by mail of the problems between his wife
and his relations, requested leave following the battle of Monterrey and
hastened home to attempt to end the domestic quarrels. He concluded
that it was Varina's fault—her willfulness, immaturity, and lack of self-
control had caused the trouble at home. Back with the army he wrote
Varina of an officer's wife who though "surrounded by annoyances," always sent letters to her husband that were cheerful and uncomplaining,
as Varina's clearly were not. She must, Davis admonished her, develop
"the good sense which skillfully avoids a collision," be less critical of others, and follow his wishes, and in his absence, those of his brother, Joseph.
Only then would she be content. "Remember," Davis advised her, "to be
responsible for ones conduct is not the happy state which those who think
they have been governed too much sometimes suppose it."[16] For women,
Davis believed, contentment could only follow obedience.

Jefferson returned from the Mexican War with a serious wound in his
foot, inflicted during the battle of Buena Vista. Varina helped nurse him
back to health, but another clash of wills soon brought their relationship
to a low ebb. Only two months after Jefferson arrived home a war hero,
the governor of Mississippi named him to fill a vacancy in the United
States Senate. Before leaving for Washington on November 11, 1847, Davis wrote a new will with Joseph's guidance and approval, which left Varina
only a small percentage of the income from Brierfield. If he died, the
property was to remain undivided, and she was to share the earnings with
Davis's three widowed sisters and two nieces.[17]

When Davis arrived in Washington, he received a bitter letter from his
twenty-one-year-old wife, whom he had left behind at Brierfield. In it she

accused him of treating her in a degrading manner and of ignoring her "rights as a woman and a wife" and blamed him for the terms of the will, for planning to have his sister Amanda and her eight children live with them, and for forcing her to "retire from the rest of the world." Jefferson exploded and responded with a belligerent letter of his own. He denied her charge that he had ignored her wishes and blamed her for their discord. Varina was, her husband claimed, unable to manage his household, contentious and unwilling to hold her temper, and unfair to him and to members of his family. Indeed, he wrote Varina, he had refused to allow her to accompany him to Washington because he could not tolerate her "constant harassment, occasional reproach, and subsequent misrepresentation." The angry husband made a point of stating that when returning to her in Mississippi, he could not call it home—"*for without hearts there is no home.*"[18] In April 1848 Davis wrote Varina that her two previous letters had not made things better between them. He wrote, "I cannot bear to be suspected or complained of, or misconstrued after explanation, *by you.* Circumstances, habits, education, combativeness, render you prone to apply the tests which I have just said I cannot bear."[19] Their marriage had broken down. Jefferson considered himself blameless and issued an ultimatum to Varina that if her conduct and attitude did not change, it would be impossible for them ever to live together again. He wrote, "I had hoped your memory instead as you say dwelling on 'the weary past and blighted future' would have grappled with substantial facts, and led you to conclusions, which would have formed for your future a line of conduct suited to the character of your husband, and demanded by your duties as a wife."[20]

Jefferson did not come back to Brierfield for ten months, until September 1848; when he returned to Washington two months later, again without Varina, at least a partial rapprochement had taken place. Varina, now twenty-two years old, realized that the initiative for resolving the difficulties of their troubled marriage rested with her, not with her husband. In the nineteenth-century South, when a marriage did not go smoothly, society normally expected the woman, not the man, to conform to her spouse's wishes. Shortly after her wedding, Varina had acknowledged that she must try harder to become an obliging and amiable wife. "I feel that Jeff's love is only to be retained," she confided to her mother, "by the practice of self control, and that it is the only mode of gaining his esteem, and confidence."[21] It took three years after that admission before she finally realized that to end their separation she must be less strong willed and more dutiful. Henceforth, Varina would send her absent husband the sorts of letters he would appreciate, full of humility and acquiescence. "Much as I have loved and valued you it seems to me I never knew the vastness of my treasure until now," she wrote in January 1849. "If you have no fear for yourself, have it for your Winnie, your thoughtless, dependent wife, and guard your health as you would my life."[22] Such professions of dependence by Varina were in fact true—what could she do if her marriage failed? Returning to her family home was not really an option; the Howells in truth depended on her and Jefferson to assist them in rearing Varina's younger siblings.

Varina's campaign to win back her husband's affection succeeded. When he traveled to Washington in late 1849 for the critical legislative session of 1850, Davis brought his wife with him after an almost two-year separation. Continuing her attempts to be the wife Jefferson wished, Varina read one of the advice books of the day, whose author, Sarah Ellis, had written, "It is impossible but that woman should feel her own inferiority, and it is right that it should be so."[23] Such reading, Varina wrote her husband, "will help 'Winnie' to be 'Wife'." She concluded her letter, "Winnie is Husband's baby and baby is your devoted Wife[.]"[24] By borrowing from the Library of Congress for her to read a three-volume, nine-hundred-page English novel entitled, *The Wilfulness of Woman*, Jefferson Davis contributed to his wife's training as a dutiful spouse. Of the book's two headstrong female characters, one died literally out of guilt after leaving her dull husband for a handsome cad, while the other found happiness with an ugly, authoritarian doctor after he cured her of a drinking problem. Husbands, the author insisted, failed their wives if they were too permissive—a mistake that Jefferson Davis was not likely to make.[25] This moral was not lost on Varina.

Her efforts to gain her husband's approval continued. "Jeff . . . says I am a good girl," she wrote her parents in August 1850, a compromise year for both the nation and for the Davises. A relieved Mrs. Howell wrote her daughter that Jeff "thinks you *now* the finest woman he knows. You cannot know how gratified we felt—the *manner he said it*—was feeling and full of pride and affection."[26]

The Davises returned to Brierfield after Jefferson resigned in 1851 from the Senate to run for the governorship of Mississippi. This bid for office ended unsuccessfully, a result that troubled him much more than it did his wife. Varina wrote her mother, "You know my heart never went with Jeff in politics or soldiering—so it does not feel sore on the subject of his defeat."[27] Soon thereafter, Varina finally became pregnant, and after seven years of marriage, the Davises' first child, Samuel Emory, was born at Brierfield on July 30, 1852.[28] The birth of a son thrilled the forty-four-year-old father. It is quite possible that some of Jefferson's early irritation with Varina and part of her feelings of inadequacy had been caused by their failure to have children.

From autumn 1851 through March 1853, the Davises enjoyed the happiest days they would ever spend at Brierfield. When Franklin Pierce became president in 1853, he asked his friend Davis to join his cabinet, but Jefferson, initially heeding Varina's urgings not to accept office, rejected the offer. At Pierce's inauguration, however, he reversed his decision without consulting his wife and agreed to become secretary of war.[29] Back in Washington the Davises rented first a house on Fourteenth Street, and then, in 1854, they leased a large mansion at G and Eighteenth, two blocks from the White House.[30] There, they entertained far more frequently than they did when Jefferson had been a legislator. He preferred working and studying to attending parties and looked on the social side of politics as an irksome chore. Nonetheless, he and Varina gave their share of receptions and other functions for the politically powerful. Varina described to her mother a typical day: "I have Nina Wood [eldest daughter of Zachary Taylor, sister of Jefferson Davis's first wife] again staying with me. She came over to go to the Brazilian Minister's ball. I did not go, but Nina and Jeff described it to me. . . . I had not intended going, but if I had[,] would have been too tired to do so, as we had a gentleman's dinner of 22 that day, and did not rise from the table until near ten o'clock." She continued, "Tell Billy, I am universally acknowledged to give the finest dinners in Washington, with the most elegant decorations—but all would I give to run round the corner with him and stuff bananas."[31] Varina, although considerably more congenial than her husband, also preferred the company of a few close friends to large gatherings. Despite her pride at her accomplishments as a hostess, Varina's letters to her parents contain far more references to the Davis children and to health than to social affairs.

On June 13, 1854, eleven weeks after Varina's festive letter of March 26 to her mother, Baby Samuel died following an illness of several weeks. Both parents were devastated. The loss of their firstborn was slightly eased by the birth on February 25, 1855, of a daughter whom they named Margaret. Four more children were to follow: the last three children arrived after their father's fiftieth birthday.[32] Besides her own children, Varina assumed the task of raising her youngest sister, Margaret, as well as her youngest brother, Jefferson Davis Howell, who had been born after Varina's marriage to Jefferson Davis and named for him.

Varina turned thirty years old in 1856. "It is getting to be a great many years," she wrote her father in 1858, "since I have ceased to do what I would, and been forced to do what I could[.] That is the lot of all flesh, I suppose—But oh it would be lovely sometimes to cut duty, and go on a *bust*." In a letter to her mother a week later, Varina wrote, "Cares do wear out one's youth."[33] Even though Varina had begun to lose her youthful looks, Jefferson found the more compliant and often pregnant Varina a more satisfying wife than the demanding teenager whom he had married. Davis concluded one letter to his wife: "God bless and preserve you all and grant me soon again to have my arms about my dearie o."[34] Jefferson, however, like other patriarchs, continued to control his wife's comings and goings and still vetoed many of Varina's requests to visit her parents. The occasions when he permitted her freedom were much rarer than his declarations of sentimental longing and appreciation.

During the 1850s and for the remaining years of their marriage, Varina increasingly sought Jefferson's approval by making herself useful to his career. In 1857 Davis returned to the Senate. While he was in Mississippi inspecting flood damage at Brierfield in 1859, she wrote him from Washington on the day after she gave birth to their fourth child that she expected soon to have 2,780 pieces of mail ready to send to his constituents. Being helpful to him in his political life was easier than convincing Jefferson to spend more time with her and the children. Varina sought to overcome her loneliness and at the same time help her overworked husband by acting as his competent secretarial assistant.[35]

Although the Davises always seemed to fall short of meeting each other's expectations, when Varina became critically ill in 1857 following the birth of their third child, a distraught Jefferson refused to leave the house for three days until his wife rallied. The next year he suffered dreadfully from the recurrence of a painful eye inflammation, and Varina spent months reading to him and answering all of his mail. She taught herself how to copy her husband's handwriting so well that few could distinguish his signature from her imitation of it.[36] Some of the personal crises during the Washington years, such as the death of their first child and the illnesses that they both endured, brought the Davises closer together, but tensions between them over his family, which had contributed substantially to their marital difficulties in the late 1840s, continued into the decade of the 1850s. In 1852 Jefferson and Varina fell out with Joseph Davis. The causes of the rift between the two brothers are not entirely clear, but one probable reason was Jefferson's insistence on changing his will to provide more for Varina after the birth of their son, Samuel. So serious was the break between the brothers that Jefferson even considered selling Brierfield plantation and moving elsewhere.[37]

The brothers had reconciled by 1856, but Varina was unwilling to forget the feud. She had never liked Joseph's childless wife, Eliza, and had long resented Joseph's influence over her husband and his attempts to direct her. When their third son was born in 1859, Varina became very irate when Jefferson insisted, over her strong objections, that the baby be named Joseph Evan Davis after his uncle, Joseph Davis, rather than William Howell after Varina's father. She did acknowledge, however, that the baby looked like her brother-in-law. "I pray," she wrote sarcastically, "he may grow out of the resemblance."[38] Varina never did totally relinquish her hostility toward her brother-in-law and his wife, several of her husband's sisters, and some of his nieces, nephews, and their children. Presumably, her lack of confidence in Jefferson's love and in his approval of her stimulated her antagonism toward those Davises, whom she viewed as competitors for his affection and financial resources. Jefferson was much more tolerant of Varina's family than she of his, but then he never felt threatened by them. His father-in-law was unsuccessful in business, and Davis lent him money, found him a temporary job as a government timber agent, and even purchased a house for the Howell family near New Orleans. His generosity toward her relatives strengthened Varina's love of him and her dependence on him.

As the Davises' marriage moved toward greater stability and mutual acceptance, the instability between the North and the South increased. From the beginnings of the debate in Congress over the extension of slavery into the territories, Davis had taken a strong proslavery position and by 1850 had emerged as a leader of the southern rights group in the Senate. However, as a graduate of West Point and as a hero of the Mexican War, he felt a deeper commitment to the union than did some of his fellow states' rightists. His reputation as a figure of both national and sectional prominence increased during his service as secretary of war from 1853 to 1857. When President Pierce's term of office expired, the Mississippi legislature elected Davis to the United States Senate. During his last Senate term, he strongly defended slavery and its expansion. However, Davis's sincere support of both nationalism and sectionalism kept him free from the bitterest battles in Congress. His compelling personality, hard work, and devotion to principle earned him the respect of men on both sides of the sectional fence and a reputation as one of the most able and statesmanlike southern politicians of the day.[39]

In their correspondence the Davises almost never mentioned slavery. Not surprisingly, they never questioned the institution, even within the privacy of their marriage. In addition, they almost never mentioned interacting with individual slaves other than their close personal servants, of whom they were very fond. They apparently accepted slavery as a given and chose to be oblivious to the moral questions rising in the North. Living mostly in Washington, they were far removed from the day-to-day operation of their plantation, Brierfield, which was operated by Jefferson's brother Joseph, a famously enlightened slaveholder.[40] Davis was well positioned to be statesmanlike.

Neither Varina nor Jefferson Davis was an ardent secessionist. Their personal letters of the late 1850s lack the hostile observations about Northerners that leap out from the correspondence of many Southerners. As the country neared schism, their letters are filled with regret over the course of political events. Even after the 1860 election of Abraham Lincoln, Varina wrote her husband from Washington that she had refused to answer all who asked what Davis's intentions were and criticized those who "talked so impudently of disunionism."[41] After all efforts at sectional compromise seemingly had failed, the Davises finally surrendered their hopes for a political reconciliation. Mississippi seceded on January 9, 1861, and twelve days later Davis, in spite of being worn out from the excruciating pain of an attack of neuralgia, resigned gracefully from the Senate in a dramatic, final speech.[42]

The Davises returned to Mississippi, where Davis received an offer to take command of Mississippi's troops. Soon, however, a messenger arrived

at Brierfield with the news that the Montgomery convention of representatives from seceding states had chosen Jefferson Davis as president of the
provisional Confederate government. Varina Davis remembered years
later that when the messenger arrived she and her husband were working
in their rose garden. When Davis read the telegram he "looked so grieved
that I feared some evil had befallen our family." In hindsight, it had. A
few days earlier Davis had doubted his ability to fulfill the office of president and stated that he thought he "could perform the functions of genl."
Varina, too, thought his talents were best suited for service as a soldier.
"He did not know the arts of the politician," she candidly wrote, "and
would not practise them if understood."[43] He accepted the presidency,
however reluctantly, and departed for Montgomery, the temporary capital
of the Confederate States of America, where he was inaugurated on February 18, 1861, at the age of fifty-three, one week before their sixteenth
wedding anniversary. In that moment Varina and Jefferson Davis became
the most famous couple in the Confederacy.

Jefferson Davis's accession to the presidency of the Confederacy was
the defining moment in his and Varina's marriage, and yet in her memoir
of him and in their correspondence there is no evidence that Jefferson
asked Varina's opinion on the matter. A proud Jefferson, writing to Varina
two days after his inauguration, wished she and the children had been
with him on his triumphal entry into Montgomery. "The people," he
wrote, "at every station manifested good will and approbation by bonfires
at night, firing by day, shouts and salutations in both. . . . I constantly
wished to have you all with me."[44] Varina and the children joined him in
Montgomery in March. After three months the president and his pregnant
wife and family moved with the government to Richmond. There they
lived at the Spotswood Hotel for one month before moving to the former
Brockenbrough home, the Confederacy's White House, a three-storied
mansion with large rooms and silver hinges on the interior doors, marble
statues of classical figures, and a lovely garden with cherry and apple trees.
The house remained their home for the next forty-five months, and it was
there that they together lived out the tragedy of the Civil War.[45]

Almost four decades after the war ended, Varina wrote that she rather
than her husband foresaw the Confederacy's defeat from its very beginning. "The dear but desperate days of my Richmond life were the more
painful to me as silence was necessary on my part, but from the first day
of secession I felt like some poor creature circulating about a whirlpool
helpless and drawing every moment nearer to the vortex. My dear husband's noble faith in the final triumph of the right I never shared. The
paper blockade quietly permitted by foreign nations and acknowledged
as binding seemed to me to close all avenues to the repair of the war's
waste—I felt the birthright of our people was well worth the war, but knew
from the first we had lost it."[46]

Unlike many other Confederate couples, the Davises were not separated for long periods during the crisis of the Civil War; thus, less is known of their personal feelings toward one another during this tumultuous period. The burdens, however, that accompanied being the president and first lady of the Confederacy were huge. Davis sought for over four years to hold off an enemy vastly superior in wealth, material, and manpower. Varina, although she was pregnant for almost one-third of the Confederacy's life span, tried even harder than she had previously done to be useful and supportive to her beleaguered, fatigued, and fretful husband. Jefferson was frequently in ill health, and Varina sometimes sought to protect him from visitors. For instance, in September 1861, "the President was stricken with a severe attack of neuralgia." Varina, it is alleged, received cabinet members and other officials to determine whose business was so urgent as to be granted bedside interviews with President Davis while "the others had to be satisfied with discussing the matters at hand" with the first lady.[47]

On December 16, 1861, Varina gave birth to their fourth son, the first child of the Confederacy, named William Howell after her father. Remarkably, Varina recuperated in time to receive callers at Christmas. A comforting wartime mother, she also consoled her weary husband, reading him novels when he was too tired to read or to sleep.[48]

Occasionally, Varina attempted to give him political advice—for example, urging him just before the death of the Confederacy not to return the unpopular, unsuccessful Braxton Bragg to high command.[49] As in the earlier years of their marriage, he frequently ignored her advice. During Jefferson's many illnesses he willingly accepted soothing and sympathy from Varina, but he rejected her proposals that she be allowed to nurse the wounded in Richmond's hospitals on the grounds that he did not wish "to expose the men to the restraint my presence might have imposed." Furthermore, he turned down her suggestions that they receive guests more frequently at the Confederate White House. Varina believed, probably rightly so, that social gatherings might win him the political support that he urgently needed but often lacked.[50] Jefferson's continued poor health and disdain for society, as well as the high cost of entertaining in the Confederate capital, prevented Varina from publicly being as much the political helpmate as she would have liked.

Even so, both Jefferson and Varina soon discovered that being constantly on display in crowded and gossip-ridden Richmond parlors was both exasperating and demoralizing. Neither of them, especially Jefferson, had a thick skin, and both increasingly found it impossible to ignore the attacks from other Confederates who blamed Davis for the South's defeats. Jefferson had long demonstrated a lack of ability to handle criticism. As Varina observed in her memoir, he "was abnormally sensitive to disapprobation: even a child's disapproval discomposed him. He felt how much he was misunderstood," she recalled, "and the sense of mortification and injustice gave him a repellent manner."[51]

Impatient with politics, Davis proved to be a poor administrator who responded negatively to most advice and to all opposition. Although he realized that excoriating others turned those who disagreed with him into permanent, personal enemies, Davis could not, as he wrote Varina, "learn just to let people alone who snap at me . . . to turn away . . . from the cats as the snakes."[52] Rebuking others in ways that provoked personal conflicts was a habit that he could not break. The sharp voices of Confederate discontentment over southern losses and defeat caused Davis to suffer attacks of stress, which often left him physically unwell for weeks at a time. He suffered especially from a nervous stomach and from relentless pain in the nerves of his face.[53]

Despite Jefferson's fragile health he devoted himself primarily to being a commander in chief who clearly wished to be in the field and enjoyed "riding off to attend a war council, visiting some general's headquarters, or witnessing battle action." In one letter to Varina, Davis wrote, "If I could take one wing [of the army] and Lee the other I think we could between us wrest a victory from those people."[54] Many critics within the Confederacy accused him of overestimating his own military abilities and of devoting "too much attention to picking, comparing, and advising generals on strategy and tactics."[55]

Varina refused to deny herself the satisfaction of attacking her husband's critics. One Virginian, after spending several hours with Varina, described her as being "a very smart, intelligent and agreeable person, quite independent, [who] says what she pleases and cuts at people generally."[56] However, Varina's sarcastic vituperations were usually in response to abuse by others of her or of the president. As early as the fall of 1861, the castigation of her husband, principally on his military handling of the war, began to reach her, and as it increased so did her indignation. She broke with Lydia Johnston, a friend from Washington days, after Lydia's husband Joseph E. Johnston, one of the Confederacy's most respected and able generals, quarreled with Jefferson. Varina retaliated, not only against those who abused her husband, but also against those who maliciously labeled her a "squaw" because her complexion was dark. Her good friend, Mary Boykin Chesnut, reported, however, that many of the stories of the Davises' maligning others were false or exaggerated.[57] During the early years of their marriage, Jefferson and Varina had faced hostility within their marriage; now it came from without, from detractors North and South. Ironically, the Civil War strengthened their relationship.

The question is, How involved was Varina in the actual guidance of the Confederate war effort? By the time of the war she had made a full commitment to their marriage on Jefferson's terms. More than a quiet helpmate, she was outspoken in defending his positions and his policies. Picturing her as a cross that he had to bear seems not just unfair but also wrong. She was not the shrew of the Confederacy. Was she the *éminence grise* of the Confederacy? Probably not. That question carries speculation too far, particularly in view of the dearth of documentation. However, a careful reading of the available materials—many of them, of course, memoirs written long after the fact and hence documents embraced by historians with extreme caution—does raise questions as to just what was going on within the confines of the Confederate White House. It is well documented that Davis was frequently incapacitated by illness during his presidency. For days, even weeks at a time, he was bedridden and frequently speechless. Eli Evans in his marvelous biography of Judah P. Benjamin, Davis's attorney general, secretary of war, and secretary of state, gives Benjamin a large but little noted role in the conduct of the Confederacy's affairs, including writing all the president's messages to Congress.[58] In addition, according to Evans, Benjamin worked closely with and through Varina in his dealings with Davis. "Benjamin," he wrote, "needed to know the day-to-day state of the President's health in order to respond to him in his office, and she needed to know in timely detail the pressures of his office in order to deal with him at home. Together and by turns, they could help him over the most difficult days."[59]

Speculation that Davis was in the hands of his wife is not new. It certainly was rife among the detractors of Davis during and after the war. These speculations of course were not raised in a kindly manner, but they usually took the form of accusing Davis of acquiescing in Varina's extravagance in equipage and entertainment. She was also accused of influencing his appointments based on her personal relations with the wives of the proposed appointees. It is interesting that people who could write most caustically of Varina's appearance, personality, and behavior never suggested she might be meddling with policy decisions or personal decisions other than those influenced by female *pique*. Discretion being the watchword, any solid evidence of Varina's involvement in running the Confederate government probably never existed, and since Jefferson was not given to sharing credit and since Varina devoted the years of her widowhood to tending the fame of Jefferson, few subsequent claims were ever made.

In evaluating her role during the war years there are several tenuous threads of evidence that can be followed: the extent, gravity and form of Jefferson's illnesses; comments, however elliptical, by the principals in later years; rumors and innuendo that floated about the couple during and after the war; and the observations of supposedly wise and judicious historians.

A recent careful compilation, of Jefferson's illnesses in the first 200 days of 1863 finds him ill at home for fifty days.[60] His illnesses were frequently very incapacitating and severe, and often confined him to his bed. On one occasion, according to Evans, Jefferson Davis who "had lain speechless for several weeks before Chancellorsville, suddenly awoke to find the upstairs of the White House almost deserted because Varina had been spending the evening at the Chesnuts, sentries guarded the door, but inside, the servants were running around frightened. Some were on their knees praying. Soldiers yelled at them that the Yankees were not that close, when suddenly a slim drawn figure appeared at the top of the stairs. Jefferson Davis was propping himself up against the bannisters with his head hanging and arms dangling with loaded pearl-handled pistols in each hand."[61]

During Davis's illnesses some authors credit his small staff of secretaries with maintaining the flow of speeches, letters, messages, and orders under his name, as well as with selecting those visitors permitted to see him. However, there is a fascinating quotation from Dr. John Burgess of Columbia University, who knew Varina in her later years in New York City: "It used to be said that she and Benjamin ran the machine at Richmond. However that may be, I can testify that she was capable of running that or any other machine, with or without Benjamin or anyone else. She was a personality with the instincts of a sensitive woman and the judgement of the strongest man. She was also endowed with tender feeling, and indomitable will. Her powers of conversation and description were superior to those of any other woman I have ever known."[62]

Late in her life, Varina wrote, "The letter you appended is not in my husband's hand but in mine—I write so like him, changing my hand as years modified his, that no one but I could distinuish between our writing."[63] Shortly before her death she wrote, "My husband's autographs are extremely rare; though thousands are sold, they are mine. For many years I wrote at his dictation all his letters, signed all his papers etc, and no one knew the difference as I had practiced his calligraphy so he even did not recognize the difference between the two."[64] These statements are usually taken to apply to letters written after the war. However, there is an interesting statement from the middle of December 1864 by J. B. Jones in his *A Rebel War Clerk's Diary* when Davis had been ill for some days: "Some people still believe the President is dead. . . . I saw his endorsements on papers, today . . . and it was a bold hand."[65] In summary, even though Jefferson was frequently very ill, directives continued to flow out of the Confederate White House over his signature. There is much evidence that Varina could readily mimic his handwriting and signature, and had been doing so for years. No one else is known to have had that skill. Varina must be recognized, in all probability, as having been heavily involved in any White House operations that covered for Jefferson when he was ill. Given her intelligence we can further speculate that she contributed more than just her skill at forgery. It seems possible that the intimate strategy of the Davises was that Varina, perhaps working with some other close presidential associates, was more involved in the government of the Confederacy than her rumor-spreading detractors imagined.

The last year of the Confederacy began with a personal tragedy for the Davises. A fall from the corner of the porch of the Confederate White House killed their five-year-old son, Joseph, on April 30, 1864. He was, wrote Varina, "Mr. Davis's hope, and greatest joy in life."[66] Mary Boykin Chesnut recalled the grieving parents at the funeral. "The dominant figure, that poor, old gray-haired man. Standing bareheaded, straight as an arrow, clear against the sky by the open grave of his son. She stood back in her heavy black wrappings, and her tall figure drooped. The flowers, the children, the procession as it moved, comes and goes. But these two dark, sorrow-stricken figures stand—They rise before me now. . . . Who will they kill next, of that devoted household?"[67] The death of little Joseph had created in the Confederacy sympathy for Varina. In a letter to Mary Boykin Chesnut at her home in Camden, South Carolina, Varina wrote, "People do not snub me any longer, for it was only while the lion was dying that he was kicked; dead, he was beneath contempt." On June 27, Varina gave birth to their second daughter, Winnie (Varina Anne), who one day would be known as the Daughter of the Confederacy. Since General William T. Sherman had begun his march on Atlanta and General Ulysses S. Grant pounded General Robert E. Lee in Petersburg, the president had little time to think of his family.[68]

As the Confederacy's fortunes declined, so did the health of its president. Celeste Clay, the wife of a high-level member of the war department, wrote in January 1865: "Every body is down on Mr. Davis. . . . He looks badly—old, gray, wrinkled. I never saw a more troubled countenance in my life."[69] Nevertheless, for better or for worse, Varina's physical and emotional support of Davis enabled him to keep going as president of the Confederacy for over four years. When Grant's army finally captured Petersburg and the fall of Richmond became inevitable, Jefferson decided that Varina and the four surviving children must be sent out of range of the approaching enemy. After selling her silver, china, some of her clothes, and other personal possessions, a reluctant Varina with the children headed south, stopping first in Charlotte, North Carolina. Davis soon followed, and for days they journeyed separately through the collapsing Confederacy. They passed through South Carolina and into Georgia, evading Yankee patrols and marauding bands of former Confederate soldiers, occasionally together, but usually apart. Husband and wife exchanged tense notes reporting the surrender of southern troops and sharing their worries for each other and for their children.[70]

Hearing rumors of the presence of soldiers in the area, Jefferson and his party joined Varina's group on May 10. That night, federal cavalry found their camp near Irwinville, Georgia. Guards took the Davises to Fortress Monroe, Virginia, where the federal government imprisoned Jefferson for two years. Varina was taken next to Savannah, where officials kept her under virtual house arrest, fearful that she might try to arrange her husband's escape. Feelings of anxiety and fear almost overwhelmed her. "If you only could know," she wrote Davis, "what an awful responsibility I feel—without your counsel, your decision." Varina claimed she could not stand alone and wrote him, "If we are not to be reunited may God take me to himself."[71]

At first, Jefferson's captors chained him and denied him communication with his guards or with the outside world. Gradually, however, his treatment improved, and in late August the authorities gave him permission to write his wife about family affairs. In one such letter, written in September 1865, Davis acknowledged to Varina how sad he felt "that public cares and frequent absence and preoccupation with disagreeable subjects had prevented me from making even the poor return which it was in my power to give." Jefferson, although he tried to maintain a confident façade in his letters to Varina, could not hide the sense of powerlessness that imprisonment had created. Despair over his fate led him to include in his letters far more declarations of religious faith than at any other time in his life. The Lord, he assured Varina, would make certain that husband and wife could eventually work together to prove his "innocence of wrong to my fellow man."[72]

A desperate Varina wrote a pleading letter to President Andrew Johnson on August 30, 1865, about her worn and exhausted husband, begging the president to allow her to go to him. "I would bear any privations . . . take and keep any parole, to be with him, even if only for an hour each day. His health is always frail, and I have been used to ministering to him at such times as he has been suffering, and consider it the chief priviledge [sic] of my life. Before you refuse me pray remember how very long I have been seperated [sic] from him and how much I have suffered."[73] Johnson never replied to this letter, and Varina was not reunited with Jefferson until May 1866.

Although other former Confederate leaders had been released from custody, many in the North viewed the former president as the symbol of secession and civil war who must be punished for the four years of national devastation. A jury in a federal circuit court in Norfolk, Virginia, indicted Jefferson Davis for treason, but the United States government refused either to bring him to trial or to release him. Davis, who then and later vehemently denied that he had committed any crime, rejected suggestions from the federal government to the effect that he might be granted a pardon if only he would apply for one. Finally, in May 1867, a year after Varina and little Winnie had joined him at Fortress Monroe, federal officials agreed to release him into the custody of the federal district court in Richmond. The court freed him on bond of $100,000, the bulk of it guaranteed by the well-known Northerners Horace Greeley, Cornelius Vanderbilt, and Gerrit Smith. Davis never went to trial. The government finally dropped all charges against him following the general amnesty order issued by President Andrew Johnson on Christmas Day, 1868.[74]

Varina had played an active role in the campaign to free her husband. While still detained in Georgia, she wrote letters to President Johnson, Secretary of State William Henry Seward, General Ulysses S. Grant, and other prominent men. From Fortress Monroe she had traveled to Washington for interviews with President Johnson and with Attorney General Henry Stanbery and to Baltimore and New York to confer with the lawyers who would finally secure Jefferson's liberation. Varina's personal pleas on behalf of her husband were not always well received. Senator William Pitt Fessenden of Maine wrote after spending an hour and a half with her in Washington: "She is a terrible talker, and presents everything in the worst light, and will do much harm. I don't know but the best thing would be to let him out and shut her up in his place."[75]

Following Jefferson's release from prison in May 1867, the Davises went to Canada, where Jefferson, although still thin, nervous, and lacking energy, recovered from his ordeal. Hoping that warm weather and familiar scenes would further restore his health, Jefferson and Varina traveled aimlessly to Baltimore, to Cuba where he checked on some funds that former Confederate officials had deposited earlier, and to Louisiana and Mississippi for reunions with his brother, Joseph, and several surviving sisters. In the fall of 1868, accompanied by their four children, the Davises left for an extended stay in Europe. There the family remained for over a year. Daughter Maggie, age fourteen, was taught by a governess and then sent to a convent school in Paris. Twelve-year-old Jefferson, Jr., and seven-year-old Billy were placed in English boarding schools. Their father, without Varina, visited Scotland and Switzerland, both of which impressed him favorably, and Paris, with her, which did not. They both enjoyed being entertained by English society and witnessing the installation of the bishop of London at St. Paul's Cathedral. Both Varina and Jefferson complained of poor health, but in Europe they could escape, if only temporarily, from the scenes of defeat and from their sense of lost power and reputation. Nevertheless, by the summer of 1869 Davis was eager to return to the United States. In the fall, he sailed for home. Varina and the children were to remain in Europe until he could find a permanent home for them.[76]

Jefferson, who had turned sixty-one in the summer of 1869, was determined, despite his age, to obtain a position that would enable him to support in style his wife and children. Since 1865, they had lived off funds that apparently had come in part from the assets of the defunct Confederacy and in part from the contributions of a few admirers of the Lost Cause.[77] While they were in Europe, their funds had shrunk, and Joseph Davis had sold Brierfield to freedmen.[78] Jefferson considered himself too proud to live off the charity of others. Soon after his arrival home from England, the directors of the Carolina Insurance Company, a Memphis-based firm, offered him the presidency of the business at an annual salary of $12,000. Prior to responding to this proposition, Jefferson wrote Varina in England asking her where she preferred to live. Before she could reply, however, he accepted the insurance company's offer.[79]

Jefferson was in Memphis and Varina and the children in Europe for much of 1870. There she suffered from nervous attacks, pain in her eyes, and other ailments. "I have been so tried," she wrote Jefferson, "for the last seven years that I think now a heavy sorrow would drive me mad." She attributed her chronic unhappiness and moodiness to her rootless and uncertain existence since the beginning of the war and lamented to Jefferson "at middle age a woman loses much of her powers."[80] Finally, in August, Jefferson sailed for Europe and returned to Memphis with Varina and the three youngest children. They settled in a rented house on fashionable Court Street, but the untroubled existence for which they must have yearned still eluded them.

All to no avail Jefferson and Varina had sought to shield their children from what had happened to them since that fateful day in 1861. Their temporary postwar residence in Canada, their stay in England, and their evaluation of possible places to live in the South were influenced in part by their parental eagerness to protect their children from the allegations of ineptness and the cloud of failure that had hovered over Jefferson Davis's head since he accepted leadership of the Confederacy in 1861. Unfortunately, here too, the Davises failed. Of the two surviving Davis sons, ten-year-old William, the first of their children born in the White House of the Confederacy, died of diphtheria in the fall of 1872, two years after the family had moved to Memphis. Of the four Davis sons, Samuel, Joseph, and now Billy were gone, and only Jefferson, Jr., born in 1857, survived. Young Jeff's bad conduct and poor academic performance, however, led his father to withdraw him from the Virginia Military Institute in 1874. The young man returned to Memphis and continued to disappoint his parents until a yellow fever epidemic swept him away too in 1878 at the age of twenty-one. The death of their last remaining son left Jefferson "crushed under such repeated and heavy blows" and set off attacks of nervous neuralgia in both parents.[81]

The two surviving daughters provided companionship and other enduring satisfactions for their parents, but with them too, there were disappointments. The Davises' older daughter, Maggie, a sensible and devoted, if somewhat overly serious girl, married Joel Addison Hayes, Jr., a promising Memphis banker, on January 1, 1876. Hayes proved to be a responsible and thoughtful son-in-law and financial adviser to both of the Davises. Varina and Jefferson were delighted by the birth of grandchildren, three boys—one of whom lived only a few months—and two girls. The Hayeses, however, moved to distant Colorado in 1884 because of Addison's ill health, and although Maggie and the children came regularly for visits, her parents missed them greatly. The Davises' youngest daughter, Winnie, a shy and bookish child, pleased both parents, but she was placed in a school in Germany from 1876 to 1881 to escape her parents' notoriety.[82]

Lack of money was another source of concern and uncertainty for Jefferson and Varina. Before the war as a planter of means, Davis had been accustomed to a large income. He had accepted the job with the Carolina Life Insurance Company because he believed it offered him the best opportunity to revive his fortunes. Like many other American insurance companies, however, the Carolina had difficulty paying the heirs of its deceased policyholders in the 1870s. Davis failed to raise additional funds to rescue the firm, and when he thought that the directors were not concerned enough about meeting the company's obligations, he resigned as president in August 1873. An unemployed and discouraged Jefferson wrote Varina that their bills exceeded their cash assets. He added that he was even considering selling some of their furniture to meet expenses. The anxiety born from all the financial uncertainty brought Davis a recurrence of the facial pain that had long troubled him. Sixty-five years old, in debt, and with no certain prospects for income, Jefferson understandably was depressed. He fell ill in a Louisville hotel on his way to meet Varina and was "at death's door." Jefferson recovered, however, and once back in Memphis, Varina succumbed to attacks of nerves.[83]

When doctors recommended a sea voyage for him to overcome poor health and depression, Davis argued that he could not leave Varina because of her bad health, but she insisted he place consideration of his health over hers. Davis left Varina in Memphis to supervise their daughters and sailed in early 1874 for England, where he spent six months recovering his health and investigating business opportunities. Before leaving for England, Jefferson wrote to his wife: "Oh my beloved Winnie how dark would be the future if deprived of your helpful, hope giving presince [sic]." Jefferson called her "the love of all my mature life, the partner of all my great efforts, and more than equal sharer of all my trials and sorrows."[84] It is difficult to ascertain what parts of sincerity, obedience to romantic conformity, and guilt for leaving her lay behind these effusions, especially since in the postwar years Davis was frequently away from Varina and his family by choice.[85]

Varina, so beautiful in the 1840s and 1850s, was losing her looks, becoming sickly and overweight, and in her letters acerbic and complaining. She was not the only object of Davis's search for someone to share his "trials and sorrows." Jefferson in the postwar era increasingly turned to other women for solace and ego reinforcement, writing Varina frankly of his many meetings and conversations with other women. There are also over sixty surviving postwar letters between Davis and Virginia Clay, the wife of Clement Clay, his colleague in the United States Senate, in the Confederacy, and in prison at Fortress Monroe. Davis addressed Virginia, a former belle who never lost the ability to dazzle men, "as the friend who most gives me joy" and wrote to her that he longed to share with her his most intimate thoughts. Clearly, Davis and Virginia Clay admired one another and enjoyed a romantic and affectionate correspondence.[86]

During the 1870s, Davis also developed a deeply emotional relationship with Mary Humphreys Stamps, the widow of his nephew who had been killed at Gettysburg. After the war Mary ran a school for girls in New Orleans, where Jefferson often visited. In one letter following a visit to the Crescent City, Davis apologized because he feared that "the love I bear you has no doubt often led me to speak to you so plainly as to bore you." He later wrote Mary from France that a statue of the Queen of Navarre in the Luxembourg Gardens had reminded him of her, "far away yet ever near."[87]

Although one must guard against the dangers of underestimating Victorian extramarital affairs, these relationships were probably innocent, but they do call into question his "stainless personal character,"[88] attributed to him later by his ever-faithful wife. Varina, apparently, tolerated up to a point his attachments to other women, but she was also jealous of them. Her strongest objections to Jefferson's involvement with other women would come, however, over his association with Sarah Dorsey.

In May 1876 Varina and Jefferson sailed to Europe where Jefferson conferred again with English businessmen. Jefferson returned home in November, leaving Varina, who was seriously ill, in England at the home of her sister, Margaret Howell De Stoess. Jefferson had by this time decided to devote himself full time to writing a history of the Confederacy, both to make money for his family and to defend his record as its president. He began to look for a quiet place to work. By the end of the year, he had settled, again without consulting Varina, at Beauvoir, the Gulf Coast home of Sarah Anne Ellis Dorsey.

Davis's hostess and friend had been born in 1829, near Natchez, the daughter of a plantation owner of great wealth. Sarah was acquainted with Varina, who was three years older than Sarah. She perhaps had also known Jefferson. Following Sarah's marriage to Samuel W. Dorsey in 1853, she traveled extensively abroad and won some notice as an author. A very intelligent woman, her literary output included four novels and several essays. In the early 1870s she became acquainted or reacquainted with Davis, whom she admired as the former leader of the Confederacy. Following her husband's death in 1875, she welcomed Davis in 1876 to Beauvoir, where he lived in a small cottage near the main house. Mrs. Dorsey served as his unpaid secretary and literary adviser on his book. Throughout 1877 they worked together on this history.[89]

This living arrangement and collaboration, not surprisingly, angered Varina who had served as her husband's scribe since the 1850s. She became especially embittered when Davis recommended that Varina stay abroad rather than join him at Beauvoir. Varina resented Sarah Dorsey, but at first her letters to Jefferson only hinted at her displeasure. Eventually, however, Davis chided his wife for not answering his hostess's letters, thus sparking an outburst. "Nothing on earth would pain me like living" at Beauvoir "in her house," she wrote Jefferson. She also complained to him that other people's questions about what parts of his book Mrs. Dorsey was writing "aggravated [her] nearly to death."[90]

Almost a year after Davis had left his sick wife in Europe, Varina crossed the Atlantic without telling Jefferson that she was coming home and arrived in Memphis in October 1877. For ten days Davis, now seventy, visited Varina, who was then nearly fifty-two but when he departed, the question of where they would live was unresolved. He returned to Beauvoir, and she remained in Memphis with their daughter Margaret. Varina wrote Jefferson in April 1878 that she would refuse to see the other woman if she called on her in Memphis. "Let us agree to disagree about her, and I will bear my separation from you as I have the last six months," she added. Perhaps thinking of herself but speaking of another woman, she continued that it was "very bitter to have to play the role of deserted Wife, and the pity of outsiders stings like scorpions."[91] One male biographer of Varina Davis proved to be most unsympathetic to Varina on the Dorsey issue. He wrote, "Interestingly, Varina made no mention of how her husband might bear separation from her." He contended that Jefferson Davis "dealt patiently with his high-strung wife."[92] Hudson Strode, another Davis biographer, considered Varina at times neurotic, and he was seemingly perplexed that Varina refused to "board at Sarah Dorsey's."[93]

A recent biographer of Jefferson Davis wrote of the Dorsey affair, "Here was an added strain Davis did not need. Middle age and years of hardship were bringing out some of those qualities in Varina that so troubled him in their first years together. Happily, he had acquired perspective and patience by now in dealing with Varina."[94]

Despite Jefferson's lack of understanding of Varina's feelings about Mrs. Dorsey and the humiliation she suffered because of the public's perception of impropriety on the part of her husband, Varina managed to isolate the issue—as her April 18, 1878, letter to Jefferson suggests—so that their strained relationship was not totally destroyed. After being separated from her husband for almost twenty months, Varina finally joined him in July 1878 at Beauvoir, where she replaced Sarah as his secretary. Ironically, Sarah Dorsey nursed Varina back to health at Beauvoir following the death of Jefferson, Jr., in October 1878. Davis snidely wrote in a letter to his daughter, Margaret, that although "Mrs. Dorsey nursed her with unwearied care . . . 'the sick man knows the Physician's step, but when he is well cannot remember his face.' "[95]

However, Sarah Dorsey did not remain long at Beauvoir after Varina arrived. Doctors discovered Sarah had cancer, and after months of medical treatment in New Orleans, she wrote Jefferson that she had agreed to have surgery "under which I may perhaps sink though of course I am in hopes to survive it." A very concerned Jefferson Davis was at Sarah's bedside when she died at the age of fifty in New Orleans on July 4, 1879. While he was with Sarah he burned—at her request, Varina tells us—all of her personal papers. He wrote Varina of the death vigil and that "I should be as mean as some of her kin, if I did not feel grateful for many kindnesses and deeply grieved at her death."[96] Before her death, Sarah had sold Beauvoir to Jefferson for $2,500 in notes, and in her will she left him not only that property, on which he had yet to make a payment, but also two Louisiana plantations and some land in Arkansas—"everything without reserve."[97] If Jefferson had predeceased Sarah, the will left the entire bequest to his youngest daughter, Winnie. Some of her relatives brought a lawsuit against Davis accusing him of using undue influence with a dying woman. Davis won the case when Sarah's lawyer testified that she had acted of her own will. The property went to Jefferson.[98]

The Dorsey bequests eased the Davises' financial plight. They now had the income from the plantations, which Davis leased out. Although both Varina and Jefferson often complained of being poor, there was enough money to employ several servants at Beauvoir, to take a three-month trip to Europe together in the fall of 1881, and to pay for their young daughter Winnie at a private school in Germany. Davis also finally regained Brierfield, following a complicated lawsuit and the failure of the former slaves to whom Joseph Davis had sold the property to make sufficient payments on their mortgage.[99]

However, the Davises never considered returning to live at Brierfield. Beauvoir remained their home during Jefferson's remaining years. Life there had its pleasant moments. In one letter Varina wrote "Hip, hip hoorah!" She had arranged the books in the Beauvoir library. "Two long days of dust and backache," she explained, "to get Poetry, Fiction and Biography, its first cousin, with Religion, History, Philosophy and Travels to stop nudging the Essayists who have time and again handled them all so roughly."[100] Also, Winnie was often with them as was Maggie Hayes and her children. Both Davises enjoyed raising roses, oranges, strawberries, eggplants, artichokes, and other flowers, fruits, and vegetables. Despite Beauvoir's seclusion, visitors, old friends, and inquisitive reporters and sightseers found them. Living at Beauvoir was a source of contentment for Jefferson, who found its "quiet . . . most desirable." Not so, however, for Varina, who chose to quote Winnie in describing it as "isolated as much as the Island of Elba."[101]

Beauvoir, with its memories of Sarah Dorsey and its remoteness, was only one reason for Varina's discontent. By 1887 Varina was sixty-one years old, and all four of her sons, her parents, and all but one of her ten sisters and brothers were dead. The previous year she had lamented the passing of her Civil War intimate, Mary Boykin Chesnut, and wrote: "My old friends are dropping off very fast, and infirmities are accumulating upon me so that my sixty years begin to be an acknowledged weariness and a trouble."[102] One recompense, although it was at best a satisfaction rather than a joy, was that Varina still felt an infirm Jefferson needed her. Davis, whom she wrote, "thinks he cannot leave home and insists that this is the only place for him—and no matter how much I need change, I must, as you know, stay where duty calls me." He would, Varina predicted, die in a month if she left him alone.[103] Therefore, she would, as she wrote, "stay here and cultivate a few roses, and take care of things."[104]

Davis enjoyed both his home at Beauvoir and receiving there the homage of former Confederate supporters, who seemed to be growing in numbers in the 1880s. Davis had attempted to answer his critics in his history of the Confederacy, completed in 1880 and published the next year, entitled *The Rise and Fall of the Confederate Government*. Its fifteen hundred pages of text and appendices demonstrated Davis's enthusiasm for constitutional, legal, and military matters and his lack of interest in politics and people. These omissions and its rambling digressions suggest that neither Sarah Dorsey, a successful writer, nor Varina, an excellent critic, played a very active role in the selection of the book's topics or its literary style.[105] A recent biographer noted, "Throughout the work the logic of his arguments was the same as it had always been, which is to say almost none at all other than the automatic assumption that his opinion, whatever it might be, was the right one."[106] Although the book was not a commercial success, its publication in 1881 reaffirmed Jefferson Davis's place as the premier leader of the Lost Cause. By 1886, when his health would permit, Davis had begun to make triumphal public tours throughout the South. Guards of honor accompanied him to the enthusiasm of the southern people who were ready to celebrate the Confederacy more than ever.[107]

As for the Davises' relationship during the Beauvoir years, Varina and Jefferson, now in the autumn of their lives, had worked out an accommodation. By the 1880s, both had come to realize that, as Varina had written Jefferson in 1875, "You and I have lived long enough to know that 'other refuge have we none.' "[108] In the 1870s, when he had "sought refuge" with Sarah Dorsey, Virginia Clay, and Mary Stamps, Jefferson had not admitted that. Now Sarah was dead, and his correspondence and meetings with the other two women had become increasingly infrequent. It was the companionship of long familiarity and common experience that came to mean so much to both Jefferson and Varina in their latter years. "We two old people live in one end of an old plantation house, and read and wish sometimes," Varina wrote an old friend.[109]

In early November 1889, the eighty-one-year-old Davis left Beauvoir on one of his regular trips to Brierfield. While en route he contracted bronchitis and became critically ill. Varina, who had been notified of his collapse, managed to intercept and to board the boat carrying him to New Orleans. She accompanied him there and nursed him through several weeks of revival and relapse until Davis died rather suddenly on December 6.

According to Hudson Strode, Varina was gripped by "uncontrolled, rack-
ing sobs."[110] The funeral in New Orleans was perhaps the biggest the
South had ever seen, with mourners numbering two hundred thousand
or more. In death the southern Confederacy and its only president were
fully restored to greatness. Every southern state "tried to claim the remains
for its own." But that day Varina chose to inter him in the Army of
Northern Virginia tomb at Metairie near New Orleans. In 1893, pressed
to select a permanent burial site for her husband, Varina chose Richmond's Hollywood Cemetery, the last resting place of so many Confederate heroes and of their son, Joseph.[111]

Years earlier, Jefferson had led Varina to view her own worth as flowing
from her services to him. His death left her at first feeling empty and
valueless. "Life seems very bitter to me now," the widow wrote several
months later. "Forty-four years I have been my husband's secretary, coun-
sellor & nurse and now my life is, as it were, a dreaded blank."[112] She
changed her name to V. Jefferson Davis or Varina Jefferson Davis, perhaps
assuming his identity to ensure that she and the personal sacrifices she
had offered up to him and to the former Confederacy would not be for-
gotten.[113] Quickly, however, Varina found an escape from her sense of
uselessness after her husband's death when she contracted with a New
York publisher to write her own memoir of Davis. Although praising her
husband's achievements as well as counterattacking his critics, Varina included in the "memoir" passages that made it clear that Davis from her
perspective had often been dogmatic, childish, unpleasant, and unable to
tolerate criticism. Indeed, her insight and candor produced some of the
most perceptive comments about Jefferson Davis that have ever been
published.[114]

Expressing in print the ambivalence of her feelings about her dead
husband may have helped free Varina from the ghost of the man who
had so long dominated her. In any case, she soon began to take actions
that were much criticized at the time, and of which, one can presume,
Jefferson Davis would not have approved. Varina, accompanied by the still
unmarried Winnie, had gone to New York City in the fall of 1890 to read
the proofs of her memoir of Davis. Mother and daughter decided to stay
in Manhattan following the completion of that task, and there Varina
lived, except for brief trips to the South and to northern resorts such as
Niagara Falls, Atlantic City, and Narragansett, for the remaining years of
her life. Varina defended her choice to live in New York City because, she
claimed, it was cheaper to live in New York residential hotels than at
Beauvoir, the heat of the Gulf Coast was harmful to her health, and, most
important, in New York she and Winnie could pursue literary interests
and careers.[115]

For whatever reason, her decision to remain in the North marked the
reemergence of the more independent woman Varina had been before
and during the first years of her marriage. Jefferson never would have per-

mitted his wife and daughter to move to New York. Moreover, within a few months of Davis's death, Varina consented to Winnie's engagement to the upstate New Yorker whose suit Jefferson had opposed. She defended her action on the grounds that she and Jefferson had given their all to the Confederacy, but she "should not surrender my ewe lamb upon an altar."[116] Winnie did not marry her fiancé and she and her mother supported themselves in part from writing occasional articles for the New York *Sunday World*. Both mother and daughter experienced modest success as authors. Varina's columns for the *World* were usually on topics such as "Christmas in the Confederacy," that allowed the newspaper to exploit her as the tragic First Lady of the Lost Cause. Her other publications included essays on manners and raising children and a small, privately published pamphlet telling the story of a tragic and futile Indian war, begun when children began to argue over a grasshopper and escalated by their mothers and fathers into bloodshed and disaster.[117]

The Grasshopper War ironically can be read as an antiwar tract on the foolishness of war, hardly a point of view shared by the author's late husband. Despite such indications of her independence, Varina continued to maintain her position as self-appointed chief defender of Jefferson Davis's reputation. Her memoir, she wrote on its first page, she undertook as a "vindication of his political action."[118] In 1898 Winnie, her youngest daughter, died at thirty-four, after months of suffering from a stomach ailment. Varina buried this doomed child, born in the Confederate White House in 1864 and known as the Daughter of the Confederacy, in Hollywood Cemetery with full military honors.

Varina sought to escape from the grief of losing Winnie, her next-to-last surviving child, by spending long hours in a sculptor's studio in New York City, supervising every detail of a statue commemorating her husband. Although she ordered Burton Harrison, Jefferson's wartime secretary and now a New York attorney, not to respond to some criticism of Davis by former General John B. Gordon in his memoirs, Varina refused to forgive General Nelson Miles, whom she held responsible for subjecting her husband to chaining and other indignities at Fortress Monroe. Varina herself explained why such activities were important to her. "In my times of sorrow and suffering," she wrote a friend, "I have wondered for what use I was spared, but suppose now it must have been to protect the blessed memory of my husband from misrepresentations against which he is powerless to defend himself."[119] Although obsessively concerned with Jefferson Davis's public image, in private letters she acknowledged her own disappointment with their marriage. Around 1903 Varina wrote cryptically, "when one of our women is married, she is, if unhappy, like Sterne's Starling, she cannot 'get out'—and she is truly miserable."[120]

Nevertheless, Varina's letters written during her New York years devoted far more space to financial and health problems than to any other topic including Jefferson's detractors, her own writing, and those who called upon her in order to meet the former First Lady of the Confederacy. Brierfield cost more to maintain than it provided in income, as was the case also with Beauvoir. A significant proportion of Varina's correspondence after Davis's death focused on her efforts to establish Beauvoir as a memorial to Jefferson Davis and their family and as a home for Confederate veterans. Varina had, in fact, received some tempting offers for the property, including one for $90,000, but she refused to sell though pressed for money, since she was convinced the home would have been demolished to build something else. To Varina's way of thinking, Beauvoir was to be the Mount Vernon of the Confederacy. In 1902 the United Sons of Confederate Veterans bought the house at Beauvoir for $10,000, and Varina received $5,000 for the land around the old Dorsey home three years later.[121]

Varina seems to have managed her remaining assets as a planter and a writer rather well and to have had enough income to do most of the things she enjoyed doing. She became the doyenne of the postwar southern colony residing in New York City and often entertained and was entertained.[122] Sickness, indeed, more than money concerns, made independence increasingly difficult for her. Varina, who turned seventy in 1896, gained more and more weight, a condition that contributed to the heart trouble that increasingly restricted her movements and often made it impossible for her to leave her room. In her last years she looked more like Queen Victoria than did Queen Victoria. In 1905 she wrote gloomily that she had "pretty well lived on nitroglycerine and strychnine for a year and a half."[123] Following her death the next year at the age of eighty, she was buried next to Davis in Richmond. Imperious to the end, Varina had requested "every mark of respect and a military funeral such as Winnie had," which she was accorded.[124]

Jefferson Davis, a man whose personal needs and inclinations fitted the patriarchal mold even more neatly than did those of many of his contemporaries, long before had insisted that his wife occupy the subordinate position she had at first resisted. There, on the whole, she remained. In 1872 Varina had sent daughter Maggie on her seventeenth birthday a list of character traits that mother urged daughter to pursue. The young woman, her mother advised, was to be "amiable," "consistent," "humble," "quiet," "respectful," and "tranquil," all the things, namely, that young Varina had not been at the age of seventeen, when she first met Jefferson Davis.[125] Given Jefferson's insistent paternalism, Varina had little choice. She came to understand and even to be able to defend his rigidity. "He is," she wrote in 1888, "a man who sees but one side because he is so freely persuaded in his own mind that he cannot understand anyone not accepting" his opinions. She added, "I envy him his strength of purpose."[126]

Thus, more than most mid-nineteenth-century marriages, the union of

Jefferson and Varina Davis approached the Old South's ideal of patriarchy. Allegedly, Jefferson Davis, during the first few months of his imprisonment in 1865, stated that "women are like the beautiful vines of the South, winding around the rugged forest trees and clothing them with beauty; but let them attempt living apart from this support and they will soon trail along the ground in muddy and trampled impurity."[127] This view of woman's utter dependency upon men he clung to until the end of his life in 1889, despite Varina's being a woman of fierce intelligence and bitingly funny wit.

Jefferson's love for her, if their letters are any indication, was more perfunctory and less emotional than hers for him. That it was not a particularly happy relationship is, perhaps, suggestive to those who believe that totally unequal partnerships between men and women are ill suited to marital joy and satisfaction. If that were true, the fault was not Varina's. There is no doubt she loved Jefferson Davis, but she also desired a far more cooperative and more affective relationship—companionate marriage based on romantic love. As an intelligent, decisive, and confident woman, Varina had in their first years together resisted subordination, finally acquiescing to preserve her marriage. The stresses of the Civil War forced them together, strengthening their marriage, and enabling Varina to play a strong role as the First Lady of the Confederacy. The years after the war were hard for the Davises; particularly for Varina as Jefferson both moved away from her and again subordinated her. It was only following her husband's death that Varina was able to enjoy the independence and recognition she had always sought but had seldom experienced. Varina had, to be sure, come to accept an inferior marital role during Jefferson Davis's lifetime as a personal and social necessity. However, for forty-four years, from their marriage in 1845 until his death in 1889, she apparently had never stopped wanting to help determine her own destiny. Ironically, Jefferson Davis probably denied her something even more precious to Varina than her independence, his enduring love.

TWO

The Lee Marriage

EMORY M. THOMAS

They married in 1831 at Arlington House, the bride's home on the southern side of the Potomac River overlooking Washington, D.C. Mary Anne Randolph Custis, only child of Mary Lee Fitzhugh and George Washington Parke Custis, married a twenty-four-year-old lieutenant on active duty (Engineer Corps) in the United States Army. Robert Edward Lee was accomplished; he graduated second in the class of 1829 at West Point, and the Engineer Corps was then the elite branch of the army. Lee was also handsome, soon to be acknowledged the best-looking man in the U.S. Army, and he came from an old Virginia family. But at the time of this wedding, his twenty-two-year-old bride was clearly the more prominent principal.

Mary Custis, the mother of Mary, was a loving woman possessed of good, practical sense and strong family roots. Parke Custis, father of the bride, was the orphaned grandson of Martha Washington by her first marriage. After his parents died, Parke Custis was adopted by George Washington as his son. Custis thus became "the child of Mount Vernon" and heir to much of the family trappings and property associated with the hero of the Revolution and the nation's first president. The Custis estate at Arlington encompassed 1,100 acres, and Custis also inherited two 4,000-acre plantations, White House and Romancock in the Virginia Tidewater, plus Smith Island in the Chesapeake Bay.[1]

On his wedding day, the groom's parents were both dead. Henry (Light Horse Harry) Lee had been a dashing commander of cavalry during the Revolutionary War, and later governor of Virginia and member of Congress. Robert Lee was the product of his father's second marriage to Ann

Carter, who proved herself to be loyal and resourceful in the extreme. Harry Lee was careless with money and truth; he left his family in 1813 when Robert was six, ostensibly to recover his health in the West Indies. Harry Lee was one step ahead of his creditors at the time, and he never restored well-being of any sort. He died in disgrace in 1818, never having seen Robert and his family again. Ann Carter Lee raised her children in genteel poverty, dependent upon the largesse of family members.[2] She died in 1829 at the age of fifty-six.

Such circumstances left an impression upon young Robert; he seemed determined to rise above his father's shame and restore his family's good name, if not its fame. And the Lee family misfortunes also gave Parke Custis pause about the future of his daughter with this prospective son-in-law. For some time after Robert asked Mary Custis to marry him and she assented, her father withheld his approval and likely blessed the union only after his wife and daughter entreated him earnestly.

Once Parke Custis agreed, Mary and Robert set the date, June 30, 1831, about a year after they had become engaged. The groom was then serving at Fort Monroe in Virginia and did with some difficulty secure leave for the occasion. At the instruction of his bride and her parents he arrived at Arlington by boat on the day of the ceremony. Meanwhile, the Custises set about a flurry of preparations. They borrowed cots and bed linens and wondered where and how their guests and twelve attendants, six bridesmaids and six groomsmen, would sleep. When the time came, double beds slept three people. And during the chaos of getting ready Mrs. Custis suffered a nervous stomach that compelled her to take to her bed.[3]

Finally the day dawned. Bridesmaids and groomsmen were all present; the groom arrived; and as he later recounted to his friend and commanding officer, "There was neither fainting nor fighting. . . ." To preside at the ceremony, the Custises engaged the Reverend Reuel Keith who had been rector of Christ Church, Alexandria, and now oversaw Virginia Theological Seminary (also in Alexandria). Keith, riding the short way from Alexandria to Arlington House, however, encountered a summer shower and arrived drenched to the skin. A hurried survey revealed that none of the guests had extra clothes for Keith. So Parke Custis offered his wardrobe. As luck had it, though, Keith was tall and slender; Custis was short and paunchy. But Keith was an Episcopalian and had his cassock and surplice to hide the short pants and sleeves he wore for the wedding.

Keith kept the service brief; as Lee recalled he "had few words to say, though he dwelt upon them as though he had been reading my Death warrant and there was a tremulousness in the hand I held [the bride's] that made me anxious for him to end." When Keith did close the service, a six-day house party began.

Most of the guests left on July 5, though a few of the bridesmaids remained some days after that. For the groom the entire time seemed a blur. Lee did ride into Washington on July 11 and called upon the chief

of the Engineer Corps; otherwise for him this was very much an interlude
en famille. When the couple left Arlington, they took the mother of the
bride with them and made a round of visits to Lee's relatives in northern
Virginia. Lee proclaimed, "I actually could not find time before I left the
District [Arlington] for anything except—."[4]

Mary and Robert Lee were married for thirty-nine years; the union
ended when Robert died in 1870. They lived in numerous places and
houses during the marriage, and Robert Lee lived in more in the course
of his service in the United States and Confederate States armies. Together they lived at Fort Monroe, Virginia; St. Louis, Missouri; Brooklyn,
New York; Baltimore, Maryland; West Point, New York; Richmond, Virginia; "Derwent" in Cumberland County, Virginia; and Lexington, Virginia. And they often returned to Arlington; they lived there together for
several extended periods, and Mary returned "home" during the times
that Robert was on duty in places where his wife felt it inappropriate or
uncomfortable to accompany him.

After the death of her parents, her mother in 1853, her father in 1857,
Mary Lee inherited a "life estate" in Arlington; when she died the place
would belong to her oldest son, Custis Lee. This was as close as Mary and
Robert Lee ever came to acquiring a home. Never, during those thirty-
nine years of marriage, did the couple ever own the house in which they
lived.

The Lees had seven children, all of whom survived to become adults.[5]
Bearing and birthing seven children in fourteen years took its toll upon
the health of Mary. And she did not enjoy robust health before she began
having babies. The year from summer 1835 to the summer of 1836, for
example, produced several crises in Mary's health and established sad
portents for her future well-being. She was expecting her second child in
July (Mary Custis, born July 12, 1835). They were living at Arlington, and
Lee was chafing from mundane duties in the Engineer Bureau of the War
Department in Washington. In May 1835, he found some relief from his
routine; he left on an assignment to the Great Lakes to survey the boundary between Ohio and Michigan,[6] leaving his wife and son with her parents
at Arlington.

Mary Lee seemed to recover from giving birth to her daughter, but
soon developed an infection in her groin that her physicians misdiagnosed. The infection persisted for more than two months while the doctors wrung their hands and drew blood. In August she wrote to her husband and begged him to come home to her. Robert was less than
understanding. He responded:

> But why do you urge my immediate return, & tempt one in the strongest
> manner, to endeavor to get excused from the performance of a duty, im-
> posed on me by my Profession for the pure gratification of my private feel-
> ings? Do you not think that those feelings are enough of themselves to con-
> tend with, without other aggravations; and that I rather require to be

strengthened & encouraged to the *full* performance of what I am called on to execute, rather than excited to a dereliction, which even our affection could not palliate, or our judgement excuse?

Lee must not have known the full truth of his wife's distress, and Mary was wont to cry "Wolf" when her comfort was at issue. Nevertheless, his insensitive response to her plea for help was dreadful indeed.[7]

When he did return to his wife (in October!), Lee became immediately alarmed and continued his concern throughout the long winter of Mary's recovery. His letters chronicle her travails:

October 12	"very slowly getting better, still confined to her bed"
October 21	"the inflammation . . . pointed and broke outwardly . . . great discharge & a relief . . . weak and helpless as ever"
November 9	"2nd Imposthume [pustule] . . . opened & by its discharge she has been much relieved . . . *soreness* is substituted for *acute* pain . . . so weak that she *cannot stand*"
November 18	"Mary gets better & better every day. . . . Her appetite is famous."
November 25	"Her hair got in such a *snarl* while confined to her bed, that she on her first sitting up, took the scissors and cut it all off."

Mary was sickly throughout the winter (1835–1836), and then in June she contracted mumps. Soon after she recovered from this, Lee reported, "she became extremely affected with fever, which fell upon the brain, and seemed to overthrow her whole nervous system. . . . Her nervous system is much shattered. She has almost a horror of crowded places, an indisposition to make the least effort, and yet a restless anxiety which renders her unhappy and dissatisfied."[8]

Robert Lee wrote this lugubrious assessment of his wife's physical and emotional state in early August 1836. Yet a month later the Lees conceived their third child! And two weeks after that child (William Henry Fitzhugh, "Rooney") was born (May 30, 1837), the father left his wife and three children at Arlington and set out for St. Louis where duty called.[9]

At the time Mary Lee ceased bearing children, in 1846, she began to be afflicted with arthritis that progressively crippled her until in 1863 she could no longer walk. She spent the last ten years of her life confined to a wheelchair.

Throughout many of her later tribulations, her husband was solicitous. He assisted her in her search for comfort and cure and even arranged for a private railroad car in the middle of a war zone to transport her to what she hoped would be "healing waters" after she became unable to endure the journey in a carriage. When he was away from her (which was often), he wrote letters to her almost daily, and in each letter he repeated a litany of concern and empathy. But still he left her, and although in his letters to her he did not repeat the self-absorbed unsympathetic nonsense that he had written in August 1835, Robert was surely frustrated by his wife's infirmities. Mary's health, or rather the lack of it, conditioned their marriage.[10]

One reason for Lee's frustration with his wife's illnesses was likely his own good health. For most of his life he enjoyed vigorous activity and seldom suffered sickness. When he finally did encounter infirmity, it was in the midst of the Civil War. In all probability, he suffered the onset of angina during the spring of 1863 while in command of the Army of Northern Virginia at a critical point in the war. Angina and cardiovascular problems annoyed and limited him during the last two years of the war and eventually killed him at the age of sixty-three. But Lee's health did not decline radically until the last two years of his life.[11]

More than health affected Mary and Robert Lee's relationship during their thirty-nine years of marriage. By most standards the Lees were incredibly unlike. Expressed bluntly, it appears to this author that Robert was careful, self-contained, ambitious, dutiful, and clever. Mary was careless, self-centered, dependent, undisciplined, and dull. Why did two such people marry each other?

Very likely, Mary recognized her husband's virtues and realized that Robert was much influenced by his father's negative example. He would never allow himself even to appear to be an irresponsible rascal like Light Horse Harry. For his part, Lee knew about many of Mary's limitations. A simple answer would be that, like other men in his family, he married wealth. But that was not fully the case. Lee consistently eschewed his opportunities to take advantage of Custis property. In fact, when Parke Custis died and left his son-in-law the chance to profit from his considerable estate, Lee demurred. He himself had inherited little from his father-in-law; but his wife and children had inherited lands that efficient management might convert to wealth and prominence. Lee termed his quandary "the question I have staved off for 20 years," and as executor of Custis's estate, he tried his hand at being a planter for two years while on leave from the army. Eventually Lee decided to resume his career in the military. He did the best he could to counter Custis's lax management, and having set his family's affairs on as rational a financial basis as he could, he left to rejoin his cavalry command in Texas. In so doing he gave firm evidence that he cared for more than his wife's wealth.[12]

One truism in the American South holds that "southern boys marry their Mommas." Robert Lee's mother and his wife were both pious women and both of them loved Robert; otherwise they seem little alike. Ann Carter Lee made the best of adverse circumstances alone and in one way or another lived to see her several children established in promising professions or marriages. Mary Custis Lee was a pampered child of wealth and privilege who never outgrew the assumption that others—parents, husband, servants—would see to her needs and comfort. Yet in a curious way,

Robert Lee did "marry his momma." He married his mother's unfulfilled hopes—for stability, status, and a loving family.[13]

For whatever reasons, the Lees did marry and within this relationship both of them demonstrated that this match was much less than "made in heaven." For his part, Robert sometimes displayed significant insensitivity to his wife's physical condition—one of the best examples was his letter to her in August 1835, quoted earlier. And he was often away from her. Lee did not always have any choice in his duty assignments with the army; but he did seem to embrace opportunities to do his duty at some distant place or post and leave Mary at Arlington to care for their seven children. Moreover, he was quite free with advice and judgment regarding her performance as a parent. Robert Lee could be a difficult mate.

Responsibilities associated with his profession and public service sometimes seemed to overwhelm Lee, though he seldom exhibited the effects of stress. Here is one example. On June 6, 1862, Mary wrote to inform her husband that their first, and at the time only, grandchild had died in infancy. Lee responded to his wife's letter and acknowledged the loss on June 10. But then on June 22 he wrote to his daughter-in-law and asked the grieving mother to "Kiss your sweet boy for me." Lee had recently taken command of the Army of Northern Virginia and he was preparing for what became the Seven Days Battles. This was his first command of a Confederate Army, and the situation seemed grave; he must have been too absorbed to remember that his daughter-in-law's "sweet boy" was dead.[14]

Later, during the war Lee revealed more evidence of the strain of command. At issue were socks. Mary, her daughters, and friends spent much of their time knitting socks for the soldiers, and when Mary accumulated several dozen pairs, she sent them to her husband. Lee, commanding general of the Army of Northern Virginia and engaged in a desperate campaign for the survival of his country, incredibly took the time to count pairs of socks and correct his wife's count in subsequent letters. Surely he had more important things to do; counting socks may have been the most reliable index of how acutely he felt the stress of command. Mary Lee was intensely proud of her husband, and she did what she could to help him. But she also bore some of the cost of his greatness.[15]

If their marriage had been a contest over which spouse endured the greater difficulty at having married the other, Robert may indeed have been the winner. Mary's limitations were not limited to her poor health.

Here are excerpts from a letter she wrote to her mother during her early months of marriage when she and her husband were living at Fort Monroe. She pronounced herself possessed of "an anxious desire to do something to show forth my gratitude to that all merciful Saviour who has done all for me." But she followed her pious statement of intention with these facts:

The only actively pious family here have not visited me. . . .

There is a Sunday School . . . but I have not seen it nor do I know how it is conducted. . . .

I am much obliged to you for the books you sent though I must confess I have not read the others yet. . . .

Mrs. Hale [near neighbor] & I commenced the life of Luther . . . have not progressed far. . . .

There is a Mrs. Haliburton at the tavern who says she is a relation of mine but I have not seen her yet. . . .

Mary Lee noted that Robert Lee's "duties require his presence daily & keep him pretty well employed." She lived with her husband in two rooms and had a servant (slave) to perform chores; what did she do all day?[16]

Robert Lee was ever tidy. When he first traveled to St. Louis, he secured a room in what was supposed to be the best hotel in the city. In a letter he wrote, "The room is intolerable, and so soon as I close this letter, I shall sally out in quest of another. I may be perhaps *over* scrupulous in this respect, but I can readily bear the *clean dirt* of the *earth* and drink without a strain the mud of the Missouri . . . this *domestic* filth is revolting to my taste." To some prospective houseguests Lee wrote, "Tell the ladies that they are aware that Mrs. L[ee] is somewhat addicted to *laziness* & *forgetfulness* in her housekeeping. But they may be certain she does her best, or in her mother's words, 'The spirit is willing but the flesh is weak.' " The combination of one person who finds "domestic filth . . . revolting" with another "somewhat addicted to laziness & forgetfulness in her house-keeping" may appeal to college administrators when pairing freshman roommates; but it would seem to portend ill for a marriage.[17]

Mary Lee retained almost a primal attachment to Arlington and her parents. "What . . . would I give for one stroll on the hills of Arlington this bright day," she wrote her mother while still a bride. And even as a bride, she managed to spend a lot of time at "home" while her husband worked and lived at Fort Monroe. The newlywed Lees lived at Fort Monroe from August 1831 until shortly before Christmas, which they spent at Arlington. Robert returned to duty at Fort Monroe in January 1832; but Mary re-mained at Arlington for what she projected would be a short time. Each time she confronted her leave-taking, however, she postponed her depar-ture until she had been at Arlington for five months without her husband. When she finally did return to him, she brought her mother with her. During their first year of marriage, Mary and Robert lived apart nearly half the time and spent a significant portion of the time that they lived together in the company of one or both of the bride's parents.[18]

The Lees had been married for about two years and were parents of one son when Robert informed a male friend that his mother-in-law had again come for a visit at Fort Monroe. Then he added, "Mrs Custis & Mary have gone up to Shirley [Plantation, home of Lee's mother's family] which is as much to say that I am as happy as [a] clam in high water."[19]

Neither Lee nor the context of his letter revealed whether his happiness was the product of the absence of his wife, his mother-in-law, or both of them. Robert addressed his in-laws as "Mother" and "Father" and apparently rendered them respect and concern for their dignity. He did seem to hold Mary's mother in high regard, feelings that she seemed to return. George Washington Parke Custis, however, was a very different case. He rested any claim he had to fame upon his adoptive relationship with the great Washington. Yet George Washington had complained of Custis's "almost uncontrollable disposition to indolence in everything that did not tend to his amusements," and had endured his son's expulsion from the College of New Jersey and the charge that he stole two teaspoons from a tavern in Alexandria.

Custis inherited significant wealth and lived well. He indulged his small talent for painting and for writing poetry and plays to no real success. He did breed fine sheep and for a time held competitions at Arlington to encourage sheep husbandry among his countrymen. But in sum, Custis's most important accomplishment was outliving his grandmother and so inheriting her lands and wealth.[20] For a brief time during the War of 1812, Custis was a staff officer with the rank of major. He clung to his largely honorific rank ever thereafter and likely did so especially when his son-in-law, the lieutenant, was around.

The contrast was striking between Custis and Lee, who had earned modest rank and station in life and aspired to achieve what he could to atone for his father's shame. Nor could Lee always overlook the obvious. He wrote to his older brother Carter, "The Major is busy farming. His *corn* field is not yet enclosed or ploughed [on May 2] but he is *rushing* on *all he knows.* 'Montgomerie' [a play about thirteenth-century Scotland] *failed.* The 'big Picture' has been exhibited in the Capitol, and attracted some animadversions from the Critics, which he says were leveled at his Politics."[21]

Early in the marriage, the question of Robert Lee's managing his father-in-law's affairs came to the surface. Apparently Parke Custis did not desire such an arrangement; Lee never had the opportunity to make his feelings known. Eventually the Lees did assume more responsibility for Custis's properties. Mary and Robert, for example, finally furnished the parlor at Arlington House after it had been a storeroom for about fifty years. Somehow Robert endured a relationship with his father-in-law that must have been often strained—especially given the long periods in which the Lees were in residence at Arlington House and the likelihood that Mary never outgrew her role of indulged only child in that setting.[22]

As parents, too, the Lees had their troubles. Because he was often away from his family, Robert attempted to oversee his children's rearing by correspondence. He was worried at one point that his wife's "discipline will be too lax, too inconsistent, and too yielding," and asked his mother-in-law "to make her do what is right." He wrote lectures to Mary, one of which stated, "I am very glad that you are all well and enjoying yourself. I wish indeed that I was with you, for I fear your *vanity* has caused you to overburden yourself with children for the purpose of *exhibition*. I am sure nothing could have induced you to take that fine boy Rob [visiting] but the pleasure of showing him & if he is not 'too good' is he to blame?"[23]

Perhaps the most symbolic event in Robert Lee's efforts at parenthood in absentia occurred at his homecoming from the Mexican War in June 1848. His family was once more at Arlington, and Lee had been away from them for twenty-one months. When he arrived in Washington, D.C., he failed to find the carriage sent from Arlington to transport him the short distance across the Potomac. Lee prevailed upon the Army for a horse and rode "home."

As he drew near the house, no one recognized the returning hero. Only the dog Spec, a terrier whom Lee himself had found and adopted, seemed to know the approaching rider and barked a welcome. Finally Mary and the children identified the "stranger" and crowded the entrance hall to greet him. They were of course embarrassed at their failure to recognize their husband and father while he was still far off.

But then Lee the father returned the faux pas. Having hugged most of his older children, he realized that he had not greeted his namesake, young Rob, now four and a half years old.

"Where is my little boy?" he asked.

Rob was on hand in the hallway. But his father swept into his arms not Rob, but his visiting playmate Armistead Lippitt instead. Martial heroism extracted a price from the Lees.[24]

Nor was Robert always convinced that his presence was good for his family. He spent an extended leave at Arlington from late 1857 until early 1860 attempting to settle his father-in-law's estate. Apparently he believed that he provoked friction in the household, for when he made the decision to remain in the military and returned to duty in Texas, after two-and-one-half years at Arlington, he wrote these chilling words to his daughter Annie:

> God knows how often I think of you and long to see you. If you wish to see me you will have to come out here, for I do not know when I will be able to go in there. It is better too I hope for all that I am here. You know I was very much in the way of everybody and my tastes and pursuits did not coincide with the rest of the household. Now I hope everybody is happier.

Likely Lee wrote some degree of hyperbole. But here is a devastating assessment of dysfunction in the Lee family.[25]

Mary and Robert Lee were, as noted, unlike each other. Her doting parents and his father's shame seemed to condition their lives separately and together. Her poor health and his extended absences compounded their differences and surely strained their marriage. And strains were certainly manifest when the Lees attempted to function as parents to their children. Was the Lees' marriage a failure sustained principally by convention and by Robert Lee's fear of bringing public censure to his family as his father had done? Did the marriage depend upon inertia, tradition, and fear—fear of gossip and the judgment of others—for survival?

At least one historian has pronounced the Lees' marriage a failure. Thomas L. Connelly in *The Marble Man: Robert E. Lee and His Image in American Society* writes of Robert Lee's "unsatisfactory marriage." He states, "The marriage may have brought him more frustration than anything else," and he also speaks of Lee as "a father who believed that his own inadequacies made him a failure as a parent."[26]

But Connelly is wrong. The catalog of differences, strains, and problems cited above does indicate that the Lees did not enjoy a blissful relationship devoid of troubles. They did, however, have a successful marriage. More than most married people, the Lees established early a series of concessions, slipknots within the marriage bond that allowed their relationship to function. Concessions evolved into accommodation and understanding; in their own ways—sometimes pretty unconventional ways—the Lees loved and supported each other. They confronted multiple frustrations and reversals of fortune and maintained their commitment to each other and to their marriage.

Clearly one of the concessions Robert Lee exercised was his perception of duty. He was a public servant, subject to orders, and he was a conscientious soldier even when stresses of child rearing, friction with in-laws, or his wife's chronic ill health threatened him. He complained about his protracted absences from Mary and the children; yet he seemed to use his sense of duty to escape circumstances in which he realized that he could contribute little of consequence and would experience little more than helpless frustration.[27]

Another concession upon which Lee relied throughout his marriage was a series of relationships with bright, young women. The pattern began early in the marriage and continued even during his final few months of life. Lee pursued these relationships most often by correspondence. Some of his letters survive, and a very little gossip or testimony by those who observed him and one or more of his female friends endures. Here are some samples of Lee's letters to his young friends.[28]

During his tour of duty in Savannah, Lee had spent time with Eliza Mackay, sister of one of his classmates at West Point. Six months after his own wedding he learned that Eliza was about to marry. On her wedding day in January 1832, Lee began a letter to his friend. "But Miss E." he asked, "how do you feel about this time? Say 12 o'clock of the day, as you see the shadows commence to fall towards the East and know that at *last* the sun will set." Lee had to abandon his letter at this point; he returned to it four days later; by this time Eliza Mackay should have been married. Lee asked, "And how did you disport yourself My Child? Did you go off well like a torpedo cracker on Christmas morning. . . ." Surely he referred to the wedding night, and the fascinating question is did Eliza Mackay Stiles understand the "torpedo cracker" metaphor? If so, it spoke volumes about her relationship with Lee.

One person who read Lee's letter and perhaps did not understand the "torpedo cracker" metaphor was Mary Lee. She appended a note offering her congratulations and affirming the joy of daughters being with their mothers, as both she and Eliza were. Although it was essentially pro forma, Mary's note is indeed significant. Throughout his lively correspondence with bright, young women Robert took pains to have his wife read his letters, or at least know that he was writing them. To the extent that Lee's clever missives were concessions, compensation for Mary's lack of wit and vibrancy, Robert made sure that he did not deceive his wife. He made her his accomplice.[29]

Robert assured Tasy Beaumont, seventeen years younger than he was and the daughter of an army surgeon with whom the Lees had shared a house in St. Louis, that his wife had given him permission to write to her.

> My beautiful Tasy;—I have just returned from Washington where your charm-
> ing letter followed me. I have brought it back with me to enjoy it. I wish you
> were here in person, for I am all alone. My good Dame not wishing to leave
> her mother so soon, even to follow such a spouse as I am. . . . Poor Alex K—I
> pity him. Comfort him Tasy, for if the fire of his heart is so stimulating to the
> growth of his whiskers there is danger of his being suffocated. What would be
> the verdict of a jury in that case? Suicide? It is awful to think of. . . . I hope
> the sympathy between himself & Miss Louise is not so intimate as to produce
> the same effect on her, for I should hate her sweet face to be hid by such
> hairs unless they were—mine.[30]

Harriet Talcott was the wife of Lee's friend and commanding officer at Fort Monroe; she was "my beautiful Talcott" in Lee's letters to her. When Harriet Talcott gave birth to a daughter, Lee wrote to propose a match between the infant girl and his son Custis who was about four months old at the time. He also suggested, at first glance anyway, that he was the father of the Talcotts' child.

> The all accomplished & elegant Master Custis Lee begs to place in her
> hands, his happiness & life, being assured that as for her he was born, so for
> her will he live. His only misery can be her frown, his only delight, her smile.
> He hopes that her assent will not be withheld from his most ardent wishes, &
> that in their blissful union Fortune may be indemnified for her miscarriage
> of the Affaire du Coeur of the Father & Mother.[31]

Lee began writing to Martha Custis Williams, his very distant cousin, in 1844, and the pair continued to correspond for twenty-six years. Here is one example:

> My dearest Markie
>
> You have not written to me for nearly three months. And I believe it is equally as long since I have written to you. On paper Markie, I mean, on paper. But oh, what lengthy epistles have I indited to you in my mind! Had I any means to send them, you would see how constantly I think of you. I have followed you in your pleasures, & your duties, in the house & in the streets, & accompanied you in your walks to Arlington, & in your search after flowers. Did you not feel your cheeks pale when I was so near you? You may feel pale Markie, You may look pale; You may even talk pale; But I am happy to say you never write as if you were pale; & to my mind you always appear bright & rosy.

Markie only married at age forty, after Robert Lee was dead.[32]

It is tempting to believe that Robert Lee physically consummated some, at least one, of these relationships. But it is highly unlikely that he did. The example of his father (and a half-brother who committed adultery with his sister-in-law) was too strong to permit Lee to risk losing control. And his resort to letters, letters that his wife read, was one way to ensure that he did not violate the letter of the marriage bond.[33]

Mary Lee had compensations as well. After all, she did spend a lot of time at Arlington where she was pampered and happy. If her children became troublesome, she had servants to care for them. She could indulge her passion for gardens and wildflowers, and she could continue close to her childhood friends and relatives. "Mr. Lee," as she called her husband, was successful in the Army, and so added luster to her status in society.

Here is a portion of a letter she wrote to her mother during a rare occasion when she accompanied her husband at his duty station. From St. Louis in 1838, she reported:

> I went out to Capt. Shreeve's to breakfast not long since & there was the most splendid cornfield I ever saw. The stalks stood as close as possible & he said it would produce from 60 to 80 bushels the acre; but all the soil here is like a rich alluvial deposit, yet rich as it is I would rather a thousands times live in Old Virginia or somewhere near it. . . . Mr Rooney is better & walks all about with his feet turned out & arms spread forward & is the most mischievous & cunning little fellow you ever saw. . . . Excuse this very stupid & unconnected letter, for Rooney is playing around me pulling my pens, paper & ink & is now trying to throw his Papa's hat out of the window. He has got on the little pink dress you sent & looks very sweet in it indeed with his little rotund figure & turned out legs.
>
> Kitty [her slave] is much disappointed at not hearing from any of her

friends. . . . You must remember me to all the servants particularly. I wish I had some of the little ones here to amuse Rooney the time Kitty is washing; for I find it rather tiresome to nurse all day such an unsettled brat, tho' his Father has come to the conclusion that there is not such another child in all Missouri & that he would not exchange him for the whole state.

In circumstances she and Robert could control, Mary did not have such a bad life. For the most part, her health excepted, she had nearly everything she wanted and more than she had reason to expect when she married her handsome young lieutenant.[34] The Lees could be lax or absent parents. Yet they, Robert especially, believed and did much that was enlightened in the course of raising their children. In fact, the ways in which the Lees acted and interacted as parents offer a pretty reliable index of the depth and strength of their marriage. Robert once wrote that children, "should be governed by *love* not *fear*." "When love influences the parent," he continued, "the child will be activated by the same spirit. . . . Dissimilar as are characters, intellects, and situations, the great duty of life is the same, the promotion of the happiness and welfare of our fellow men." Lee believed this latter statement and acted upon it as more than a parent. He also believed the reverse: if the "great duty" be selflessness and giving, then the great evil is selfishness and taking.[35]

Sometimes Lee as parent revealed himself existentially, in deeds far more than words. Once when his son Rooney severed the ends of two fingers in an accident, Lee wrote a letter to Custis, his older son, to inform him of Rooney's misfortune. Following the then prevalent notion that parents should use life experiences to teach moral lessons, Lee wrote very stern judgments about Rooney. He wrote of "the fruits of disobedience," the "calamity," Rooney's proclivities to be "heedless, obstinate, disobedient," his "evil ways," and the prospect of his being "ruined for life." "Do take warning," Lee counseled. But tucked into all this doom and gloom was a sentence very easy to overlook—"I am now watching by his bedside lest he should disturb his hand in his sleep." Lee sat with his son for several nights to guard against him tearing at the dressings on his fingers and ruining all hope that the severed ends would knit. As it happened, Rooney did lose the ends of his fingers; but his father did all he possibly could to heal Rooney's injury. All the time that Robert was writing his didactic letter to Custis, he was acting out absolute love, sacrificing his own comfort and well-being on the chance that his child might need his help.[36]

Later in Rooney's life the young man enrolled at Harvard. He was, however, an indifferent student and spent much of his time and energy in pursuit of pleasure with his friends. Robert Lee knew that his son was not thinking or working very hard, and he complained to his wife that the lad "thinks entirely of his pleasures" and was "running about amusing himself." But every semester when Rooney's tuition came due, his father punctually mailed him a check to cover the expense. Rooney would have to make decisions about his education; Lee supported his son—even in folly—to honor the young man's integrity.[37]

More direct in his attempt to shape the lives of his children was Lee's counsel to Custis when the oldest son was at West Point. The young man complained of what modern college students describe as the "sophomore slump" during the early spring of his second year at the Military Academy. His father responded:

> Shake off those gloomy feelings. Drive them away. Fix your mind & pleasures upon what is before you. . . . All is bright if you will think it so. All is happy if you will make it so. Do not dream. It is too ideal, too imaginary. Dreaming by day, I mean. Live in the world you inhabit. Look upon things as they are. Take them as you find them. Make the best of them. Turn them to your advantage.

In time Custis graduated number one in his class at West Point, better than his father's number two. Yet he seemed an unhappy person, perhaps never able to escape his father's famous shadow. Robert Lee, however, certainly beset with more frustrations than his son, took his own advice and made the best of his circumstances, both personal and professional.[38]

Lee could and did do more for his children than support them and preach to them. His youngest son Rob remembered the period his father spent with the family at Arlington following the Mexican War. In the mornings, Rob recalled, Lee invited his younger children to crawl into bed with him. They would, Rob said, "lie close to him, listening while he talked to us in his bright, entertaining way. This custom we kept up until I was ten years old or older." With his older children, Lee organized family races and built a high-jump standard in the yard. He enjoyed having his feet tickled and read stories to his children while they tickled his feet. Both Lee parents developed nicknames for their children. They hugged them and kissed them on their mouths.[39]

To the end of his life, Robert Lee had fun with his family. In January of the year he died, he wrote to his youngest (twenty-four-year-old) daughter Mildred about a letter she had written that must have been illegible:

> I received your letter of the 4th. We held a family council over it. It was passed from eager hand to hand and attracted wondering eyes and mysterious looks. It produced few words but a deal of thinking, and the conclusion arrived at, I believe unanimously, was that there was a great fund of amusement and information in it if it could be extracted. I have therefore determined to put it carefully away till your return, seize a leisure day, and get you to interpret it. Your mother's commentary in a suppressed soliloquy, was that you had succeeded in writing a wretched hand. Agnes thought that it would keep this cold weather—her thoughts running on jellies and oysters in the

storeroom; but I, indignant at such aspersions upon your accomplishments, retained your epistle and read in an elevated tone an interesting narrative of travels in sundry countries, describing gorgeous scenery, hairbreadth escapes, and a series of remarkable events by flood and field, not a word of which they declared was in your letter. Your return, I hope, will prove the correctness of my version of your annals.[40]

Mary Lee shared in the family fun. Indeed, she was the parent most creative in the nicknaming of her children. Custis, for example was Bun, Bunny, Boo, Boose, Bouse, and Dunket. She once presented the infant Custis to Andrew Jackson, when as president he came to inspect Fort Monroe.

> I carried Bouse [Custis] in to see the President who took him in his arms and held him some time. Bouse looked at him with a fixed gaze, put his hand over his nose, but did not pull it hard, and put his fingers in his eyes. The old man gave him Rachael's [Jackson's dead wife] picture to play with, which delighted him much, and then presented him with a half dollar & told me to put a hole in it and put it round his neck; said he was a fine boy & a good boy and that I must take off his shoes and let him run about barefoot.

Add courage to Mary Lee's virtues; very few people ever tweaked Jackson's nose or poked fingers in his eyes and survived the experience.[41]

The standards and stories of Mary and Robert Lee's family reveal that both the mother and father were engaged with their children. Whatever their limitations as parents, the Lees loved their children and let them know it. They established a happy, functional family in the midst of circumstances that rendered happiness hard to get. Their capacity to love their children and do their best to meet their various needs provides a pretty reliable gauge of their capacity as spouses.

Certainly the American Civil War challenged Mary and Robert's relationship. Robert treated his service as a "foreign war," although he was seldom far from Mary and at least a few of his children. During the war the Lees endured the death of their daughter Anne, and of their daughter-in-law Chass, a battle wound to Rooney, captivity for Rooney, and the uncertainty of having three sons in the army. They also lost Arlington, much of the Custis wealth, and the war.

Mary was a refugee very early and lived with friends behind enemy lines for most of the first year of the war. She obtained passage through federal lines in June of 1862 and lived in Richmond for most of the remainder of the conflict. In Richmond, the inhabitants, many of whom shunned the Davises, revered Mary Lee. There she with her daughters established her sock-knitting enterprise and so set an example for others on the home front.[42]

Robert Lee wrote his wife quite often and gave her candid summaries of the situations and prospects of his army. In fact his descriptions of his battles were usually more vivid and descriptive than those he sent President Jefferson Davis and the Confederate War Department.[43]

Mary Lee, like her husband, had prayed fervently that the war would not happen. On the eve of Abraham Lincoln's inauguration, she wrote:

> I pray that the Almighty may listen to the prayers of the faithful in the land & direct their counsels for good & that the designs of ambitious & selfish politicians who would dismember our glorious country may be frustrated.

As the war came and continued, however, she became ever more a rebel— especially after the United States took possession of Arlington and buried so many Federal soldiers there that no one would ever be able to use it as a residence again. In the end, even as her husband evacuated Richmond and led his army in desperate flight, Mary proclaimed to visitors, "The end is not yet," and "Richmond is not the Confederacy." And afterward, Mary displayed herself much less reconstructed than her husband. She wrote in 1867: "It is bad enough to be the victims of tyranny, but when it is wielded by such cowards and base men as Butler, Thaddeus Stevens, and Turner, it is indeed intolerable. The country that allows such scum to rule them must fast be going to destruction." Robert Lee was less than happy with the fruits of failure; but he established himself as a model American and counseled reunion both publicly and privately.[44]

During his final five years of life, Lee was president of Washington College (now Washington and Lee University) in Lexington, Virginia. Within the limits of his cardiovascular decline, he accomplished great feats as an educator; he took charge of an impoverished tiny college and laid the foundation for a fine, modern university.

One of President Lee's achievements at the college was the construction of the president's home. Very probably Lee and his builders used plans from a "pattern book," but he reformed the design to fit his family. The children all had rooms and among the outbuildings were a greenhouse and even a "cat house" for his youngest daughter's pets. A stable adjoined the house so that Lee's warhorse, Traveler, would be under the same roof as his master. Mary's bedroom was on the first floor and opened upon a redesigned porch enabling her to roll her wheelchair from her room to the porch and around three sides of the house. Robert's favorite space in this home was a bay window in the dining room. There he enjoyed a view of the campus and the mountains, and he napped after dinner in his chair. And there he died.

For many years Robert Lee had done all that he could to ease his wife's pain and improve her health. When he became seriously ill with misdiagnosed cardiovascular disease, Mary returned her spouse's favors as well as she could. He, however, needed more than attention and concern, and on September 28, 1870, he suffered a stroke that proved fatal two weeks later.[45]

On October 10, 1870, Mary Lee sent a note to Francis Smith, superintendent of the Virginia Military Institute, also in Lexington.

> My Dear Gen'l:
> The Drs. think it would be well for Gen'l Lee to have some beef tea at once & as I cannot get it at market before night I send to beg a small piece, if it can be found at the Institute, lean & juicy if possible; a pound would answer for the present, as I can get some more tonight.
>
> In great hast Yrs.
> M. C. Lee.

Smith complied with the request, and the stricken Lee drank the "beef tea" or broth.[46]

Enormous irony attends this effort of Mary to help heal her husband. The best speculation now possible about the medical circumstances of Lee's death concludes that he suffered a stroke—a rare stroke that did not provoke any paralysis. His stroke did impair his will, however, and he lapsed into passive silence, dozing much of the time. In such a condition he was going to die of some complication of his stroke or possibly of another stroke or heart attack. The complication that killed him was pneumonia; "a change came," daughter Mildred Lee recalled, on October 10.

One of Lee's functions apparently damaged by his stroke was his cough reflex; none of the witnesses or the physicians' notes mentions his coughing. The nourishment administered by family and friends got into his lungs and produced pneumonia in the weakened patient who was unable to cough. It is entirely possible that the "beef tea" Mary sought so ardently killed Robert.[47]

Robert Lee died on October 12, 1870; Mary survived him only about three years. She died November 5, 1873, five months after she saw Arlington for the first time since the war and the last time in her life. About this visit she wrote:

> I rode out to my dear old home but so changed it seemed but as a dream of the past—I could not have realized that it was Arlington but for the few old oaks they had spared & the trees planted on the lawn by the Genl & myself which are raising their tall branches to the Heaven which seems to smile on the desecration around them.[48]

The "desecration," of course, was the graves and headstones of her husband's enemies, and they were multitude.

_____

THREE

"A Sweet Solace to My Lonely Heart"
"Stonewall" and Mary Anna Jackson and the Civil War

_____

SARAH E. GARDNER

It is something of a mystery that Mary Anna Jackson never publicly condemned biographers and novelists who insistently proclaimed that her late husband, General Thomas "Stonewall" Jackson, liked to suck lemons. Indeed, she expended a great deal of energy in her waning years combating accounts of him that included, among other foibles, his rather unusual penchant for citrus fruit, yet she never singled out this particular character trait.[1] Anna's concern for her husband's image developed long before her husband's death, however. Despite her husband's requests to the contrary, for example, Anna sent her husband, away at the war, pantaloons with gold braiding. Her idea of a proper uniform befitting a general in the Confederate States Army did not mesh with that of her husband. "I became so ashamed of the broad gild band that was on the cap you sent," the general notified his wife, "as to induce me to take it off. I like simplicity." More important, throughout the general's tenure with the Confederate Army, Anna sought glory for his exploits in the war. Perhaps as perplexing as the postwar accounts that failed to champion her husband accurately or adequately, however, was General Jackson's own reluctance to aid his wife in her wartime efforts at glorification. Although Anna extolled the general's modesty in the years following his death, she found this trait quite exasperating when she tried to extract information from him during the war. "Stonewall" Jackson received his wife's requests for graphic details of the war with good humor, but in the end remained largely silent, forcing his wife to make do with the unceremonious accounts of him published in the newspapers. "Don't trouble yourself about representations that are made of your husband," the general wrote Anna in the fall of 1862. "These things are earthly and transitory. There are real and glorious blessings, I trust, in reserve for us beyond this life." He later advised, "It would be better for you not to have anything written about me."[2] Anna found her husband's reticence maddening and her desire to see his reputation celebrated intensified in the postwar years. By the end of the nineteenth century she had become involved in a number of controversies surrounding the literary and historical representation of her husband's character. The concern for his image that in part fueled her wartime relationship with "Stonewall" Jackson guided her through the years following the Civil War.

On Thursday, July 16, 1857, Mary Anna Morrison, the daughter of Mary Graham and Robert Hall Morrison, a Presbyterian minister, married a hero. The wedding took place in the bride's family mansion, Cottage Home, some twenty miles outside of Charlotte, North Carolina. Of Cottage Home, Anna wrote, "In those good old times before the war many wealthy families lived upon their plantations, and the neighborhood in which my father lived was noted for its excellent society, refinement, and hospitality." Anna was born into this "refined society" on July 21, 1831, the third of the six Morrison daughters. Anna's mother was the daughter of Revolutionary War general Joseph Graham and sister of William A. Graham, a governor of North Carolina, U.S. senator, and secretary of the navy under Millard Fillmore. Her father had a distinguished record as a student at the University of North Carolina and the Princeton Theological Seminary and served as the first president of Davidson College.[3]

The bride's newly betrothed, Thomas Jonathan Jackson, a graduate of the U.S. Military Academy, had distinguished himself in the Mexican-American War and returned from that conflict to a hero's welcome. His early life did not suggest such an auspicious course. Born on January 24, 1824, to the chronically indebted Jonathan Jackson and Julia Neale Jackson, Thomas was left fatherless at the age of two after his father died of typhoid fever. Julia Jackson, in poor health and forever teetering on financial ruin, married Blake Woodson on November 4, 1830, hoping to provide security for her three young children. Woodson, faced with economic woes and the imminent arrival of an additional child, encouraged his stepchildren to find a home elsewhere. In 1831, Tom and his sister Laura were taken away by an uncle to live in Jackson's Mill, Virginia. They stayed in Jackson's Mill for four years, during which time their mother and stepfather died. In 1835 Laura was sent to join her mother's family in Parkersburg, Virginia, and Tom joined his Aunt Polly and Uncle Isaac Brake until he ran away from this abusive uncle and returned to Jackson's Mill. Tom devoted many of his teenage years to earnest, albeit haphazard, study, and in 1842, Jackson, grossly unprepared, secured an appointment to the U.S. Military Academy at West Point, New York. Four years later, as he stood ready to leave West Point, the United States declared war on Mexico. Jackson desperately hoped to be sent to Mexico. As one of his biographers noted, the almost-sure alternative—life on the western frontier—provided little excitement for those who wished to be tested in warfare waged "with equal arms against an equal enemy." In July 1846, Lieutenant Thomas J. Jackson's wish was fulfilled. He was ordered to report to Captain Francis Taylor, commanding Company K of the First Artillery.[4]

Jackson performed valiantly at Veracruz and Churubusco, earning the praise of his superiors. As George Henderson, one of Jackson's early biographers, remarked, "Within eighteen months of his first joining his regiment he was breveted major. Such promotion was phenomenal even in the Mexican war, and none of his West Point comrades made so great a stride in rank. His future in his profession was assured."[5] Moreover, Jackson had returned from the war, according to a recent biographer, with the firm conviction that "the military was his true vocation and war his natural element."[6]

The young Anna Morrison first met Jackson, then a professor of natural and experimental philosophy at the Virginia Military Institute, while visiting her sister Isabella Morrison (Mrs. Harvey) Hill in 1853. His military bearing struck her immediately. Anna later recalled that "he was more soldierly-looking than anything else, his erect bearing and military dress being quite striking. . . . His uniform, consisting of a dark blue frock-coat with shoulder straps, double breasted, and buttoned up to the chin with brass buttons, and faultless white linen pantaloons was very becoming to him." To the young North Carolina belle, Jackson was clearly "not an ordinary man."[7] She would carry that image of him for the rest of her life.

On that hot and humid day in July 1857, Mary Anna Morrison married more than a hero, however. She also married a widower. Shortly after Jackson had met Anna Morrison he married Elinor Junkin, whom he had been courting for some months, in a private ceremony.[8] Commenting on Jackson's first marriage, historian James I. Robertson, Jr., remarked that "Jackson had spent his life—especially the impressionable years of his youth—longing for a home, for a family atmosphere, for the collective love that such an association fosters. Now at last he had it. Jackson was happier than he had ever been."[9] His marital happiness did not last long. A little more than a year after his marriage, Elinor died while giving birth to their stillborn infant.

Jackson seemed prostrated by grief. His nephew, Thomas Jackson Arnold, described his uncle's anguish. "A period now came in Major Jackson's life where [*sic*] his faith and trust in God was subjected to its strongest tension. To a man of his temperament and nature, his love was intense. To have the object of this love turn from him without warning was a death blow to him, save for his implicit childlike trust in God. No one will ever know the weight of that blow, and the veil should not be lifted that concealed the wound."[10] Informing his sister, Laura Jackson Arnold, of Elinor's death, Jackson wrote, "She has now gone on to a glorious visit, through a gloomy portal. . . . I look forward with delight to the day when

I shall join *her.*" He later noted, "I will have joy and hope for a future reunion when the wicked cease from troubling and the weary are at rest." Indeed, Jackson's father-in-law, Dr. George Junkin, remarked that Major Jackson was "growing heaven-ward faster than I ever knew any person to do. He seems only to think of E[llie] and heaven."[11]

Jackson sought consolation from his sister-in-law, Margaret Junkin. The death of Elinor Junkin Jackson had similarly devastated Margaret, who had also recently lost her mother. Elizabeth Preston Allan, Margaret's biographer, recorded that "of such friendly consolers, her brother-in-law, Major Jackson, was easily first. His place, as a son of the household, was as near to Margaret's heart as that of her own brothers, and his constant presence encouraged an intimacy." She later noted that Margaret Junkin "frankly claimed that Jackson never revealed his inmost thoughts and feelings to any human being as he did to her during the first four years of his widowhood."[12] Jackson's letters to his sister-in-law were undeniably effusive and heartfelt. But Jackson had picked an odd choice to be his confidante. Margaret had never been one of Jackson's supporters. In fact, she so opposed her sister's decision to marry Jackson that Elinor called off the engagement for a brief time out of deference to her sister's opinion.

The death of Elinor, however, brought the grieving husband and sister together. By February 1855, the two had begun a long and intimate correspondence. Clearly Elinor provided the common thread between the two, at least in the beginning. Margaret initiated the correspondence, offering her sincere condolence for her brother-in-law's loss. Writing to his brother-in-law, George Junkin, in early February 1855, Jackson exclaimed, "And dear Maggie! How can I ever make an adequate return for her deep solicitude? My heart yearns to see her; and yet it may be best that we should not so soon meet; for my tears have not ceased to flow, my heart to bleed."[13] Jackson chose to respond to Margaret's letter on February 14, 1855. Evoking their mutual loss, Jackson wrote, "You and I were certainly the dearest objects which she left on Earth and if her emancipated spirit carries back to Earth, and sees how we are bound together, and how we have a mutual [. . . ?] of strong affecting for *Her,* do you not suppose that it thrills her with delights?"[14] And although Elinor always provided the link between the two, by late summer of 1855 a deepening affection for his sister-in-law clearly motivated Jackson to continue the correspondence. "I want all your letters to be full of yourself and more so than heretofore received," he announced to Junkin. "Never be afraid of saying too much about yourself to me; but always remember that the more they abound in self the more interesting they may be to me." He closed the letter by inviting her to "come to me with every joy, and every sorrow, and let me share them with you."[15]

Despite the deepening bonds of affection and Jackson's growing desire for a more meaningful home life, Jackson could never find permanent consolation with Margaret. As his recent biographer has noted, Presbyterian law expressly forbade a man from marrying his deceased wife's sister. "Jackson and Maggie knew Church law; they lived in the home of a leading Presbyterian cleric. Church doctrine and family ties could not be disgraced. To do so would be to live in sin and disgrace." And so Jackson had to "look elsewhere" for permanent companionship.[16]

Major Jackson looked to Mary Anna Morrison. With no small degree of modesty, Anna later recalled the major's burgeoning interest in her. She remarked, rather disingenuously, that Jackson "began to realize that life could be made bright and happy to him again and in resolving this problem in his mind his first impulse was to open communications with his old friend Miss Anna Morrison, and see if she could not be induced to become a participant in attaining his desired happiness."[17] Jackson soon entered into a correspondence with Anna that rivaled the one he had with Margaret Junkin. "In my daily walks I think much of you," he wrote her in the spring of 1857. "And as my mind dwells on you, I love to give it a devotional turn, by thinking of you as a gift from our Heavenly Father."[18] After a brief courtship, the couple married, but not before Jackson instructed Margaret to select Anna's engagement ring. "I have made an estimate such as I suppose would more than cover your selecting from what you have stated," he informed her in the letter that accompanied the checks, "and this has been done with the view of having every thing so elegant as to meet with Anna's cordial approval for I should dislike very much to have her not entirely satisfied with what I hope to see her wear through her life." Trusting Margaret's good taste, Jackson suggested only that the accompanying pearl necklace be "longer than yours, yet lighter than Ellie's with a massive fastening."[19] Apparently Margaret selected the jewelry to everyone's satisfaction and on August 6, 1857, the Lexington [Virginia] *Gazette* carried a brief announcement of the Morrison-Jackson wedding that had taken place a few weeks earlier. Significantly, the paper carried another wedding announcement directly below it. "On the 3rd of August, by Rev. George Junkin, D.D., a President of Washington College, Major John T. Preston of the Virginia Military Institute to Miss Maggie Junkin, daughter of the officiating clergyman."[20]

Anna Jackson remembered the early years of her marriage fondly. When writing for a postwar audience that was familiar with "Stonewall" Jackson's military exploits, she tried to balance his heroic image with accounts of their wedded and domestic bliss. "Those who knew General Jackson only as they saw him in public would have found it hard to believe that there could be such a transformation as he exhibited in his domestic life," she recalled.

He luxuriated in the freedom and liberty of his home, and his buoyancy and joyousness [*sic*] nature often ran into playfulness and *abandon* that would have been incredible to those who saw him only when he put on his official dignity. The overflowing sunshine of his heart was a reflection from the Sun of Righteousness, and he always said we could not love an earthly creature too much if we only loved God *more*.[21]

Major Jackson undoubtedly found much comfort with his new wife and home. Despite his recent happiness, he nonetheless brought to his second marriage a sense of grief over the loss of his first wife and child. That loss was surely compounded when the couple's first child, Mary Graham Jackson, died in infancy in the summer of 1858. The major also brought to his second marriage a profound and real fondness for Margaret Junkin Preston that Anna could never understand or acknowledge fully. For her part, Anna brought to her marriage a fierce pride and at times overwhelming concern for her husband's reputation. The things they carried would greatly influence their marriage in the Civil War years.

After a northern honeymoon, one that nearly duplicated the route Jackson took with his first wife, Ellie, the newlyweds settled in Lexington, where Jackson resumed his tenure as a professor at VMI. But the coming of the Civil War disrupted the Jackson home. The reality of that disruption, suggested Anna, prompted her husband to offer the following prayer from Corinthians upon receiving orders to bring Virginia Military cadets to Richmond in late 1861: "For we know that if our earthly house of this tabernacle be dissolved, we have a building of God, a house not made with hands, eternal in the heavens." Lest Jackson's postwar readers believe, however, that her husband, the consummate and dutiful soldier, relished abandoning his domestic life, she noted that, "although he went forth so bravely from his cherished and beloved home, he hoped confidently to be permitted to return again." Jackson left Lexington on April 21, 1861, and "from this time forth," his wife noted, "the life of my husband belonged to his beloved Southern land, and his private life becomes public history."[22]

Anna remembered her husband's departure with a deep sense of melancholy. She recalled, "our home grew more lonely and painful to me from day to day." Anna took small comfort in the recognition that the women around her were experiencing the same apprehension and dread. Noting that she was cut off from family, Anna recalled that "kind friends did all in their power to prevent my feeling this need, and all hearts were drawn together in one common bond of trial and anxiety, for there was scarcely a household upon which had not fallen a part, at least, of the same weight and sadness which flooded my own home."[23] The departure of men for war engendered a fundamental shift in the structure of southern households that compounded the emotional stress of the physical separation of husbands and wives. Anna noted that although she tried to manage the family household, including the slaves, the disruption was too great. "Without the firm guidance and restraint of their master, the excitement of the times proved so demoralizing" to their slaves that her husband advised her to disperse the slaves and move back with her parents in North Carolina. "Thenceforward my home was with them throughout the war, except during the few visits which I was permitted to pay my husband in the army."[24]

Not surprisingly, a voluminous correspondence sustained the couple during their long stretches of separation.[25] Anna and Thomas Jackson did not, however, always agree on the proper content of that correspondence. Anna craved news of the war. She continually beseeched her husband for military updates. "Little one," he playfully responded to one of her requests, "you wrote me that you wanted longer letters, and now just prepare yourself to have your wish gratified." To her complaint that he never provided her "any news," he answered, "I suppose you meant military news, for I have written you a great deal about your *esposo* and how much he loves you."[26] Although he maintained that it was "unmilitary and unlike an officer to write news respecting one's post," he did occasionally satisfy her penchant for information. In a letter dated November 9, 1861, for example, he tediously updated her on his command and rank.

My command is enlarged, and embraces the Valley District, and the troops of the district constitute the Army of the Valley, but my command is not altogether independent as it is embraced in the Department of Northern Virginia, of which General Johnston has the command. There are three armies in this department—one under General Beauregard, another under Holmes, and a third under my command. . . . A major-general rank is inferior to that of a full general. . . . At all events, the President appoints them in the Provisional army of the Confederate States, and these appointments are only for the war. As the regulations of the army of the Confederate States do not require the rank of major-general there is no pay and staff appointed for it; but I expect to have two aides, and at least one adjutant-general.[27]

More often than not, however, "Stonewall" Jackson left his wife's curiosity unsatisfied.

Anna seemed especially anxious to get reports from her husband to supplement the newspaper accounts, which she found wholly inadequate, of her husband's exploits. Jackson sent a brief note to his wife, for example, after the battle of Manassas, where his heroic (or cravenly) performance earned him the nickname "Stonewall." As Jackson's recent biographer noted, at Manassas occurred "one of those dramatic moments in history when legend is born." General Barnard Bee of South Carolina rode up to Jackson to inform him that the enemy had broken his lines. Jackson, "with brutal determination etched in his face," replied " 'Sir, we

will give them the bayonet.' " General Bee, his confidence renewed, rejoined his men, shouting " 'Look, men, there is Jackson standing like a
stone wall! Let us determine to die here, and we will conquer.' " Perhaps
Bee's confidence was misplaced, for he died there later in the day.[28] Jackson later explained the event to his wife with little hint of pride: "Yesterday
we fought a great battle and gained a great victory for which all the glory
is due to God *alone*. . . . My preservation was entirely due, as was the glorious victory, to our God, to whom be all glory, honor, and praise. Whilst
great credit is due to other parts of our gallant army, God made my brigade more instrumental than any other in repulsing the main attack."
Fearing that he had overstepped the bounds of discretion, he back-
pedaled, warning his wife: "This is for your own information only . . . say
nothing about it. Let another speak praise, not myself." Unfortunately for
Anna, others did not speak loudly enough to quell her desire to see her
husband glorified. Jackson tried to console his wife. "You must not be
concerned at seeing other parts of the army lauded, and my brigade not
mentioned," he wrote. " 'Truth is powerful and will prevail.' "[29] Apparently, truth did not prevail to Anna Jackson's immediate satisfaction. The
Lexington [Virginia] *Gazette*, for example, made no mention of Jackson
in its early reports on the battle save for a brief letter it reprinted in the
August 1, 1861, edition. "General Jackson, too, was riding along the
front," the letter read, "urging our men to their duty—his whole appearance was that of a man determined to conquer or die."[30] Apparently, Anna
found blurbs such as this one wanting.

Anna never confessed the reason behind her desire to see her husband's image glorified. She surely understood that if her countrymen and
women recognized her husband's importance to the Confederacy her
place as his wife would be ensured as well. As the granddaughter of a
Revolutionary War general, perhaps she hoped to see her husband earn
as exalted a place in American history as that of General Joseph Graham.
Whatever her motivation, Jackson found his wife's complaints exasperating. "And so you think the papers ought to say more about your husband!
My brigade is not a brigade of newspaper correspondents." The general
found the seemingly un-Christian nature of his wife's appeals especially
aggravating. In a telling rebuke, Jackson wrote: "I am thankful to my ever-
kind Heavenly father that He makes me content to await His own good
time and pleasure for commendation. . . . My darling," he continued,
"never distrust our God, who doeth all things well. In due time He will
make manifest all His pleasure, which is all His people should desire."[31]
Anna apparently believed she should expedite God's timing.

General Jackson, however, remained unmoved by her pleas. Henry M.
Field wrote in the introduction to Anna Jackson's posthumous biography
of her husband that "of the war itself she has but little to tell us; for he
did not confide his plans even to her. It was not that he distrusted her
womanly discretion; but, in the midst of thousands of watchful eyes, had

he disclosed to her the dangers into which he was going, her cheek might have blanched with fear, or a shade of anxiety passed over her countenance that would have set all to wondering what it meant." Field later noted that even when the general wrote after a battle, "There is no attempt to describe it, and hardly an allusion to it, except in a general way, in the expression that often recurs in his letters that 'by the blessing of Almighty God their arms have been crowned with victory.' "[32] Not surprisingly, then, little evidence exists to suggest that Anna Jackson influenced her husband's military decisions in any way.

Despite Anna Jackson's insistence on receiving news from the front line, her husband remained content to relate much more mundane matters. "Don't you tremble when you see that you have to read such a long letter," he warned her lovingly in a letter dated November 16, 1861, "for I'm going to write it just as full as it can hold." Jackson then described in great detail his winter quarters in Winchester, Virginia. "This house belongs to Lieutenant-Colonel Moore," he explained to his wife. "The building is of cottage style and contains six rooms. I have two rooms, one above the other. My lower room, or office, has a matting on the floor, a large fine table, six chairs, and a piano. The walls are papered with elegant gilt paper. I don't remember to have ever seen more beautiful papering, and there are five paintings on the wall. . . . The upper room is neat, but not a full story, and is, I may say, only remarkable for being heated in a peculiar manner, by a flue from the office below." Jackson's efforts to recreate his prewar home are significant. As one cultural historian of the Civil War has noted, men in both armies "wove reminders of domesticity into military life to simulate family sentiment," which had become so critical to the formation of the Victorians' identities and understanding of themselves. Because the war forced men to abandon their homes, albeit perhaps only temporarily, the recreation of a domestic setting "allowed the Victorians to rededicate themselves to domesticity in a society where actual families felt the weight of numerous pressures." Jackson concluded his letter to Anna by admitting, "If I only had my little woman here, the room would be set off."[33]

Not surprisingly, the possibility of a campside visit generated a great deal of excitement for both husband and wife. Many officers did indeed bring their wives to camp. Unfortunately for the Jacksons, wartime exigencies made such treats rarities. "I received your precious letter," General Jackson acknowledged in the spring of 1861, "in which you speak of coming here in the event of my remaining. I would like very much to see my sweet little face, but my darling had better remain at her own home, as my continuance here is very uncertain." Later in that spring, he told his wife that if she had not already begun her journey to Winchester by the time she received his letter, "do not think of coming."[34] Despite the difficulties involved, Jackson, like countless other military men "responded to the war's impositions with a determination to involve their families" in the conflict. In fact, so determined were officers to maintain some semblance of prewar domesticity, argued one historian, "that they violated their own notions of propriety concerning the sexes' separate spheres in order to keep their loved ones close by."[35] General Jackson was no exception. He asked his wife, "In reference to coming to see your *esposo*, what would you do for privacy in camp?" He then warned, "I tell you there are more inconveniences attending camp life for a lady than little pet is aware of; and worst of all is the danger you might encounter in such a trip, as the cars are so crowded with soldiers." Nevertheless, he concluded, "I would dearly love to have my darling here at this time, and I think I might be able to get a room for you with a kind family in whose yard I have my tent."[36]

Anna did visit her husband in the fall of 1861. She noted that her husband's warnings about the perils of traveling and camp life were hardly exaggerated. She and her escort made an unremarkable journey to Richmond but because "her young man" was neither in the army nor about to enter it, he was denied the passport needed to complete the rest of the journey. Anna Jackson refused to turn back, although she was unaccustomed to traveling alone. She telegraphed her husband and, mustering her strength, boarded the train, "filled with apprehension—the cars being crowded with soldiers and scarcely a woman to be seen." She later noted that a "lady seemed to be a great curiosity to the soldiers, scores of whom filed through the car to take a look." Anna eventually met a family friend, Captain J. Harvey White, who escorted her to Manassas where she was to meet her husband. The rest of her trip did not proceed smoothly, however. Her husband failed to receive the telegram that she had sent from Richmond telling him to meet her at Manassas. White, unwilling to leave Mrs. Jackson unattended in Manassas, persuaded her to travel on to Fairfax Station, thus delaying the Jacksons' reunion for a day. Because "not a place to accommodate a lady was to be found," Anna Jackson was forced to spend the night on the train. "I was all alone, and had nothing to read, so it can be imagined that the few anxious and dreary hours spent in that little place of horrors seemed an age."[37] That Anna willingly risked traveling, unescorted at least part of the way, and endured a lonely and frightening night locked in a railway car suggests the degree to which her husband had come to be an integral part of her sense of happiness.[38]

Significantly, Jackson took his wife during that visit on a tour of Manassas, the site of the Confederacy's first great battle, suggesting that although he was still bound by many of the gender conventions of the antebellum south he was willing to expose his wife to the scene of a bloody struggle. "Much of the *debris* of the conflict still remained," Anna noted of her trip to the battlefield. "The old Henry House was riddled with shot and shell; the carcasses of the horses, and even some of the bones of the poor human victims were to be seen. It was difficult to realize that these now silent plains had so recently been the scene of a great battle, and that here the Reaper Death had gathered such a harvest of precious lives, many of whom were the very flower of our Southern youth and manhood." Although still protected by her husband, Anna nonetheless pushed on the boundaries of antebellum southern gender conventions when she rode through the battlefield, listening to stories of the movements and positions of the two armies.[39]

In the late fall of 1861 Jackson received orders to report to Winchester, Virginia. He immediately wrote his wife of his new assignment, adding, "I trust I may be able to send for you after I get settled." He later promised her "a very nice house" if she were to come. The news heartened Anna, who, by now a seasoned traveler to military camps, "without waiting for the promised 'aide' to be sent on as my escort," joined some friends who were going on to Richmond. From there she met an elderly clergyman who escorted her for the rest of the trip. Anna Jackson remembered her second visit to her husband fondly. "Winchester was rich in happy homes and pleasant people, in social refinement and elegant hospitality; and the extreme kindness and appreciation shown to General Jackson by all, bound us both to them so closely and warmly that ever after that winter he called the place our 'war home.' "[40]

Shortly after Anna arrived in Winchester, General Jackson set off on the Bath-Romney campaign. During his absence, Anna stayed at the home of the Reverend James R. Graham. Graham remembered well the general's insistence that his wife should be provided a proper home in the midst of war. "On his return from this memorable expedition," Graham recalled, "he declared that it would be cruel to turn Mrs. Jackson out of her *home*, and if Mrs. Graham would allow her to remain, *he* would stay and help to take care of her." Anna recalled that upon her husband's return from Bath and reunion with his wife at the Graham home, Jackson exclaimed, "*Oh! this is the very essence of comfort!*" For the next two months the Jacksons stayed with the Grahams, and the general referred to the house as "his *home*."[41] Anna left Winchester in the winter of 1862. She did not see her husband again for thirteen months.

Early in Anna's stay in Winchester, stories filtered back about Jackson's mistake in the Bath-Romney campaign. Jackson, determined to shore up western Virginia's support for the Confederacy, had devised a plan to take the strategically important town of Romney. On New Year's Day, an unusually warm day for that time of the year, Jackson's men, reinforced by 6,000 of General William W. Loring's troops, set out to march. By the end of the day, the weather turned brutally cold. The supply wagons lagged far behind the marching men, leaving the soldiers cold and hungry. Jackon pressed his men onward, despite their obvious fatigue, and on January 14, 1862, they finally reached a deserted Romney. Only then did Jackson apparently realize that many of his men openly complained about Jackson's strategy, earning him the name "Fool Tom Jackson."[42] Anna later determined to counter that version for her postwar reading audience by suggesting that the general's men trusted him implicitly. She recounted the story, for example, of a conversation she overheard between a Confederate officer and a woman from Winchester. When asked for his opinion of General Jackson, the officer replied, "I have *the most implicit confidence in him*, madam. At first I did not know what to think of his bold and aggressive mode of warfare; but since I *know* the man, and have witnessed his ability and his patriotic devotion, *I would follow him anywere*." She also suggested that the rumored discontent of the men on this expedition came not from the general's troops but from General Loring's. Although the severe weather made the campaign difficult, she admitted, "his own command bore up with great fortitude and without murmuring, but the adverse weather had the effect of greatly intensifying the discontent of Loring and his men." She intimated that the discontent stemmed less from the severe weather and Jackson's insistence with pressing forward, however, than from Loring's opposition to a winter campaign. Moreover, "an unfortunate jealousy" developed between the two commands, causing "an immense amount of trouble and disappointment to Jackson, and frustrated much of the success for which he had reason to hope." To shore up her version, she included in the second edition of her biography of her husband a series of reminiscences of men who had served with him as testimonials to his military genius.[43]

Significantly, General Jackson never visited his wife at home during the war. Responding to Anna's plea that he take a furlough, he explained, "I can't be absent from my command, as my attention is necessary in preparing my troops for hard fighting should it be required." Moreover, because the men serving under him were unable to visit their families, Jackson was unwilling to risk the morale of his troops by seemingly abandoning his post to visit his wife. Jackson seemed particularly concerned with absenteeism in the Confederate ranks and believed that furloughs encouraged such spurious behavior. On Christmas, 1862, shortly after the birth of their daughter, Julia, he wrote to his wife that "it appears to me, that it is better for me to remain with my command so long as the war continues, if our ever gracious Heavenly Father permits. The army suffers immensely by absentees. If all our troops, officers, and men were at their posts, we might, through God's blessing, expect a more speedy termination of the war." Although he longed to see his wife, he believed he needed to set an example to his men.[44] Henry Kyd Douglas, who served under Jackson, noted that although furloughs "were freely granted in some divisions of the army; few in Jackson's brigade. . . . His troops stood it with little grumbling when he refused them, officers or men. His brigade was a good school of war."[45] Anna, however, was apparently not as sanguine about her husband's policy as were his troops.

Despite Jackson's refusal to leave his troops, he was most anxious to see her, especially after Anna became pregnant. One historian of Confederate women has suggested that because of the "general medical realities and . . . conditions specific to wartime," white women of the Confederacy feared childbirth. Surely the death of Elinor Junkin Jackson during child-birth and the death of the Jacksons' first child caused the couple to be concerned. Following the rules of Victorian propriety, Anna made scant comment on her second pregnancy. Moreover, the letters for her husband that she excerpted in her biography of him make no reference to her condition. Yet she commented effusively on the birth of their daughter, Julia. "We now approach an event in the life of General Jackson which gladdened his heart more than all his victories, and filled it with devout gratitude to the Giver of all good," she noted. "To a man of his extreme domesticity and love for children this was a crowning happiness." Writing to his wife after he received word of the successful delivery of his daughter, Jackson acknowledged the danger his wife faced in childbirth. "Oh! How thankful I am to our kind Heavenly Father for having spared my precious wife and given us a little daughter!"[46] The Jacksons welcomed their child, despite the hardships of pregnancy and delivery, and despite the wartime exigencies that kept the family apart.

General Jackson did not see his wife and child until mid-April 1863. Julia's bout with the chicken pox prevented the mother and child from visiting him earlier in the year. He still refused to ask for a furlough, despite his wife's pleading. Nonetheless, his desire to see his family only intensified, especially after "Mrs. General Longstreet, Mrs. General A. P. Hill, and Mrs. General Rodes" came to see their husbands. "It made me wish I had Mrs. Jackson here too," he admitted to his wife. The general delighted in his family's company during their nine-day spring visit. His wife noted in her biography, however, that he "did not permit the presence of his family to interfere in any way with his military duties," that when he returned from headquarters, he devoted all of his leisure time to his family.[47] The next time Anna would see her husband, he was on his deathbed.

On May 2, 1863, during the battle of Chancellorsville, Confederate soldiers who mistook Jackson for a Union officer shot him in the left arm. Eight days later he died of pneumonia. The Confederacy surely suffered a great loss with the death of General Jackson. Upon hearing the news of Jackson's death, General Robert E. Lee, who scored one of the most important victories of the war at Chancellorsville, claimed, "It is a terrible loss. I do not know how to replace him. Any victory would be dear at such a cost."[48] His death forced many white Southerners to ponder seriously the possibility of Confederate defeat.[49] The story of the fatal wounding soon acquired the aura of legend. Dr. Hunter McGuire, the attending physician, wrote perhaps the most famous account, which Anna Jackson reprinted in her biography. Only after she retells others' versions of his fall did she offer her own thoughts to her reading public. She recalled seeing her husband dying:

My own heart almost stood still under the weight of horror and apprehension which then oppressed me. The ghastly spectacle was a most unfitting preparation for my entrance into the presence of my stricken husband; but when I was soon afterwards summoned to his chamber, the sight which there met my eyes was far more appalling, and sent such a thrill of agony and heart sinking through me as I had never known before! Oh, the fearful change since last I had seen him. It required the strongest effort of which I was capable to maintain my self-control. . . . His fearful wounds, his mutilated arm, the scratches upon his face, and above all, the desperate pneumonia, which was flushing his cheeks, oppressing his breathing, and benumbing his senses, wrung my soul with such grief and anguish as it had never before experienced.[50]

Equally as shocking was Anna's realization that she was soon to become a widow with a five-month-old baby. She took only small comfort in knowing that "his name and memory are enshrined in the hearts of his countrymen, and of the good and noble of all lands."[51]

After the death of her husband, Anna, age thirty-one, returned to Cottage Home in North Carolina where she remained for the last fifty-two years of her life. Jackson's recent biographer has noted that although the fall of the Confederacy wiped out the Jackson estate, worth close to $22,000, in December 1865, "a nationwide appeal was made 'for the relief of the widow of the brave Jackson.' " An unfounded rumor circulated that Anna " 'had been compelled to sell everything,' in order to survive." Anna Jackson eventually earned the name "Widow of the Confederacy" and enjoyed a successful career as one of the most popular women in the country. Her daughter Julia, too, became well known as the "Daughter of Stonewall," appearing as the guest of honor at various Confederate veteran events, parades, and dedications. Julia died at the age of twenty-six, but her own young children continued to make public appearances on behalf of their grandfather's memory.[52]

Not surprisingly, the death of "Stonewall" Jackson strengthened Anna's resolve to see her husband's Civil War exploits celebrated. Initially, she concentrated her efforts on the enshrining of his grave. "I was gratified to see from the Lexington [Virginia] paper," she wrote her late husband's sister-in-law, Margaret Preston, "that the railing . . . had been put up [around his grave] and that the dear people there had commemorated the 10th of May. It is a sweet solace to my lonely heart to see his name and memory so dear and so honored by his countrymen." In addition to the glorification of his name and memory, however, Anna wished the physical monument—his grave—be "honored" as well. "I am so anxious to visit the grave again," she continued in her letter to Preston. "Please write me a full description of it. I do trust it will not be so desecrated now, by persons pulling grass +c off it. I might not call it *desecration* for I know that those who do it are activated by feelings of [. . . ?] for him, but still it is very painful to friends to see graves left in that condition. . . . If the Col. did not have it all sodded, I would be greatly obliged if he would have it done yet, and I do hope the sacred spot will be kept neatly and *left alone*."⁵³ Anna was not alone in her quest to maintain General Jackson's grave and commemorate his deeds. Many communities chose May 10, the anniversary of Jackson's death, as Confederate Memorial Day.⁵⁴ Ironically, then, the idolatry that General Jackson so abhorred in life surrounded him in death.

In addition to maintaining his grave, Anna devoted her time and energy to ensuring a place for her husband's memorial at the Confederate Museum in Richmond, Virginia, and at Confederate bazaars held throughout the postwar South. She sent, for example, a box of her husband's relics to a Mrs. Tegmeyer for a bazaar that was to be held in 1898. Anna Jackson apologized for not sending more, "but as I wrote before the most of my relics are in the Confederate Museum." Buttons seemed to be an especially popular item for Confederate bazaars. Anna sent a note to Mrs. John Gresham of Baltimore, Maryland, that accompanied a button. Apparently there was some dispute over the authenticity of said button because Jackson had not cut it off the coat herself, but rather found it lying among his other effects. "I hope, however, that you will not look upon this . . . button as a *fraud* but still cherish it as having belonged to Gen. J." Although buttons were plentiful, autographs were hard to come by, even for the General's widow. "I get letters from all over the land asking for General Jackson's autograph," she admitted, "but I am unable to meet the demand." At times Anna Jackson considered "the penalties" of being the widow of a cherished war hero "rather heavy, but then there is also the light side to it, for the blessed name brings me so much reverence, love, and [. . . ?] which I can never appreciate enough."⁵⁵ Despite her periodic bouts of self-pity Anna recognized the important cultural position she held.

Anna exerted her influence over her late husband's literary image as well. Robert Dabney's 1866 biography of "Stonewall" Jackson, *The Life and Campaigns of Lieutenant-General Thomas J. Jackson,* appeared with the imprimatur of Anna Jackson. Anticipating those who might question his qualifications for writing the late general's biography, Dabney gave his first response: "My answer is, that it has been entrusted to me by the widow . . . of General Jackson."⁵⁶ Lest there be any confusion, Dabney let his readers know that Anna Jackson had "authorized" his biography. Thirty-five years later, Anna authorized William C. Chase's biography, *The Story of Stonewall Jackson.* "I am grateful to hear that you are progressing so well with your book," she wrote Chase. "I am satisfied your work has been executed very carefully, and unmistakably in a marked degree of devotion for my husband's memory, and that the book will prove a most interesting one upon General Jackson's life and career."⁵⁷ Anna, however, remained discontent to let military men publish accounts of her late husband. Ten years before Chase's biography appeared, Jackson's widow published her own biography of "Stonewall" Jackson, engendering a literary controversy that she was quite unprepared to handle.

This controversy had its roots in an article titled "Personal Reminiscences of Stonewall Jackson" published in *Century* magazine the fall of 1886 by Margaret Junkin Preston, Jackson's sister-in-law. It appeared in the *Century*'s highly successful Battles and Leaders of the Civil War series.[58] Although the series concentrated on articles written by former Union and Confederate officers, the *Century* did publish a handful of articles by women. Those articles selected for publication were generally of a lighter fare than the formal and stilted prose of the former combatants. Specifically, the editors encouraged stories that told of the "human side of affairs, avoiding the dry bones of history."[59] Preston certainly fulfilled the requirements established by the editors. As Jackson's sister-in-law and intimate confidant, she believed that she "held a key to his character" and was thus eminently qualified for the task of biography. Rather than focusing on Jackson's military career, Preston chose to highlight his religiosity, compassion, morality, and devotion to the state of Virginia, claiming that these principles, and not necessarily his military prowess, fueled the man who "to the end was the popular idol of the South."[60]

Preston's essay undoubtedly captured the imagination of many of her readers but perhaps none more than that of Anna, who used much of it in her own biography of her late husband. Mary Anna Jackson's *Life and Letters of General Thomas J. Jackson*, published by Harper and Brothers five years after Preston's essay appeared in the *Century*, borrowed heavily from Preston's discussion of "Stonewall" Jackson's early career and character development, for which Preston was present, but Anna was not.[61] Prevailing practice may have allowed for the absorption of public discourse into personal narratives, but Preston did not feel so generous. Incensed by Anna Jackson's plagiarism, she informed her editors at the *Century* of Anna's intellectual dishonesty and vehemently expressed her disgust at this act. "I was . . . very much surprised," she wrote Richard Gilder, "to find some of its [the original essay's] most illustrative anecdotes and as many as fourteen partial pages in Mrs. Jackson's book copied for this Century article, without any credit given to author or Edition. . . . [T]his is an inadmissible appropriation of another person's literary property." Preston fully expected the Century Company to challenge Harper and Brothers and Anna Jackson on this matter, not only to protect one of its favorite contributors, but also to safeguard its own interests as publishers of the original essay. The circulation of the widow Jackson's biography "will be immense in the south," Preston predicted, and she wished to be acknowledged as the creator of the narrative, as well as to be guaranteed a portion of its profits.[62]

While mere carelessness might explain Anna's omission of the proper reference to Margaret Preston's essay, it is equally as likely that Jackson, as the late general's widow, believed she held a proprietary claim to his life and life story, even the part that did not include her. She was surely unwilling to share that life story with another intimate of "Stonewall" Jackson. Anna Jackson cited other sources from which she lifted long, descriptive passages. "It is the Rev. Dr. Dabney," she informed her readers in one instance, "who thus sketches the figure of the chief." She then pulled two paragraphs from Dabney's *Life and Campaigns of Lieutenant-General Thomas J. Jackson*, published in 1866.[63] Here lies the crux of Preston's argument with Jackson's widow. To be sure, Anna alluded to Margaret Preston. Prefacing an extensive quotation from Preston's Battles and Leaders series' article, she identified her source as "a lady who was a relative, with whom he [Jackson] lived under the same roof [for] several years."[64] But she never named Margaret Junkin Preston. Preston voiced her frustrations with Anna's affront to the editors of the *Century*. She noted, "as Acknowledgment is given everywhere through the book, even when the extracts are slight, it is a most unaccountable thing that it is invariably omitted where I am concerned. Almost everywhere you read of what a 'friend' or 'person' has said or done," she continued, "you may credit it to me."[65] Moreover, Margaret Junkin Preston was hardly a "mere lady who was a relative," and Anna's failure to acknowledge Preston as an authority on her late husband insulted the general's former confidante mightily. By lifting portions on the formation of Stonewall Jackson's character from one of his contemporaries and intimates, and presenting them as her own, Anna Jackson was, in effect, writing herself into a critical stage in "Stonewall" Jackson's career. In lionizing her late husband, she was also giving herself a more prominent role in his history.[66]

Anna, of course, made no such admission. Rather, she claimed that she wrote her version of the late general's life so that her grandchildren could appreciate "that tender and exquisite phase of his inner life, which was never revealed to the world." She explained her long-held public silence by noting "for many years after the death of my husband the shadow over my life was so deep, and all that concerned him was so sacred, that I could not consent to lift the veil to the public gaze." She later noted that she had intended to "keep myself in the background as much as possible," when discussing the general's early life. In explaining her account of their married life, however, Anna noted that "in what follows, my own life is so bound up with that of my husband that the reader will have to pardon so much of self as must necessarily be introduced to continue the story of his domestic life and to explain the letters that follow."[67] This statement appears directly following the passages Anna Jackson took from Margaret Preston's essay. She could now easily explain her "intrusion" into the narrative.

Twenty-five years after Anna's tangle with Preston, the general's widow found herself embroiled in another literary battle over her husband's image. In 1911, Virginia novelist Mary Johnston published the first of a two-volume novel of the Civil War, *The Long Roll*, offering, according to some of her readers, including Anna Jackson, a slanderous portrayal of "Stone-wall Jackson" at the Bath-Romney campaign. According to Johnston, the general's men had little confidence in " 'the damned clown,' " Fool Tom Jackson. " 'The individual at the head of this army is not a general,' " opined one soldier while addressing his compatriots; " 'he's a peda-gogue—by God, he's the Falerian pedagogue who sold his pupils to the Romans.' " Finishing his analogy, the soldier continued, " 'Oh, the lamb-like pupils, trooping after him through flowers and sunshine—straight into the hands of Kelly at Romney, with Rosecrans and twenty others just beyond.' " At the protestations of a V.M.I. cadet, the soldier concluded his rant with a summation of Jackson's character: "stiff, fanatic, inhuman, callous, cold, half mad and wholly rash, without military capacity, ambi-tious as Lucifer and absurd as Hudibras—I ask again what is this person doing at the head of this army."[68] Although Jackson garnered the support and confidence of his men throughout the course of the novel, Johnston's initial characterization of the general was tantamount to blasphemy to some, deserving the most serious rebukes. This portrayal seemed espe-cially loathsome to Anna because she had attempted to counter the image of "Fool Tom Jackson" in her biography published nearly twenty years before the publication of *The Long Roll.*

Anna thanked her good friend Mrs. John Jones Gresham for being "a good angel to me in all my trials with that awful novelist—Miss Johnston." Despite Gresham's advice to Jackson to avoid "any controversy," the gen-eral's widow did *"just what you told me not to do*! I have at least contradicted her outrageous misrepresentations. . . . All the honor and glory which she has to accredit to her *professed* hero, cannot atone for the miserably *untrue* and *unjust* portraiture which she seems to revel in making of him."[69] Anna retaliated by writing a scathing review of *The Long Roll* in the *New York Times*, claiming that although her opposition to "publicity and newspaper controversy" had heretofore impelled her to remain silent, she felt she must set the historical record straight. "Pity 'tis true that fiction is more read by the young than history," Mrs. Jackson lamented, "and it would be a great injustice to General Jackson that such a delineation of his char-acter and personality go down to future generations." According to Anna, Johnston rendered the general "rough, uncouth, boorish, slovenly, and unbalanced." Even worse, "Miss Johnston acknowledged that she never saw or knew General Jackson, which fact is very evident from the hideous caricature she uses as her frontispiece [by artist N. C. Wyeth] representing him and his little sorrel and which alone is enough to condemn the book." And though Johnston's " 'presumptuousness' " may be dismissed as the folly of a young mind, literary success, which acts like a "fine wine," has dulled her senses to the detriment of history. "Will not all true Confed-erate soldiers who followed Stonewall Jackson," she pleaded at the end of her review, "give an expression of their opinion of 'The Long Roll,' " and if they approve of it let them say so candidly but if not will they unite in

such a protest against this false and damaging portraiture of their commander as will settle the question for all time."[70]

Former soldiers most willingly picked up the gauntlet thrown down by
Anna. Captain J. P. Smith, who served on the staff of the general, charged
Johnston with unjustly portraying Jackson as "harsh, hostile, pedantic, awkward, hypochondriachal, literal, and strict." Worse than these sins of commission, however, according to Smith, were Johnston's sins of omission.
Johnston provided "no adequate conception of the religious character of
Stonewall Jackson," Smith fumed. And although Johnston described the
general as obsessive, bordering on the fanatical, and utterly unfit for duty,
he was, according to Smith, "devout and reverent, humble, steadfast,
prayerful in spirit and faithful in duty." Convinced that Johnston had in-
vented her own peculiar image of "Stonewall" Jackson, Smith doubted the
author had consulted any historical or biographical source. "It will be an
unmeasured loss to generations to come," he wrote "if a picture so marred
be retained in the thought and memory of our people."[71]

Mary Johnston challenged her detractors, including, by implication,
Anna, to support their claims on the novel's historical inaccuracies. In
order for her critics to levy their complaints, she noted, they "must really
strike out of existence the hundred and odd volumes of the official records, the whole series of Southern Historical Society papers, all the newspapers of '61–65, the articles contributed by Southern officers to 'Battles
and Leaders,' as well as those contributed to Mrs. Jackson's life of her
husband, Henderson's biography, histories, memoirs, and diaries without
number, forms of records too numerous to mention." Although Johnston's detractors believed her characterization of "Stonewall" Jackson rendered the general an uncouth boor, Johnston believed it made him human. Her novel, she proclaimed, "has done a service to Virginia and the
South." Convinced of its importance, Johnston noted finally, "Jerusalem
is not the only city that stones her prophets, nor antiquity the only time
that preoccupies itself with some blemish—it may be reality, may be fancied only—on the forehead of a great and real service."[72]

Not all readers took offense at Johnston's characterization of "Stonewall" Jackson. After reading Anna Jackson's attack in a local paper, Joseph
Ames, future president of the University of Chicago, dashed off a letter
to Johnston. Intimating that she never "wish[ed] to see the name Jackson
again," Ames felt "as if I must write to tell you how much I . . . enjoyed
your picture of the great General." He later thanked Johnston for deliv-
ering those "who never knew the war, an *impression* which we shall never
forget."[73] William Terrence published his spirited defense of Johnston in
the Richmond *Times-Dispatch*, citing "an embarrassment of riches" to au-
thenticate her portrayal of General Jackson. Moreover, "as an artist, it is
Miss Johnston's right to take what ever she knows to have been true of
the man and use it to the advantage of her characterization." Those who
accuse Johnston of "poison[ing] the minds of the young," had failed to

prove that she had falsified any public record.[74] Even Ferris Greenslet, Mary Johnston's editor at Houghton Mifflin who continually worried about the public's reception of his client's novel, reassured Johnston, "It is a pity that the writer of fiction should have the trouble of the biographer. . . . I think you will find, however, that in the long run even Mrs. Jackson will take a different view."[75]

Despite Greenslet's prediction, Anna Jackson remained unmoved. To the end of her life, she stood by her version of Stonewall Jackson's life. Mary Anna Jackson died four years after the publication of *The Long Roll*. At the 1915 National Convention of the United Daughters of the Confederacy, Jackson's niece, Eugenia Hill Arnold, gave the eulogy. "She lived all the years in that long half century [after General Jackson's death] in the hallowing light of a supreme loyalty to that one dear memory, and as every sacred loyalty must, it illuminated her life with a radiance that shone more and more to the perfect day."[76] That loyalty to his image, of course, in part guided Mary Anna Jackson throughout her brief married life with General Jackson. She was acutely aware that she had married a war hero, and she wanted him to be treated with the proper respect. The war intensified her desire to see her husband glorified. For General Jackson, however, the war increased his desire for domesticity. His descriptions of "home" stand in stark relief against his wife's pleas for detailed accounts of his actions on the battlefield. The war may have disrupted the Jackson home, but the general endeavored mightily to keep the ties of his home life intact during the conflict. In the end, of course, the war disrupted their home permanently. Anna Jackson was left with only her memories and her hero-image of her husband. And as she sought to magnify his image in a region that already championed its heroes, she wrote herself into his story, ensuring that she, too, would be remembered.

FOUR

"Cupid Does Not Readily Give Way to Mars"

The Marriage of LaSalle Corbell and George E. Pickett

LESLEY J. GORDON

LaSalle Corbell Pickett liked to tell her readers that she first spotted her husband George as he wandered alone on the beaches at Old Point Comfort, Virginia. It was the summer of 1852 and her parents, John and Elizabeth, had taken their family to the seaside on holiday. Precocious and inquisitive well beyond her nine years, Sallie recalled "a solitary officer on the sands, reading, or looking at the ships as they came and went, or watching the waves as they dashed to sudden death against the shore." He seemed the perfect picture of a gallant soldier and ideal man. She noted his physical exterior, especially his hair, "which hung in shining waves almost to his shoulders," his neat attire, and erect gait. Learning that he was a Mexican War veteran, Sallie remembered: "It seemed impossible to me. How could anyone so immaculate and so beautiful to look upon have really fought and killed people?" To the girl he appeared the " 'Good Prince' in the fairy stories my grandmother told me."[1]

Sallie Corbell's "Good Prince" had grown up on a plantation called Turkey Island not far from Old Point Comfort on the James River. George Edward Pickett was born on January 25, 1825, to Robert and Mary Pickett of Henrico County, Virginia. By the time George reached adolescence, his parents had begun to worry about his prospects. The tobacco market was unstable and George seemed unconcerned about his economic prospects. At first, Robert and Mary sent their son to study law with an uncle in Quincy, Illinois, but law held little interest for young George. His parents hoped the United States Military Academy would instill in their gregarious son the discipline and focus he so sorely lacked. After four years bucking the academy's system, and nearly facing expulsion for excessive demerits, George Pickett graduated from West Point in 1846 and became a professional soldier. During the Mexican War he earned brevets for meritorious combat and at the battle of Chapultepec in September 1847, he experienced one of the most exhilarating moments of his life: his friend and comrade James Longstreet fell severely wounded, and Pickett quickly scooped the American flag from Longstreet's hands and hoisted it over the ramparts of the captured fortress. George Pickett had found his life's calling. He traded the antebellum South's world of planters and slaves for the seclusion and monotony of the frontier army. The army became an adoptive home, his fellow officers his surrogate family. In January 1851, Brevet Captain Pickett married Virginian Sally Minge and brought her to his army post deep in the Texas frontier. Ten months later Sally died in childbirth; nor did the infant survive. Inconsolable in his personal grief over the loss of his wife and child, George went away without leave for several months from the army. Some of that time twenty-seven-year-old Brevet Captain Pickett may have spent wandering alone on the beaches near Old Point Comfort.[2]

LaSalle claims that she observed George sitting quietly reading under an umbrella one warm afternoon. She innocently interrupted his solitude and asked if he had whooping cough. The child was sick with the ailment and wondered if George shared her illness and thus, like her, had to stay away from friends and parties. According to LaSalle, George denied having the illness, but explained that he had "something worse, a broken heart, and he did not like to make others sad with his sorrow." LaSalle asked how he broke his heart. He answered, "God broke it when He took from him his loved ones and left him so lonely." She claimed, "In his solitude I felt that we were comrades in sad experience."[3]

"He drew me to him," LaSalle remembered, "telling me that he had lost his wife and little girl, and that he was very lonely. I asked him their names; they had both been called Sally.

" 'You can call me Sally,' I offered. 'I'll be your wife and little girl.'

" 'That's a promise,' he replied. 'You shall be named Sally and be my wife.' "[4]

The soldier and child spent the rest of the day playing games, building sand castles, and singing. They both felt a bond, LaSalle recalled. "In return for his confidence," she later wrote, "I promised to comfort him for his losses and to be his little girl now and his wife just as soon as I was grown up to be a lady." To symbolize their pledge, he gave her a ring and gold heart with the inscription "Sally" on it. "Then and to the end," LaSalle affirmed, "he was my soldier, and always when we were alone I called him 'Soldier.' "[5]

LaSalle would later mark that day in 1852 when she encountered Brevet Captain George Pickett as her "point of beginning—a period back of which life to present consciousness, was not." She insisted that she knew at that very moment that one day their fate would be joined.[6]

The historical "facts" of this first meeting between LaSalle Corbell and George Pickett are hard to prove. There are no other sources besides LaSalle's many published writings to corroborate this account, and little authentic correspondence has survived from their wartime courtship and marriage. LaSalle's tendency to fabricate and romanticize her past make using her writings as reliable historical evidence difficult. Still, there are some significant meanings and elements of "truth" to the images she con-veyed in her postwar recollections. Her books and short stories tell us a great deal about the nature of this couple's powerful if not always idyllic relationship. Their story, imagined and real, was in some ways unique; yet it also had elements of timeless wartime romances where two lovers strug-gle to rise above the pain of war, defeat, exile, and death. Their devotion to one another is undeniable.[7]

LaSalle was born Sallie Ann Corbell on May 16, 1843, to John David and Elizabeth Phillips Corbell. She apparently grew up in modest wealth on her family's plantation at Chuckatuck, not far from Fort Monroe on Virginia's eastern shore. According to LaSalle, her childhood was bucolic; she was surrounded by faithful slaves and doting parents. Still, she claimed that her parents were initially displeased that their firstborn was not a son. Her "poor disappointed, heart-broken mother turned her face to the wall" when she learned her baby's sex and her father greeted the news that he had a daughter rather than a son by exclaiming: "How did it happen?"[8] No doubt, it was expected that she would grow up to be a proper lady and suitable match for men in her class.[9]

It is entirely possible that the Corbells knew the Pickett family through the social circles of the Tidewater elite. Maybe the grieving army officer did briefly encounter young Sallie during her beach holiday in eastern Virginia, and perhaps George innocently played with the nine-year-old girl, finding that she made him temporarily forget his pain and loneliness. But despite LaSalle's talk of fate and destiny and her insistence that he promised his heart to her, George left Virginia in 1854, probably with little thought of returning. He assumed command of a fort in the Pacific Northwest and remarried. He built his wife, a Haida Indian, a modest house and settled into his new life. Tragically, his second wife died soon after the birth of a baby boy. George could not bear to stay in their home, or take care of little James. He gave the child up to a white foster family. When George left to join the Confederacy in 1861, he never saw his son again.[10]

LaSalle's publications made only limited mention of George's life in Washington Territory. She described his experiences in the "Pig War" where he confronted angry British settlers over possession of San Juan Island. She praised his ability to speak Indian languages and to keep the peace in the region. She even credited Pickett and William Harney for deliberately causing the Pig War in the hopes of unifying the country in 1859 and avoiding civil war. But, although she privately acknowledged

George's Indian son, and even tried to support him financially after her husband's death, she never revealed to readers the existence of George's Indian family.[11]

The Civil War defined the Pickett marriage both in reality and in fantasy. Indeed, the Civil War brought George and Sallie together. George returned to Richmond in September 1861, and whether it was for the first time or the second, he fell in love with Miss Corbell, eighteen years his junior. War would leave its imprint on both Picketts, melding them as lovers, but also leaving lasting and painful scars.

Their ardor was not immediately apparent. During the first several months of war, George focused on promotion and field command. By the end of 1861, he was a colonel responsible for the lower Rappahannock River. He won promotion to brigadier general in February 1862, largely due to his fifteen years of professional army experience and the Confederacy's need for brigadier generals. Participating in the siege of Yorktown and the battles of Williamsburg and Seven Pines, Pickett and his all-Virginia brigade earned high marks from several superior officers, including George's good friend James Longstreet. Sallie meanwhile was attending a ladies' seminary in Lynchburg, Virginia. At the Battle of Gaines' Mill on June 27, 1862, while leading his brigade forward, George suffered a shoulder wound. His injury was serious enough to keep him from participating in the remainder of Lee's successful Seven Days campaign and the important battles of Second Manassas and Antietam. Sallie attested to her postwar readers that she rushed to Richmond and remained at George's bedside during his long convalescence, nursing him back to health. During their many hours together, LaSalle recalled playing the role of nurturer, comforter, and moral protector—roles that defined the Victorian ideal of wife, and roles that she would increasingly assume.[12]

It was not until after George's return to the army in the fall of 1862 and his promotion to major general that their romance became obvious to others. For George, his growing passion for Sallie Corbell became an obsession; he increasingly defied danger, censure, and acceptable military protocol to see his sweetheart whenever possible. Miss Corbell, tall with dark hair and dark eyes, was equally attracted to her Soldier. She later called these nocturnal visits "glimpses of heaven," but they made a poor impression on George's military contemporaries.[13] In the spring of 1863, a Virginia colonel complained to his wife that General Pickett was "continually riding off to pay court to his young love, leaving the division details to his staff."[14] Major G. Moxley Sorrel criticized George's "frequent applications to be absent" to visit Sallie, remarking: "I don't think his division benefited from such carpet-knight doings on the field."[15] George's constant requests to leave camp also irritated close friend and corps commander, James Longstreet. In her book, *The Bugles of Gettysburg*, LaSalle recounted supposed dialogue between the two men:

Longstreet remarked: "I do not go galloping through forests and over rivers and past hostile sentries . . . just for a look and a word and come dashing back to the field with the first glint of morning."

"A look and a word?" George rejoined. "But they are worth the hardest ride that ever a soldier took."[16]

George and LaSalle most certainly exchanged more than a look and a word: there must have been letters, although no original and authentic correspondence between them has yet to surface. George's wartime correspondence first published by LaSalle in 1913 has proven highly problematic for critical scholars. Some historians have argued that LaSalle purposefully constructed the published letters long after her husband's death. Others have wondered if LaSalle did not merely heavily "edit" original letters. Indeed, a comparison of the published correspondence to her many short stories and books shows her to be at least the co-author of George's letters.[17]

But like LaSalle's fabled story of meeting her "Good Prince" at Old Point Comfort, these "fraudulent" letters lend authentic insight into the Picketts' relationship. The missives depict a man so distracted by his lover that he wrote her even in battle. LaSalle was his salvation in a cruel, painful world. In one letter, dated just after the battle of Fredericksburg in December 1862, George recounted the horrors of battle and the admiration his men had for the brave, but futile Union charges on Mayre's Heights. "Oh, my darling," he mused, "war and its results did not seem so awful till the love for you came. Now—now I want to love and bless and help everything, and there are no foes—no enemies—just love and longing for you."[18]

Other sources affirm that George Pickett was losing his appetite for fighting. There are several accounts of George ducking bullets or seeking shelter during attacks.[19] One officer later blamed LaSalle for George's loss of focus and cowardly behavior on the battlefield. Eppa Hunton, a former colonel in Pickett's brigade, claimed that Pickett was "a gallant man," but his courtship and marriage changed him. "Up to the time he was married," Hunton maintained, "I had the utmost confidence in his gallantry, but I believe that no man who married during the war was as good a soldier after, as before marriage." Hunton believed that marriage during war "seemed to demoralize" men.[20]

Before the Civil War, the regular army had served as a surrogate family for George. It seemed to give him direction and identity, and reaffirm his masculinity, especially during times of trouble and pain. LaSalle replaced the army, reassuring George that he was an honorable man and courageous soldier, even when others said he was not. And she, a woman, limited in the roles she could play in a man's war and world, found purpose in George's desperate eyes. Is it no wonder that she later insisted on the veracity of the cheerful portraits she painted of her marriage and husband? No doubt these were the same fairy tales that she doggedly but reassuringly told her troubled Soldier.

Pickett saw little action during the first several months of his tenure as major general. His division was in reserve during the Confederate victory at Fredericksburg on December 13, 1862. And in early May 1863, when Robert E. Lee and Stonewall Jackson masterminded their brilliant win at Chancellorsville, Pickett was miles away, engaged in the siege of Suffolk.

Pickett's first real opportunity to lead his division in battle came during Lee's campaign into Pennsylvania in the summer of 1863. During the first two days of the battle of Gettysburg, Pickett and his men worried that they would miss an important and perhaps the final engagement of the war. When Pickett learned that his division, along with portions of other commands, would make a frontal attack on the Union center on the afternoon of July 3, he was thrilled. Fellow Confederate E. P. Alexander remembered Pickett "sanguine of success" just before the charge commenced.[21] But Pickett's mood quickly changed as he witnessed his division shattered in the futile charge. Several officers recall observing the general staring into space and crying uncontrollably. When Lee ordered him to round up survivors and prepare for a counterattack, Pickett sobbed, "General Lee, I have no division now."[22] Repeatedly, he returned to that day in July and aired his angry disappointment. He was convinced that others prevented him and his men from a definitive victory. Left without infantry or artillery support, his men, Pickett believed, were led to the slaughter. Three weeks after the battle he wrote LaSalle: "If the charge made by my gallant Virginians on the fatal third day of July had been supported, or even if my other two Brigades had been with me [,] we would have been in Washington and the war ended."[23] When it came for Pickett to write his official report of Gettysburg, he repeated what he told LaSalle and lashed out at superiors and subordinates. He was convinced that if his men had been supported, the charge would have succeeded and the war would be over. Lee demanded that Pickett destroy the document and replace it with one that reported casualties only. Pickett refused and never filed an official report of the battle.[24]

LaSalle told a very different story of George Pickett at Gettysburg and she almost always mentioned the famed charge in her writings and public lectures. In 1913 she wrote: "Time has not lessened the fame of Pickett's charge at Gettysburg, and it never will; for the changes that have taken place in the science of war leave no possibility that future history will produce its counterpart." Gettysburg, she wrote was "the greatest battle of the western continent" and Pickett's Charge was "one of those deeds of arms that are immortal."[25] She declared: "With its imperishable glory—overshadowing all other events in martial history, notwithstanding its appalling disaster—is linked forever the name of my soldier."[26] LaSalle Pickett did not hide the fact that the general was devastated by the charge. She merely used this to enhance her portrait of him as the tragic and fallen leader. In her book *The Bugles of Gettysburg*, she described George's face changing as he witnessed the last few terrible moments of the charge: "The battle ardor had died out and left it pale with the sorrow of great loss,—perhaps the greatest loss that had ever come to man since the first battle for supremacy was fought in a wildly ambitious world. For over each dead form that lay on that blood-crimsoned field his heart mourned as a father-heart mourns over the grave of a son." The sight of so much senseless death and suffering, LaSalle claimed, stunned General Pickett: "The tiger-eyes that had flamed with the fire of the coming conflict were softened in a gray tender light sadder than tears." But an even greater alteration had occurred deep within the man. In that "short time" her husband "traveled the road to immortality."[27] Confederate and Union soldiers witnessed the change. She pictured Confederates awed by Pickett's "motionless, erect figure under the falling shot and bursting shells." When Federal soldiers took aim at the general, LaSalle claimed that they suddenly changed their minds:"We can't kill a man as brave as that."[28]

After Gettysburg, LaSalle alleged that George was even more eager that they marry. "The future is uncertain," she recounted him saying, "and it is impossible for me to call a moment my own. Again, with all the graves I have left behind me, and with all the wretchedness and misery this fated campaign has made, we would not wish anything but a very silent, very quiet wedding, planning only the sacrament and blessing of the church, and after that, back to my division and to the blessing of those few of them, who by God's miracle, were left."[29] Though not quite the dutiful, humble soldier LaSalle idealized, George Pickett was a man increasingly sobered and sickened by war. Marriage to the vivacious, outgoing Sallie Corbell was perhaps his only salvation.

"Cupid does not readily give way to Mars," LaSalle explained in her autobiography, "and in our Southern country a lull between bugle calls was likely to be filled with the music of wedding bells."[30] A lull finally came in mid-September 1863 and George and LaSalle quickly arranged to be married.

LaSalle's account of their wartime wedding reads like a romantic novel. When her warrior-groom requested a furlough it was denied, but he managed to obtain assignment for "special duty" and slip away from the front. Word leaked to Union troops stationed close to the Corbell home in Suffolk, so the couple chose to meet in Petersburg. Sallie, the "smuggled bride," traveled with family members by mule, ferry, and train to reach her lover. They were reunited at St. Paul's Episcopal Church in Petersburg only to discover another problem. Since neither George nor Sallie were Petersburg residents, they would have to have a special court decree to obtain a marriage license. Somehow, the decree was obtained and the ceremony held on September 15, 1863. A good deal of celebrating followed. Guns, cheers, chimes, and bugles hailed the happy couple as they boarded a train for Richmond. In the Confederate capital, there was music and dancing. Guests included Jefferson and Varina Davis, and Robert E. Lee's wife, Mary. Sallie remembered feeling like a child "who had been given a bunch of grapes, a stick of candy. Oh, I was happy."[31]

Very little of LaSalle's description can be corroborated. About a week after their marriage a Richmond newspaper briefly listed the event under marriage announcements: "In Petersburg, at St. Paul's Church on Tuesday 15th inst. by the Rev. Mr. Platt, Maj. Gen. George E. Pickett to Miss Sallie Corbell, daughter of J. David Corbell, Esq. of Nansemond Co., VA." There was no mention of crowds or gun salutes or a large wedding reception.[32]

LaSalle did feel obliged to defend the absence of a proper courtship and a traditional ceremony. "Had we been living under the old regime," she explained to readers, "nothing would have been easier than to prepare for a grand wedding in the stately old Southern style."[33]

It is significant that LaSalle insisted that she was a "child-bride" on her wedding day when she was actually twenty years old. In fact, she repeatedly depicted herself as a child throughout her writings. Telling readers she was only six when she first met George, LaSalle maintained: "Almost from babyhood I knew him and loved him." When she married him, she claimed to be fifteen years old, instead of her actual age of twenty. By assuming the identity of a young girl, it seems that LaSalle wanted to deemphasize her own independence and autonomy as a successful writer and single mother. By stressing her own delicacy and innocence, she fit herself into traditional conceptions of southern womanhood, and she simultaneously bolstered her husband's troubled image. Her childishness and naiveté served to heighten his maturity and strength.[34]

LaSalle's published recollections of their first months of marriage depict a young wife trying to live, as much as the war would allow, a normal traditional domestic life. She was not like Jessie Frémont, Libbie Custer, or Elizabeth Lee, who actively and publicly promoted their husband's military careers. Instead, she claimed that she exerted her influence more privately and subtly. She yearned to recreate a stable and peaceful household in the middle of a horrific war, assuming the role of moral superior, working to check her husband's bad habits and monitor his drinking and swearing. In her autobiography she recounted a member of George's staff remarking, "Before the General was married he would not allow any of us to swear at all. He said he would do the swearing for the whole division. Now that he is married we have not only to do our own swearing but his, too." LaSalle tried to be the ideal Victorian wife. It would not be until after the war and many years after her husband's death, that she would become a tireless defender of her husband's military record.[35]

Although, she was close to George's headquarters, LaSalle recalled having a good deal of time to herself. She befriended other officers' wives, read novels and newspapers, took long walks, rode horses, and danced. She also brought food and clothing to nearby hospitals and prisons. It seems likely that these accounts are true; women on both sides of the war faced similar trials and sought ways to feel useful and stay busy.[36]

George Pickett had plenty to keep him occupied. His appointment to the Department of North Carolina in September 1863 removed him from field command, but made him responsible for one of the most volatile places in the Confederacy: eastern North Carolina. By late 1863 Unionists and Confederates had severely splintered the Tar Heel State into warring factions. Disaffection plagued its troops, and residents grew increasingly resentful of impressment, conscription, economic hardship, and military defeats. Bands of destitute deserters roamed North Carolina communities, plundering homes and wreaking havoc, often upon their own neighbors. These were trying circumstances for anyone in command. For an embittered and distracted man like George Pickett, they were doubly straining.[37]

In addition to trying to keep the peace among North Carolinians, George had military operations to oversee. In early February 1864 he received orders from Lee to retake New Bern, North Carolina, from Union control. He tried, but failed, blaming subordinates and overly ambitious orders for the defeat. Soon after the botched attack on New Bern, Pickett learned that his men had captured a number of North Carolinians identified as former Confederate soldiers. A court-martial was ordered, and in three separate hangings, twenty-two men were executed in Kinston, North Carolina. Most of the men were from the area and family and friends witnessed the hangings in horror and shock. Union officials were outraged and demanded an explanation. Pickett responded with haughty language and threats to hang ten men for every one Confederate prisoner executed by the Federals in retaliation. A Confederate soldier later recalled hearing Pickett personally threaten two of the prisoners: "God damn you, I reckon you will hardly ever go back there again, you damned rascals; I'll have you shot, and all other damned rascals who desert."[38]

Three months after Kinston, Pickett faced an aggressive Federal offensive on the James River at Bermuda Hundred. Reduced to district command of Petersburg, Pickett managed to keep the Federals at bay with few men, limited resources, and a hasty and scattered defense and he held out until reinforced. The crisis at Bermuda Hundred brought months of bitterness, frustration, and exhaustion to a head. Lacking sleep, eating little, and sick with worry, George collapsed—mentally and physically exhausted. On May 10, 1864, he crawled into bed and remained for a solid week. When he finally regained his strength, he returned to field command in the Army of Northern Virginia.[39]

LaSalle Pickett glossed over these difficult months and never publicly acknowledged the North Carolina hangings. Like so many other details of her husband's life, the Kinston episode was just too troubling to acknowledge openly. It is unclear how much she knew about the entire incident, but she must have witnessed his anger, frustration, and resentment. She may have comforted him and assured him that he had done the right thing, even when others said he acted hastily and inappropriately.

Instead, LaSalle focused on her husband's performance in the Bermuda Hundred Campaign, where, she attested, he saved the city of Petersburg. Her Soldier was constantly cool and courageous, even prophetic.[40] "Though my Soldier had been ordered a few days before to report to the Army of Northern Virginia," she wrote, "he could not leave Petersburg to destruction. In defiance of orders he remained in the beleaguered city."[41] He refused sleep, she maintained, so concerned was he with protecting "a whole city full of helpless, defenseless women and children at the mercy of an oncoming army."[42] LaSalle recalled joining other "heroic, unselfish wives and daughters of the Confederacy" who carried dispatches, conveyed food to hungry soldiers, and cheered on imaginary troops at the railroad station.[43] She barely saw her husband at all, except "when I carried to him on the lines a dispatch or his bread and soup and coffee."[44]

LaSalle maintained again that George's thoughts remained solely on her. He allegedly beseeched her, in the middle of the enemy attack, to explain why she had quipped, "Never mind" to him at their last meeting. "It troubled me all night," he claimed. "I wanted to follow after you and ask you what you meant, but couldn't. I would have jumped on Lucy [his horse] and ridden in to Petersburg and found out if it had been *possible* for me to leave. I was so troubled about it that I was almost tempted to come in anyhow." He wondered if he had hurt her feelings by telling her she need not come to the front anymore, that he had enough men to do soldiers' work: "Were you aggrieved because your blundering old Soldier told you there was no necessity for your coming out to bring dispatches any longer, that, thank heaven, the recruits and reinforcements were coming in now and that we could manage all right?"[45]

George was not managing well. In mid May, a weak but somewhat recovered George Pickett traveled north to resume command of his reconstructed division. He arrived in the midst of Ulysses S. Grant's determined campaign to outflank and annihilate Lee's Army of Northern Virginia. Pickett and his men missed the most intensive combat of the 1864 Virginia campaign. Portions of his division shifted frequently to lend support north of Richmond and outside Petersburg, but his troops essentially served as a "mobile reserve" under the direct command of Lee. When siege operations began, Pickett's division settled into place on the Howlett Line northeast of Petersburg.[46]

LaSalle too settled in with her husband near his Petersburg headquarters. She recalled living in a tent and then a rustic log cabin and befriending other officers' wives. LaSalle wrote: "There was no lack of social diversions. In a small way, we had our dances, our conversaziones and musicales, quite like the gay world that had never known anything about war except from the pages of books and the columns of newspapers. True we did not feast." She emphasized yet again how she looked for the "rifts of sunshine to break the gloom."[47]

During the summer of 1864, LaSalle gave birth to their first child, George, Jr., her "new little soldier." Dubbed the "little general," the new baby was allegedly a favorite among the troops. Once during a visit to camp, LaSalle claimed that several soldiers clamored for the chance to hold the baby. "I am ashamed to confess it," she wrote, "but notwithstanding the gentleness of the soldiers, baby's quiet, peaceful mien, and the

General's continued assurance that he was all right, I, his very new and solicitous mother, suffered agonies of torture and anxiety until he was back again in my arms; and oh, dear, what a greasy, dirty, grimy little bundle it was when I did get it back."[48]

Motherhood apparently did not lessen LaSalle's devotion to her husband. She alleged that she came frequently to the front to see him, alone or with her baby. She described an incident when she accompanied George as he inspected the lines and shells began to explode dangerously close. The general pleaded with her to leave.

" 'No indeed,' I said. 'I'm not a bit afraid, and if I were do you think I would let Pickett's men see me run?'

'Come, dear, please! You are in danger, useless danger, and that is not bravery.' "

She told readers that she stayed at the front, snatching a pair of field glasses to gaze across the lines, even catching a glimpse of General Grant and his wife.[49]

Some of the wartime stories LaSalle recounted revealed the lasting horror of war. She told of once witnessing the decapitation of a young officer, just after he warned her of the danger of her visiting the front. She watched him "riding in that graceful way which the Southerner has by inheritance from a long line of ancestors who have been accustomed to ride over wide reaches of land."[50] Regretting her "obstinate resistance to his appeal" that she take shelter, LaSalle was mortified to see his death. "Impulsively I sprang from my horse," she wrote, "and ran and picked up the poor head, and I solemnly believe that the dying eyes looked their thanks as the last glimmering of life flickered out."[51]

This is indeed a disturbing tale, but perhaps it can be seen as a metaphor for Sallie Pickett's war experience as a military wife. It underscores the vast destruction, death, and personal suffering she saw firsthand but had no power to control. In many ways, this war must have truncated her dreams and hopes for the future. Her husband, almost two decades older than she, was a failed, short-tempered, complaining general. His health was poor and he drank sometimes excessively. Sallie was utterly devoted to her Soldier, or at least the ideal of him. Although there is no evidence to indicate that she directly influenced her husband's military career, LaSalle became his comfort and support when things went terribly wrong After the war, she and other ex-Confederates would do their best to celebrate their idealized albeit racist antebellum past in the myth of the Lost Cause, and in the process of doing so, rewrite history. Occasionally the raw pain of civil war came back to LaSalle Pickett in full force, and no amount of romanticizing could excise the ghosts. "Years away from that time of anguish and terror," she wrote, "I awaken suddenly with the crash of those guns still in my ears, their fearful sounds yet echoing in my heart, only to find myself safe in my soft, warm bed."[52]

General Pickett's demons continued to haunt him during war's final months. His health was bad and the conditions of his division poor enough to warrant a reprimand from Lee. Lee complained to Longstreet that Pickett's division lacked discipline and proper military instruction. "Unless the division and brigade commanders are careful and energetic," Lee warned Longstreet, "nothing can be accomplished."[53] Pickett's men were also deserting in disturbingly high numbers, hemorrhaging some 10 percent of his force during only one week in March 1865. The taint of unreliability lingered, and although Pickett was the army's most senior major general, he lacked any sort of independent command following his mixed performance at Bermuda Hundred in May 1864.[54]

George Pickett's final ignominy came on April 1,1865. Entrusted with a special task force of cavalry, infantry, and artillery, Pickett had set out on March 30 to stop the threat of a strong Union attack on Lee's right flank. The Battle of Dinwiddie Courthouse on March 31, 1865, was a Confederate victory with Pickett successfully pushing back the Federal advance. But the next day, Pickett disappeared from the front, and as he leisurely ate shad and drank whiskey, the enemy struck again. By the end of the day, Federals had broken through the Confederacy's right flank and Lee was in desperate retreat. Just eight days later, on April 9, 1865, Lee surrendered to Grant at Appomattox Courthouse. Spotting Pickett at the surrender, Lee reportedly exclaimed: "Is that man still with this army?"[55]

While her husband faltered and failed through those final days of war, LaSalle recalled waiting anxiously in Richmond for news. On April 2, 1865, the Confederate government abandoned their capital, and the next day, Union troops entered Richmond. LaSalle described being alone with her baby; her slaves had long gone, and rumors circulated that her Soldier was dead. Fires set by Confederates spread, and frenzied crowds looted stores and warehouses. Broken furniture, shattered glass, and other wreckage filled the muddy streets. LaSalle likened the experience to a "reign of terror": "The yelling and howling and swearing and weeping and wailing beggar description. Families houseless and homeless under the open sky!"[56] The surreal, hellish picture was made complete by the presence of black Union soldiers. LaSalle remembered, "They were the first colored troops I had ever seen, and the weird effect produced by their black faces in that infernal environment was indelibly impressed upon my mind."[57]

LaSalle's description of the Confederacy's last days includes one of her favorite and best-known stories. The day after the city fell, she maintained, she had an unexpected visitor. "With my baby on my arm," she wrote, "I opened the door and looked up at a tall, gaunt sad-faced man in ill-fitting clothes." It was President Abraham Lincoln who, LaSalle repeatedly told her readers, was an old friend of her husband's and had taken time to check on Pickett's young family. Kissing George, Jr., Lincoln declared, "Tell your father, the rascal, that I forgive him for the sake of your bright eyes." She asserted that Lincoln was instrumental in obtaining George his appointment to West Point and that George would never allow anyone to speak badly of the Yankee president.

LaSalle's Lincoln-Pickett stories have little factual basis. George's Uncle Andrew Johnston did apparently know Lincoln, and Pickett may have met the Illinois lawyer during his brief stay in Quincy. John Stuart, Lincoln's law partner, was the congressman responsible for George's appointment to West Point. But there is no evidence that there was any sort of friendship between the two, and certainly nothing to support her story that Lincoln saw her during his visit to Richmond.

It is more likely that these stories originated from LaSalle's efforts to appeal to a broad national audience at a time when reconciliation ran high and Lincoln stood as the great hero of the war. LaSalle published most of her writings in the 1890s and early decades of the twentieth century. Making the martyred president her husband's close friend seemed to be her deliberate attempt to reflect the renewed nationalism of the 1890s and also to attract northern audiences. And it was yet another way for her to lessen publicly the magnitude of her spouse's failings.[58]

The war's end brought a broken and bitter George home to his wife and infant son. Sallie joyfully remembered their reunion and her relief that he had returned to her safely. Just hearing his voice, she wrote, swept away "all the privation and starvation and bloodstains of the past four years, all the woes and trials, griefs and fears, of the last dreadful days." Sallie excitedly slid down the banister to greet her Soldier with open arms. "I do not know how to describe the peace, the bliss of that moment—it is too deep and too sacred to translate into words."[59]

Their peace was only momentary. Financial struggle, exile, illness, and death marked George and LaSalle's postwar marriage. George's childhood home at Turkey Island just east of Richmond was in ashes, and after nearly twenty-five years in uniform, the forty-year-old ex-general had no occupation. They sought temporary shelter with LaSalle's parents in Nansemond County in southeastern Virginia. They were horrified to learn that the Federal government was investigating George for war crimes. Facing indictment for his actions at Kinston, he fled to Montreal, Canada. LaSalle and the baby soon followed.[60]

The Picketts rented a modest room in a boardinghouse, ate cold leftovers, and borrowed money from family and other exiled Confederates. Too ill to work, George stayed in bed, weak and depressed. LaSalle secretly sold her jewelry and took a job teaching Latin to support the family. She became her family's main provider to her husband and young son. Twenty-two-year-old Sallie embraced these roles with vigor, later remembering those several months in Canada rather ironically as the happiest times of her life. LaSalle very much valued having her Soldier all to herself and living anonymously in a foreign land. They were far removed from the harsh reality of defeat in the postwar South. And his dependency on her made her feel needed and important. Like that moment on the beach at Point Comfort, she would be his wife and his little girl. She would become his all.[61]

But George needed others besides his loving wife to help him in this crisis. In desperation, he turned for help to his West Point classmate and Mexican War comrade, Ulysses S. Grant. On March 12, 1866, he wrote a pleading letter to Grant begging him to intercede and procure a "guarantee that I may be permitted to live unmolested in my native State, where I am now trying to make a subsistence for my family, (much impoverished by the War), by tilling the land." Pickett described "certain evil disposed persons [who] are attempting to reopen the troubles of the past, and embroil me for the actions taken whilst the Commanding Officer of the Confederate Forces in N. C." He insisted that he had merely followed the rules of war by executing these deserters. George pledged his honor "as an officer and a gentleman" and asked for "some assurance, that I will not be disturbed in my endeavor to keep my family from Starvation, and that my parole, which was given in good faith, may protect me from the assaults of those persons desirous of still keeping the War which has ended in my humble opinion *forever*." Grant sent an endorsement to President Johnson on the day he received Pickett's letter. Admitting that Pickett had used poor judgment in ordering the North Carolina hangings, Grant asked the president to overlook the incident as a personal favor. He immediately issued Pickett a parole exempting him from arrest unless ordered by the president or secretary of war.[62]

Grant's timely intervention apparently stopped the United States government from formally pressing charges against George Pickett. After two separate military boards of inquiry, the investigations ended with no indictment issued; nor did George ever succeed in obtaining a personal pardon. He eventually obtained a full pardon under President Andrew Johnson's general amnesty in December 1868.[63]

The Picketts had already returned to Virginia in December 1865, and with Grant's help in stopping the Kinston investigation, they were soon able to start life anew. They built a small cottage near the ruins of the Pickett family plantation house at Turkey Island. In 1866, Sallie gave birth to their second son, Corbell.

George failed at every occupation he attempted. He struggled with farming, and tried selling real estate and insurance. He turned down state and federal government positions and an offer from the Egyptian army. His health remained feeble and his spirits low.[64]

LaSalle worked daily, doing household chores and caring for the two boys, and perhaps helping George with the farming. The labor was so demanding that LaSalle could at one point "scarcely hold a pen, her fingers being very sore from hard work." Her concerned husband confided to his brother-in-law that he felt "miserable" for not providing her with "the comforts which I expected for my darling wife when I married." He felt that he had failed as a husband and chief provider. "I must say," he wrote of his wife, "that she bore up bravely under her trials."[65]

George began to dread the future "a thousand times more than I did any battle I have ever been in." The "physical discomforts and personal dangers" of war paled "when a woman is in danger and duress," particularly "one [who] is so dear." It made George Pickett feel helpless and declare, "I *am* a child."[66] A sympathetic family member expressed his concern over the Picketts' "domestic troubles," maintaining that these were particularly difficult for the man of the family to bear. "The[se] infernal hard time[s] are bad enough to make a man mad," the cousin stated, "without having family afflictions to to[r]ment his feelings."[67]

Financial problems and illness persisted through the Reconstruction years. In the spring of 1874 Corbell became severely sick with measles and died. LaSalle's published version of her youngest son's death is again less important for its veracity than the meaning it conveys. Corbell was only eight years old, but according to LaSalle, he had a Christlike quality, withstanding his suffering without complaint. While Corbell lay dying on Good Friday, he asked his parents to help a stranger whom he had heard scuffling with police outside his window. Corbell picked out his pallbearers and cheerfully asked that they wear white and bring flowers to cast on his grave. As Easter Sunday dawned, LaSalle dramatically described her son's final moments: "Through the open window the voices were sounding 'Christ is risen' as he turned his head and laid his face against mine and reached out his little hand to my Soldier and [his nurse] Mary. I felt his spirit flutter and go." Her perfect marriage could only produce perfect angelic children.[68]

In July 1875, the Picketts had planned a vacation at White Sulphur Springs, but unexpectedly George had to go to Norfolk on business. LaSalle recalled: "Very much against his advice, I insisted on accompanying him." In Norfolk George suddenly fell seriously ill with "gastric fever" and died two days later. LaSalle claimed that his last request was to be alone with her: "I do not want anybody but my wife." He was fifty years old.[69]

When her husband died, thirty-two-year old LaSalle and her eleven-year-old son George, Jr., had little financial support. "The future is a dark one to me," she confessed privately, "I dare not look into it, for I see only loneliness and desolation if I do." LaSalle lamented, "The light of my life is gone out."[70] When she later published her autobiography in 1917, she ended her life story with her husband's death. As he sighed his last breath, LaSalle recalled dramatically: "Darkness came."[71]

In reality, LaSalle Pickett's life did not end in 1875. She lived for five more decades, facing her uncertain future with her stubborn determination. She broke a time-honored antebellum taboo by setting out to support herself and her son financially without a man. LaSalle left her native Virginia, traveled to Washington, D.C., and found a job as a government clerk in the Federal Pensions Office.[72]

LaSalle left little public or private record of her first twenty years of widowhood. Her primary responsibility after George's death was raising their son. She apparently taught George, Jr., at home for a time, and when he reached college age, she enrolled him in the Virginia Military Institute. It is not known how she afforded to send her son to this prestigious southern academy, but somehow it was determined that young George would follow his father and become a professional army officer. She also maintained correspondence with her husband's first son, James, whom she addressed as "son" even to the point of being willing to support him financially. James Tilton Pickett had grown up to be a talented young artist but died tragically in 1889 at the age of thirty-one from tuberculosis. As he lay dying in a Portland boardinghouse, James asked that a friend read letters from his famous father and the stepmother he had never met.[73]

Sometime in the late 1880s, Sallie Pickett decided to write about the past. Effusive eulogies at her husband's funeral in 1875 may have inspired her as much as a need for money. It seems that she also sought a way to transform a painful and difficult past into something inspiring and admirable. Either way, by the late 1880s, Mrs. Pickett was a common sight at veteran reunions and monument dedications. She was the toast of the twenty-fourth reunion at Gettysburg, signing autographs and handing out flowers. On the field of battle, Pickett's men formed into a line to meet their commander's widow and shake her hand. The *New York Times* reported, "She had a word for all and all had a word for her."[74] She thrilled veterans and journalists with her charm and vivaciousness.

In 1899, Sallie published her first book, *Pickett and His Men*. She plagiarized large portions from a division history written by a staff officer and introduced readers to her idealized Soldier. Gone was the bitter, bad-tempered, and sickly man. Instead, readers found a duty-bound soldier full of compassion, honor, and good humor. "The general possessed the greatest capacity for happiness," she wrote, "and such dauntless courage and self-control that to all appearance, he could as cheerfully and buoyantly steer his way over the angry, menacing, tumultuous surges of life as over the waves that glide in tranquil smoothness and sparkle in the sunlight of a calm and clear sky."[75] Her Soldier was affectionate and amiable, a man of "classic taste and perfect harmony and simple, pure heart" who loved nature, singing and most of all his wife, Sallie.[76] He fought because duty bade him to, but preferred peace over war making and never felt anger or bitterness toward his enemy, only love and respect. LaSalle dedicated the book to her husband and his men, but confessed: "I would gladly inscribe this book—to him alone, to whom my life has been dedicated."[77]

Pickett continued her public career for the next twenty years producing half a dozen books, numerous short stories, poems, and an autobiography. She toured nationally on the Chautauqua lecture circuit, attracting enthusiastic crowds in both North and South. Her books and public lectures followed many of the basic tenets of the Lost Cause mythology of the 1890s and early twentieth century. She participated in veteran reunions, monument dedications, parades, and other postwar rituals. Pickett upheld a romanticized portrait of the Old South, and the Confederacy, but she also supported a unified nation. The 1890s ushered in a new period of national reconciliation and Pickett shaped certain aspects of her stories, most notably the erroneous claim that Abraham Lincoln was her husband's close friend, to appeal to northern readers. And while she celebrated the myth of the traditional Plantation South and a legendary southern soldier, she also embraced the new American woman of the early twentieth century. She lived as a single working mother and many of her writings, including *Across My Path* and *Literary Hearthstones of Dixie,* described famous women Pickett admired and sought to emulate in her own life.[78]

The marriage Pickett described in her writings was always idyllic. She was the innocent "Child-bride," he was the brave but doting Soldier-husband. In 1913, she published *The Heart of a Soldier: As Revealed in the Intimate Letters of General George E. Pickett, C.S.A.* So intent was LaSalle in promoting her mythical husband and their mythical marriage that she apparently fabricated personal correspondence between her and her husband. The collection was reprinted in 1928 and is still in print and widely cited. A recent historian has remarked: "If he [George Pickett] didn't write such eloquent letters, he should have."[79]

LaSalle Corbell Pickett never remarried. She died in 1931 at the age of eighty-seven, lauded as "Mother Pickett" and the protector of her husband's memory. When LaSalle died, her grandson George E. Pickett, III, tried to bury his grandmother next to her beloved Soldier in Richmond's Hollywood cemetery. But the Ladies Hollywood Memorial Association, fearing to set a precedent for other soldiers' wives, refused to allow LaSalle's remains to be placed alongside those of George in the venerated Soldiers' section of the cemetery. Relatives raised a ruckus and threatened to dig up George and re-bury the two together in Arlington National Cemetery in Washington, D.C. In the end, George's grave was not disturbed, and LaSalle's ashes were placed at a mausoleum near Arlington Cemetery.[80]

As the years passed, the mausoleum became dilapidated and plans were made for its permanent closure. In 1998, over 120 years after George Pickett's death, the Virginia Division of the United Daughters of the Confederacy removed LaSalle's cremated remains from the neglected vault and had them reinterred next to George's grave in Hollywood Cemetery. The UDC Virginia Division president stated: "The motto of the Virginia Division is 'Love Makes Memory Eternal.' For us to bring Mrs. Pickett back is a very inspiring thing."[81]

Civil war brought George Pickett and LaSalle Corbell together as lovers, as husband and wife, and as soul mates. The heroic, admirable, soldier-husband, submissive child-wife, and happy romantic marriage were mainly LaSalle's postwar literary creation. The Picketts did share deep affection and lasting attachment to each other. They must have had moments of true happiness. But given George Pickett's spotted military career, his near arrest for war crimes, and the harsh realities of war and defeat, daily disappointments, stress, and even fear plagued their life. As the wife of a general, LaSalle endured frequent separations and constant anxiety about her husband's safety. There is no evidence to suggest that LaSalle acted as her husband's military adviser; instead, her role was more traditional and intimate. She shared in his many military disappointments and became his anchor and his comfort. After the war, exile, poverty, illness, and the loss of their youngest son cast a dark shadow over their marriage. George felt helpless that he could not provide financially for his wife and young sons. Having lost two wives in death, nearly indicted for war crimes, and left with no profession, he had grown, it seems, wholly dependent on his much younger third wife LaSalle for her emotional strength and her financial help. In the end, he gave LaSalle the only thing he could: his passionate love and undying devotion. After George's death, LaSalle eventually repaid his fidelity by rewriting the historical record and refighting his foes. She dedicated her life to making him the Confederate hero he never was.

FIVE

"All Say They Are under Petticoat Government"

Lizinka Campbell Brown and Richard S. Ewell

PETER S. CARMICHAEL

In nineteenth-century America, the community defined and enforced gender and family conventions. All men agreed that marriage should subordinate women to male authority. When roles were reversed and a husband found himself under a "strong-minded" wife, a couple's personal life often became a community issue, a topic of intense scrutiny. Elizabeth Campbell Brown and Confederate General Richard S. Ewell's unique relationship endured such a trial. The fundamental assumptions of patriarchy did not define their wartime marriage, largely because she had succeeded outside her appointed "sphere" as a single woman, ranking as one of Tennessee's wealthiest planters. Her fierce independence, tacitly accepted by her husband, brought them under the public microscope almost as soon as they were married in 1863. Lee's soldiers deeply resented her attempts to manage Ewell's military affairs, and many officers unfairly blamed her for Ewell's poor generalship and repeated battlefield failures. Some even charged that officers who married during the war suddenly lost their courage in battle and their efficiency in camp. The perception that Richard was henpecked made him a popular topic of army gossip. The idle chatter tended to alienate the couple from acceptable social circles. It is also possible that it upset the chemistry of their relationship. During the first two years of marriage, Ewell deferred to his wife and often followed her advice. In the postwar years, however, he rarely followed her lead. Over the bitter protests of his wife, he took frequent business trips, leaving her alone and isolated on their Tennessee farm. By restricting her to the role of the plantation mistress, Richard had reduced her public voice while demonstrating to the community that he was committed to male honor. Public shame drove him to reestablish male hegemony.

Elizabeth Campbell Brown Ewell fiercely resisted her husband's attempts to reassert male domination after the war. Prior to her nuptials with Ewell, contemporaries noted her unrelenting determination to control her own affairs. As a wealthy widow and one of Tennessee's most prominent antebellum planters, she had the unique ability to pursue an independent course. Her money came from the estate of her father, George Washington Campbell. When he served as James Monroe's ambassador to Russia, his daughter was born in St. Petersburg in 1820. Her close friends called her Lizinka, a Russian nickname for Elizabeth.[1] Marriage to James Percy Brown in 1839 consolidated the wealth of two slaveholding families at the price of Lizinka's happiness. Percy Brown admitted on his wedding day that he did not love his bride. To drive home this point, he proceeded to have numerous affairs. He felt no shame or remorse, torturing Lizinka with the intimate details like some dungeon master joyously turning a rack, deriving pleasure from his victim's pain. Her pleas never ended the abuse; with every demand for restraint he seemed even more determined to wreck their marriage. When Brown returned from a trip to Mississippi, he asked Lizinka what she would say if he had impregnated a mutual friend. Lizinka responded by packing her bags, fleeing her brutish husband, only to reunite shortly before Brown took his own life in 1844.[2] Although the circumstances surrounding his death are sketchy, a history of suicide ran in the family. Brown's grandfather had killed himself, and a son he fathered with Lizinka (Campbell Brown) also committed suicide after the Civil War.

In death, Percy Brown inflicted one last cruelty on Lizinka. His will provided that his sons receive the family fortune with the condition that they change their last names to Percy.[3] Why Brown insisted on such a stipulation is a mystery when his grandfather Percy had left a reputation of bigamy and suicide. With one last arrow in his quiver, Brown aimed at Lizinka and wrote her out of the will. She refused to accept the document, headed straight to the courtroom, and demanded her dowry rights provided by the law. Two years later, in 1846, she asked the court to grant her and her children an allowance from the estate. Shortly afterward she finally won her case; the will was nullified, and Lizinka added to her already massive fortune in land and slaves. A friend believed that Lizinka's property was worth more than five hundred thousand dollars in 1854.[4]

As a wealthy widow, Lizinka's popularity among Tennessee's most eligible bachelors soared. Her striking looks only enhanced her status. She possessed soft features, delicately thin lips, and dark hair that curled around her ears. Her eyes were sad-looking, almost melancholy. She did not consider remarriage an attractive option after the monstrous Percy Brown. She poured her emotions and energy into her children and business obligations. Making the transition to head of household proved difficult at times, but she sought the counsel of friends and family. In no time she mastered her varied duties. With this newfound power, she boldly asserted herself, injecting opinions often when they were not welcomed. One relative complained that she has a "tendency to interfere where she is not wanted." A friend pointed out that Lizinka "criticizes others with biting, disparaging remarks" and "looks upon everyone with skepticism."[5]

Lizinka tried to control every aspect of her professional and personal life. Over the protests of some male relatives, she followed her son Campbell Brown to the University of Virginia and Georgetown University. Motherhood and a deep sense of family shaped Lizinka's identity, giving her life meaning and purpose as it did with most women in the antebellum period.[6] Her experience outside the home, where she oversaw the vast operations of her plantations, provided Lizinka a unique opportunity to enter an exclusively man's world. In this arena she furthered her sense of independence, became more certain about the correctness of her views, and grew even more suspicious of men. In her business dealings she demanded exacting perfection from those around her and reprimanded relatives who tried to take advantage.[7] Any violation of her autonomy must have reminded her of Percy Brown's cruelty. Remarriage threatened Lizinka's independence, but in Richard Stoddert Ewell she found a man who could be controlled, at least initially. Ewell was a genuine eccentric, highly excitable, and at times neurotic. Legends persist that he had mental problems and that he sometimes hallucinated he was a bird. He would chirp softly in his tent for hours at a time, accepting only sunflower seed or grains of wheat at mealtime. His big, hawkish nose and impressive bald dome made him look like a feathered creature, complementing his already birdlike tendencies.[8]

Ewell's peculiar behavior did not keep Lizinka from befriending the general, who was also her first cousin. Born in Georgetown on February 8, 1817, he spent most of his childhood on the family's modest farm in Prince William County, Virginia. His father, Thomas Ewell, was an alcoholic who suffered bouts of depression. A man of excess, he destroyed his successful medical practice and squandered the family's financial reserves. He died when Richard was nine. They had never been close. In Richard's subsequent correspondence, he never mentioned his father, whose irresponsibility had placed his family in the most tenuous situation. He turned to his mother, Elizabeth, for guidance and inspiration. She was a proud woman, deeply religious, and determined to teach her children the importance of duty and responsibility. During the difficult financial times that followed her husband's death, she taught school while Richard and his brothers managed the farm. She constantly reminded her children that they came from a distinguished lineage, the finest blood of Virginia, and that their economic woes were temporary. Despite her best efforts, the family hovered just above the poverty line. Dinner often consisted of nothing more than cornbread.[9]

One of the more memorable incidents of Ewell's childhood occurred when Lizinka visited his family in Virginia. Richard immediately fell in love with her, but she did not reciprocate his affections. Ewell coincidentally declared his vow of bachelorhood the same year Lizinka married Percy Brown.[10] Without sufficient funds, Richard, like his siblings, sought educational opportunities that did not impose on the family's lack of finances. In July 1836 he accepted an appointment to the United States Military Academy at West Point. Although Ewell suffered few demerits or other difficulties, he looked upon a professional career in the army with dread. "I think I have nearly as much aversion to that life as yourself," he wrote his mother on the eve of graduation, "but you know that the education we get here does not qualify us for any other than a military life, and unless a man has money he is forced to enter the Army to keep from starving." In July 1840, Ewell graduated from West Point, ranked thirteenth out of forty-two cadets, carrying an officer's commission in the First Dragoons.[11]

As Ewell had predicted, he intensely disliked army life, especially on the western frontier where the tedium and loneliness severely tested one's resolve. The Mexican War temporarily interrupted the mind-numbing routine, providing a new venue for Ewell's wonderful sense of humor. When General Winfield Scott approached Ewell and his immediate superior Major Edwin V. Sumner, he complimented the officers for "the extraordinary vigilance of our scouts who, as he said, were peering at him from behind every bush as he approached the camp." Unaware that the drinking water had caused a diarrhea epidemic in the ranks, Scott mistook these men who were relieving themselves for scouts. Ewell believed the mistake made the general look ludicrous. "When we go to drill, the men have to leave the ranks by dozens," he added, "and as the Plain is bare as a table, make an expose of the whole affair. The effect is unique as they squat in rows about a hundred yards from the battalion, and when we deploy as skirmishers, we run right over them." Ewell faced more serious danger once active campaigning began. He saw heavy fighting at Tete de Pont where the fortification of Churubusco covered the narrow causeway leading to Mexico City. Ewell received a brevet for gallantry, but he considered the commendation lacking in distinction.[12]

Ewell maintained a regular correspondence with his cousin while serving in the United States Army during the 1840s and 1850s. Slow advancement and the harshness of military life continued to frustrate Ewell. When Lizinka learned of her cousin's disenchantment with the army, she contacted influential friends in Washington to secure promotion. She never bothered to inform Richard of her plans, a trend she continued during the Civil War. After the couple's 1863 marriage she consistently entered the public world of army politics as Ewell's advocate without the slightest regard for the inevitable backlash that awaited such a violation of male authority.

Lizinka's efforts prior to the war did not bring Ewell immediate rewards. Nonetheless, she still felt compelled "to do something for Dick." After considering his options, she reached the conclusion that the military did not suit Ewell's peculiar personality and suggested he become a farm manager on one of her plantations. Lizinka explained her assessment of Ewell to another relative: "The truth is I am excessively anxious about Richard, all the more for the sensitiveness which I fear unfits him for any position out of the army."[13] The offer tempted Richard, who solicited the advice of many friends. Their varied opinions only seemed to confuse him. His vacillation irritated those who waited for his decision, including Lizinka's cousin Thomas Gantt, who offered a prescient forecast of Dick Ewell as a Confederate general: "It is chiefly the agonies of indecision which rack him and make him act so foolishly. Yet he is a good soldier, I believe. It is clear that he could never rise above very subordinate place however. When executing orders given by a superior, no doubt he would do well. If it became necessary to decide between a certain sacrifice and a possible or probably great recompense, he would be paralysed [*sic*]."[14]

After much agonizing, Ewell in 1855 decided to stay in the army. He informed Lizinka via Thomas Gantt who reported that "he [Ewell] would not hesitate to accept your [Lizinka's] proposal if you were a man, but he fears to take advantage of a poor weak woman in the matter of a bargain."[15] His excuse was thinly veiled. Lizinka's prosperous situation and prominent position in Tennessee society made such an offer a trifling matter. He must have regarded Lizinka's proposal as a threat to his identity as a southern man. Depending on a woman's generosity violated the cardinal rule that a man must provide for and protect the household.[16] The title of farm manager posed an additional threat to community acceptance. Some might equate the job with the detested but accepted position of overseer.

In war, Richard and Lizinka were united. Her son, Campbell Brown, accepted a position on Ewell's staff a few months after the beginning of hostilities at Fort Sumter. While visiting Campbell in Virginia, Lizinka's relationship with Richard quickly moved beyond friendship, and they announced their engagement in December 1861. Why Lizinka had a sudden change of heart is difficult to say. She must have loved him, but her son never thought they would reach the altar.[17] Concern for Campbell Brown and a desire to protect him through Ewell might explain why she accepted the general's proposal. Engagement would ensure that Ewell served as a protector and advocate for her son. She frequently reminded her fiancé that injury or death to Campbell would be a devastating blow. Whatever her motives, the general seemed not to care. He eagerly looked to the future, telling Lizinka that her "expression 'in life or death we shall be united' " was "fraught with promise."[18] Lizinka's religious bearing and influence also renewed Ewell's commitment to serve God. More than ever, he desired to live according to the teachings of Jesus Christ.

Like other southern women, Lizinka assumed the role of the family's moral guardian. Her eagerness to serve as Ewell's moral caretaker did not signal a retreat. She did not defer to his judgment, nor did he try to interfere in her personal affairs. When the Federals advanced toward Nashville in the spring of 1862, Richard desperately wanted to assist her. Separation made him feel helpless, irrelevant, a shell of a man. If the Yankees threatened her property, he bluntly told her, "You can judge best what to do on the spot." Without the restraints of the army, he assured her that he would make a sacrifice "consistent with duty and honor."[19] At this early stage of the war, when gender relations still resembled prewar patterns, most plantation mistresses remained dependent on their absent men for advice. Lizinka, however, followed her own instincts. An invading Union army did not shake her self-reliance.[20] Ironically, Federal authorities did not confiscate her property until she married Ewell in 1863.

Like a good Confederate patriot, Lizinka served in the Ladies Hospital Association of Nashville in 1861 and the following year she held the superintendency of one of the city's hospitals. While Lizinka cared for the sick and injured in Nashville, her husband emerged as one of the Army of Northern Virginia's most promising officers. In the 1862 Shenandoah Valley Campaign, Stonewall Jackson compiled a series of impressive victories with Ewell as a primary subordinate. He excelled as a divisional commander, but Jackson's secretive ways exasperated him. When Stonewall battled the Federals at McDowell on May 8, 1862, he left Ewell with vague orders to remain at Swift Run Gap. "I tell you, sir, he is as crazy as a March hare," Ewell exploded to a subordinate. "He has gone away, I don't know where, and left me here with some instructions to stay until he returns, but Banks' whole army is advancing on me and I haven't the most remote idea where to communicate with General Jackson. I tell you, sir, he is crazy and I will just march my division away from here."[21] Ewell wisely stayed put, but he still could not understand why Stonewall considered the Shenandoah Valley the Confederacy's epicenter. Ewell believed that Jackson did not care whether the rest of the nation collapsed as long as the valley remained in southern hands.[22] Over time Richard came to appreciate and admire his eccentric superior. Both officers jelled on the battlefield, united by their penchant for the offense, their desire to hold the initiative, and their advocation of slashing attacks. Impressive victories in the valley brought wide acclaim, especially for Stonewall whom Southerners championed as the nation's savior. The favorable press also cast a few rays of the national spotlight on Ewell, whose stock dramatically rose in the Confederate War Department. All of the publicity must have pleased the ambitious Lizinka, who did not want her future husband's career to languish in the Confederacy as it had in the regular army.

After a credible performance during the Seven Days Campaign, Ewell accompanied Jackson during his famous march around John Pope's Union army. When the Federals located Stonewall's troops near Brawner's Farm on August 28, Ewell's battle lines slammed into the Union column. As the general observed the enemy's movements, a bullet shattered his right knee. Ewell became extremely weak, his body hemorrhaging from the grievous wound. At a field hospital the respected Dr. Hunter McGuire amputated his leg.[23] Recuperation was excruciatingly slow and painful, casting some doubt on the general's future in the army. Not until November was he able to complete the journey to Richmond. While convalescing, he disobeyed doctor's orders, left his bed, taking a hard fall that resulted in another hemorrhage. Lizinka could not convince Richard to strictly adhere to the doctor's instructions, causing the entire family to wonder if his condition would ever improve. By the spring of 1863, he could not ride a horse or wear a wooden leg.[24]

After the war Campbell Brown speculated that his mother would never have agreed to marriage if it had not been for the general's crippling injury.[25] Campbell Brown admired Ewell and had no reason to stop his mother from going to the altar. It appears that pity, more than romantic love, played the deciding factor in Lizinka's decision. She wrote an extremely revealing letter to her fiancé while he was resting in Richmond. The loss of his leg, she believed, made her more "necessary to you" than ever before. Until this unfortunate incident, Lizinka believed that Richard should "marry a younger woman, [but] now I will suit you better than any one else, if only because I will love you better." "The truth is," she added, "I have grown old very rapidly during the last six months [and] my eyesight is not good & my hair is turning grey, besides being thin & sallow."[26]

When Richard returned to Lee's army in the spring of 1863, he received a promotion to lieutenant-general and command of Jackson's old Second Corps. A day later on May 26, Ewell and Lizinka were married at Saint Paul's Church in Richmond. The notable minister, Charles F. E. Minnigerode, presided.[27] Shortly after the ceremony, Ewell rejoined the army of Northern Virginia for its Pennsylvania raid. Controversy has surrounded the general's actions at the ensuing battle of Gettysburg. On the first day of fighting, when the Federals had been routed and were madly retreating through town, the commanding heights of Cemetery Hill seemed to beckon the Confederates. Capturing this important ground would have compelled the Army of the Potomac to abandon the field completely.[28]

Ewell understood the importance of Cemetery Hill and believed he could take the position with the assistance A. P. Hill's Third Corps. Lee was also anxious for Ewell to attack, but he gave his subordinate vague instructions, allowing for any course of action as long as Ewell did not destroy his command. Without firm direction from above, caution overwhelmed Ewell. When he realized that A. P. Hill would not provide support, he called off the attack. Why Lee did not order a combined assault between Ewell and Hill's troops remains a mystery. The commanding general was on the field, near the Third Corps, and in plain view of the heights. He had the ability to control the flow of the battle, not his lieutenants.[29]

A number of ex-Confederates, especially Jubal A. Early and William Nelson Pendleton, shielded Lee from criticism after the war. After trouncing their favorite target, James Longstreet, they turned on Ewell and blamed him for failing to take Cemetery Hill, thereby squandering the South's best chance for victory. Early and Pendleton and a host of other Lost Cause disciples conjured up Stonewall's ghost to argue that Gettysburg's outcome and the fate of the entire war would have been different if Jackson had lived. The ever-aggressive Stonewall, runs the argument, would have pressed the advantage, cleared the heights of Yankees, and delivered another impressive victory to the Army of Northern Virginia. This interpretation, a hallucinatory vision at its most fundamental level, has captured the popular imagination at the expense of Ewell's reputation. In the process, Lee has been neatly removed from the army's tactical miscues, exonerated for one of the Confederacy's most devastating defeats.[30] Immediate reaction after the battle reveals a strikingly different assessment of southern leadership. Alexander "Sandie" Pendleton, Ewell's chief of staff, thought Cemetery Hill would have fallen into Confederate hands if Hill's troops had supported the Second Corps. "There has been some mismanagement in this affair & while the fault may be with others," Pendleton concluded, "the blame must & should fall on Gen. Lee."[31] Despite the lack of wartime evidence, Ewell's military reputation suffered irreparable damage from the Gettysburg controversy.

Most of Ewell's contemporaries and even some historians believe marriage to Lizinka derailed his military career. His subordinates were especially critical of Lizinka, blaming her for Richard's shortcomings as a general and an administrator. One officer summed up the dominant opinion of the army: "From a military point of view the addition of the wife did not compensate for the loss of the leg. We were of the opinion that Ewell was not the same soldier he had been when he was a whole man—and a single one."[32] This officer touched on a popular idea that had gained acceptance among Lee's troops during the latter stages of the war. Once a soldier took his wedding vows, ran the common argument, he lost his aggressiveness in battle, his sense of duty to his men, and his overriding purpose as a soldier. Womanly influences, not a lack of courage in the ranks, provided an acceptable explanation of the army's decline to many Confederate soldiers. In reference to another Confederate general who married during the war, an officer from Virginia observed "that no man who married during the war was as good a soldier after. . . . It was a singular fact, because those men who came into the war as married men were as good soldiers as the single ones, but marriage during the war seemed to demoralize them."[33]

In the eyes of many observers, Lizinka must have represented the fall of the plantation mistress because she had seemingly lost her womanly traits. Her aggressive personality, her apparent control of her husband, her bold entrance in the public world of army affairs shocked the sensibilities of most men. She did not live according to the traditional image of the docile, submissive woman who subordinated her interests to male authority. Her brashness more closely conformed to the image of a Yankee woman. Contrary to most Confederate women who used their femininity to expand their voice, assume new roles, and take political action against the invading Yankees, Lizinka was viewed as a threat to feminine behavior because she did not use women's weapons. Playing the part of a naive, fragile woman must have been incomprehensible to the strong-minded Lizinka.[34]

A number of officers felt threatened by Lizinka's alleged spell-like control of Ewell. She stayed at Second Corps headquarters during the winter of 1863–1864, like countless other upper-class women who lived in their husbands' camps. Their numbers, far greater than anyone had anticipated, alarmed the rank-and-file. This practice, critics argued, subverted discipline, distracted officers, and undercut morale among enlisted men who were prohibited from bringing their wives to quarters. After Ewell and his family made a short visit to a Charlottesville hospital in late November, Jedediah Hotchkiss predicted that all "will be back, though all are much opposed to having women in camp, as officers neglect their duties to attend their wives & when any movement takes place instead of seeing their commands off."[35] Letters appeared in Richmond newspapers in the winter of 1863 and 1864 demanding that women no longer live with the army. In the Richmond *Enquirer,* one soldier complained that the "General 'fares sumptuously every day' " with "his wife and loved ones." In stark contrast the private receives repeated denials to return home, having no choice but to stay "manfully" at his post where he "sees his leader—the man who speaks to him of self denial and endurance—enjoying the luxury of a house, and the pleasant society of his family. Ladies, stay at home, and knit gloves and stockings for your husbands," the same soldier concluded. "Officers, attend to your duties, leave your wives to attend to theirs, and when your troops are called on to do or dare, they will not be found wanting."[36]

If Lizinka even noticed the article, she dismissed every word, rebelled against every sentiment. Instead of submitting to a more acceptable domestic role, she saw herself as Ewell's chief of staff. In her self-appointed position, Lizinka tried to convince her husband that certain subordinates and fellow generals conspired against him. With just cause she worried about the intentions of the ambitious Jubal A. Early, the Second Corps' senior divisional commander, who often exerted undue influence on the pliable Ewell. A consummate bachelor who intensely disliked Lizinka, he mocked Ewell for being "desperately enamoured as if he had a blooming young wife." He also criticized Richard for bringing Lizinka to winter quarters, saying that "camp [was] no place for a woman."[37]

Chief of staff "Sandie" Pendleton found his name near the top of her hit list. Pendleton probably ranks as one of the finest staff officers in Lee's army, a man of integrity, intelligence, and remarkable bravery. Lizinka thought Pendleton was Ewell's Judas. Although he never tried to sabotage the general's career, she probably was not imagining that Pendleton was her enemy. Her low opinion of Pendleton probably stemmed from the young man's outspoken position against women in camp.[38] Sandie believed Lizinka pulled the general away from his responsibilities. On November 25, 1863, he called Ewell a "superannuated chieftain worn out as he is by the prostration incident, in a man of his age, upon the amputation (of his leg) and doting so foolishly upon his unattractive spouse."[39]

Although Sandie grew increasingly disenchanted with Ewell after Gettysburg, he never allowed his personal feelings to interfere with his duties. When Pendleton accompanied Early to the Shenandoah Valley in 1864, Lizinka crowed with delight, interpreting his departure as proof of disloyalty. In a rare moment, Ewell reprimanded his wife, not so much for her slanderous accusations, but for insinuating he lacked fortitude and wisdom. He replied that "in one of your recent letters you speak of Pendleton's going off as leaving the setting sun, &c & unless you are mistaken in my strength of character, he is destroying his chance for promotion." Even if the man "were my worst enemy," Richard countered, he would still promote an officer who could "whip the Yankees." After Campbell Brown and another staff officer brazenly disregarded an assignment, Ewell sent Pendleton on a "more troublesome duty." He "was ready at once & returned promptly doing his duty well." After relating the incident to Lizinka, he asked: "Which is the best friend?"[40]

Lizinka's efforts to win her son promotion and shield him from combat angered Ewell's staff. Interfering on behalf of her son violated their sense of fairness, even though such political wrangling often determined the course of an officer's career. Once a woman entered the arena of army politics, the rules changed, and acts of favoritism were no longer viewed as a necessary evil but as a gross violation of military protocol. When a new bill before the Confederate Congress would have enlarged the general staff of the Confederate army, a few officers charged that Ewell was maneuvering to promote Campbell Brown. "Old Ewell," wrote Colonel James Connor, "acted upon by feminine influences, is dead bent on pushing Campbell Brown, Mrs. Ewell's son, up to be a Colonel, and to do it, he is trying to engineer his other staff officers out of the way." Such rumors reflected the perception that Ewell was merely a puppet-general, a figurehead manipulated by his wife. Connor wrote with disgust that "Old Baldy" was a "fond, foolish old man . . . worse in love than any eighteen-year older that you ever saw."[41] Although the staff bill received a pocket veto, the incident revealed the troubled state of affairs in the Second Corps. On the eve of a major campaign against Grant, when Lee needed harmony and cooperation among his subordinates, Lizinka's maneuvering had brought a fair amount of dissension to the Army of Northern Virginia's command structure.

Lizinka did not concern herself exclusively with issues of promotion and rank. She also tried to shape Richard's conduct on the battlefield, warning him to stay clear of enemy fire. Persuading Ewell to avoid danger would also increase the chances that her son would remain safely tucked away from the Yankees. In a conversation with the priest, James B. Sheeran, of the Louisiana Brigade, Lizinka asked the clergyman if a general "is justified in carelessly exposing himself on the battlefield." Sheeran unequivocally said no. "A general in my opinion should keep himself as far as possible out of danger," he explained, "but in such a position as to see or hear of the movements in battle." He considered the general "the soul of the army, and his fall always causes despondency and sometimes greater disaster to his command." Lizinka then triumphantly turned to Richard and chirped: "There now General, you see that the Father is just of my opinion."[42]

While Lizinka never convinced Ewell to avoid enemy fire, she succeeded in keeping Campbell Brown a comfortable distance from the Yankees. Whether other women had a similar effect in shaping battlefield behavior remains to be seen. During the Spotsylvania Campaign, Ewell had a horse shot from underneath him but escaped without injury. Campbell Brown reluctantly reported the incident to Lizinka "because you are likely to hear exaggerated stories, perhaps of his being wounded." He assured his mother that Ewell "has insisted on my staying in the rear since last Thursday, which is very repugnant to me until I think of you and what your situation would be if we were both killed at once." The likelihood of the general receiving a fatal wound, Brown added, seemed improbable, for "really the Gen'l is conscientious about it & does not expose himself more than required." The famous cartographer, Jedediah Hotchkiss, offered a similar appraisal during the Spotsylvania campaign, writing that "Gen. Ewell sleeps and stays in the trenches, but he will not let any of his staff stay where there is any danger if he can help it—sending them off as soon as they have done any duty he may require."[43]

Ewell confided to a staff officer named Turner that "he had never exposed [to enemy fire] Campbell but once, and then was so miserable until he came back, that he did not know what to do." "If anything had happened to him," Ewell added, "I could never have looked at his Mother again." Turner repeated this story to a friend and then exclaimed: "Hang him [Ewell] . . . he never thinks of my Mother, I suppose, for he pops me around, no matter how hot the fire is." After Turner left, another staff officer remarked: "'Well, Turner is safe, but I am in a tight place. Campbell Brown hangs onto his mother's petticoats, and Turner is engaged to the little Brown girl (Lizinka's daughter), and she will prize him up, but I have to fight against the pair."⁴⁴

Lizinka's influence in the Second Corps' operations caused some of Ewell's staff to wonder whom they served. Colonel James Conner noted that Lizinka "manages everything from the general's affairs down to the courier's who carries his dispatches. All say they are under petticoat government."⁴⁵ General Robert Rodes sardonically asked who commanded the Second Corps: the Widow Brown, Ewell, or chief of staff Sandie Pendleton. Rodes hoped that it was the last one. The snide comments had made it abundantly clear that the men resented Lizinka's presence at camp. General Lee ordered all women to leave winter quarters on April 12, 1864, but Lizinka defied the commanding general's edict. She lingered at Ewell's headquarters for ten extra days before departing. Just before she left, she turned to the staff and told them that "she knew every one here was glad to get rid of her." Without Lizinka's presence, the tension at Second Corps' headquarters must have eased considerably, but its commander appeared lost, a man without direction. "Mrs. Ewell has gone away," Hotchkiss wrote, "& the poor old General is almost disconsolate—gets up early in the morning & walks about nearly all day."⁴⁶

As the army prepared for Grant's spring offensive, Lee entertained serious doubts about Ewell as a lieutenant general. His uneven performance at Gettysburg and recurring health problems raised troubling questions about his leadership abilities. Those fears were not misplaced. At the Wilderness, Ewell fought exceptionally well on May 5, probably his finest moment in the Army of Northern Virginia. The next day, however, he succumbed to a fit of mental paralysis when Grant revealed his right flank. Instead of immediately exploiting the advantage, Ewell hesitated. He possibly cost the Confederates a grand opportunity to punish the Army of the Potomac. Lee expected too much from Ewell in this situation, when ample reserves were not plentiful, but his subordinate's inaction reinforced the growing perception that Ewell lacked the aggressive instincts necessary for command.⁴⁷

The stress and demands of active campaigning overwhelmed Ewell physically and emotionally. After the Federals broke the Confederate lines on May 12, at Spotsylvania, an agitated Ewell lost his composure as he tried to rally some fleeing soldiers. One witness described the general as a "tower of passion" as he hurled a "terrible volley of oaths," calling some of the stragglers cowards. "Yes, goddamn you, run," he shouted. "The Yankees will catch you. That's right, go as fast as you can." When Ewell started to hit some of the fleeing soldiers with the flat side of his sword, Lee ordered him to restrain himself. "How can you expect to control these men when you have lost control of yourself?" Lee asked. "If you cannot repress your excitement, you had better retire." Seven days later, Ewell suffered a complete emotional breakdown when he inspected Grant's flank. In a postwar conversation with William Allan, Lee recounted that "he (Ewell) lost all presence of mind, and that he found Ewell prostrate on the ground, and declaring he could not get Rodes's division out." The sight of Ewell lying helplessly on the ground infuriated Lee, who told his subordinate that he would find another officer to move Rodes.[48]

Shortly after this incident Ewell left on sick leave but sought reinstatement, as Jubal Early left for the Shenandoah Valley in mid-June. Lee tried to put him off because of his sickness. Ewell insisted that he was physically capable of resuming command. The commanding general reluctantly informed him that he had been permanently relieved and that his replacement, Early, was better suited to lead a corps. It was a wrenching decision, Lee told Allan, but one necessary for the good of the cause.[49] Ewell's loss of command to Early must have embittered Lizinka, who had long maintained that her husband's primary subordinate sought his job. Ewell received a secondary assignment to the Richmond defenses near the end of the war, a duty he performed well even though he would have preferred a more important post. He accompanied Lee's army on its retreat to Appomattox, only for the Federals to capture him at Sayler's Creek, three days before the surrender.[50]

Federal officials withheld paroles to Confederate generals captured just before Appomattox. Consequently, Ewell, Campbell Brown, and some other officers were shipped to Fort Warren, Boston, for internment. Just before their train reached Providence, Rhode Island, the news of President Lincoln's assassination was received. A mob gathered at the railroad station to greet the prisoners, including some men carrying weapons and stones. In the end only harsh words were hurled at the Confederate prisoners. One impassioned citizen yelled to the crowd: "Three groans for Ewell."[51]

Lizinka wanted the immediate release of her husband and son and the return of her property. She thought she could capitalize on her prewar connections with Andrew Johnson and his family, even though Johnson despised the planter class and remained a staunch Unionist. Instead of directly petitioning the president, she wrote a strange letter to Mrs. Johnson, calling her mother and referring to Andrew Johnson as the governor. Not only was Mrs. Johnson incapable of assisting Lizinka, but her letter for some unexplainable reason infuriated the president who promptly had her arrested and detained in St. Louis. Johnson's forceful response stunned Lizinka. She had never been subjected to such unyielding authority as the military arm of the federal government. In the face of such power she did not know what to do, nor where to seek counsel. Lizinka considered the arrest "a mystery & is beginning to have on my mind the evil affect of a ghost story—some thing unseen & dreadful because you cannot get hold of it." She assured Ewell that she had "been careful &

quiet, not even visiting the kindest people for fear of giving offense or getting into trouble that I feel injured & indignant as well as mortified & provoked."[52]

In late June President Johnson relented, allowing Lizinka to see Richard in prison on the condition that she not visit Tennessee. On June 28, Lizinka met with Johnson for three hours. Over dinner he told her that Ewell could not be released yet, but pardons would quickly follow for Campbell Brown and herself if she returned in three days with the proper petitions. Lizinka reminded Johnson that she had been pardoned by Lincoln and that she had been a loyal citizen ever since. Just before the end of the war, when the cause appeared hopeless, she took the oath with Richard's knowledge and approval. (It appears that Richmond authorities did not know of the matter.) When Lizinka reapplied, Johnson granted her amnesty under Lincoln's pardon of March 23, 1865, not under his own generous proclamation. She was also permitted to go to Tennessee and resume control of her Nashville property and two farms in Maury County. Upon her return, she found her land barren, her livestock gone, and her buildings dilapidated, but she did not despair. "I do not mention these things to complain," Lizinka wrote Ewell, "but to shew [sic] how important it is that we should go to work at once to repair damages & make a living."[53]

In midsummer she made a final appeal, begging Johnson to free her husband and son. "You told me to address you not with the formality due to your high office," she wrote on July 13, "but with the freedom of a friend. I do so with fear and trembling." She remembered that an earlier petition resulted in her arrest. Another mistake, she worried, might prolong their imprisonment. Lizinka could not suppress images of her loved ones behind bars, haggard looking, frail, and suffering from the effects of a poor diet. Their sickly condition and general helplessness necessitated action. "I am too restless and miserable to be quiet, and I appeal to you as a weak woman to a strong man, and entreat you by all that makes life dear to you to give me back my husband and child." Johnson must have chuckled at Lizinka's transparent attempt to portray herself as a "damsel in distress." By the end of the letter, she grew tired of playing the defenseless woman. She mustered all her wrath and vented in classic Lizinka style: "If Richard dies at Fort Warren, I shall hate you—wicked as it is to hate any one."[54] Her strong words to Johnson revealed the inner struggle that Lizinka could never resolve. She rightly saw herself as a strong-willed, determined individual, but the gender conventions of nineteenth-century southern society often rendered her helpless.

For portions of June and July Lizinka resided with a prominent Rhode Island family to be near her husband and son. Prison did not insulate Ewell from his wife's stern advice and controlling ways. After complaining about his eyesight, Lizinka bluntly told him: "Do get over your delusion about a stigma—it is a queer idea. Read the 46th Psalm."[55] Not until late

July were Campbell Brown and Richard released from Fort Warren. Initially, Ewell's movements were restricted to Virginia, but other officers who left the same prison had been granted more generous terms. In a polite letter to Johnson, Ewell asked for the same liberties. With executive permission granted, the reunited couple returned to Spring Hill, Tennessee.

Although Ewell quickly adapted to civilian ways, Lizinka wanted to escape her Tennessee plantation. She felt isolated, cut off from proper society. The attractions of Nashville and Richmond appealed to her.[56] Richard refused and immersed himself in farming. From the years 1866 to 1868, he turned Lizinka's Spring Hill property into a prosperous stock farm. Relations soured between the two when Richard decided to oversee Melrose and Tarpley plantations in Mississippi. In what must have evoked painful memories of Percy Brown for Lizinka, Ewell frequently left her for business trips to Mississippi. He seemed obsessed with Melrose, which he did not even own. Lizinka had inherited the property from Percy Brown. Refusing to sit idly by while Richard speculated with her money, Lizinka decided to remodel the Spring Hill farmhouse because Ewell would never move to the city. She sought his advice, but he was too busy to respond. "R. Wont say a word," Lizinka complained to her son, "and I have to decide every-thing for myself but I'll do it—& do it vigorously too."[57]

On the battlefield Ewell preferred a conservative course, but in his financial dealings he was a gambler. He risked a considerable sum of his wife's capital in trying to revive Melrose and Tarpley. Lizinka could not understand her husband's motives. Any proposal that did not appear financially sound she rejected. She rightfully took a vested interest in the management of her landholdings. "After the utter want of affection evinced in your leaving me as you have done this winter in a singularly uncomfortable & unladylike position," she wrote, ". . . you cannot of course expect me to go to Mississippi or any new & uncomfortable place & risk a similar neglect should you fancy digging a ditch elsewhere." Lizinka had warned Ewell not to visit the Mississippi property because "it would separate us so much." That was bad enough, but what angered her the most "was your *individual* interest & as I was to gain no money by it."[58]

Percy Brown had frequently left Lizinka on the pretense of taking care of Melrose to cover his illicit activities. Now Richard's repeated absences seemed to remind her of those past fears and humiliations. "[I] hope you will make enough money at Tarpley to pay you for all the pain & mortification your absence has caused me," she wrote. "I *wonder* sometimes whether I'm taken now for a lady or a washerwoman. I have tried to write amiably but I cannot. My feelings are too bitter & my mortification too great."[59] In another venomous letter, she condemned him for abandoning her, writing that "I think it is due to the woman you considered respectable enough to be your wife not to be left as I have been this winter with the additional mortification when asked, when will your husband be home? To be compelled to answer, I have no idea. Looking back, I can't see how I have deserved it. I have declined leaving you even to go to my children & I thank you for teaching me the folly of so doing."[60]

Their relationship reached a crisis point on January 3, 1870. A worker from Melrose had returned to Tennessee and innocently told her that Ewell seemed happier there than at Spring Hill. Deeply hurt by this off-handed remark, she gave her husband an ultimatum: "If you choose to stay at Melrose & let business here go to the dogs do so, but I'll stay here now until Hattie's visit is over & then if you decide to stay away months at a time I'll just go somewhere else, where I can have quiet & rest. . . . I won't stay here. O how I hate it."[61] Although Richard hurried home after this angry letter to mollify Lizinka, he did not change his behavior. Except for a summer excursion to New York with his wife, he spent much of 1870 in Mississippi. Lizinka, it appears, eventually resigned herself to the situation, blaming her husband's obsession on "cotton fever." "It seems to do him so much good to go down there & turn savage for awhile that I cannot object to it," she wrote her son, "tho' I think this place suffers very much from it." On the occasions the general returned to Spring Hill, he seemed distracted, always worried about Tarpley.[62]

Under Ewell's management, his farms in Mississippi turned a profit for three years, despite floods, insects, and labor difficulties. When his lease came to an end in 1871, he had decide whether he would buy Tarpley, find another tract of land, or quit altogether. He agonized over the matter and his position changed from day to day. Lizinka considered cotton mania Ewell's addiction, his downfall, and she never disguised her opposition. Their near estrangement over the issue must have been one of the factors that convinced Ewell to get out of the cotton business. The decision threw him into a depression, but the sadness did not last long. The farm at Spring Hill and family obligations eased the transition. His return to Tennessee was a salve to their relationship. While the reunited couple enjoyed their grandchildren, Ewell continued to work long hours on the farm. Without sufficient rest, his weakened body contracted typhoid fever. The general lingered with the sickness, infecting Lizinka and other members of the household. She was the first to perish, passing away on January 22, 1872. The family did not immediately inform Ewell of his wife's death. They waited for a day, when it seemed certain that he would not recover. A family member recalled that "he was dreadfully agitated" when he heard the news. He called "for her picture to be hung around his neck, which he put over his heart." Death came two days after that. Richard was buried next to Lizinka in the Old City Cemetery, in Nashville, Tennessee.[63]

Few military couples during the Civil War received such intense outside scrutiny as did the Ewells. And few military wives were as outspoken and brazen as Lizinka Brown Ewell. Her repeated intrusions exposed Richard's embarrassing failings as a man, husband, and soldier for all to see. After the war, Richard sought to reaffirm his power as husband and male patriarch by leaving his wife alone on the farm and trying to recast her as the traditional plantation mistress. But Lizinka was not a woman to take such treatment lightly. She had gained her brash assertiveness long before Fort Sumter and she struggled against Richard's behavior angrily, threatening to leave him if he did not return home. In the end, Richard did come home and the Ewells seemed to reconcile. But tragically, their harmony was short-lived and both Ewells died quite suddenly of a killer disease. The deep tensions in their marriage were finally put to permanent rest.

SIX

The Marriage of Amelia Gayle and Josiah Gorgas

SARAH WOOLFOLK WIGGINS

"Minnie," Josiah Gorgas wrote wistfully in 1858 to his wife, Amelia, "I wish we had come together early in my life. It seems to date only from my marriage."[1] To Josiah, his marriage was the defining moment in his life. For most men, marriage shapes their personal lives. Josiah's marriage to a southern woman also shaped his career. As Amelia's partner, life opened before him in ways that he had not previously known. She returned his devotion, and their love became the keystone of a strong marriage.

To the casual observer, Amelia Gayle and Josiah Gorgas were an unlikely couple to build a successful marriage. She came from a distinguished Alabama family. Her maternal and paternal ancestors included decorated Revolutionary War veterans. Her father was John Gayle, Alabama governor, congressman, and judge. Her mother was Sarah Haynsworth, descended from a prominent South Carolina family and known as a great beauty. Sarah Haynsworth Gayle died of lockjaw in 1835 when Amelia was nine years old, and two years later John Gayle remarried and began a second family.[2] The Gayles were comfortable, but never rich, Southerners who were content with their place in the aristocratic social circles of antebellum Alabama.

The third of six children, Amelia, born in 1826, attended classes with local teachers in Greensboro and Tuscaloosa, Alabama, before attending Columbia Female Institute in Tennessee. Back in Mobile as the oldest girl at home after the marriage of her older sister, Sarah, Amelia spent her teenage years assisting her stepmother with the care of John Gayle's young second family. When she was twenty, her father was elected to the U.S. Congress; Amelia accompanied him to Washington. When that magical year ended, Amelia returned to Mobile, where she again assisted her step-mother with the care of the family's young children.[3] The network of support from family members was always important to the Gayles.

In contrast, Josiah, born in 1818, was the youngest of the ten children of Joseph and Sophia Atkinson Gorgas of Running Pumps, Pennsylvania. Joseph was a clockmaker and a farmer who was not particularly successful financially. When Josiah was seventeen, he was sent to live with one of his older sisters and her husband in Lyons, New York. There as an apprentice in a printing office he caught the eye of the local congressman, who secured an appointment to West Point for the young man. After graduation Josiah began his career as a professional soldier in the ordnance corps. His first assignment was at a federal arsenal in upstate New York, and after three years there he obtained leave to travel in Europe for a year to study European forts and armaments. He returned to the United States to serve as an ordnance officer under General Winfield Scott in the Mexican War. In these years Josiah grew away from his family. After several brief assignments he was sent in July 1853 to the federal arsenal at Mount Vernon, Alabama, located on high ground north of Mobile. There, at age thirty-five, his life changed forever.[4]

Victorian America saw the decline of arranged marriages and the rise of marriages based on romantic attachment as the circumstances of the Gorgas engagement and marriage illustrate. Amelia met Josiah in August 1853 while he was commandant of the Mount Vernon Arsenal. Responsible for two of her older sister's children while the parents traveled abroad, Amelia had fled Mobile's 1853 yellow fever epidemic to the safety of the home of her older brother, Dr. Matthew Gayle, then the arsenal surgeon. Each after noon she read to the children on her brother's verandah next door to the commandant's quarters. Josiah overheard her reading. He always maintained that he fell in love with her voice before they met. They were married in December 1853. Amelia was twenty-seven, and Josiah was thirty-five. Theirs was a genuine love match between best friends. Six children were born between 1854 and 1864. Although both parents were deeply involved in child rearing, this marriage was never a child-centered one.[5]

For the next three decades Josiah's career shaped the Gorgases' world. Between 1856 and 1861 army assignments took the family to Maine, South Carolina, and Pennsylvania. When the Civil War began in 1861, Josiah resigned his U.S. Army commission, enlisted in the Confederate army, and became chief of the Confederate Ordnance Bureau. In this post Josiah became known as the most capable administrator in the Confederate government, as a "genius at improvisation." Although the army frequently lacked food, clothing, shoes, and medicine, Confederate soldiers after 1862 did not experience shortages of munitions. During the Civil War the Gorgases lived in Richmond until Josiah fled with the Confederate government, leaving Amelia and the children with Amelia's younger sister, Maria Bayne.[6]

At the end of the Civil War Josiah opened an ironworks at Brierfield, Alabama, a venture that proved to be unsuccessful. In 1869 he became headmaster of the junior department at the University of the South at Sewanee, Tennessee. When Sewanee fired him in 1878, he was elected president of the University of Alabama at Tuscaloosa, and there the family made their last move.[7]

The Gorgas marriage, which spanned the Civil War and its aftermath, epitomized the Victorian concept of separate spheres for husband and wife. The husband was the financial provider for the family, while the wife remained at home to create a refuge for the husband and to bear and rear their children. The arrangement presumed the primacy of the husband's role in the marriage and his dominance in decision making for the family. Josiah was the provider and decision maker in the Gorgas marriage, and Amelia was the keeper of the home sphere. However, Josiah's power was constrained by his devotion to Amelia, and her preferences always tempered his decisions.

The couple were together during most of the years of the Civil War, but in the aftermath of the war Josiah's lifelong profession in the army was gone. Economic circumstances now dictated separations as Josiah sought a new occupation to support his family. With Josiah absent, Amelia stepped forward into Josiah's sphere. When the separation ended, Amelia stepped back into the home sphere and returned Josiah's leadership role to him. Each time she acted in these changing circumstances, she grew stronger and so did their marriage. Unwittingly, Amelia prepared for a time when Josiah's physical collapse made her the primary family provider. When separated from each other, the couple wrote to each other almost daily. This flood of correspondence, combined with Josiah's journals (1857–1878), provides a window through which their marriage may be viewed.

The two personalities who emerge from these sources were articulate, assertive partners who deeply respected each other. They could disagree without being unpleasant or judgmental, and they solved problems without projecting blame on the other partner. Three qualities shaped the Gorgas marriage: their unselfish concern for each other, their compromises in family decision making, and their management of separations.

Amelia and Josiah enjoyed an intimacy that permitted differences but did not require one personality to subordinate itself to the other. They were simply miserable when separated. Whether the separation was early in their marriage (1858) or late (1878), the feel of their correspondence remained the same. In 1858 while Josiah was in South Carolina and Amelia and their three young children stayed in Maine, Josiah was "lost" without her.[8] "I would give anything to have my arm around your waist." "I do love you so dearly so entirely." He complained that he slept too much: "I want something to keep me awake—babies or *something!*" And, he confessed, "I have hardly known myself how my heart is wrapped up in you until I am so far away." And, "Will there never be an electric telegraph between two hearts that yearn for each other which will annihilate distance?" He had "no peace or happiness away" from Amelia.[9] When her letters arrived, he was jubilant: "Your loving words always comfort me, and just now your expression of affection & trust are doubly dear to me. What should I do without you, . . . my pride, my joy, my best beloved." Two letters from Amelia in one day made him as "elated" as if, he said, he had been promoted or won a lottery. When no letters came, he despaired.[10]

Separation also left Amelia "lost & lonely." She felt that "I should be well & happy if you were only here." And "My heart fairly aches for you." For Amelia, writing to Josiah provided solace during his absence. "I have been so impatient all day to write to you a little note; it is a poor substitute indeed for our long afternoon chats but they give me a world of comfort." Interruptions in her letter writing to Josiah annoyed Amelia, and she allowed herself to indulge in the luxury of writing to him only every other day.[11]

In 1862 when the federal army threatened Richmond, Amelia fled southward with her children. By this time the couple had been married nine years and had a family of five children, a son and four daughters, ranging in age from eight years to less than one year. No correspondence from Amelia to Josiah in this period has survived, but Josiah's letters to her again reflect their intimacy. He wrote that he lived for her letters, and when one arrived, he declared that he was as happy as he could be away from her, "without whom the world is indeed very dull." "When shall we all be together again?" he asked in another letter.[12]

Neither Josiah's journals nor his few wartime letters to Amelia suggest that the general discussed ordnance matters with his wife, let alone asked for her advice. Nor is there evidence in his letters or journals that she offered any advice. However, the couple were together for most of the war, and we do not know what they discussed in private or across the dinner table. Still the tranquility of their home life, free of turmoil, gave Josiah emotional support to concentrate his thoughts on meeting the ordnance needs that kept the Confederate war effort afloat.

Even before the Civil War the devotion of Josiah and Amelia to each other had profoundly affected how they arrived at family decisions. She acknowledged and appreciated his decision, for her sake, to apply for an assignment in Charleston, South Carolina. A sister, Mary Aiken, lived there. "What will I not do for you darling in compensation for so many sacrifices." She loathed being separated from her husband, and she urged him to arrange somehow for the family to be reunited. "Make any arrangement you think best . . . & I will cheerfully accede."[13]

Another example of this pattern of accommodation in the Gorgas marriage occurred during the secession crisis in 1861. Amelia's sympathies were deeply southern, probably influenced when she was a young woman by the views of her father, John Gayle, and of the statesman of South

Carolina, John C. Calhoun. Her father had been a strong states' rights governor in Alabama in the 1830s, and his influence laid the foundation for the states' rights movement later in the state. In the 1840s while Gayle was a U.S. congressman, father and daughter had lodged at the same boardinghouse as Calhoun. Amelia and Calhoun became great friends, and the two took regular morning walks on the grounds of the national capitol. They discussed everything from politics to housekeeping. "I enjoy of all things a walk with him," she wrote her older sister, Sarah Crawford.[14]

Josiah's background was different. A poor Pennsylvanian, he had spent his adult life in the U.S. Army, and all of his family lived in the North. His first exposure to the South had come when he was posted to Mount Vernon in 1853, and the region won him over completely. In 1859 he admitted that "the South has . . . wooed and won me. Its blandishments have stolen into my senses, and I am its willing victim."[15]

In 1861 he was stationed at Frankford Arsenal at Philadelphia, and in February he declined a commission in the Confederate Army. Amelia told him to decide his future according to his own conscience, and wherever duty called him, she would go also.[16] Although no evidence exists to imply that Amelia consciously or unconsciously tried to influence him, Josiah's devotion to Amelia certainly affected his decision to join the Confederacy.

Equally as important as Amelia's southern sympathies in Josiah's decision in the secession crisis was his strained relationship with his army superiors. The problem had a long history. In 1845 when Josiah had been an impatient young army officer about to travel in Europe for six months, he wrote to Secretary of State James Buchanan, announcing his plans, asking if he could deliver any diplomatic messages abroad, and requesting letters of introduction to U.S. officials in European capitals. Buchanan replied that no transmission of dispatches was needed and ignored the request for letters of introduction. Immediately, Josiah wrote directly to Buchanan in what was apparently a petulant letter that was forwarded to the war department. Josiah then sought letters of introduction through an old friend, U.S. Chief of Ordnance George Talcott, but without success. Once in Europe Josiah learned how seriously he had offended the secretaries of state and war, and yet he applied for an extension of his leave. His friend, Talcott, soothed the angry secretary of war and won a six-month extension for Josiah.[17] But the damage was done, and the staff in the war department had a long memory.

In the 1850s Josiah irritated his superiors in Washington with complaints about his post assignments and requests for relocation. Unfortunately for Josiah, a new ordnance chief, H. K. Craig, replaced Josiah's friend, Talcott. Josiah and Craig began a sparring contest that continued through the rest of the decade. One leave extension denied by Craig was overruled for Josiah by his friend, Secretary of War John B. Floyd, who also changed one undesirable assignment for another post for Josiah. A month after Josiah declined the Confederate commission, Craig transferred Josiah to foundry duty under U.S. Inspector of Ordnance Benjamin Huger. Josiah had quarreled with Huger during the Mexican War, and the idea of serving under Huger was repugnant to Josiah. Given his wife's southern sympathies and his own strained relationships in the U.S. Army, it was not surprising that he resigned effective April 3, urged, he said, "by my own sympathies & likings, & importuned by my Southern friends." He confided to his journal that he had been ordered from Frankford "(very wrongfully) & so I thought I might as well make one move of it & go where I should ultimately have to go."[18]

The year 1861 marked more than a change in Josiah's career. His years in the old army had seen him frequently display a prickly impatience that made him quick to reply to what he had perceived as slights to him. That quality had caused his strained relationships with his superiors in Washington in 1845 and had precipitated his quarrel with Benjamin Huger during the Mexican War. After his marriage to Amelia his personality softened, with fewer willful outbursts toward his superiors in the 1850s. After 1861 Josiah definitely mellowed and grew more patient, probably because of the serenity of his relationship with his gentle and charming wife. Such new patience perhaps explains how he maintained a successful relationship with the often difficult and prickly Jefferson Davis and why he would respond so calmly to a crisis at Sewanee in 1878.

Josiah's decision to join the Confederacy cut whatever feeble ties remained with his relatives in the North. After his marriage in 1853 his contacts with his family had been infrequent, except between 1856 and 1858, when he was stationed at the federal arsenal in Augusta, Maine. As his absorption into Amelia's family grew, his contact with his own family declined. After 1861 and his decision to cast his fortunes with the South, his family cut him off completely.[19]

It was not the Civil War but rather the depressed southern economy during Reconstruction that seriously threatened the Gorgas marriage—separating the parents, wiping out their savings, and bankrupting their dreams. After Richmond fell in April 1865, Amelia and the children, who now numbered six, remained in Richmond while Josiah fled southward with the remnants of the Confederate government. No evidence exists to suggest that he attempted to contact any of his family in the North. Instead, he sought refuge with Amelia's family in Alabama; they welcomed him. His profession as a soldier was now gone. At first Josiah worried that as an ex-Confederate chief of ordnance he might be arrested and deported, but that fear never materialized. As months passed, he considered immigration to another country or to a border state. If only he and Amelia were to be considered, he said, "I should *gird* up my *loins* & seek other lands." But if "all quit the South, she will be left to her destroyers; and what *all* cannot do, no *one* ought to do." His letters in the summer and fall of 1865 repeatedly expressed his longing to see Amelia "to talk over our future."[20]

Amelia knew that responsibility for her and their children deeply affected Josiah's deliberations about his future. "Go abroad if you think best," she urged. "I can manage for myself & children until you send for us." Responsibility for herself and their children was creating a new self-confidence in Amelia, and in no way did Josiah try to stifle her independence. "I shall settle myself in some economical village . . . & make the means you left support us." Ever philosophical, Josiah saw these as unsettled times for his family: "we are all like passengers in a boat suddenly upset—floundering about in unknown depths, & striking out we hardly know whither."[21]

Although Amelia's younger brother, Dick, recently had been released from a Union prison and continued to suffer physically from that imprisonment, the Gayle family's primary surviving wartime tragedy was Amelia's older brother, Matt. A Confederate surgeon, Matt had suffered a nervous breakdown at the end of the war, and he was "incapable of doing anything for himself" for the remaining ten years of his life. Although Josiah himself was unemployed and living alternately with Amelia's older sister, Sarah, and their stepmother, Clara Gayle, he took the initiative to provide for his brother-in-law. So that Matt's care be "no heavy tax" on Amelia's stepmother, Josiah set aside "a month's pay in gold" for this purpose and proposed that Dick and Tom Bayne (husband of Amelia's sister Maria) join him in purchasing a home for Clara and Matt. "The care of Matt will devolve on her, & besides we owe her a great deal."[22] The Gorgas manuscripts reflect that Josiah assumed this responsibility without even a suggestion from Amelia. The Gayles were his family, and their problems were his.

While the ex-Confederate general floundered in Alabama trying to find a new occupation in the summer of 1865, Amelia and her sister Maria left Richmond, finding that their expenses exceeded their expectations and that the city was not healthy for their children. Earlier, Josiah, concerned for the family's safety in Richmond, had advised Amelia to go to New York or "some green lawn in New Jersey" where her "means" could sustain her for a "couple of years." He did not advise her to seek refuge with any of his relatives in the North. By July, however, some communication between Josiah's sister Eliza in New York and Amelia apparently occurred because Amelia wrote to Josiah that his sister "does not hint at a visit" from Amelia and the children. Now the Gayle sisters accepted an offer of hospitality from the family of Bayne's roommate at Yale and moved first to Baltimore and then settled in Cambridge, Maryland. In October Maria and her children went home to New Orleans, while Amelia and her children remained in Cambridge until April 1866.[23]

In 1865, forty-seven-year-old Josiah went to work to support his family as he had gone to work to arm the Confederacy. Unfortunately, his success in arming the Confederacy lulled him into believing that he could achieve the same success in a peacetime business. He was sure that the "good opinion" of his management of the Ordnance Bureau would eventually secure for him "some desirable position." "I am not yet old, & the world is open to me." Regularly, he described each new prospect to Amelia, always wishing to discuss these possibilities with her in person before "making a final selection." He knew that reviving an iron furnace in Alabama would require the family to live in an isolated rural area. The couple had decidedly different tastes. "You like the city, I the country," Josiah admitted. More bluntly, "I know you abhor the country, & yet with our limited means city life would be simply *absurd.*"[24]

Amelia was as desperate to reunite the family as was Josiah, and she urged him to hurry preparations for a reunion. "As to our future I know you will decide for the best." She was willing to do anything, go anywhere. "I am more than willing to go to the woods . . . if your interests or happiness are thereby promoted & we can *only be together.*" And "I will cheerfully live in the bottom of a well." She dreamed of the "long, cozy evenings" they would have, "I sewing while you read some charming book."[25]

For Amelia the presence of family and friends and their emotional support was vital. By January 1866 she was exhausted with separation from Josiah and the Gayle family and was surviving only because of the devotion of friends in Maryland. She wrote Josiah that "beyond the pain of separating from my family" she would pack up for "Mexico or California as soon as any where else." If Josiah could find "agreeable or congenial work in Ala, I think we ought to make our home in that state; we have good & strong friends there."[26] Ultimately, Josiah decided to go into the iron business in the wilderness at Brierfield, Alabama: for him the proximity of Amelia's family was as powerful a reason for that decision as it was for Amelia. Josiah recognized the benefits for children that came from growing up amid a large extended family. He did not wish "to separate them from their relatives."[27]

By 1865 Josiah had began to involve Amelia in family finances. He respected her intelligence and her capacity for growth. Earlier correspondence and entries in his journals mention no consultation with Amelia about money. But now as this postwar separation stretched from weeks to months to a year, financial discussions had begun. Josiah found Amelia already quite self-reliant. When the Gayle sisters had made plans to move from Richmond to a less expensive location, they informed their husbands of their intentions. The sisters did not seek advice for or approval of what they were about to do.[28]

Gradually, Josiah's advice became specific. "I hope you are making good use of your gold—small as it is," he wrote, "buying Greenbacks at the *highest* rates & you *purchasing* at the lowest." He instructed Amelia about handling financial resources set aside earlier. He owned 4,100 pounds of cotton stored near Greensboro, Alabama, and Winnsboro,

South Carolina, the home of Amelia's sister, Mary Aiken. Also, he advised Amelia about handling a note for money owed to Josiah by the husband of one of his sisters and money owed to Josiah by his older brother, Solomon. He also wrote Amelia about the contents of a "little leather trunk" that he had prepared in Greensboro and of a black trunk that he had left at her sister's home in Winnsboro.[29]

Still, he continued optimistic about their financial prospects. "Don't stint yourself to save money. It is not worth while. We will find more when that is spent," he wrote to Amelia in Maryland. He was relieved to learn that Amelia and the children were comfortable, and he reassured her that her arrangements were "sufficiently economical." He jokingly admonished her "to make your mind as easy as you can & grow fat! not that I think you can be improved, but *the more* there is of such a paragon of wife, why *the better!*"[30]

When Josiah visited the Baynes in New Orleans in the fall of 1865, he thought of Amelia and the children as he passed attractive residences in the Garden District. He wrote her that he knew she would be so happy "if I could command one of them for you, and how pleased I would be in rendering you and the children happy."[31]

Amelia regularly reported her financial condition to Josiah. By September 1865 Josiah commended her growing skill. "Your statement of finances is quite satisfactory & does great credit to your learning in that branch."[32]

As the months of separation continued, Amelia prepared for winter in Maryland. She wrote her husband that she had "laid in" her winter's supply of oak and if necessary could move to a less expensive lodging. She was thinking ahead and weighing the costs of "keeping house against that of boarding." Early in 1866 she found schools for the older children and dutifully reported the monthly costs to Josiah.[33]

Amelia worried that the children's separation from their father was affecting them adversely. She particularly grieved that their eldest son, Willie, was "removed even temporarily" from Josiah's influence. She feared that she lacked "sufficient decision of character to train children particularly boys," and she was anxious "to shift the responsibility." Amelia astutely realized that Willie loved her "dearly" and that she controlled him "entirely through his affection." However, she said, "I am too weak to insist upon duties repugnant to him."[34]

One of Amelia's letters contained her wistful description of her daydreams for the future. She amused herself talking of a "charming house in the mountains where each child is to have a pony, a squirrel, a pig & children of their own. . . . I shall live like a fine lady, dear, & have you read to me every evening."[35]

After Josiah had moved to Brierfield, his alarm about the wisdom of his decision to open the ironworks mounted rapidly. "I am really disinclined to bring you here," he wrote, because everything "looks so ruinous and uninviting." The place was "very, very lonely."[36] Amelia, the eternal optimist, tried to cheer her husband, to affirm and support his decision. If she had private reservations, she never expressed them any more than she blamed him later when Brierfield proved to be a financial disaster. She pronounced that the family would be happy in their "iron home, even without the society you promise." She felt grateful for what they had, as they were "so much more fortunate" than some of their friends. They would not regret the move to Brierfield, Amelia daydreamed. He would make a fortune and regain his health, the children would be "happy & healthy & I perfectly contented to bide the time when we can afford to introduce your daughters into N.O. society. . . . Did you ever know a woman of such perverted tastes!!!"[37]

But Amelia was already planning to liven up life at their "wild new home." Her sisters and their children would visit, and, she said, "I will bring out some nice playing cards and we will live Mt. Vernon days over again." She facetiously asked Josiah if they could hire a particular old friend and "let him take a hand at whist occasionally?" On a more personal matter she promised Josiah that she would bring with her from Maryland "a change of bed linen" so that "we may begin our 'love in a cottage' without delay."[38] Throughout this long separation, as in all other separations, Amelia never whined about her hardships or played for sympathy from her absent husband.

No sooner had the Gorgas family been reunited at Brierfield in April 1866 than Amelia's relatives began a steady stream of visits to break the monotony of life in the Alabama wilderness. They came in large numbers and stayed for months at a time. At Brierfield Josiah and Amelia settled into a routine of simple pleasures not unlike their early days of marriage. On his birthday Amelia baked two big blackberry pies for Josiah. The couple resumed their delight of his reading aloud to her. They were "much interested" in reading Jefferson Davis's *Prison Life*.[39] But most of all they enjoyed the pleasure of each other's company.

The ironworks' financial problems increasingly overshadowed the contentment of domestic life at Brierfield. Economic circumstances of the times made Josiah unable to succeed at Brierfield as he had at the Confederate Ordnance Bureau. The growing specter of financial disaster reduced Josiah to a state of severe depression. He poured his anguish into his journal: "for no imaginable recompense would I live this life over again. I can now understand how these poor, doomed, destroyed wretches whose self-destruction we daily see chronicled, are forced to their doom. To many annihilation must be the only thing left. Nothing is so terrible as despair." And "God grant that we may not fail."[40]

As the ironworks tottered toward bankruptcy, Amelia never blamed Josiah for his unfortunate decision to go into the iron business. She offered only encouragement while Josiah sought other employment. Relief at the offer of the position as headmaster of the junior department at the University of the South at Sewanee, Tennessee, was tempered by the specter of another separation. Josiah and Willie, then fourteen years old, moved permanently to Sewanee in July 1869, leaving the five younger children with Amelia at Brierfield until a new home was ready. Amelia was to salvage what she could from their financial investments at the ironworks. Josiah instructed her in great detail about their financial matters. He directed her on how to sign his name ("Write a little heavier than usual") and how to handle bills. Then he moved to domestic matters—the care of calves, cows, peach trees, and the sale of hay and feed.[41]

Amelia kept Josiah informed about the progress of the furnaces. The news was rarely favorable, but Josiah discussed business matters with Amelia as an equal. He determined not to dwell on the financial disaster. "I don't want you to sigh over it," he wrote Amelia. When prospects for the sale of the ironworks increased, he assured Amelia of his confidence in her business judgment. Still, he worried about her having enough money to meet her needs in his absence. Then prospects for a quick sale evaporated, and Josiah leased the ironworks to Captain Thomas Alvis in August 1869. Amelia and the younger children continued to live at Brierfield awaiting word from Josiah that he had a place for them to live at Sewanee.[42]

Soon after his move to Sewanee, it became obvious that the family's financial troubles had not ended. The school had been founded in 1860 and had languished until Josiah's arrival in 1869. At that time no residences existed for the staff, and the limited physical plant was uncleaned and in disorder. During his first months at Sewanee Josiah built dormitories, classrooms, and residences, while he lived in a campus dormitory with another faculty member. Then he realized that the Sewanee trustees expected him to recruit students, teach classes, lead the junior department, and raise money, especially the latter. Like the ironworks, the school verged on bankruptcy, and no money was available to build the new headmaster a place to live. Amelia again faced the crisis positively, proposing in a letter to Josiah that she take in boarders at Sewanee to provide some income, although she admitted that she did not "hanker after them." Meanwhile, at Brierfield she busied herself "overhauling" the children's last year's winter clothes, determined to purchase nothing new.[43]

For months Josiah struggled to have a house built so that the family could be reunited in Tennessee. Having lost so much money invested at Brierfield, Josiah was determined not to incur debt by building a house of his own at Sewanee. He wrote Amelia almost daily about the problem, describing the various obstacles and options; he was convinced that the "difficulties of housekeeping" at Sewanee were even greater than those at Brierfield.[44] By August 1869 Josiah was disgusted with the dilly-dallying of Sewanee's Episcopal bishops. He wrote Amelia that unless he had the prospect of a house by the next spring, he would look for another job. When a house finally was built for them, he fretted that it was not as comfortable as he had hoped. Still he believed their separation must end, "even at the risk of some discomfort." Not so many years remained to them that "we can throw them away."[45]

As the months of separation dragged on with Amelia and the children still at Brierfield, forty-three-year-old Amelia suffered a miscarriage in September 1869. Josiah wrote, "I fear our living would have been less fruitful if we had been less loving." Amelia never expressed apprehension about childbirth or complained about the pain involved. However, childbirth did worry Josiah, who had confided his fears to his journal at the birth of their second son in 1864, saying that such events caused "terrible suffering."[46]

One Sunday letter from Sewanee described how bleak Josiah's life was without Amelia's presence. He sat alone, cheered only by her "dear" letter. The weather was horrible—rain, sleet, snow, howling winds. "I am just *drawing* the cork of my last bottle of Stout, . . . & intend to *make a night* of it, on this & a biscuit" brought from a neighbor's supper table. "So you can see I am not in bad spirits, tho' a bit lonely, without you, my love." He longed, he said, to settle "somewhere & know & feel that I am to stay until I die." He foresaw trouble at Sewanee: "people are very impatient and are but too apt to require in Schools what is impossible." Also, he sensed dissension among the school's trustees, and he warned Amelia that he was unsure that "we are to be the 'magnificent success' that has been trumpeted of us."[47]

By May 1870 a house was finally ready at Sewanee, and the family was reunited. Life for the time being was uneventful except for concern over the career choice of Willie and for Josiah's declining health. After Willie's failure to be admitted to West Point and his lack of interest in the law, he enrolled in medical school in New York en route to what became an illustrious medical career. He was then twenty-two, but his parents still bombarded him with endless advice. A particularly telling comment came from Josiah, who urged Willie to establish social relations with a congressman's family. "Women move the world you know," he wrote, reflecting his awareness that Amelia made his own life comfortable in the haven that was his home.[48]

When fund raising for Sewanee took Josiah to New Orleans, he stayed with the Baynes, whose great wealth and lavish lifestyle painfully contrasted with those of the Gorgases. Despite the financial success of his in-laws, he wrote to Amelia, he found his own life preferable. He doubted whether there was a home anywhere "more thoroughly enjoyable than ours, thanks to its presiding divinity." Relatives, friends, old army comrades royally entertained him. But he thought constantly of home and Amelia. "I wish," he wrote, "all these civilities could be bestowed on *you*."[49]

In 1872 the Sewanee trustees appointed Josiah as vice-chancellor of the university. By this time it was clear that Sewanee's reputation was Josiah's reputation. The bishops' continued expectations that he could miraculously improve the school's financial situation disturbed Josiah. His experience had been that "expenditures estimated" always occurred, while "resources confidently relied on" were "seldom fully attained."[50] Unfortunately for Josiah and Sewanee, his predictions were correct.

During the next several years, Sewanee enrollment grew as did financial pressures and Josiah's workload. In 1873 he informed the board that he needed an administrative assistant and wished to teach only one class. The board acceded only to the latter request. Over Josiah's objections the board reduced the teaching staff to save money, damaging the quality of instruction and discipline. Josiah feared an enrollment drop was next. Despite the deteriorating relationship between Josiah and the board, the trustees elected him in 1875 to a five-year term as vice-chancellor.[51]

Meanwhile, Josiah's health declined precipitously. By early 1876 he described the constant pain in his left arm and leg as venomous. He lost patience with medicine and wished "to throw it to the dogs." Given his health problems, Josiah worried about financing Willie's medical education. But his brother-in-law, Tom Bayne, promised that he would advance funds if necessary.[52] Although Willie's educational future was secure, the financial prospects of the rest of the family were not.

The relationship between Josiah and the Sewanee trustees steadily worsened as did the financial condition of the institution, and by 1876 meetings were "stormy and disagreeable." Josiah quietly began to look for another job. His loyal, uncritical wife felt that the trustees treated Josiah with the "greatest ingratitude," and she expected to be a happy woman when he could turn his back on Sewanee and the family could "forget the existence of such a place." She was convinced that the stress at Sewanee aggravated Josiah's health problems. Amelia's assessment that Josiah has "more brains than all these meddle-some Bishops put together" was not surprising for a devoted wife in such precarious financial circumstances.[53]

While Josiah traveled to recruit students and raise money for Sewanee, he directed Amelia about managing the family hogs and cows. After all, with his meager salary these animals provided food for the Gorgas table, and this advice was as important as any monetary instruction.[54]

At the August 1877 meeting of the trustees, Josiah's stormy relations with the bishops came to a head. The trustees adopted a resolution that the vice-chancellor should be a clergyman and that this change would take effect "within the twelve months next ensuing." The meaning of the board's action was clear: the trustees were firing Josiah.[55]

Facing unemployment, in February 1878 Josiah traveled to Washington on a job hunt. Quickly, he saw the effort was futile, even for the ex-Confederate chief of ordnance: "no southern man of any record can get any appt. under the administration." In the face of such circumstances, he wrote Amelia, "I keep a stiff upper lip & pretend I don't want anything."[56] As he called on old army friends, one officer related a recent visit to an arsenal in upstate New York where Josiah had been assigned in the 1840s. Former servants had asked about Josiah and were told that "I had lost everything & was doing the best I could." The reply of one former servant said much about Josiah's character: "Mr. Gorgas was always mighty good to me, & if a matter of a thousand dollars would do him any good I wouldn't be behindhand in giving it to him."[57]

Josiah spent a lonely month in Washington. This separation from Amelia was as difficult as any of the previous ones. Daily he wrote her, expressing how much he missed her company. "I fear you don't sleep warm at night, in my absence."[58]

Once home, he steeled himself for the approaching showdown with the Sewanee trustees at their August 1878 meeting. Then a miracle occurred, or so it seemed. Without warning, Josiah learned that the University of Alabama trustees had elected him as president of that university in July. Josiah wrote Willie, now in medical school in New York, that "this piece of good fortune" was due entirely to the efforts of an old friend then serving on the board of trustees of both the University of Alabama and the University of the South. Josiah immediately accepted the offer and made plans to go to Tuscaloosa. Now there was no problem about a place for the family to live, as the university provided a mansion for its president. Still, a family with five children at home could not relocate instantly, so Amelia and the children remained behind at Sewanee until Amelia could move their children and household goods to Tuscaloosa.[59]

Suddenly, the attitudes of the Sewanee bishops changed, and even the most censorious could no longer find fault with Josiah's management of the school. Nevertheless, Josiah left Sewanee in July 1878, saying he never wanted to see the place again, and he never returned. As Amelia phrased it, "We all leave Sewanee without regrets."[60]

Only Josiah's separation from Amelia once again and his constant physical pain dampened his pleasure at leaving Sewanee. He had given up hope of ever being free of physical pain. "I pray God fervently only so to inflict it that I may do my duty to my family."[61]

Tuscaloosa would receive the Gorgases as their own come home. Many remembered Amelia's father from the 1830s when he had lived in Tuscaloosa as Alabama's governor and as president of the university's board of trustees.[62] One lady remembered Amelia as a child and classmate, a lady "very faded now," he wrote, "not bright & joyous like my wife." Impressed as Josiah was with his warm reception in Tuscaloosa, he was desperately lonely without Amelia, and again he wrote her almost daily. He enjoyed receiving her letters, but he preferred "to hold the hand that wrote them." He counted the days until his busy wife would join him. "How happy we shall be."[63] He wrote Amelia that her gentle presence would be an "advantage" at the university where he found the meals to be "very unstylish" without "lady supervision." Amelia would be a partner in his new job. As Amelia prepared to move the family to Tuscaloosa in December 1878, he asked her what furniture he should purchase and what household arrangements should be made for the president's house. He advised her in detail about insurance for their furniture and house at Sewanee. His directions for packing and moving were even more careful: what to bring, what to sell and for what price, how to pack, and what to do with their livestock.[64] His helpful instructions notwithstanding, it was Amelia who had to contend with the difficulties of the actual move.

Amelia and the children finally joined Josiah in Tuscaloosa a few days after Christmas 1878, and he became "more bright & cheerful & hopeful." Unfortunately, within weeks Amelia hurried back to Sewanee to nurse her sister, Mary Aiken, who had fallen seriously ill. Mary had moved to Sewanee in the summer of 1872. Separated once again, husband and wife wrote frequently. He missed her terribly. "No, my love," Josiah assured Amelia, "we won't grow old nor cold, toward each other. I dreamed of you night before last, & my last dreamy thought, as I drop off, is certainly of my absent love, whom I miss so much."[65]

Suddenly, Josiah suffered a massive stroke on February 23, 1879. Amelia hurried back to Tuscaloosa and wrote their son, Willie, of her "frantic grief" when she first saw her beloved husband. She immediately assumed responsibility for the family, as she sent instructions to Willie in New York and organized how each of the children still at home would contribute financially to the welfare of the family. In March Mary Aiken was well enough for Amelia to move Mary and her family into the Gorgas household in Tuscaloosa.[66] In 1879 Amelia permanently crossed the boundary into Josiah's sphere.

Josiah, conscious of how desperate were their circumstances, drew Amelia down to him one day, saying "my poor darling! what will become of you if I do not recover." After a few weeks Amelia proposed that the university divide Josiah's salary between the Gorgas family and the professor who was performing Josiah's duties, but the trustees insisted on continuing the full salary to Josiah. Amelia's optimism alternated with despair: "Brighter & better times I know are coming," and "I can scarcely keep back my tears." As months passed and it was clear that Josiah could not resume the presidency and must resign his post, she again made plans to take in boarders to supplement the family's income. "I will not flinch," she wrote, "when the time comes."[67] Then more miracles occurred. The trustees created the post of university librarian for Josiah, provided the family a rent-free house on campus, and gave Amelia the position of hospital matron.[68] Amelia and her daughters could ghost Josiah's job as university librarian, and with a place to live and a steady income Amelia began sending money to Willie for his medical education as Josiah had done. For the next four years Amelia nursed her "darling" and grieved over his declining health. He died at the age of sixty-six on May 15, 1883, Amelia kneeling beside his bed.[69]

Amelia lived another thirty years on the university campus in the house provided to Josiah when he resigned the university presidency in 1879. She now became the university librarian in name as well as fact and continued as hospital matron also. In 1886 a post office was authorized for the university, and Amelia assumed the position as postmistress. The student newspaper called her the "college mother" to the boys who "loved her and recognized her home as their own."[70] Amelia retired from the university on January 1, 1907, and continued living in the house that was now known as the Gorgas Home until her death on January 3, 1913. Her children lived in the same house until the last surviving child died in 1953.

This marriage was a genuine partnership of strong individuals. Each understood, trusted, and depended upon the strength of the other. Josiah usually led. Yet, Amelia instinctively knew when she must assume his role. After the war, necessity separated the couple on several occasions for lengthy periods, leaving Amelia with the responsibility for rearing five or six children and the burden of supervising the family's moves to another town for another job for her husband. Such circumstances forced her to grow strong, and her abilities were maximized as the couple coped with the changes that came at various stages of their lives. These repeated separations trained Amelia for the day when she became head of the household of six children and a disabled husband.

Although Civil War experiences dramatically changed many southern women, for the Gorgases it was the struggle to survive in the postwar years that most changed Amelia and the Gorgas marriage. She not only shouldered domestic responsibilities alone, but also she salvaged what she could at Brierfield and proposed to augment the family income at Sewanee and Tuscaloosa. Hardship made her grow, and Josiah encouraged her growth and took pride in it. After her death, one of her daughters remembered Amelia as the one upon whom the entire family leaned because Amelia knew better than anyone "just what to do & did it all with so much ease."[71]

Despite having immense responsibilities and hardships thrust upon her, Amelia never developed those attitudes that have been ascribed by Drew Faust to southern women who coped with hardships during the Civil War. Amelia did not face the post–Civil War or post-Reconstruction world with "self-doubt," "deep-seated bitterness," or a new conception of herself as a person "with needs, interests, and even rights, not just duties and obligations."[72] On the contrary, her son, Willie, said that Amelia "sacrificed" without consciousness that she was sacrificing.[73] She never complained about the hard circumstances of her life after the war, seeming "perfectly content wherever she was." Amelia "did her duty" and lived a most "useful life doing a woman's work in this world."[74]

In the 1850s, Josiah said that his life began with his marriage. For thirty years he never wavered in that belief. For him, Amelia was "Heavens last best gift." The "happiest periods" of his life, he wrote Amelia, were "our courtship—our wedding—& the birth of . . . our babies—what events! Talk of battles, politics, travels! A man has no experience worth mentioning until he loves the woman he weds, & has children born to him by her."[75]

PART TWO

UNION
MARRIAGES

SEVEN

A Marriage Tested by War
Ulysses and Julia Grant

JOHN Y. SIMON

Of the leading figures in the Civil War, Ulysses S. Grant had the happiest marriage. Julia Dent Grant wrote a sunny account of their life together.[1] Varina Davis, perhaps a more talented writer—although a less congenial wife—published a defensive memoir of her husband, Jefferson Davis. Although Mary Lincoln wrote nothing for publication, her side of the tortured Lincoln marriage has frequently engaged sympathetic biographers. The reclusive Mary Custis Lee remains an enigma to most Robert E. Lee scholars. Although a solid and affectionate marriage was not a prerequisite to Civil War achievement, notable benefits followed in Grant's case.[2]

Julia Dent, an eighteen-year-old schoolgirl, first met twenty-two-year-old Brevet Second Lieutenant Ulysses S. Grant in 1844 at the Dent family estate of White Haven in south St. Louis County. Born in St. Louis on January 26, 1826, Julia was raised at White Haven. She was the fifth child in a family that already had four boys. Three more girls followed, one of whom died in infancy.

Julia's father, Frederick Dent, was called "colonel" through wealth and social standing rather than military service. Born in Maryland in 1786, he had prospered as a St. Louis merchant and real estate speculator. He had acquired a country estate of nearly 1,000 acres, which originally supplemented his downtown residence. He gradually withdrew from business to enjoy country life and domestic pleasures, at some cost to his once considerable wealth. A Southerner by birth and inclination, he farmed White Haven with slaves and never doubted the propriety of the institution nor his opinions on any subject. Neighbors considered him indolent, irascible, and litigious.

Julia's mother, Ellen Bray Wrenshall Dent, born in England and raised in Pittsburgh, was educated in Philadelphia. Her father, an importer and Methodist preacher, established a strong religious and genteel tradition. She was remembered as cultured and quiet, perhaps uncomfortable in frontier society. From her father, Julia acquired assertiveness and from her mother, a persistent use of feminine wiles.

Julia remembered her girlhood as idyllic. Her father's pet, she had young slave girls as attendants. Her schooling began nearby at a log schoolhouse, which she recalled fondly. Required to learn "those dreadful roman numerals" or face punishment with a rod, she faltered in class but was given a reprieve by a kindly schoolmaster, John F. Long, who later became a close friend to both Grants.[3] At age ten, Julia was sent to a St. Louis boarding school, where she remained about seven years. She remembered her years there as filled with reading romantic novels while neglecting English grammar and multiplication tables. Noticeably cross-eyed and rarely considered beautiful, she was nonetheless a belle. Willful and charming, she captivated Lieutenant Grant.

Ulysses was born at Point Pleasant, Ohio, on April 27, 1822. His father, Jesse, was the son of a Revolutionary War veteran too fond of drink, whose many children scattered on the frontier after the death of his second wife, Jesse's mother. Jesse received assistance from his prosperous half-brother Peter and from kindly families that took him in as a bound boy, including the family of Owen Brown, father of abolitionist John Brown. Jesse eventually learned the tanner's trade and established himself in Point Pleasant, where he married the daughter of a nearby farmer. Hannah Simpson was an educated young woman from Philadelphia noted for her Methodist piety.

Young Ulysses, the oldest of six children, apparently had an ordinary boyhood in Georgetown, Ohio, where he grew up and attended school. The Grant home was across the street from the tannery, which Ulysses came to detest. He preferred farm work and anything involving horses, for which he seemed to possess a special aptitude. After Ulysses spent two terms at nearby academies, Jesse arranged his appointment to the United States Military Academy. Ulysses immediately said, "I won't go." Jesse responded that "he thought I would, *and I thought so too, if he did.*"[4] The unwilling cadet, who did not study "with avidity," enjoyed reading novels.[5] A natural talent for mathematics carried him to graduation in the middle of his class. This brought him a commission as brevet second lieutenant and assignment to Jefferson Barracks, then the largest military post in the United States. His West Point roommate, Frederick Dent, encouraged Ulysses to visit his parents at nearby White Haven. Ulysses enjoyed the company of two of Fred's brothers still living at home and two young sisters—Nellie, age fifteen, and Emma, eight or nine—as well as the hospitality of the Dent parents.

In February 1844, when Julia returned from a social season with the family of Colonel John O'Fallon in St. Louis, Ulysses and Julia met and soon found themselves in love without fully realizing the depth of their attraction. Orders in May sending Grant's regiment to Louisiana forced both to recognize the truth. Ulysses left with at least an informal engagement, not yet blessed with parental approval, something that Ulysses eventually wrung from Colonel Dent one year later, despite Dent's concern about whether his daughter would be happy as an officer's wife.

Neither of the young people shared Colonel Dent's apprehensions, and Ulysses hoped to leave active service soon for teaching. He had already corresponded with his mathematics teacher at West Point about returning there and eyed academic opportunities elsewhere. Military movements carried the regiment from Louisiana into Texas, and then interfered with Ulysses's teaching plans. As Grant's regiment became entangled in the preliminaries of the Mexican War, then the war itself, the young couple's separation was bridged solely through ardent correspondence.

Julia carefully saved Ulysses's letters. Although he treasured her letters, they have not survived. His letters attest to the strong bond between them, intensified by separation. After the war, twenty-six-year-old Ulysses hurried to St. Louis to marry twenty-two-year-old Julia. Their quiet wedding on August 22, 1848, at the Dent house in St. Louis was conducted in accordance with Methodist practice. All three groomsmen later fought for the Confederacy, including James Longstreet, Julia's cousin as well as Ulysses's friend. None of the Grant family attended, a portent of trouble to come.

Although Ulysses and Julia had many common bonds and were deeply in love, the similarities in their backgrounds came from their quiet Methodist mothers. Their fathers differed enough to presage trouble. Jesse Grant held strong antislavery views and was a Whig; Colonel Dent was an opinionated slaveholder and Democrat. Julia was too fond of her father to challenge him; Ulysses had experienced his father's authoritarian personality when forced to attend the military academy but respected his financial success. By the 1850s, a partner in two tanneries and several leather stores, Jesse Grant had a net worth of some $100,000, although his grandson remembered him as "at no time a liberal man."[6] Jesse Grant was probably wealthier than Frederick Dent, but the Dents lived as if they were rich, the Grants as if they were poor.

For four years, the young couple experienced the normal life of a young officer's family. Expecting an assignment at Detroit, the Grants found instead an unwelcome posting to Sackets Harbor, New York, a cold, dreary, lonely place to spend a winter. Nonetheless, they found enough society for comfort, enough privacy for bonding. Julia remembered that her husband once invited other officers home for dinner after church without informing her. She begged him to rescind the invitation until she could determine that her cook was sufficiently skilled. This he did, telling her later that his friends went without dinner that day. Later, they joined him in teasing Julia, pretending that they were afraid to enter the Grant home without her special permission.[7]

In spring 1849, the Grants went to Detroit, where they spent a pleasant year in a larger city with more society. Julia returned to St. Louis to give birth to Frederick Dent Grant on May 30, 1850. While she was gone, regimental headquarters moved to Sackets Harbor, where her husband found them a comfortable home.

The greatest trial of their marriage came with Ulysses's assignment to the Pacific Coast in 1852. Again pregnant, Julia and two-year-old Fred might not have survived the journey across the Isthmus of Panama, a nightmarish trek across fever-ridden swamps that cost the lives of many women and children who had accompanied the troops. Left behind for her safety, Julia gave birth to her second son, Ulysses S. Grant, Jr., on July 22, 1852, while staying with the Grant family in Ohio, so he was nick-named "Buckeye," later shortened to Buck. Assigned to Fort Vancouver, Ulysses tried to supplement his pay through various investment and farm-ing ventures to enable him to bring Julia and the two boys to Oregon Territory. Everything he tried turned out badly. As the months dragged by, Julia went to St. Louis to await fruitlessly a summons to the Pacific Coast. Reassigned to the dreary and isolated post of Fort Humboldt, Cal-ifornia, commanded by a martinet with whom he had quarreled years earlier, troubled by malaria and other ailments, and despairing of pro-motion beyond captain, Ulysses resigned in 1854 after two years of family separation, planning a new career as farmer on land given to Julia by her father.

In his *Memoirs,* Ulysses wrote little about the seven years between his resignation from the army and the start of the Civil War, and that chapter dealt chiefly with the politics of the period. His financially troubled ad-justment to life outside the army threatened his capacity to support his family. Whatever the economic stresses of the time, the marriage thrived. Shortly after Ulysses's return from the Pacific Coast and the happy reun-ion at White Haven, the family traveled to Bethel, where Jesse proposed to set his son up in the leather business in Galena, in the northwestern corner of Illinois, an attractive prospect before Jesse revealed his thrifty intention to have Julia and the children stay with the Grants or with her father while Ulysses learned the trade.[8] Indignantly declining the offer, Ulysses returned to Missouri, where he began to farm just in time to be overwhelmed by the Panic of 1857. At least once during her farm life Julia succumbed to despair about her future, and she hated the log house, Hardscrabble, that her husband had built himself. After Julia's mother died in early 1857, the Grants moved from Hardscrabble to the family mansion of White Haven, but eventually Ulysses had to move to St. Louis in search of employment.

In the spring of 1860, the Grants finally moved to Galena, where Ulysses worked with and for his two younger brothers. The Grants had a seven-room rented home. Fred and Ulysses, Jr., had been joined by Ellen (Nellie), born on July 4, 1855, and Jesse, Jr., born at Hardscrabble on February 6, 1858. Although Ulysses received only a small salary, Julia had a servant who did all the cooking. Ulysses disliked his employment and Julia missed St. Louis, but family life provided compensations.

The outbreak of war impelled Ulysses, conscious of his obligations as a trained soldier, to volunteer immediately. He presided over a Galena war meeting, accompanied a local company to Springfield, and found employment in the governor's office. Acquiring a commission proved more difficult, but after two months Grant became colonel of a regiment of Illinois Volunteers. Julia sent eleven-year-old Fred to join his father in Springfield, and Fred accompanied the march to the Illinois River and the railroad trip to Quincy, where his father put him on a steamboat headed toward home. Julia protested because Fred had been sent alone, although both Grants later recalled that Julia protested that Fred should have stayed with his father.[9]

During the summer of 1861, Grant received promotion to brigadier general and both Grants realized that the war would not end soon. Where should Julia and the children live? Galena did not seem like home to Julia without her husband, and Simpson, her favorite of Ulysses's brothers, slipped deeper into illness, dying in September. Ulysses considered sending Julia to live with his parents in Covington, Kentucky, but, remembering previous disagreeable talk about money, only as a paying guest. The Confederate sympathies of too many family and friends made St. Louis uncomfortable. Although Julia's eldest brother Fred fought for the Union, her father and brother John sympathized with the South. Julia's love for her Dent family was overshadowed by her devotion to Ulysses, whose political views became hers as well. In part because the Grants truly had no other home, the family reunited at Cairo, Illinois, in November 1861. Grant had recently fought his first battle at Belmont, Missouri, an inconclusive engagement; the family remained in Cairo until Grant left for Fort Henry, Tennessee, in early February. Julia remembered the superior quality of the mess and the companionship of Mrs. William S. Hillyer of St. Louis, whose husband served on Grant's staff.

Other women, including Mary Logan, wife of John A. Logan, by then an Illinois colonel, joined their husbands at Cairo. Located farther south than Richmond, Virginia, Cairo was nonetheless a city in a northern state. Grant's advance into the rebellious South presented new problems for officers' wives, especially those with young children. Few officers were as frequently accompanied by their families as Grant. Julia, who brought a welcome domesticity to her husband's army headquarters, also nursed Ulysses through devastating migraines.

Julia wept piteously as she left her husband at Cairo; being together meant much to both. Grant, however, now advancing southward, had wrung grudging approval from his commanding officer, General Henry W. Halleck, for a campaign to open the Tennessee River. They were separated during Grant's campaign against forts Henry and Donelson. When Confederate General Simon B. Buckner accepted Grant's terms of "immediate and unconditional surrender" at Fort Donelson on February 16, 1862, Grant suddenly became famous. He had achieved the first major Union victory of the war, had captured some fifteen thousand prisoners, and had won promotion to major general. Grant's aggressive and successful campaigning increased the jealousy of Halleck, whose efforts to displace Grant after his success at Fort Donelson failed largely because of an injury to General Charles F. Smith, Halleck's preference for commander of the Tennessee River expedition.

Restored to command, Grant was surprised by an attack on his troops at Shiloh. A few miles away, waiting to meet the army of General Don Carlos Buell, joining him for an attack on Corinth, Mississippi, Grant had not anticipated that the enemy might strike first. Hurrying to the field, Grant rallied his forces and created a line on the banks of the Tennessee River to protect his army. The next day, reinforced by a dilatory division of his own army and forces under Buell, Grant more than redeemed the losses of the first day and drove Confederates from the field. The bloodiest fighting of the Civil War to date brought Halleck to the field, reacting to Grant's victory as if it had been defeat, and northern newspapers attacked Grant's unpreparedness and alleged inebriation.

Not until Halleck left the western armies for Washington, D.C., in July 1862 did Grant emerge from a cloud of suspicion and neglect so debilitating that he considered resignation. Once free of Halleck, he sent for Julia, who joined him at Memphis in July and then accompanied him to Corinth. During the summer, all their children stayed with them. In the fall, after they were placed in school, Julia returned to army headquarters with Jesse, Jr., who was still too young for school.

Julia's frequent visits to her husband in the field fueled speculation that her presence kept Ulysses from drinking. Old army gossip that Ulysses had drunk himself out of the army in 1854 pursued him through the war, leading observers at headquarters to comment frequently on his sobriety. He did not drink when Julia was around but also abstained when she was not with him. Soon after the battle of Shiloh, Ulysses reassured Julia that he was "as sober as a deacon no matter what is said to the contrary."[10] Charging him with drunkenness at Cairo in late 1861, an anonymous writer demanded "pure men in habits and men without secesh wives with their own little slaves to wait upon them."[11] As Julia joined her husband whenever possible during the campaign that ended at Vicksburg, at least one slave given to her by her father was much in evidence through the early years of the war. When the Grants had moved from St. Louis to Galena in spring 1860, they left behind four young slaves. When Julia left St. Louis in 1861 to follow her husband, Jule, or "Black Julia," accompanied the Grants, especially to care for young Jesse. Julia gave little indication of consciousness of any incongruity, however much the scene startled others. In early 1864, concerned that an impending trip to Missouri might return her to slavery, Jule ran away. Residence in Mississippi should have freed her under the Emancipation Proclamation; in Missouri she could have become another Dred Scott.

Julia Grant, raised on a farm worked by slaves, owner of slaves in her own right, a southern belle by disposition and training, tolerant of the Confederate leanings of members of the Dent family, was nonetheless devoted to her husband. In Holly Springs, sharing a house with rebel sympathizers, her position was quite easily misunderstood. The young women of the family invited Julia to join them in the parlor to listen to rebel songs, and those who saw Julia out shopping with Jule made similar assumptions. Julia set the record straight: "I am the most loyal of the loyal," she explained, and to arguments about the constitutionality of secession she responded that she "did not know a thing about this dreadful Constitution."[12] Her belief in her husband and his cause was strong and unwavering.

Grant's overland campaign in Mississippi failed when Confederate General Earl Van Dorn raided the Union supply base at Holly Springs on December 20, 1862. Narrowly avoiding capture, Julia had left Holly Springs shortly before the raid. During the early months of 1863, as Grant attempted to reach Vicksburg from a base across the river in Louisiana, Julia remained in St. Louis, but she had joined him when Union gunboats and transports ran the Vicksburg batteries in April. She always remembered the exciting nighttime spectacle. When Grant crossed the river in late April to campaign on dry land, she returned home to St. Louis, but thirteen-year-old Fred, who had gone ashore by subterfuge, accompanied his father through the campaign that ended on July 4 with the capitulation of the Confederate citadel.[13] Although Fred recalled the campaign as an adventurous lark, he returned to St. Louis seriously ill.

Julia rejoined her husband in occupied Vicksburg. The Grants lived on the first floor of the Lum mansion; the family lived above. Julia did favors for the Lums (including interceding with her husband to revoke the banishment of a family friend) that eventually changed their attitudes toward the Union; she also made friends elsewhere in Vicksburg by intervening in cases that touched her tender heart. She had established a circle of friends before she left at the end of the summer of 1863 to make arrangements for her children's schooling. She later returned to Vicksburg to nurse her husband, seriously injured when his horse fell in New Orleans, and accompanied him as far as Louisville when he was called to take command at Chattanooga. After Grant's great victories in the battles at Chattanooga in late November, she joined Ulysses at headquarters in Nashville.

Julia soon hurried to St. Louis upon receiving word that Fred was gravely ill with dysentery and typhoid. In late January 1864, Ulysses was called to his son's bedside, uncertain whether he would arrive in time.[14] As it turned out, Fred had already begun to recover before Ulysses reached St. Louis. In the meantime, Julia's persistent problems with her eyes had reached a crisis, and she thought that a long-deferred operation to cure her strabismus might improve her appearance as the wife of the great soldier. When a surgeon told her that it was too late, Ulysses reassuringly reminded her that he had fallen in love with those same eyes.

Grant's growing prominence in the Civil War gave Julia greater responsibilities and prominence. Willingly or not, she began to represent her husband. St. Louis neighbors scrutinized her actions and conduct for clues to her husband's beliefs. Those who knew the southern sympathies of some of her Dent kinsmen expected some reflection of them. Although St. Louis held a substantial Unionist majority, Julia's prewar social circle represented the minority. Some of her St. Louis neighbors went so far as to assume the disloyalty of this southern slaveholder. Julia eventually found living in St. Louis uncomfortable.

Grant's own distaste for burgeoning public recognition of his military achievements encouraged shifting the spotlight of publicity and attention to his wife. Because of her troublesome eye problems in early 1864, Julia did not accompany her husband to Washington in March for the ceremony marking his promotion to lieutenant general and assignment as general in chief, commanding all the armies of the United States. Instead, Fred accompanied his father. At a crowded White House reception where Grant first met President Abraham Lincoln, Grant had to stand on a sofa to allow all to see him. At a quieter ceremony attended by cabinet officers the following day, Lincoln made a brief speech investing Grant with authority; Grant responded with an even briefer speech, written out in advance, delivered awkwardly, and omitting points that Lincoln had specifically requested for inclusion. After a visit to General George G. Meade's headquarters in Virginia, Lincoln invited Grant to a state dinner. Grant declined, complaining privately that he had enough of "this show business."[15]

Julia arrived in Washington later, after Grant had decided to accompany the Army of the Potomac on its overland campaign in Virginia. As General William T. Sherman traveled with the Grants from Nashville to Cincinnati, Julia asked Sherman's advice on Washington etiquette, an apt subject since Sherman had been raised by a politically prominent family and had a brother serving in the U.S. Senate. Sherman advised Julia to return all calls, something that she eventually found impossible. One day in Philadelphia gave Julia an opportunity to improve her wardrobe. After

Ulysses left Washington for the army, Julia attended her first White House reception escorted by Admiral David G. Farragut and two of her husband's staff officers. Both the president and Mary Lincoln graciously welcomed Julia, who displayed impressive self-assurance and eluded flattering efforts by strangers to place her under obligation. Standing by Farragut's side, receiving the welcome of the most prominent leaders in wartime Washington, Julia gave every indication of relishing the attention that her husband abhorred. Asked if she thought her husband would capture Richmond, Julia answered that he would: *"Mr. Grant always was a very obstinate man."*[16]

Before rejoining her children in St. Louis, Julia went to New York City as the guest of the Hillyers. Again she enjoyed meeting "many distinguished people."[17] Daily telegrams of war news received from Secretary of War Edwin M. Stanton reflected her new prominence. She also attended the great Sanitary Fair, an event organized to raise money for charitable work in military hospitals. For each dollar donation, fair-goers received one vote for a handsome jeweled sword for presentation to the most popular general. The two leading contenders were Grant and General George B. McClellan, the first commander of the Army of the Potomac, removed in November 1862, and the inevitable Democratic opponent of Lincoln in the presidential election of 1864. Julia cast her vote for McClellan on grounds of "good taste" and "etiquette."[18]

Newspaper attention given to Julia's gallant gesture distressed her husband, less because the vote went to McClellan than because the story was widely reported.[19] Like it or not, Julia had acquired some of the celebrity of her husband and enjoyed the spotlight. Grant won the sword but still regretted that Julia's name had been involved. Julia contentedly dawdled in New York, later claiming that she awaited a suitable escort to St. Louis. Nonetheless, she had previously traveled without one and was aware that her children were in the capable hands of her relative, Louisa Boggs.

As the spring campaign of 1864 opened, Ulysses wrote Julia that he did not "know exactly the day when I will start or whether Lee will come here before I am ready to move. Would not tell you if I did know."[20] Through much of the grim fighting that took such a terrifying toll on the Union army and on Grant himself, the lighthearted relationship between Grant and his family provided some measure of relief. Ulysses planned to bring Julia to his army, first intending that she stay at nearby Fort Monroe with Sarah Butler, wife of General Benjamin F. Butler. During the summer, the entire family joined Grant at City Point. Staff officer Horace Porter once came upon Ulysses flushed by exertion after wrestling with his boys.[21] Determined that his children receive an education, Ulysses looked that fall toward finding a home in Philadelphia before discovering that nearby Quaker-dominated Burlington, New Jersey, offered even better prospects. Julia put the three older children in school, then, with Jesse, rejoined her husband at City Point. Ulysses lived in a small cabin built by engineers in the shadow of Hopewell Manor, an elegant mansion that he declined to commandeer. Although the cabin contained few comforts, neither Grant complained. They were together. "I am snugly nestled away in my husbands Log cabin Head quarters," wrote Julia. "I enjoy being here, have such long talks with my husband, when all have retired."[22]

As a professional soldier, Grant shared the conservatism of the old army. Fifteen years in the army dating from admission to West Point had provided him with close friends among rebel commanders. Marriage into a family of border state slaveholders strengthened his southern ties, notably those to Longstreet. A prewar St. Louis slaveholder, Grant had voted in only one presidential election, casting a ballot for Democrat James Buchanan. Although famed for demanding "unconditional surrender," he had not yet been tested by Confederate offers to negotiate.

At the end of January 1865, Confederate emissaries arrived at City Point requesting permission to visit Washington to confer with Lincoln about terminating the "existing War."[23] Lincoln sent a war department official to insist that no conference could take place unless the commissioners discussed a "common country." By welcoming and dining with the commissioners, Grant had already exceeded what Lincoln thought proper. To underscore that point, Lincoln ordered Grant to allow "nothing which is transpiring, change, hinder, or delay your Military movements, or plans."[24]

In a telegram to Stanton, Grant forced Lincoln's hand by asserting that the commissioners had shown him "that their intentions are good and their desire sincere to restore peace and Union."[25] "Induced by a dispatch of Gen. Grant," Lincoln wired Secretary of State William H. Seward, "I Join you at Fort-Monroe so soon as I can come."[26] Grant was not invited to the unproductive Hampton Roads conference where Lincoln insisted upon reunion and emancipation. Jefferson Davis had empowered his emissaries to concede neither but only to promote an unrealistic alternative, first suggested by Lincoln's adviser Francis P. Blair, Sr., to unite North and South in an expedition to drive the French from Mexico. Lincoln, who gained nothing by conferring, reported to Congress that he would not have gone without Grant's urging.

Grant was soon drawn into one of the most bizarre episodes of the war. Confederate commissioners at City Point had been favorably impressed by Grant's friendliness and especially that of Julia, who hoped that Confederates might be induced to release her brother John Dent, held prisoner in the South despite his ardent rebel sympathies. Grant refused to exchange any soldier for his civilian brother-in-law, especially since Dent had foolishly thought that his outspoken support of the Confederacy gave him license to travel freely in the South. Remembering Mrs. Grant's cordiality, though perhaps forgetting its cause, Julia's cousin Longstreet proposed to Union General Edward O. C. Ord that Louise Longstreet and

Julia Grant, old friends from St. Louis, exchange social visits as a first step toward conversations between officers of both sides that might end with Grant and Lee suspending hostilities to negotiate. "How enchanting, how thrilling!" exclaimed Julia; "Do say I may go." Grant dismissed that proposal as "simply absurd."[27]

Conversations between Ord and Longstreet ostensibly concerning political prisoners wandered toward peace negotiations. Ord reported that Longstreet had asserted that Lee believed the southern cause to be hopeless although Davis insisted on continuing the war. Ord suggested that Lee threaten to resign to force Davis to negotiate.[28] Lee requested a meeting with Grant, who forwarded the message to Washington and received an unequivocal reply from Stanton that was actually penned by Lincoln himself. "The President directs me to say to you that he wishes you to have no conference with Gen Lee unless it be for the capitulation of Lees army, or on solely minor and purely military matters He instructs me to say that you are not to decide, discuss, or confer upon any political question: such questions the President holds in his own hands; and will submit them to no military conferences or conventions—mean time you are to press to the utmost, your military advantages."[29] Even more vigorously than Grant, Lincoln pushed toward what Confederates considered to be unconditional surrender. Julia's presence at headquarters may have strengthened Lincoln's determination to limit Grant's peacemaking authority.

As the war neared its end, Grant appointed Lincoln's son Robert to serve on his staff. Robert had previously attended Harvard College and remained in its law school. Well aware of the precarious nature of Mary Lincoln's mental health after the death of Willie in 1862, the president acquiesced in protecting Robert from danger. Finally, he requested Grant to appoint Robert to a staff position, something Grant agreed to do, not without a bit of grumbling, but did accede to Robert's request to attend his father's second inauguration.[30] Once at Grant's headquarters, Robert had little to do more essential than escorting his parents. At Julia's suggestion, Ulysses invited the Lincolns to visit City Point.

Mary Lincoln's behavior during this visit tested Julia. "How dare you be seated until I invite you," Mary said.[31] Worse followed when the two women, escorted by Grant's staff officer Adam Badeau, rode together in an ambulance to witness a review of the Army of the Potomac. Mary learned from Badeau that while other women were sent away from the army when campaigning loomed, the wife of General Charles Griffin had received special permission from Lincoln to remain. Mary exploded. "Do you mean to say that she saw the President alone? Do you know that I never allow the President to see any woman alone?" Julia later agreed with Badeau that neither would ever mention the dreadful episode again.[32] The next day, the same party started off for a review of the Army of the James, joined by Horace Porter, another staff officer brought along by Badeau for support. Mary soon discovered that Mary Ord, wife of General Ord, commanding that army, was on horseback by the side of President Lincoln. Mary Lincoln behaved even more irrationally and hatefully than the day before, finally turning on Julia, who had tried to mollify her. "I suppose you think you'll get to the White House yourself, don't you?" Meeting Mrs. Ord at the review, Mary brought her to tears through insults and refused to cease her abuse. Even at dinner she kept after the poor woman, demanding that Lincoln remove General Ord from command.[33] Julia learned to avoid Mary Lincoln.

On March 29, 1865, Grant left City Point for what he planned as the final campaign against Lee. Ulysses advised Julia to move to the dispatch boat anchored in front of their City Point cabin. She did so, along with the wife of General John A. Rawlins, Grant's principal staff officer. Mary Emma Hurlbut, a Connecticut governess stranded in Mississippi by the war, had married the widower Rawlins after the fall of Vicksburg, and Julia had been a delighted witness to their courtship. When Julia invited Mrs. Rawlins to come with her to City Point in November 1864, Rawlins raised a flurry of objections, but Julia eventually got her way.[34] Rejoicing in the success of Union arms, the two women now anxiously awaited the return of their husbands. One general sent Julia a bouquet picked in the gardens of Petersburg immediately after its occupation on April 2.

On April 7, the day Grant first asked Lee to surrender, the two women received a telegram from Ulysses telling them to return home. Grant expected to be absent ten or twelve days longer, to go to Danville, and to unite with Sherman, who was then in North Carolina, in crushing the remnants of the rebel forces. Julia proudly noted on the telegram that she "did not obey" but remained at City Point and eventually returned to Washington escorted by victorious generals.[35]

While Grant cornered Lee, Julia visited the Lincolns on the *River Queen*. She understood that Mary Lincoln did not welcome her company. Somewhat miffed that Lincoln had visited Richmond without her, Julia made her own visit to the Confederate capital, weeping when she reflected on the human cost of war. When she returned, she learned that the Lincolns, about to return to Washington, had not invited her to a final reception on board their boat. Julia decided to embark upon a James River cruise with her friends, took along a band, and had it play "Now You'll Remember Me" as her boat passed the *River Queen*. Julia had acquired a sense of social standing that eclipsed that of her husband.

Soon afterward, a telegraph operator delivered to Julia the news of Lee's surrender on April 9 before sending the telegram to Washington. When Ulysses returned, he rejected the idea of visiting Richmond, although Julia joined the chorus of those urging a triumphal entry. Grant had decided to return to Washington promptly to end the war. As always, Grant focused firmly on the business of war, leaving ceremony to others.

Back in Washington, however, even Grant could not evade the rejoicing over Lee's surrender. On April 13, all Washington was ablaze with lights to celebrate the triumph. Mary Lincoln had invited Grant to escort her to view the spectacle. Intending to accompany Secretary Stanton and his wife to view the illuminated public buildings, Julia insisted that her husband escort her. This he did, joining Mary Lincoln later, and remembering her bitterness when crowds cheered Grant instead of her husband.

Under the circumstances, Julia was determined to reject the theater invitation from the Lincolns for the following evening. An overdue visit to the children in Burlington served as an effective excuse as well as a legitimate reason for absence. Julia believed that the conspirators followed her to lunch that day and that John Wilkes Booth himself trailed the Grants to the railroad station. The Grants reached Philadelphia before learning of events at Ford's Theatre; Ulysses then returned to Washington, leaving Julia in the comparative safety of Burlington. In the aftermath of the assassination, none could predict the extent of the conspiracy. Julia believed that a locked railroad car door had foiled a plan to kill Grant on the train traveling to Philadelphia.[36] For his part, Grant regretted his absence from the theater, where he might have stopped Booth.

With Lincoln's tragic death, Grant became the North's single greatest living Civil War hero. Wherever he traveled crowds gathered to honor the victor. Ulysses's innate modesty and Julia's sense of propriety allowed the Grants to move unscathed through a tempest of adulation.

The Grants had come a long way from Galena. Then a couple in modest financial circumstances, still dependent upon Ulysses's father and younger brothers for employment, exiled by circumstance from the Missouri farm life that both preferred, their rise to prominence had been meteoric. Observers then and now have been quicker to marvel at this ascent than the Grants themselves. Julia had always believed that her husband possessed extraordinary qualities that eventually others would discern. Two years of prewar separation had prepared her to live independently during the Civil War. Her own social skills had been acquired in sophisticated St. Louis rather than some backwoods village. She was better prepared than her husband for the world of celebrity and leadership into which both were now thrust.

During the war, Ulysses wrote scores of lengthy letters to Julia, almost all closing with "kisses" for her and the children. Once after Julia visited military hospitals in Nashville and returned with petitions for discharges, her husband reminded her that he dealt with such matters daily. "I want and need a little rest and sunshine."[37] She needed no further reminder. Through victories and defeats in battle, vicissitudes of command, burdens of administration, and crushing responsibilities, Ulysses's love for Julia provided his core of strength and stability.

Grant continued to command the armies during the administration of Andrew Johnson. Detesting the political intrigue of Washington, Ulysses first attempted to commute from Philadelphia. Finding this impractical, the Grants moved to Washington, living comfortably in a house purchased for them by wealthy admirers.

Grant became entangled in the turmoil he had sought to avoid. He found himself trapped when Johnson pushed a policy of rapid Reconstruction without fundamental southern changes and congressional Republicans insisted on protection of the civil rights of freedmen. Johnson tried to harness to his cause Grant's immense popularity through having him replace Secretary of War Stanton during a congressional recess. When Congress reconvened and insisted upon Stanton's return, Grant resigned, touching off an acrimonious quarrel with Johnson that led to the impeachment trial, and Grant in turn became the inevitable Republican candidate for president in 1868.

When the Grants moved into the White House in 1869, Julia initially relied on Julia Fish, wife of Secretary of State Hamilton Fish, for guidance in the duties of first lady. Neither Mary Lincoln nor Eliza Johnson, a reclusive invalid, had provided effective role models. Julia plunged into refurbishing the White House; she replaced carpets and reupholstered furniture, hired an excellent chef, and served elegant state dinners.

As in wartime, Julia played little role in executive matters. Her sphere was, instead, personal and domestic. Unlike wartime, the Grants were rarely separated, and both treasured summertimes away from steamy Washington at their cottage in Long Branch, New Jersey, amid their closest friends.

When the Civil War ended, the Grants had four school-age children. Fred left for West Point in 1866, Buck for Harvard in 1870, and Nellie for Miss Porter's School in Farmington, Connecticut. Both boys graduated, but Nellie returned almost immediately, preferring Washington society to education. When not quite nineteen, Nellie married Algernon Sartoris in 1874, a much publicized wedding at which her father was tearful. Sartoris was a dashing Englishman and nephew to abolitionist and actress Fannie Kemble, but the marriage proved a mistake and eventually ended in divorce. The same year as Nellie's wedding, Jesse entered Cornell University, but Buck soon returned home to serve as his father's secretary.

The Grants also brought Colonel Dent to live at the White House. Before his death in 1873, he enjoyed sharing outspoken and outrageous political opinions with Republican visitors, to the delight of both Grants. When Jesse Grant visited Washington, he stayed in hotels, and Hannah never visited. President Grant appointed so many relatives to office that nepotism charges arose. The preponderance were, however, Dents rather than Grants.

Ulysses never wanted to be president and served two terms through a sense of duty and responsibility. On the other hand, Julia loved her years in the White House and made it a pleasant home for her family. Even more delightful were the two-and-one-half years following, when the

Jefferson Davis in a portrait by
George Lethbridge Saunders, 1849.
*National Portrait Gallery, Smithsonian
Institution, Washington, D.C.; gift of
Joel A.H. Webb and Varina Webb Stuart.*

Varina Howell Davis in a John
Wood Dodge portrait, 1849.
*National Portrait Gallery, Smithsonian
Institution, Washington, D.C.;
gift of Varina Webb Stewart.*

Varina Davis and her
daughter Winnie, after
the Civil War.
The University of Kentucky.

Robert E. Lee as a
young officer, in a portrait
painted by William West,
circa 1838.
*Courtesy of the Virginia Histori-
cal Society, Richmond, Virginia.*

Mary Custis Lee some
seven years after her
marriage to Robert E.
Lee, in a portrait by
William West.
*Courtesy of Stratford Hall,
Stratford, Virginia.*

General Thomas "Stonewall"
Jackson in 1857.
*Courtesy of the Stonewall Jackson
Foundation, Lexington, Virginia.*

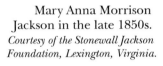

Mary Anna Morrison
Jackson in the late 1850s.
*Courtesy of the Stonewall Jackson
Foundation, Lexington, Virginia.*

Photograph of miniature in
ivory of George and LaSalle
Corbell Pickett probably done
in 1863, about the time of their
wartime marriage.
*The Museum of the Confederacy,
Richmond, Virginia.*

Confederate Lt. General Richard S. Ewell.
Courtesy of Donald C. Pfanz.

Lizinka Campbell Brown Ewell.
Courtesy of Donald C. Pfanz.

Northerner Josiah Gorgas
served as the Confederacy's
Chief of the Ordnance Bureau.
*Courtesy of Hoole Special Collections,
University of Alabama, Tuscaloosa, Alabama.*

Amelia Gayle Gorgas and her eldest son, William
Crawford Gorgas, around 1911 in Tuscaloosa, Alabama.
Courtesy of Hoole Special Collections, University of Alabama, Tuscaloosa, Alabama.

In this rare photograph, Lt.
General Ulysses S. Grant stands
beside his wife, Julia, who poses
sideways to hide her "lazy eye"
or strabismus.
James A. Bultema—Grant Collection.

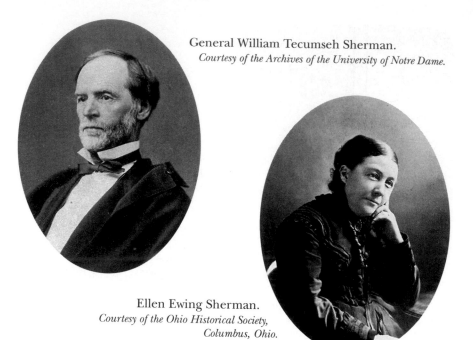

General William Tecumseh Sherman.
Courtesy of the Archives of the University of Notre Dame.

Ellen Ewing Sherman.
Courtesy of the Ohio Historical Society,
Columbus, Ohio.

General Lawrence Chamberlain in 1862.
Courtesy of the Pejepscot Historical Society.

Fannie Chamberlain in 1862.
Courtesy of the Pejepscot Historical Society.

Libbie and Armstrong Custer
and their black servant Eliza,
photographed on April 12, 1865,
just three days after the Confederate
surrender at Appomattox.
*Courtesy of the Little Bighorn Battlefield
National Monument.*

John Charles Frémont,
painted in his Civil War uniform
in 1867 by Giuseppi Fagnani.
*Missouri Historical Society,
St. Louis, Missouri.*

Jessie Benton Frémont in 1856, the
same year her husband made his
unsuccessful bid for the presidency.
*National Portrait Gallery, Smithsonian
Institution, Washington, D.C.*

Navy Lieutenant S. Phillips Lee,
in a Thomas Sully portrait painted
one year after his marriage.
Courtesy of the Blair Lee Family.

Elizabeth Blair Lee, in a
1844 portrait also painted
by Thomas Sully.
Courtesy of the Blair Lee Family.

Grants traveled leisurely around the world. After they returned, supporters failed in an 1880 attempt to nominate Grant for a third term. The Grants settled in New York City, where Ulysses became a silent partner in Buck's investment firm of Grant and Ward, which collapsed in 1884 through the swindles of Ferdinand Ward. Impoverished and suffering from cancer, Ulysses began to write memoirs to support his family, completing that heroic task shortly before his death in 1885. The grieving widow was unable to attend the funeral.

A few years after Ulysses's death, Julia began to write her own memoirs, perhaps initially intending only to provide her children and descendants with a tribute to her beloved Ulysses. Accepting conventions of the day, she emphasized her husband's strength and wisdom and her own frailty and inadequacy. Although she repaid some scores with her husband's enemies, her memoirs generally present an affectionate and cheerful portrait of the life of both Grants. Civil War chapters provide delightful accounts of her naiveté in strategy and politics.

She gave herself less credit than she deserved. For four years she had balanced the needs of four young children with those of her husband. A resident of Galena for only one year before war began, she had no local network of family and friends to assist her with the children or other household responsibilities. Rebel sympathies of too many St. Louis friends and neighbors hindered her from using her old home as a base. Tensions in the Grant family pervaded Covington. Julia had no true home except with her husband. Otherwise she moved from place to place, sometimes boarding with distant relatives or strangers. With her husband's guidance, she assumed responsibility for the children's health and education, and the management of the family finances. Simultaneously, she provided Ulysses with relief from the overwhelming cares and responsibilities of command. Her children and her husband needed the affectionate health care that only she could provide. The Grants together prevailed during the Civil War in ways creditable to both. A love story that began at White Haven endured until 1902, when they lay together in Grant's Tomb.

EIGHT

General and Mrs. William T. Sherman, a Contentious Union

JOHN F. MARSZALEK

It was 1829. The five-year-old girl watched with curiosity as her father walked along the street and up the hill to their large white house, holding the hand of her nine-year-old friend. Both man and boy looked stern, and the girl knew why. Her friend's father had recently died, his brothers and sisters were departing to other friends and relatives, and he was coming to live with them, to become part of their family. Ellen Boyle Ewing was witness to what would prove to be a major event in her and her friend's life. Tecumseh Sherman, Cump as everyone called him, was becoming a Ewing. Ellen was now his foster sister, but in the future, she would become his wife. Later, however, all she could remember about that day was, "I peeped at him with great interest."[1]

At the time of his death, Charles Sherman, Cump's father, had been a judge of the Ohio Supreme Court, but a debt incurred earlier while he was a federal internal revenue collector had forestalled any chances of his financial success. He could have declared bankruptcy, but he insisted on trying to pay back everything. Consequently, when he died, he was nearly penniless. This poverty was the reason for the breakup of the family and Cump's move to the house on the hill. While he became a Ewing, his mother continued living in the house that, until now, had been his home. She did not die until the 1850s, and he saw her regularly. It was all very strange to the young boy.[2]

Thomas Ewing was one of the area's leading attorneys. He was to become a United States senator, the nation's first secretary of the interior, and a leader in the Whig party. Nine-year-old Cump Sherman could not have understood all this at the time, but in later years he came to recognize what an impressive person his foster father was. Unfortunately, this recognition made him feel increasingly insecure, particularly when he compared his father's failure to Thomas Ewing's ever-growing success. At the same time, Ellen idolized her father beyond usual daughterly affection.[3]

Other aspects of life in the Ewing household proved equally disconcerting to the young boy. The Ewings absorbed Cump fully into their household of seven children (four of their own and three relatives). Yet, he always felt like an outsider. Soon after the switch of houses and families, Cump also changed religions, from Presbyterian to Catholic. Maria Boyle Ewing, his foster mother, was a staunch Catholic and insisted that he be baptized into the family's Catholicism as a precondition for his entry into their home. When a priest came to their hometown of Lancaster, Ohio, for his monthly visit, he baptized the young Tecumseh, adding the Christian name, William. (The day was allegedly the feast day of St. William.) William Tecumseh Sherman had lost his father, his family, his home, his religion, and even his name. He understandingly felt unsure about his entry into the Ewing family, and this uncertainty was to influence him and his later marriage to Thomas Ewing's favorite daughter. Ellen, meanwhile, watched the ceremony with religious awe.[4]

Lancaster, Ohio, situated on the Hocking River in the southeastern part of the state, had been settled in 1800 as a result of the construction of the nearby Zane's Trace. By the time Cump and Ellen were born, he in 1820 and she in 1824, Lancaster had a population of about a thousand people. It contained a courthouse, a jail, a bank, two newspapers, and a variety of merchants and mechanics. Stage coaches regularly arrived, bringing mail and people and providing a link to the outside world. Lancaster was a small town, but its favorable location gave it closer contact to the rest of the nation than most frontier communities enjoyed.[5]

In 1829, the nine-year-old Cump and five-year-old Ellen lived a comfortable existence in this prosperous community. They seemed to have the usual brother-sister relationship while they were growing up. Cump and Phil Ewing were only a year apart, so they were inseparable, but Ellen tagged along, too, not always with her two brothers' approval. In school, she and Cump were both good students, and Cump helped her whenever she needed tutoring, especially with her arithmetic. She enjoyed the attention and began looking up to him, as she later said, as her "protector,"[6] reflecting contemporary society's view of the relationship of the allegedly weak woman and the powerful male. Her attachment to her father also grew ever stronger, however, a fact that significantly limited Cump's status as protective male and helped fuel his insecurity.

When they reached their teenage years, Cump and Ellen went their separate ways. In 1836, through Thomas Ewing's influence, Cump entered the United States Military Academy at West Point, while Ellen began attending a Catholic school for girls in nearby Somerset, Ohio. She immediately became his most faithful correspondent, their four-year age difference melting over the distance and in the similarity of their maturation. He told her about cadet life at West Point. She kept him informed on the latest happenings in Lancaster and at her school. They did not see each other again until his summer furlough in 1838 when he was eighteen years old and she fourteen. He was impressed enough with what he saw to send her an invitation to a cadet ball. She was unable to attend, but in May 1839 when Cump thought there was a possibility of her visiting West Point, he wrote her an exuberant letter, "delighted with the probability of your coming here during the coming summer." Once again, Ellen was unable to visit him. She was accompanying her father to Washington for early entry into Georgetown's Visitation Convent school.[7]

After Cump's graduation from the military academy in 1840, he returned to Lancaster on furlough, and Ellen accompanied her senator father home from Washington. The highlight of that summer was a formal party that Ellen organized. Cump, in his new U.S. Army uniform, proved to be the hit of the evening when he drove an invading bat out the front door. Partygoers laughed at "General Sherman's first battle," and Ellen joined in the relieved hilarity, no doubt impressed at her foster brother's quick action.[8]

At the end of the summer, Ellen returned to Washington to complete her education. Cump was assigned to Florida to fight in the Seminole Wars, then to reopen Fort Morgan in Mobile, Alabama, and serve garrison duty in Charleston harbor's Fort Moultrie. Ellen went home to Lancaster and to a life of ease.

Throughout this period, Ellen and Cump maintained their regular and increasingly personal correspondence. Ellen acted as family scribe but expressed her own opinions as well. She put increasing pressure on Cump to quit the army and undertake a civilian occupation; he resisted. At the same time, she pointedly asked him about his religious practices. Cump admitted that since his departure from the Ewing home and its regularized religious ceremonies, he had practiced no religion at all. It was obvious that he no more planned to become a practicing Catholic than he planned to leave the army. Ellen was clearly unhappy at his attitude, but Cump was unmoved. Their correspondence continued unabated anyway.[9]

It was during his 1843 furlough to Lancaster that matters took a serious turn. The two fell in love. How this happened is uncertain because Cump and Ellen never discussed it in their otherwise full correspondence. They had, after all, lived together as brother and sister. They had, however, grown from childhood to adulthood apart from one another. On their few brief occasions together, they were two strangers who knew each other only from dried ink on letter paper.

Perhaps, however, there was more to it. Ellen never seriously considered anyone else, and Cump, falling in love with Ellen and making plans to marry her, became a son-in-law to Thomas Ewing, a far more acceptable role than that of ward. Cump and Ellen accepted marriage as simply a matter of course and proceeded toward it without much thought. Ellen, however, hoped that Cump would become a practicing Catholic, if not before then certainly after their marriage.[10] She was determined, too, that he become a civilian and find employment with her father in Ohio.

Ellen and Cump knew that they could not marry until Cump's career and finances permitted it. He returned in 1844 to Fort Moultrie, and she remained in her father's home in Lancaster. Their relationship depended once more on the mails. They had serious disagreements that needed resolution, and they struggled with them from their distant writing desks. Now that she was engaged to him, Ellen pushed harder than ever for Cump to resign his army commission and return to a civilian occupation in their hometown. At the same time she continued to insist that he become a practicing Catholic. How else could he protect her against the anti-Catholicism that was so prevalent in the world? "When you become my protector," she wrote, using that most significant word again, "how can you be sincere in your defense unless you *have* proved and *can* prove the truth of that which I claim to be true, pure and holy?" Cump continued to refuse to resign his commission or to practice Catholicism. He hurried home in early 1845 to try to resolve their disagreement. The reunion was a disaster. She continued to insist on a civilian profession, Catholicism, and the city of Lancaster, and he continued to refuse to consider any of it. In the process, Lancaster came to represent the whole complex of disagreements. Ellen saw the city as home, family, and religion; Cump saw it as continued dependence on Thomas Ewing. He could not budge or he would never feel independent of the revered father of his bride to be. The couple decided finally to put matters aside. They silently agreed to disagree—a position they were to maintain throughout their married life together.[11]

The nuptials of Ellen and Cump slipped further into the future when Cump received orders to sail for California that late June 1846. He knew that he had to get into the Mexican War if he hoped to have any career in the army. At the same time, he did not want to leave Ellen. He came close to tears "at the thought of the trouble my wayward life has already given you. . . . You will think of me will you not?" he beseeched Ellen in a farewell letter.[12]

For the next four years, Cump never saw battle against the Mexicans, but he had to deal with obstreperous gold miners and the rising inflation that resulted from their discoveries. Mail service was excruciatingly slow, letters between Cump and Ellen taking six months to a year to travel the distance between them. Ellen, waiting and waiting for Cump to return, suffered from harsh headaches, recurring boils, and gynecological problems. Her pessimistic letters about her health kept Cump continually on edge. At the same time, he developed depression over his inability to participate in the war, worried that his army career was doomed. The stress he felt manifested itself in the worst kind of asthma attacks. Ellen, upset at his reports of ill-health, stoically offered him encouragement. When she wrote him, anxious over her own health problems, that he find another potential wife because she was too unwell for marriage, he roused himself to disagree in terms that demonstrated his affection for her: "My love for you has never abated, never wavered in the least and upon it you may constantly rely." Cump looked to Ellen as his anchor, the person he could always depend on and reach out to, even if it was only through the mails. Ellen saw him as the only man in her life. Theirs was a relationship less of romance and more of mutual dependence.[13]

Finally, after almost giving up hope, Cump received orders to return to the East, arriving in New York in late January 1850 to deliver dispatches to Winfield Scott, the army's commanding general. He rushed to Washington and surprised Ellen who was living there with her family, Thomas Ewing serving as secretary of the interior. Plans for marriage followed quickly, and the May 1 ceremony was one of the major Washington social events of the year; President Zachary Taylor and his cabinet were among the three hundred distinguished guests. Ellen carried a silver bouquet holder given her by Henry Clay, and Cump's army friends were present in large numbers. Like him, they each wore a full dress uniform. The twenty-six-year-old bride was beautiful and the thirty-year-old groom handsome, but beneath it all, the old problems of his occupation, religious beliefs, and hometown resentment remained. The couple's differences were evident in the wedding itself: although the Jesuit priest-president of Georgetown University officiated at the evening ceremony, it did not take place in a church. Cump's lack of Catholic standing prevented a church wedding. Ellen was disappointed, but Cump said nothing. The popping of champagne corks exemplified the festive nature of the event and camouflaged any discomfort over religion.[14]

Cump and Ellen took an extended honeymoon trip, ending in a month-long stay in Lancaster. There the Ewings pressured him to become manager of the family saltworks in nearby Chauncey, Ohio, so he and Ellen could live in Lancaster. Cump hoped for autonomy, but his family pushed him toward continued dependence. Ellen felt drawn to fulfill her parents' wishes, yet she wanted to be a loving mate to her husband, too. Marriage had hardly solved Cump and Ellen's differences.[15]

This dichotomy of feeling manifested itself immediately and often after that. Cump remained in the army and in the fall of 1850, received orders to St. Louis. Ellen, however, remained behind in Lancaster to await the birth of the first Sherman child. Cump's letters that fall and spring were filled with loneliness and hurt. He let it be known to Ellen that once she had delivered their child, he expected her to join him and to follow him wherever his army career took him. He wanted her to be a loyal wife and adopt her proper role as helpmate, as other women of the age did. She remained noncommittal to her husband's demands, still drawn to her father and family: "I fear I shall be terribly homesick," she told a brother. After giving birth on January 28, 1851, to a girl the new parents named after Ellen's mother, but quickly came to call Minnie, Ellen finally joined Cump in March. She came reluctantly, sadly watching Lancaster fade into the distance as she left it.[16]

For the next year, Cump, Ellen, and Minnie lived together as a family in St. Louis. They seemed happy, but Cump maintained a strange distance from the child, frequently insisting, for example, that she was only "like a thousand other babies," although relatives maintained that she was somehow special. Cump seemed unwilling to commit his affections to this new daughter, perhaps fearing that her mother might, any day, decide to return to Thomas Ewing's home in Lancaster and leave him once more alone in St. Louis. Ellen's desire to be near her parents remained strong, and it adversely affected her marriage.[17]

During 1852, Ellen returned to Lancaster to spend the summer, and Cump's depression and asthma returned. He felt the Ewings stood between him and Ellen, but he found it difficult to express his frustration directly to Thomas Ewing, the man to whom he owed so much. Instead, he directed his unhappiness toward Lancaster, that city continuing to represent all that bothered him about his relationship with his wife. "I have good reasons to be jealous of a place that virtually robs me of my family and I cannot help feeling sometimes a degree of dislike for that very reason to the name of Lancaster." For her part, Ellen could not understand how her husband could feel this way.[18]

Cump was transferred to New Orleans in October 1852. Once again he traveled alone because Ellen was in Lancaster preparing to deliver their second daughter on November 17, 1852. This girl was named Mary Elizabeth (Lizzie) after Cump's recently deceased mother, and she, Ellen, and Minnie arrived in New Orleans in December. With the family growing larger, Ellen continued to pressure Cump to leave the army for a civilian profession—Thomas Ewing's saltworks near Lancaster. Once again Cump refused. Nevertheless he worried about his finances, concerned that he was not making enough money to support his family, and remembering with fright his father's death and the family's subsequent problems. When in February 1853 a former army friend from California days, Henry S. Turner, offered him the job of managing a California branch of a St. Louis bank, Cump accepted and resigned his army commission.[19]

When Cump announced his decision to go west, the Ewings urged him yet again to come back to Lancaster and join the family business interests, the saltworks. He refused once more, and then they protested the idea of Ellen going with him. As a compromise, they made the suggestion that little Minnie be left behind with her grandparents. Ellen readily agreed to this arrangement, convincing a reluctant Cump to go along with the idea. Cump, Ellen, and Lizzie traveled to California, but Minnie remained behind in Lancaster. Cump wrote his father-in-law: "I think I have ever shown a disposition in all things to conform to your wishes and now assert my continued wish to do so." Cump was unable to break the bond that held him and Ellen to Thomas Ewing.[20]

Upon her arrival in California in late October 1853, a homesick Ellen complained about the area, their house, and seemingly everything else associated with her life there. "This is El Dorado—the promised land," she complained. "I would rather live in Granny Walters cabin [in Lancaster] than live here in any kind of style." Cump took a completely opposite position. "I would rather be at the head of the bank in San Francisco, a position I obtained by my own efforts, than to occupy any place open to me in Ohio." He attempted to make a new life for himself and his family in California, while his wife wistfully looked back to Ohio, to her parents and her firstborn child, Minnie.[21]

The Shermans' time together in San Francisco, therefore, was less than idyllic. He suffered from asthma; she had problems with boils and headaches. When their third child, William (Willy) Tecumseh Sherman, Jr., arrived on June 8, 1854, Cump once more demonstrated little excitement, showing again no desire to make an emotional commitment to the new baby, clearly worried that Ellen might satisfy her yearning for Lancaster. When he saved the bank during a February 1855 financial crisis in the state, Ellen responded by expressing disappointment about his success, since she wanted to return to Ohio. In the spring of 1855 she decided to go home anyway. Startlingly, she left Cump, Lizzie, and Willy behind. For the next seven months, Cump and Ellen could once again talk to each other only through the mails. Her attachment to Lancaster and all it represented continued to overwhelm her affection for her husband.[22]

Ellen returned to California in December 1855 and seemed more content. She still missed her parents and the absent Minnie, but she tried to assuage her homesickness by hanging pictures of the Ewings and her missing daughter throughout the house. She had Lizzie and Willy talk to these likenesses as though they were real people. She even dressed Willy in a girl's headgear "to make him look like Minnie." Still, things were better. The birth of their fourth child, Thomas Ewing Sherman (Tommy), on October 12, 1856, was a joyous event and was followed by one of the happiest Christmases in their married life. Hopefully, the young couple had turned the corner toward a future that would be happier than their past.[23]

Unfortunately, the good times did not last. Officers of the main bank in St. Louis, worried about continuing problems with the California economy, ordered the closing of Cump's San Francisco branch on May 1, 1857. Cump, however, irrationally blamed Ellen for the failure. Her repeated insistence on their departure for Ohio and her unwillingness to spend money carefully had hurt his chances for financial success, he insisted. Once again, the unresolved problems surfaced. Ellen happily prepared to go home, while Cump mourned the death of his bank. The short-lived hopes for a happier future faded away.[24]

Cump, Ellen, and family left California that spring. In July 1857, Cump traveled to New York City to open a new branch bank, while Ellen contentedly returned to her father's house in Lancaster. The Panic of 1857 doomed Cump's new venture, and once again, he angrily lashed out at Ellen. "No doubt," he told her, you are "glad at last to have attained your wish to see me out of the army and out of employment." He was deeply depressed, worried not only about his economic failure, but even more concerned about huge debts he had contracted in making failed bank investments for army friends. His life seemed to be crashing around him just as his father's had when Cump was a nine-year-old boy. And in the background, yet again, loomed the massive figure of Thomas Ewing, Ellen's father. It began to look to Cump as if he would have to depend on his foster father once again, just what he had been trying to avoid since that fateful walk up the hill in 1829. At the same time, Ellen hoped these difficulties would result in Cump's finally agreeing to live and work in Lancaster.[25]

The next several years saw Cump fall to the pits of dejection as failure piled upon failure. He escaped the Ohio saltworks by joining his brothers-in-law, Tom and Boyle Ewing, in Kansas in a legal and real estate business, only to see it flounder. Desperate, he contacted everyone he knew who might be able to get him back into the army, but all he received for his efforts was the possibility of a superintendency of a newly established Louisiana Military Seminary. The Ewings, with Ellen in agreement, offered him the position of manager of an American bank in London. He hesitated before settling on the military position, considering it more stable and more appealing than the uncertain banking venture. In October 1859 he traveled down to Louisiana alone, leaving his wife and family in Lancaster, Ellen having determined never to join him there. She preferred that he go to England, and she remain in Ohio.

Her pressure and that of her family finally wore Cump down. Even though he was enjoying his work and was making a success of something for the first time in his life, he acceded to Ellen's and Thomas Ewing's wishes and submitted his resignation from the military seminary superintendency on March 1, 1860. "I have made desperate efforts to escape but I see it as inevitable, and so might as well surrender," he lamented. When he traveled north, however, he quickly found that the London bank offer was dangerously uncertain. He returned south by the end of March 1860 and withdrew his resignation, determined to stay there and confident that once the school built him a house, he would have his wife and family with him. Cump seemed to have gained control of his life. He and his family would live far south of Lancaster, Ohio. Ellen still hoped it would not happen. And then the war came.[26]

As Cump Sherman prepared to join the Union army in the spring of 1861, his marriage was filled with difficulties. He and Ellen had produced six children, the most recent being daughters Eleanor Mary Sherman (Elly) born on September 5, 1859, and Rachel Ewing Sherman born on

July 5, 1861. But there had been no clear resolution to the problems that had begun during their courtship days. Ellen still looked to her father rather than to her husband; she also remained unhappy with the jobs Cump held, and beyond the normal nineteenth-century wife's concern about a husband's religious life, she was displeased that he refused to practice the Catholicism that was so dear to her. She always expressed these feelings in the same way, by yearning to return to Lancaster. There, her father and family lived, there Cump could work for the family business interests, and there he might be coaxed into become a practicing Catholic.

In 1861, Cump was forty-one years of age, and Ellen was thirty-seven. Both had aged markedly in the eleven years since their marriage, although Ellen seemed to have grown older faster. She had had a child on average every twenty-one months and regularly suffered from boils, weight gain, and chronic anxiety. The stresses of being disappointed in her husband's profession and religious life, and her own poor health and numerous pregnancies drained the youth from her. Ellen increasingly retreated into her church life and showed less interest in any nonfamily social activities. Although Cump maintained his reddish brown hair and his slim figure, wrinkles had begun to appear on his face. When he was not depressed or suffering from asthma, he exhibited a high energy level that kept him ever fidgeting, constantly moving, and talking in rapid bursts of conversation. The older he became, the more eccentric he seemed to be, although his ability to charm people seemed undiminished. As Ellen withdrew, Cump grew more outgoing.[27]

Adding to their problems was the amount of the Shermans' married life they spent apart—Cump searching for financial success and Ellen taking the children to her father's home in Lancaster. Their correspondence, however, was regular, full, and explicit. They did not shrink from telling each other exactly what they felt, holding nothing back, and frequently arguing as though they were actually together. Through it all, the two loved each other, though they hardly viewed their relationship through the mists of emotional romance. She talked of Cump being her protector, but Ellen Sherman was no subservient wife in the nineteenth-century meaning of that term. She disagreed with the most fundamental aspects of her husband's life, and she told him so whether he liked it or not. Cump did not see Ellen as an inferior to be coddled. He treated her as he treated everyone else he dealt with: bluntly and honestly. They both wished for more from the other, but they were willing to settle for what they had: a matter-of-fact love. Theirs was hardly the superior male and inferior female relationship of the Victorian era, but it worked for them. They stayed together not simply because religion and society expected it but because they accepted their frequently exasperating love for each other and never thought of life with any other partner.[28]

The Civil War produced additional pressure on this strained yet surprisingly steady marital relationship. Matters were especially difficult in the early years of the conflict, as Cump struggled to find his proper place. He had entered the war, after all, worried about the Union's determination. When, on several occasions, he met Abraham Lincoln, he was appalled at what he considered to be the president's nonchalant attitude toward the conflict. Serving briefly as Commanding General Winfield Scott's inspector general, he saw the North's unpreparedness, which only further convinced him that his fears were correct. When he commanded a brigade in Irvin McDowell's invading army at the battle of Bull Run in July 1861, he became depressed and panicky over what he experienced. "I have read of retreats before," he told Ellen, "have seen the noise and confusion of crowds of men at fires and shipwrecks, but nothing like this. It was as disgraceful as words can portray." And when he saw how newspaper reporters made the debacle look even worse, he added the press to his concerns about the Union effort. Ellen tried to offer solace by suggesting that she and the children come to Georgetown, a loving suggestion considering her consistent desire to remain in Lancaster. Cump, however, told her to stay in Ohio, a complete reversal of his normal position. He believed that his wife's presence would set a bad example for his civilian volunteers whom he was trying to mold into reliable soldiers. Cump decided, early on, that his marriage had to take second place to his war efforts, even if this meant his wife and family had to live in Lancaster with Thomas Ewing.[29]

Cump remained disgusted and worried about the military situation around Washington, so he jumped at the chance to go to Kentucky and serve under an old friend, the hero of Fort Sumter, Major General Robert Anderson. He arrived in Louisville in early September 1861, after spending a week with Ellen and the children in Cincinnati, and found to his disappointment that matters in Kentucky were as confused as they had been in Washington. When Anderson had to resign command because of physical and mental exhaustion, Cump was forced to take over on October 8, despite an earlier promise from the president that he could avoid such a fate. He bombarded Washington with dire predictions of military catastrophe and when Secretary of War Simon Cameron passed through on an inspection tour on October 17, Cump presented a gloomy assessment of Union prospects. Although a number of leading Kentuckians agreed with his pessimistic telegrams to Washington, his eccentric behavior before the local populace and visiting newsmen elicited whispers about his mental condition. He paced the floors of his hotel every night; he looked disheveled; and he spoke and moved with a rapidity and passion that stunned onlookers. Ellen grew so worried when these stories of Cump's nervous behavior reached Lancaster that she convinced her brother Phil, Cump's close friend from childhood days, to accompany her to Louisville to try to calm her husband down. She stayed a week, but Cump remained upset. Meanwhile, Assistant Secretary of War Thomas W. Scott expressed loudly what others were whispering. "Sherman's gone in the head, he's luny."[30]

Cump had long been demanding replacement, and on November 13, 1861, Don Carlos Buell took over his command in Kentucky and Cump went to Missouri to serve under an old California friend, Henry W. Halleck. Sent on an inspection tour soon after arriving, Cump once more began expressing his deeply felt worries about possible Confederate attacks. He so frightened everyone he encountered that Halleck ordered him back to headquarters, where he was bowled over to find Ellen waiting for him. A number of his subordinates had telegraphed Ellen to come, to take him home for a brief rest to give him a chance to recover his equilibrium. Cump protested mildly but, in late November, he traveled to Lancaster with his concerned wife. Ellen was taking her husband to her father's house for revival, an act of love but one fraught with hurt. Once more, Thomas Ewing was saving Cump in a time of need, just what Cump had been trying to avoid all his married life. Making matters worse, on December 11, 1861, the *Cincinnati Commercial* published an article that publicly declared him insane.[31]

To see himself openly stigmatized in this manner only depressed Cump even more, but he pressed forward anyway. Just before Christmas 1861, he returned to Missouri where Halleck gave him a less stressful job, training recruits at Benton Barracks near St. Louis. Ellen, her father, and the rest of the family took up the cudgels for him. They contacted newspapers all over the nation, cajoling and demanding retractions of the story of Cump's insanity, while Ellen wrote the president and then visited him personally. Abraham Lincoln took no action, but from that time on, he so charmed Ellen that she always considered him to be fair to her husband.[32]

The fact that Cump was once again the beneficiary of Ewing help did not sit well with him, but there was nothing he could do about it in his depressed and vulnerable state. He kept performing his lowly job as well as he could, and soon Halleck had him back in a command position in Paducah, Kentucky, forwarding troops to the increasingly successful general, Ulysses S. Grant. The two men developed the friendship that was to sustain them for the rest of the war. At the same time, the need for continued Ewing defense of his sanity faded. Cump became one of the heroes at Shiloh in April 1862, restoring his reputation through his own, and not the Ewings', efforts. Still, he was clearly happy when Ellen told him that Thomas Ewing was "exceedingly well pleased" and "very proud" of him and could "hear nothing" of him "without emotion." Despite his desire for independence from Thomas Ewing, Cump still craved his approval. He wanted his foster father to acknowledge his military achievements and thereby allow him to stand on his own and to supplant the great man in Ellen's devotion. Cump wanted both independence and approval. He was still struggling with these issues. Meanwhile, Ellen felt increasing worry about her husband's future in the nation's military effort.[33]

As the war progressed and Cump advanced in the army hierarchy, he continued to have his ups and downs, but generally he now had control over his emotions and he grew confident in himself and the Union war effort. Ellen, who had proven such a steadying force during the time of the insanity charge, continued to maintain her support of him. Whereas earlier she had seen Cump as her protector, now she assumed that role toward him. She even offered suggestions about which general to trust and which one to hold at arm's length, but Cump regularly ignored her advice. Her support was to his emotions, not his military judgment. In one area, however, she continued to pour forth negative comments. She kept insisting that Cump actively practice Catholicism. In one letter, for example, she phrased her love in a characteristic way. "You only want Christianity to make you perfect." Cump ignored such caveats and concentrated on her affection and her steadfast support in his time of emotional need. Leaving aside his usual reticence about expressing his affection, he told her that her support caused him to "love and honor" her "more than ever."[34]

After the success at Shiloh in April 1862, Cump participated under Halleck in the capture of Corinth, Mississippi, in May. Then in the fall, he moved to Memphis as military governor. In December 1862, he helped plan a joint operation with Grant against Vicksburg. His friend and colleague did not arrive because of the loss of his supply base, however, so Cump suffered a terrible repulse at Chickasaw Bayou in his solo attack. In February 1863 he vented his frustration by court-martialing a newsman for his unauthorized presence with the attacking flotilla, and then he shared in Grant's glorious July 1863 victory at Vicksburg. Through it all, Ellen remained in Lancaster with the children, but she constantly prodded him to allow her to pay a visit. Cump insisted that he would not mix the public and the private; he, not surprisingly, still concentrated solely on winning the war and was determined to make the necessary personal sacrifices to achieve the victory. In mid-August 1863, with Vicksburg safely captured, he relented and allowed Ellen and the children to come and spend time with him in his camp some twenty miles outside the city.

Relaxed because of the great victory at Vicksburg, Cump was extremely happy to see Ellen, twelve-year-old Minnie, eleven-year-old Lizzie, nine-year-old Willy, and six-year-old Tommy when they arrived in August 1863 for a six-week visit. The boys slept in the tent of a Ewing uncle who was on Sherman's staff, and the rest of the family stayed in the two tents that Cump had pitched together to form a little house. Cump was particularly happy to see Willy, clearly his favorite child. The young boy loved the military as Cump did, and during this visit, he accompanied his father on all his inspection tours. To Cump's extreme pleasure, the men of the Thirteenth Regiment, the headquarters detachment, made Willy a sergeant and included him in all their ceremonial activities. Ellen, too, watched with satisfaction as Cump and the other soldiers doted over the children, demonstrating a contentedness she had rarely displayed before.

The Sherman family was together after a very long time apart, and they enjoyed each other's company and the attention of others. They socialized with the Grants and found the experience of camp life exhilarating. Once again, their future together looked bright.[35]

In late September 1863, Cump received orders to relieve William S. Rosecrans at Chattanooga; he immediately began moving his troops toward the Mississippi River, planning to take his family with him as far as Memphis. As the river boat prepared to pull away, Cump had to send a soldier to fetch Willy who was spending time with General James B. McPherson. Soon after his arrival aboard ship, Willy complained of sickness and soon developed a severe diarrhea. Ellen called in a physician, and he diagnosed the child with dysentery and malaria. He urged Cump to order the boat to proceed as quickly as possible to Memphis. Along the way, Willy grew increasingly ill, and nothing any physician on the ship or later in Memphis could do seemed to help. The boy was deathly ill. Ellen called in a Catholic priest, and Willy remained stoic in the face of his impending death, upset only that he was leaving his parents behind. The chaplain reassured him that he would see his mother and father again in heaven, and he became resigned to his fate. When Ellen began sobbing, he reached out and held her face in his hands, dying peacefully with his family around him.

The loss of their nine-year-old son devastated Ellen and Cump; in fact, neither ever got over the trauma. They blamed themselves for placing him in danger of fever and wondered how they would ever survive his loss. This tragedy, like the insanity controversy, tightened the bond between them. The problem was that they could not express their sorrow together. Cump had to go off to war, and Ellen went back to Lancaster. There was a significant difference this time, however; she wished she could have stayed with her husband. Once again, difficulty brought them closer together.[36]

Cump participated in the successful Grant-led lifting of the siege at Chattanooga in November and then spent Christmas 1863 with his family in Lancaster. It was a gloomy affair, the first real chance husband and wife had to grieve together over Willy. On his way back to the war, Cump brought Minnie along, to take her to a school in Cincinnati, thus gaining a bit more time with at least one member of his family. But war duties called, and he pressed on, his family left behind again in Lancaster.

The new year of 1864 was to prove conclusive for Sherman's military reputation. He became one of the major military leaders of the Civil War. In February, he conducted the successful Meridian Campaign through Mississippi, the first implementation of his philosophy of destructive war against civilian property. Then in May he began the Atlanta campaign against Confederate General Joseph E. Johnston, culminating his efforts by capturing the crucial inland city in September. Following this sensational success, he marched to the sea in November and December, dramatically demonstrating the effectiveness of destruction to break the will of the Confederate populace and its army. His place in American military history was set.

As Cump implemented his Atlanta Campaign, Ellen remained in Lancaster. On June 11, 1864, she delivered another boy, Charles Celestine Sherman, the baby conceived in Vicksburg before the death of Willy. When General James B. McPherson, the family friend and Sherman subordinate, was killed in battle in July, the Shermans had new grief to share. Willy's connection with McPherson was not lost on them, so in grieving for McPherson, they once more grieved for Willy. Their son's death seemed impossible to overcome, but it continued to draw them together.[37]

A major change in the relationship between Cump and Ellen now took place. In July 1864, while he was still in the midst of the Atlanta Campaign she told him that she was planning to leave her father's house and take the children to South Bend, Indiana. She wanted to send the boys to Notre Dame and the girls to neighboring St. Mary's. Ellen said she moved out of her father's house because her mother's recent death had made the place too big for her to care for. She had always loved her mother, but she idolized her father, so Maria Ewing's death could not have caused Ellen to leave her father's house for that reason alone. Thomas Ewing's dominating presence and his refusal for her to live anywhere else in town may finally have proven to be too much for her, especially since she had grown closer to Cump. Ellen decided to leave Lancaster entirely. Cump, who had spent his entire married life trying to separate his wife from her father, could not understand the inconvenience and extra expense of a move just now. Deep down, however, he had to rejoice at the development. Perhaps after thirteen years of marriage and seven children, his wife was finally prepared to separate herself from her beloved father and look to her husband as the dominant male figure in her life.[38]

So while her husband was marching to the sea and his name was becoming a household word, Ellen was living in South Bend, in a house rented from the future vice-president of the United States, Schuyler Colfax. She missed Cump, but by now she was used to long separations, and her pride in his martial achievements dampened any exasperation over his absence. Unfortunately, a new personal tragedy quickly replaced the public euphoria over Cump's Atlanta success. Baby Charles, just a few months old, died on December 4, 1864, and was buried on the Notre Dame campus, a large artillery shell serving as a temporary marker. Meanwhile, a thousand miles away, Sherman's soldiers were detonating Confederate land mines hidden in the road leading to Savannah. Ellen had to suffer the baby's death alone, because sadly, she could not contact her husband, cut off as he was from the outside world. She did not reach him by mail until the end of December and immediately connected his new success with their mutual grief over the death of Charley—and Willy. These deaths, she reminded Cump, were "a lesson to us of the vanity of human glory." He had never seen the baby, but deep in his heart he had hoped that this child would be the replacement for the dead Willy. As for glory or honors, if they were worth anything, Cump said, "they will accrue to you and the children." What particularly pleased him, however, was that he had finally shown Thomas Ewing how successful he could be on his own. "Of course I feel just pride in the satisfaction you express," he wrote Ewing, "and would rather please and gratify you than all the world beside." William Tecumseh Sherman was no longer simply the ward of a great man. He was a great man, and Ewing acknowledged it. Ellen's change of attitude—the result of personal tragedies, not military successes—was also encouraging. While he mourned, Cump simultaneously rejoiced at his military success and the new approval from his wife and father-in-law.[39]

Cump had little time to continue grieving or celebrating because he was soon marching through the Carolinas, extending his attempt to break the will of Confederate society so that Southerners would stop their battle against the Union. Meanwhile, Ellen stayed in South Bend, mourning the loss of her baby but keeping busy with the planning for and participation in the Sanitary Commission Fair in Chicago, gathering money to aid in that organization's charitable work for soldiers. Husband and wife remained apart, she mourning her loss by doing charitable work, he methodically wreaking destruction on Confederate society to end the war.[40]

As the conflict drew to a finish, Cump increasingly became recognized as one of the heroes of the Union war effort. After a late March 1865 meeting in Virginia with Grant, Lincoln, and Admiral David Dixon Porter to plan the inevitable end of the fighting, Cump returned to his army in North Carolina. In mid-April, after Lee had already surrendered to Grant, Cump met with Confederate General Joseph E. Johnston to end the war in the West. He gave his Confederate opposite such generous terms that Secretary of War Edwin Stanton, leading the new Andrew Johnson administration after Lincoln's assassination, wondered about his loyalty. Even Ellen could not believe her husband's generosity: "News electrified us on Monday of your mild terms to Joe Johnston. You know me well enough to realize that I would never agree to any such policies as that towards deserters from our Union." When Stanton and the press began berating Cump as a traitor, however, Ellen ceased her criticism and joined the rest of her family in his defense. Once more she stood ready to do battle for her husband's good name.[41]

Unlike the insanity controversy, this imbroglio with Stanton and the press quickly faded away. Public euphoria at the war's end smothered any suspicions about the victorious Sherman. His own hard feelings, however, did not go away so quickly. On May 24, 1865, when his army participated in the Grand Review of Union troops in Washington, Cump got his revenge on Stanton by refusing to shake his hand. Ellen proved to be more forgiving. She sent Mrs. Stanton some fresh flowers and even paid the secretary of war a social call. Cump was unmoved. He remained angry at Stanton until time eased the resentment. Ellen, meanwhile, kept a bad situation from getting worse.[42]

Cump exited the great war as he had entered it—the subject of controversy and with his marriage unromantically steady. Now, however, he was a famous national hero, and he and Ellen had a lengthy period together for the first time since the 1850s. They savored the opportunity, made better by the cheers of the people they met on a tour of the country. Cump became commander of army troops in the West, and when Grant entered the White House in 1869, Cump took over his post as commanding general. The honors and the presents poured in. Lancaster demonstrated its affection by undertaking a $100,000 fund-raising drive for the family. St. Louis and New York instigated their own efforts to raise money, and by the time Cump became commanding general in 1869, he and Ellen had houses in St. Louis and Washington as well as a substantial bank account. On January 9, 1867, the final Sherman child was born, Philemon Tecumseh Sherman (Cumpy). In October 1874, the eldest daughter Minnie wed in a ceremony that Ellen, ever the chauvinistic Catholic, made as grand as possible to show Protestant Americans that Catholics were as good as the nation's majority religious group. In 1871, the death of Thomas Ewing ended any lingering ambiguities Cump and Ellen felt about him. Everywhere they turned, General and Mrs. Sherman had seemingly found the home and hearth that they had never had before.[43]

Peace was not to come to Cump and Ellen, however, because major problems still existed between them. Thomas Ewing was gone and with his absence, Ellen's attraction for Lancaster faded. But she still pressured Cump to become a Catholic, and he continued to worry about money. At the same time, another old problem intensified. As commanding general, Cump had a myriad of social obligations which he, a social being, enjoyed. Ellen, on the other hand, increasingly withdrew into herself. She refused to play the social role expected of Victorian wives. She avoided even the smallest parties. She put on weight and regularly complained about her lack of energy and good health. Cump grew steadily more irritated at her attitude and went off to social events by himself, harboring resentment at her behavior. When his friend General Philip Sheridan married a younger woman, Cump's inner feelings came out. He complimented Sheridan on marrying someone "who can go with you to the camp or a palace with equal grace and happiness." Ellen found Cump's criticism unwarranted; she felt that fulfillment of her family duties satisfied her obligation as a wife. She had no social responsibilities, no matter what Cump thought.[44]

Cump had long been able to tune out Ellen's lifelong nagging about Catholicism. Then something happened that convinced him that her insistence on her religion was not only bothersome, but it was also sinister. Over the years, Cump had settled on his son Tommy as the replacement for the deceased Willy. He reluctantly agreed to Ellen's demand that Tom attend Georgetown University, but insisted that he follow this Catholic schooling with a stint of education at Yale. He prepared the young man, a lawyer, to become caretaker for the family, to prevent it from falling into the bankruptcy that Cump had suffered as a child and which had haunted him all his life. Then, the unthinkable happened. On May 28, 1878, Tom announced in a letter to his father that he was going to become a Catholic priest, a Jesuit no less. Cump was devastated and did all he could to try to prevent his son from following this calling. When he failed and Tom sailed away to a seminary in England, Cump blamed Ellen. He believed that her Catholicism had caused him to lose one of his two surviving sons. Her insistence on his education in Catholic schools had provided the opportunity, he said, for the church to steal him. Harsh letters passed between them, and there was a crisis in their marriage. She moved to Baltimore, and he remained in Washington.[45]

Tom's decision to become a priest and Cump's certitude that Ellen was responsible for it exacerbated the long-existing religious strain in their marriage. This coupled with Ellen's lack of sociability no doubt encouraged Cump to reach out to others. He had always enjoyed the company of young women, joking that his postwar hobby was kissing them. And he certainly developed that reputation; newspaper articles frequently laughed about his propensity for kissing and the willingness of young women to go along. Even Ellen joked about it, saying, however, that she did draw the line at widows. "You are the only man in the world I ever could have loved," she said, "you are true to me in heart and soul." Then she added a significant caveat—"even if your prejudices do run away with you sometimes." Ellen loved Cump despite their differences, and he shared the feeling. Cump never forgave Tom for becoming a priest, but over time, he forgave Ellen.[46]

Yet, Cump did enjoy being around other women, and they were attracted to the famous general. Confederate leader Robert E. Lee was also a flirt, and his comments to young women were also frequently frank. While there is no conclusive proof that either man went beyond flirting, it seems evident that Cump had a fling with sculptress Vinnie Ream. His letters to her between 1873 and 1878 are full of allusions to his physical attraction. In the early 1880s, Mary Audenreid, the widow of his military aide, threw herself at him, but Cump fought off her advances, insisting that she was like another daughter to him. He allowed himself to be seen in public with both of these women and others besides, which might very well indicate that there was more flirtation than intimacy in these encounters. It seems improbable that he would have systematically threatened his marriage by indulging in and then publicly flaunting infidelity.

Ellen did destroy Mary Audenreid's letters to Cump, but her apparent motive seems to have been religion not jealousy. She never confronted her husband over any dalliance, though she boldly confronted him about everything else and certainly would have done so had she even suspected him of sexual or any other sin. Similarly, the only public commentary about Cump Sherman's relationship with other women (other than the joking about his kissing young women) was a ridiculous newspaper claim that he had fallen in love with Mrs. Grover Cleveland. If the fifty- to sixty-year-old Cump was involved in extramarital activity, he certainly kept it discreet, and it seemed to have no discernible effect on his marriage or his public persona.[47]

Otherwise, the life of Cump and Ellen Sherman in the years after the Civil War resembled their relationship before the conflict. Cump traveled regularly and widely across Europe and out West. He went to the theater and to a variety of dinners. Meanwhile, Ellen stayed at home. He avoided churchgoing, and she attended daily Mass whenever she could. He worried about family finances, and she spent money with little compunction. After 1871, Thomas Ewing was no longer around, but Tom's entrance into the priesthood made the Catholicism issue ever more divisive.

Clearly the marriage of Cump and Ellen remained no life of bliss. Yet the two stayed together, communicating as bluntly through the mails as they always had. She allowed him to travel and go to his parties, experience the praise of the public, and then return home to find her always there, always supportive, albeit in her own way. As a Victorian wife and mother, she was expected to act that way, but obligation was not the explanation for their relationship. They truly loved each other. Their marital bond remained what it had always been: one of mutual dependence but hardly one of passion. They were used to one another and contented in that relationship.

When the time came for Cump to retire from the military as he did in late 1883 at the age of sixty-three, their relationship changed but little. The Shermans moved to New York to be closer to their children, several of whom were now married. Minnie's 1873 high society marriage to a St. Louis, later Pittsburgh, businessman resulted in one financial crisis after another for the family, while Elly's 1880 wedding to a naval officer and later businessman proved steadier. Tom was a Jesuit priest, while Lizzie in her thirties, Rachel in her late twenties, and Cumpy soon to graduate from Yale, all still lived at home. Lizzie and Rachel often took their mother's place at social functions. By then, Ellen, at age sixty, was practically a recluse.

For a time the Shermans lived in New York City's Fifth Avenue Hotel, an exclusive address. Then in late September 1888, because the sixty-four-year-old Ellen increasingly blamed her poor health on hotel living, Cump purchased a house at 75 West 71st Street. He hoped that such a change of residence would improve her health, which he insisted was not heart trouble, as she and her doctors said, but hypochondria. The sicker and weaker she became, the more he went into denial. Finally he had to admit that she was not imagining her physical ailments; she was gravely ill. On November 28, 1888, as he sat reading in his office, the nurse he had hired to stay with her, shouted down to him that Ellen had taken a turn for the worse. In anguish, he sped up the two flights of stairs to her room: "Wait for me Ellen, no one ever loved you as I loved you," he cried out mournfully. He arrived too late. She had died. In the end, although he sank into depression at her passing, he was willing to let her go. "To her the world was a day—Heaven Eternity—and could I, I would not bring her back," he said. In his love for his wife of thirty-eight years and his foster sister of sixty years, Sherman never could take her religion to his own heart, but he accepted its validity for her. He overcame his depression over her death, aided by his concerned children. Still, he died himself less than three years after Ellen's demise, succumbing on February 14, 1891, at the age of seventy-one.[48]

The relationship of Cump and Ellen Sherman was, therefore, turbulent and unusual. Despite in-law problems, resulting from his being her foster brother and her attachment to her father, and despite disagreements over religion, job, and home, they stayed together and remained in love. Clearly William Tecumseh Sherman's marriage to Ellen Boyle Ewing governed his life—at times in a positive way as when she provided crucial support during the insanity controversy, at other times negatively as when she helped make his time in California more difficult than it already was. Her life centered on him and their family after she was able to extricate herself from her obsessive devotion to her father. Still, she always found Cump's lack of religion exasperating and worrisome. Cump stubbornly refused to accept the help the Ewings offered and never understood the complex emotions that tied Ellen to her family. Neither was an ideal mate. Neither fulfilled the expectations of the other completely. In their marriage, they demonstrated that the relationship of any husband and wife is complicated, and that there is no one way to live it. They had a contentious union during their lifetime together, and even in death they display this tension. They lie next to one another in St. Louis's Calvary Cemetery, her grave marked by a large granite cross, his by military flags of the same material. In death, as in life, they remain together, side by side, but their debate, it seems, goes on.

NINE

The Reconstruction of "Home"

The Civil War and the Marriage of Lawrence and Fannie Chamberlain

---

JENNIFER LUND SMITH

Fannie Chamberlain spent the blustery night of September 1, 1862, in a tent at Camp Mason, in Portland, Maine. Three weeks earlier her husband, Lawrence Chamberlain, had taken leave from his teaching position at Bowdoin College to become the lieutenant colonel of the newly formed 20th Maine regiment. Against the backdrop of a raging southeaster, they bid their final farewells, and the next morning he was off to war. Fannie left no written record of her reaction to her husband's decision to enlist in the Union army, but Lawrence recalled that she was unhappy about his actions. In a letter she wrote to him on Thanksgiving 1862, Fannie shared her loneliness and told him, "[Y]ou ought to be at your own home." In 1862 Fannie Chamberlain did not realize how profoundly the war would alter the relationship that had defined their "home." The way in which the Civil War changed civilians into soldiers has received much attention. Less documented, however, is how the changes wrought by the Civil War in both civilians and soldiers affected their relationships with their spouses, particularly among Northerners.[1]

Frances Caroline Adams probably met Joshua Lawrence Chamberlain in Brunswick sometime after he arrived at Bowdoin College in 1848. Bowdoin required all of its students to attend First Parish Church on Sundays where Fannie's father served as pastor. It was in this place that the lives of Fannie and Lawrence, different in many ways, began to converge.[2]

Fannie grew up in a gray area between two families, not feeling clearly a part of either. She was born in Boston in 1825, the biological daughter of Ashur and Emilia Adams, but she spent the majority of her childhood with Ashur's nephew, the Reverend George Adams, and his wife, Sarah, in Brunswick, Maine. The extant family correspondence provides no explicit explanation for why Fannie's parents decided not to rear her themselves. But Ashur was a businessman in his mid-forties when Fannie was born, and he already had six children: three children from a previous marriage and three more from his union with Emilia. Letters do suggest that the Adamses experienced economic strains at times, and the expanding family may have taxed Ashur's finances. Also, even as a child, Fannie suffered from chronic eye problems that caused her a great deal of discomfort; perhaps George and Sarah Adams had more resources available to help her. For whatever the reasons, when Fannie was about five years old, she moved to Brunswick with her adoptive parents, George and Sarah.[3]

George Adams was a Yale graduate who taught school for two years in New Hampshire before entering Andover Theological Seminary. In 1829 he assumed the pastorate of the First Parish Church. Sarah had also taught school in New Hampshire before following her husband to seminary and eventually on to Brunswick, Maine, where he was ordained.[4]

George and Sarah never had any children of their own, but they kept the parsonage full nevertheless. In addition to fostering Fannie, they took in Anna Davis, the granddaughter of a Bowdoin faculty member in the medical department, and Deborah Folsom, an unmarried member of Sarah's family.[5]

Although Fannie's adoptive parents seem to have doted on her, the lack of connection with her family of origin left her feeling vaguely isolated. When Fannie was eight years old she took the initiative to reacquaint herself with her family by writing to her older sister Charlotte, and later to her mother Emilia Adams as well. Both women expressed pleasure, but surprise, to hear from her. One particular exchange between Fannie and her mother provides insight into how her estrangement from her family of origin affected her in a small, perhaps, but profound way. A letter from Emilia Adams contained the poignant postscript: "A question you asked Mary [Fannie's half-sister], I will answer now, your *birth*day my dear, is the 12th of August." Fannie, according to this letter, did not even know the date of her birth until she was twelve and a half years old, and apparently neither did her adoptive parents.[6]

Both Fannie's families probably loved her, but it was difficult for her to feel truly secure in her relationships. The letters from her family in Boston contained reminders that she was, in many ways, a guest in Brunswick. A letter from Emilia Adams admonished eight-year-old Fannie to "try in every way to make them [George and Sarah] happy and strive in some measure to return your many obligations." It was a clear reminder to young Fannie that she bore a heavy responsibility in accepting George and Sarah Adams's care and affection.[7]

There is no indication in the family papers that either George or Sarah

Adams treated Fannie as anything other than a member of their family. But a letter Fannie wrote home to Brunswick in the summer of 1838 illustrates her insecurity about her relationship with them, as might be expected in a child who had been separated from her family when she was old enough to remember, but not old enough to understand why. The summer Fannie turned thirteen, Emilia Adams invited her to spend time with her "Boston family" in Jamaica Plain. The stay in Massachusetts no doubt allowed her to become acquainted with her family of origin, and hence in some ways with herself. But the visits did little to ease her anxiety about her position in her family. In August she wrote a letter to the Reverend Adams describing a delightful summer full of nature walks and music and drawing lessons, but in her postscript she added, "Sister Mary tried to make me think you were going to keep Charlotte instead of me; but I told her that if all the people in Boston should tell me so, I should not believe it." Her inclusion of the story of Mary's taunt, however, suggests that it unsettled her, and it reads more like a plea for reassurance than an affirmation.[8]

George Adams's diaries reveal that he did truly think of Fannie as his daughter. And so did the residents of Brunswick. As she was growing up, Fannie was subjected to the scrutiny that comes with being a member of a minister's family. Fannie never joined the church, and this must have caused Dr. Adams some anguish, as well as providing a topic for discussion among the congregation. Indeed, in her reluctance to join her father's church, Fannie displayed an independence that probably raised some eyebrows in Brunswick.[9]

As a young woman, Fannie did not consider herself a happy person. A photograph of her taken in 1862 captures a wistful rather than a happy-looking woman. She was an introvert, a dreamer who expressed herself through painting and music. And while she did share her passion for art with a gentleman in Portland at one point, and she and Charlotte shared gossip about a Mr. Ward, presumably a suitor of Fannie's, she displayed reserve in her relationships with men.[10]

As she matured, Fannie's artistic talents were encouraged by both of her families. Her half-sister Catherine gave her some drawing lessons when she was young, and both Emilia Adams and Fannie's sister Charlotte sent her paints from Boston. In Brunswick, George Adams engaged organists to instruct Fannie, who began to play regularly in church. Emilia Adams made it clear that she viewed Fannie's artistic skills as more than mere genteel talents. She told Fannie that "it may prove a delightful resource, and also a profitable one, if had should be, in future." Perhaps she envisioned Fannie teaching, as her half-sister Catherine did. The Adamses, it seems, did not object to stretching the boundaries of the women's sphere, if necessary.[11]

For the moment, however, Fannie's paintings and music provided an emotional outlet and a source of enjoyment for her. By her early twenties she often accompanied, on the organ, the church choir that was led by Lawrence Chamberlain, an intent theology student.[12]

Three years younger than Fannie, Joshua Lawrence Chamberlain was born September 8, 1828, in Brewer, Maine, the eldest of the five children of Joshua and Sarah Dupee Chamberlain. Unlike Fannie, Lawrence possessed a clear sense of his identity. His ancestors had resided for generations in the area that became Maine and included veterans of both the French and Indian and the Revolutionary Wars. From his father, a farmer and an officer in the local militia, Lawrence learned the values of honest work and tenacity. As a young man Lawrence worked hard on the family farm. In Chamberlain's biographies, a story is repeated about an incident that occurred during his childhood on the farm in Brewer: he and his brothers came up against a boulder in the field that would not budge. When they reported their dilemma to their father, he reportedly offered no suggestions as to how to deal with the rock; he simply told them to move it. Ultimately, the young Chamberlain did.[13]

Lawrence's mother imbued in him strong religious convictions. With the family roots deep in New England, it is no surprise that the Chamberlains attended Brewer's First Congregational Church and adhered to its prescribed code of behavior. Surely it pleased his mother that Lawrence joined the First Congregational Church in Brewer when he was sixteen years old, taking the responsibility of church membership very seriously.[14]

When he was eighteen, rejecting both his father's wish that he embrace a career with the military and his mother's desire that he become a minister, Lawrence decided to prepare himself to become a missionary to foreign lands. To that end, he began making plans to enter Bowdoin College. He spent a year and a half with tutors studying to pass the entrance exam, which he did in the winter of 1848.[15]

At Bowdoin, Chamberlain was an earnest student who excelled in his classes, particularly languages. Although the standards he set for his own behavior precluded his involvement in many of the college pranks that entertained his classmates, they appeared to respect him and enjoy his company. Despite his dedication to his studies, Lawrence did not deny himself the pleasure of attending all social events. He especially enjoyed music and singing, and he even became adept at playing the organ at the college chapel. There were many opportunities for him to meet other young people, one of them being the local minister's daughter. In 1851 Lawrence became the conductor of the church choir, which surely afforded him additional time with Fannie.[16]

Lawrence and Fannie became close at a time of great turmoil in her life. In February 1850, her adoptive mother Sarah Folsom Adams died after a protracted illness. Her death had a profound impact on her husband and family. For months after his wife's death, George Adams seemed lost; he filled his time fretting about his daughters. Then, in the summer of 1851, he met Helen Root while at a convention in Chicago. In December of that same year, he brought her to Brunswick to become his wife.[17]

Helen Root Adams's arrival in Brunswick caused a furor in the Adams household. To Fannie, Anna, and Deborah Folsom, it seemed that Helen, who was much younger than her husband—indeed, she was virtually Fannie's age—had caused Dr. Adams to undergo a personality change. The tension became so great that within a year, all three women—Fannie, Anna, and Deborah—fled the Adams home in Brunswick. Anna received a position to teach music in Mississippi, and Deborah Folsom moved to Hoboken. After spending several months studying music in New York, Fannie accepted a position to teach voice and piano at a private school for girls in Milledgeville, Georgia.[18]

In the wake of her mother's death and the changing family dynamics that ensued, Fannie and Lawrence began their courtship. In June 1851 Fannie wrote perhaps her most romantic letter to Lawrence, describing a recent visit with him as "a dream," and dwelling on the "blessed gift!" of the memory of the time they shared. But the letter also reveals what may have come to concern Fannie about her relationship with Lawrence, as well as what drew her to him. She wrote, "Are you yet oppressed with that feeling of unrest + are you yet striving for the unattained (perhaps unattainable) until your very soul is wearied as you used to do? Do you not feel that the wants of your soul may never be met until your earthly pilgrimage shall have ended the storms of life for ever [unclear]?" Fannie must have been unsure about her ability to satisfy Lawrence's searching soul and make him happy. "Yet," she added admiringly, "yours is the true life, which is 'a thing of intensity of depth.' "[19]

As their relationship deepened, the passion Fannie had felt in June gave way to caution. Her father's seeming betrayal by his recent marriage to a woman so unlike her mother, and the upheaval that union had engendered, surely contributed to Fannie's wariness about intimate relationships in general, and men in particular. Indeed, her foster sister Anna seems to have suffered the same disillusionment about men following George Adams's remarriage. Anna confided in Fannie that spring, "I don't think much of *the men*—and I *know you* do not." Moreover, since childhood Fannie had experienced some anxiety about her familial relations, and this may have extended to romantic relations as well.[20]

Early in 1852 Fannie consulted with her friend Stephen Allen to solicit a male opinion regarding her relationship with Lawrence Chamberlain. Drawing from the description Fannie gave him, Allen concurred that a man of the "jealous, sanguine, and ardent temperament" that Fannie described might be "hard to please + satisfy." Feeling undecided, Fannie admitted to Allen that she did love Chamberlain, but she feared that she did not feel "that sort of love . . . of which [she had] for years dreamed, so wildly."[21]

Although they approached the relationship differently, both seem to have been dreamers who embraced the romantic ethos of the nineteenth century. While Fannie expressed uncertainty about a future with Lawrence, he seems to have felt quite sure that he had found a life companion in the educated and artistic minister's daughter. Fannie could not have found a suitor more fiercely romantic than Chamberlain, and it pained Lawrence when Fannie's letters suggested her passion did not match his. In May 1852 he moaned that in her last letter, "There was no answer to my love. It seemed as if it was only the common part of it that you recognized—as if it would have been just as well for you if I had loved you as others love—and all beyond that, all that is *mine* in love was lost." This was to be an issue for the couple during most of their courtship: she felt uncertain that he could arouse in her the intense passion about which she fantasized, and he worried that she would not give him her whole heart.[22]

By the end of 1852, after returning from New York to her home in Brunswick, Fannie felt she could no longer stay in the house with her stepmother Helen, and so she retreated from the battlefield of her father's house to Georgia. In so doing, Fannie was leaving a town in Maine with a strong antislavery tradition and heading to the heart of the slave South. It had been in Brunswick's First Parish Church in the spring of 1851 that Harriet Beecher Stowe received the vision that compelled her to write the novel *Uncle Tom's Cabin*. In February 1852, George Adams marked in his diary, "Anti-Slavery Convention," suggesting that he had attended, and in March he noted, "Read 'Uncle Tom,' + am delighted with the book; it must do great good."[23]

Fannie, too, was familiar with the book. One of the first letters she sent back to New England from Milledgeville, Georgia, contained reports of her first encounter with the institution of slavery. On her trip from Savannah to Milledgeville she was approached by a "queenly, black woman with a very stylish turban" who briefly mistook Fannie for her "dear old Missis come from Savannah." Though the woman had seemed pleased with the prospect of seeing her "old Missis," Fannie made it clear that she did not believe the encounter was representative of "the happiness of the slaves with, and their attachment to their masters." She also seemed pleased to see a "well thumbed" copy of *Uncle Tom's Cabin* on the mantel of the home in which she stayed when she first reached Milledgeville. The book was banned in the South and shunned by most Southerners, but Fannie's hostess was originally from Massachusetts, which explains the book's presence, as well as its prominent place on the mantel.[24]

Lawrence, too, was acquainted with Harriet Beecher Stowe's work. While studying under Professor Calvin Stowe at Bowdoin, Chamberlain had been invited to Mrs. Stowe's "Saturday Evenings" during which she often read excerpts from *Uncle Tom's Cabin* while it was appearing in *The*

National Era. Although neither Fannie nor Lawrence was an abolitionist, they did share a disdain for the slave system.[25]

Notwithstanding the cultural and political differences between the North and the South, and Fannie's concerns about them, she seemed extremely pleased with her reception in Georgia. She received a great deal of attention, which buoyed her spirits despite an illness that disabled her during her first few days in Milledgeville. She wrote Charlotte early in 1853, "I have had a great many 'calls' since I've been here, and have been treated with great attention and kindness on all sides." And she immediately gained self-confidence in her abilities as a musician. She confided in her sister, "Between you and I; [*sic*] their standard of music here does not terrify me in the least; and my confidence has been regularly increasing ever since I came."[26]

During the two and a half years Fannie spent in Georgia as a school-teacher, she and Lawrence continued their courtship through the mails. The letters they wrote reveal a great deal about how they related to one another and what they expected of their marriage. Additionally, their correspondence seems to suggest a period of prenuptial negotiation between two strong individuals. Since Fannie was three years older than Lawrence—during the antebellum period it was unusual for the suitor to be younger than the woman he courted—it may have made Fanny slightly bolder than other young women in her position.[27]

The couple engaged a great deal of paper discussing the role of sex and passion in their relationship, and Lawrence's frank enthusiasm for the topic clearly unnerved Fannie. Sometime after she arrived in Georgia, Fannie tested Lawrence's reaction to the idea of a platonic marriage, telling him she believed children were the "result of a tyrannical cruel abuse + prostitution of women." She asserted that she was prepared to "rebel at all the Bible says about it + deem a man unreasonable who presumes to think of children as a *natural* offspring of marriage." It was obvious to Lawrence that Fannie was musing not on the dangers of childbirth, but rather intimate marital relations. He interpreted her remarks as an offense to his manhood and desirability, and proclaimed that her proposition could "cool a passion about as effectively as if it were soaked in the Dead Sea." Although he stated that he was willing to abide by her wishes, he wanted her to admit that it would require "as much self denial on your part as on mine—that your love for me was to some extent a love in which difference of sex was an interesting + important feature."[28]

Although many northern middle-class couples in the mid-nineteenth century were fairly open in their discussions with each other about sex, Fannie probably did feel some hesitancy about sexual relations. She was inexperienced, and she had no mother with whom she could discuss such a delicate subject. Moreover, her suggestion of a nonsexual union may have been a way of feeling out her influence on her future husband.[29]

On the subject of most intimate matters Fannie hesitated to write her innermost thoughts, suspecting her letters would fall into someone else's hands. Lawrence, however, seems to have raised his frequent musings about sex to an art form. In response to Fannie's suggestion of a platonic marriage, Chamberlain tortured her with an elaborate tale about sleeping with another woman. He teased her, ". . . you do not care, do you? You know you are above all such things—they are '*cruel*' + '*unnatural*'! If I am never to *touch* my wife, nobody can blame me for *this*." In the same letter he boldly admitted, "I have such a terrible passion for you tonight that I hardly dare to go to bed . . . it stirs me all up, making my physical existence rather inconvenient." He then admonished her to "be careful how you kiss my lips, or you will set me all on fire." Later he informed her "I am just getting ready to make out a list—for my own amusement mind you—of studies for my little "_____" next year! . . . I shall not tell you what sort of studies they are, only I have been thinking for a year or two + making up my mind. You know you will not have anything else to do—(for *one year* at least!)." His study sessions obviously had little to do with academics. He chuckled gleefully, "I am going to have a nice little time with *somebody*."[30]

While Fannie was generally timid about baring her heart through the mails, she was not shy about asserting her opinions when they pertained to her future with her prospective husband. Finding that she enjoyed Georgia, Fannie urged Lawrence to consider employment in the South, and she lobbied actively on his behalf at various schools. She must have been fairly persuasive with him; at one point he seems to have considered one of her proposals quite seriously. Significantly, Fannie was trying to find him teaching positions. Chamberlain's plan had been to become a missionary, and Fannie knew that, but she did not want to be the wife of a minister or a missionary. In one letter she told him, "I never felt so strongly before, my peculiar unfitness for being a minister's wife; it is not that her trials and troubles are so great, believe me it is not so selfish a feeling, but is that my whole mind, character and temperament are entirely inappropriate for that position, and I never could be useful in it." As George Adams's daughter, she knew how busy a minister was, how often his work cut into family time, and that the minister's wife was constantly under intense scrutiny. In all probability she was being quite honest about the limits of her ability to conduct herself in a manner that would help further his career. Her reluctance to join the church surely demonstrates reservations about organized religion. In steering Chamberlain away from the ministry, not only was Fannie trying to gain some control over where they would settle, but also her fiancé's career choice.[31]

The time Fannie spent in Georgia lent her a feeling of self-reliance that empowered her. By the time she returned to Brunswick, she was thirty years old; she had traveled away from home on her own and had had a chance to discover that her musical talents measured up quite well. Having a job for the first time added to her sense of independence. Although she found herself in debt frequently, when Lawrence offered to send her money to help her with her debts she replied, "No darling, *no indeed.* You shall not think of sending me anything as you proposed; I would not have you for the world. I should think it very, very hard if with all my labor and strivings, I could not support *myself* here." In reality she did not manage her finances successfully while in Georgia, but her experience fostered the confidence that she could supplement the family income if called upon to do so. She also became quite sure about her commitment to Lawrence.[32]

In the summer of 1855, Ashur Adams called Fannie home from Georgia to be with her sister Charlotte who was dying. Fannie also assumed she was returning to Maine to marry Lawrence Chamberlain. When Fannie returned home, however, she found a hesitant Chamberlain who preferred, he said, to postpone the wedding until he could more comfortably support a wife. Embarrassed and feeling rebuffed, she spent a great deal of September writing to Lawrence, "or in crying."[33]

Lawrence's apprehension must have particularly stung Fannie, the thirty-year-old who had remained loyal to him despite her family's concern about their compatibility and his economic prospects. In the end, Fannie prevailed, and after a flurry of sewing by the young ladies of Brunswick, the couple wed on the afternoon of December 7, 1855. The family remained dubious. Deborah Folsom, who could not attend the wedding, sent a letter to Fannie the week preceding the event with the caustic message: "My love to Lawrence. Hope he is prospering as well as he could expect." The Reverend Adams wrote in his diary the evening of the wedding, "*I feel sadly about poor Fanny,* fearing greatly she will not make herself happy."[34]

Despite everyone's fears, the marriage did seem to make both Fannie and Lawrence quite happy. After a little more than a year of marriage Lawrence told Fannie, "I am happier dear Fanny + *growing happy* every day—"[35]

Once they were married and living together, the Chamberlains seem to have found a comfortable balance in their relationship. Although Lawrence often failed to recognize Fannie's self-reliance, preferring to view her as his "little wife" and exaggerating her innocence—reflecting the patriarchal views of the nineteenth century—as their relationship continued to develop, Lawrence did break from the prevailing stereotype on wives to consider Fannie's opinions when he made decisions that affected both their futures. For example, before the couple married, Lawrence had accepted a teaching position at Bowdoin, not the missionary post to which Fannie had objected. Although the job did not pay very well, Fannie must have been delighted that her protests against becoming a minister's wife had had some influence with Lawrence.[36]

In their marriage, the Chamberlains seem to have found the elements that they regarded as vital to a successful union: Lawrence the passion, Fannie the security, and both the romance for which they had been searching. The letters they exchanged after their wedding display none of the power struggles that characterized their courtship. During a separation in the winter of 1857, they shared memories of their wedding night. Lawrence recalled coming to her "most desperately—almost too much awful desperate power in it, for the [peace?] and safety of a frail sweet honeysuckle girl." Fannie responded with an uncharacteristically romantic passage, sharing her recollections of the "*dear* little sacred chamber where I first pillowed my head upon your bosom,—your own beloved wife."[37]

In the first years of their marriage Lawrence occasionally exhibited the "jealousy" and "intensity" that Fannie had feared, but she seemed able to assuage his anxieties. When Lawrence found some old letters, from an old beau of Fannie's, she reassured him that it had not been a serious affair, and she explained that she would have shown him the letters, "only those fearful, morbid states of feeling into which you so often fall, are beyond endurance for me, they kill my very soul." But endure them she did, and she declared, "Lawrence[,] God knows that I love you in such a way as it would satisfy even *your* heart to know."[38]

Both Lawrence and Fannie faced their antebellum separations with a great deal of reluctance. Nearly two years after their wedding, when Fannie was tending to family business in Boston, Lawrence, who was suffering a bit of a cold, wrote her of a nightmare that had plagued him the previous night. He recounted, "[You] would go away to amuse yourself + never once cast a look at poor Nonny whose heart was bound up in you." When he woke and realized Fannie was not due to return for another week, Lawrence professed "I could not keep the tears from my eyes." Feeling a bit sheepish about his fears and not wanting her to feel she had to rush away from her responsibilities in Boston to be with him, he apologized, "Perhaps I am too much of a lover for a husband, as the world goes." Several years later, during another absence, Fannie wrote to Lawrence, "I am *terribly lonely* for you." As usual, she dared not express her emotions further, for she feared "the sacred expressions of affection" would find their way to "other eyes than those from who it was meant."[39]

Finances were strained during the first years of their marriage, and although Fannie had assured Lawrence she was willing to teach to help make ends meet, she never had the opportunity. She must have been a keen student of the "studies" Chamberlain had alluded to in his letter to her during the time she was in Georgia; their daughter, Grace Dupee, nicknamed Daisy, was born in October 1856, ten months after they were married. The birth did not go easy for thirty-one-year-old Fannie. After the delivery, she suffered for months with erysipelas, a puerperal fever that was often fatal at the time, and understandably, she worried a great deal about her health. A premature baby arrived the next year but died within hours. Another healthy child, this time a boy they named Harold Wyllys, arrived in the fall of 1858, but the Chamberlains later suffered the loss of two more daughters before the babies reached their first birthdays.[40]

During the latter half of the 1850s, Fannie lost in numbing succession not only several children but also most of the members of her Boston family. Emilia Adams had died in 1854 and Charlotte, her sister and confidante, in 1855. In 1858 Fannie's sister Mary died, and in 1860 both her brother George and her father, Ashur, passed away. About that same time, she also lost her foster-sister Anna. With the deaths of so many of her family members, and because her relationship with George Adams never fully recovered after his marriage to Helen, Fannie's emotional ties became increasing focused in the family she and Lawrence created together.[41]

Despite their heartbreaks, the Chamberlains also had a good deal for which to be thankful. By 1862, they had bought a house near Bowdoin College, Lawrence had just received a promotion, and they were raising two healthy children. But like so many families, North and South, the Civil War that had erupted in 1861 eventually invaded their personal lives.[42]

Lawrence's decision to join the army marked the first alteration in their married relationship. In 1862 the Union had not yet resorted to conscription; Lawrence's enlistment was completely voluntary. And unlike many of the men who became prominent officers during the Civil War, Lawrence had not attended West Point or received formal training as a soldier. Whereas Fannie had exercised influence in decisions affecting their family before the war, she apparently could not dissuade her husband from becoming a Union officer. Lawrence's unilateral decision to join the military signified the first breach in their union, their experiences during the Civil War further transformed their relationship.

As a soldier, Chamberlain led an existence that could not have been more different from that of a college professor. Not only did he witness atrocities that civilians could hardly imagine, but even the daily routine that constituted most of the soldiers' time was alien to those at home. The month after he departed from Maine, Lawrence exclaimed to Fannie, "Does your innocent little head imagine that I could get a *photograph* (!) taken here? My stars! I fear you have not a *high* idea of my position . . . if we can find a bit of paper, or get a little thimble full of ink . . . if we can see a house that is not riddled with shot + shell, or left tenantless through terror . . . we think we are in Paradise."[43]

In that same letter, written in the fall of 1862, shortly after he witnessed the carnage at Antietam, Chamberlain tried to express the changes he detected in himself. He told Fannie, "[L]et me say no danger + no hardship ever makes me wish to get back to that college life again. I cant breathe when I think of those last two years. Why I would spend my whole life in campaigning it, rather than endure that again. . . . My experience here + the habit of command, will make me less complaisant [*sic*]." His experiences as an officer, surprisingly, had a liberating effect on Chamberlain that prevailed over even the most atrocious scenes of war.[44]

Fannie must not have been pleased to receive that letter for several reasons. While Lawrence embraced the war and was eager to see battle— he complained bitterly to Fannie when his regiment was quarantined due to a smallpox outbreak and risked missing a battle he felt was imminent— Fannie it seems, worried a great deal about combat, as surely did all soldiers' wives. From his position hundreds of miles away, Chamberlain tried to console his wife. He wrote, "You were too sad, Darling, when you wrote. . . . I do not think you can have any particular occasion to feel apprehensive either for yourself or for me." Fannie's apprehension probably transcended the issue of his physical safety; the fact that he was away from home, away from her, making decisions that affected not only his life, but the lives of his family as well, was unsettling. She was not qualified to assist him with military strategy, and it appears she did not attempt to do so. Moreover, Lawrence had obviously made a unilateral decision not to return to teaching, an occupation for which Fannie had actively campaigned.[45]

Chamberlain need not have feared missing a battle. During his first year as a soldier, he participated in most of the most important battles in the eastern theater. In September 1862, the still green volunteers of the Twentieth Maine marched to Sharpsburg, Maryland, in time to witness the battle at Antietam on September 17. That day, an estimated 20,946 men were killed or wounded and an additional 1,771 listed as missing. While the members of the Twentieth Maine remained on the periphery during the bloodiest single day of the war, it offered them a sobering baptism as soldiers. Three months later, the regiment participated in the Federal debacle at Fredericksburg, where they fought against both the Confederates and the cold. There, Chamberlain narrowly avoided serious injury from a musket ball that "grazed his neck and right ear." In the spring of 1863, he and his men had the less than romantic, but important, task of patrolling Hooker's telegraph lines during the battle at Chancellorsville.[46]

Even away from the battlefield, soldiering took its toll on the human body. In addition to the near miss he experienced at Fredericksburg, he collapsed from sunstroke on a march in June 1863; contracted malaria, which would continue to plague him for the rest of his life; and following the battle at Gettysburg, suffered from "exhaustion of the nervous system produced by the severity of the campaign."[47]

In the face of the dangers and hardships the war offered, Chamberlain consistently embraced his duties. This characteristic, as well as his keen mind and tenacity, impressed the military and earned him the respect of his commanding officers, even as it often put his life in jeopardy. Through

Lawrence's military experiences, Fannie was flirting with widowhood, and it was completely out of her control.

Lawrence's letters home did not impart the explicit horrors of war. Instead, he described his living conditions and informed her of his actions as well as he could. He did list casualties, but he did not intend that Fannie should have to bear the details of death and or the atrocities he witnessed. He did anticipate that she would share his glories, however, and he could not wait to tell her about his victory at Gettysburg.

On the second of the three awful days at Gettysburg, Chamberlain distinguished himself as an exceptional commander, even while facing the most dire of situations. On July 2, 1863, Colonel Strong Vincent volunteered his Third Brigade to occupy the strategically essential piece of high ground known as Little Round Top. The Twentieth Maine took its position holding the "extreme left of the entire Union line,"[48] with orders from Vincent to "hold this ground at all costs."[49] Failure would not only enable the Confederates to flank the Union line but could also give them access to the roads that led to the Federal capital. After an afternoon of anxious waiting, Confederate troops began pouring down from Round Top, just south of Little Round Top, and engaging the Third Brigade. As the battle intensified, Chamberlain noted that Confederate troops had already initiated a flanking maneuver on his left. Recognizing that the traditional response, using the entire regiment to charge front, was impossible under the present conditions, Chamberlain had to think creatively. He deployed the "left wing . . . of the regiment to the left and rear, facing it at right angles with the original line." The Twentieth Maine, positioned virtually behind the Union line, took the Confederates off guard and saved the Union rear. All that grueling afternoon the regiment held its ground against repeated waves of assaults from the Fifteenth Alabama Infantry under the direction of Colonel William C. Oates. By approximately 6:00 P.M., Chamberlain's men had no ammunition left to fire. Once again, Chamberlain took command of a seemingly impossible predicament by orchestrating a bayonet attack that swept from left to right. The move was so desperate, bold, and unexpected that it sent the Confederates running. The Twentieth Maine took four hundred prisoners as a result of the attack, but their victory came at great cost. The regiment had begun the day with 358 armed men; ninety of those had been wounded and forty had died in the battle. As darkness descended on the Gettysburg battlefield, Chamberlain and his diminished as well as exhausted troops climbed Round Top and secured it for the Union. Though they met with limited resistance, it was a long, tense night. By the time the Twentieth was allowed to rest the next morning, the deeds of its commanding officer and soldiers had already become well known among Union troops. Chamberlain's ingenuity had saved the Union position.[50]

Two days later, on the Fourth of July, 1863, Lawrence, in a hurriedly scribbled letter to Fannie from a field near the battle site exclaimed, "We are fighting gloriously. Our loss is terrible, but we are beating the Rebels as they were never beaten before," adding, "The 20th has immortalized itself." He quickly recounted what had happened and inserted, "I am receiving all sorts of praise, but bear it meekly."[51]

Fannie probably did not receive that letter for some time; she did not wait patiently in Brunswick to receive letters from Chamberlain at the front. Fannie seems to have coped with the absence of her husband primarily by traveling, sometimes to meet Lawrence and other times alone. One consequence of these sojourns from home was that she began to exhibit the independence she had displayed prior to her marriage. In commenting on Fannie's frequent absences from home, Helen Root Adams wrote, "She is a strong woman." Her journeys away from her children, however, evoked a great deal of criticism from relatives. Furthermore, Fannie seems to have eschewed the auxiliary groups that many women formed to support the war effort. She had no interest in sustaining a war that she felt had already cost her so dearly by separating her from her husband.[52]

The Chamberlains had occasional opportunities to see each other during the war, but often their reunions occurred when Lawrence was suffering one of the maladies he incurred as a soldier and Fannie was called upon to act as his nurse. Two months following the battle at Gettysburg Lawrence returned home to recuperate from "nervous prostration." Later that year, in November 1863, Chamberlain was sent to Georgetown to recover from an attack of "malarial fever." As a result, Fannie joined him in Washington, D.C., and Trenton, New Jersey, to attend to him as he performed court-martial duty, the assignment he drew during his rather lengthy convalescence. Occasionally they enjoyed more relaxed visits; in the spring of 1864, they toured Gettysburg together. It was an opportunity for Lawrence to share his war experiences with his wife on the site of his triumph. Unfortunately, her thoughts of the tour went unrecorded.[53]

Then, in June 1864, the war almost took everything away. Early in the month Chamberlain had assumed control of the newly reorganized First Brigade of Brigadier General Charles Griffin's First Division. The brigade spent much of the month marching toward Petersburg, where General Grant was planning an attack. On June 18, Chamberlain's troops participated in an assault in front of the city. Their task that afternoon was to lead an attack on substantial enemy fortifications in front of the city. To reach their goal they would have to make their way down an incline, cross a stream at the bottom, and continue up a slope, facing full exposure as they advanced. Most in the brigade viewed their orders as a suicide march, but Chamberlain rallied them with his example. He moved to the front of the line, and as he attempted to issue visual commands in the din of cannon fire, a shot pierced his hip. Despite having sustained a near fatal wound, Chamberlain refused to let his troops see him falter; he kept himself upright by using his sword as a cane until he finally collapsed. His biographer describes the gruesome effect of the enemy weapon: "The minie ball had torn through his whole body from the right thigh to left hip, severing blood vessels, nicking the urethra and bladder, and crushing bone before it stopped." Believing he would not survive the wound, Chamberlain took up a pencil and wrote what he believed to be his last letter to Fannie. He summed up his feelings for her, made more acute by his imminent death, "To know + love you makes life + death beautiful," and then he implored her to "Cherish the darlings." It is noteworthy that the penultimate sentence in that letter was, "Oh, how happy to feel yourself forgiven." It reflects not only Chamberlain's unswerving faith in his God and his religion, but also in himself. In recognition of Chamberlain's leadership on the battlefield, and believing he was on his deathbed, General Grant approved his promotion to brigadier general.[54]

To the surprise of his commanding officers, the doctors, and Chamberlain himself, he survived. Fannie rushed to him in Annapolis. For five months Chamberlain convalesced in hospitals and finally at home in Maine. His recuperation period in Brunswick must have been an anxious time for both Fannie and Lawrence. He was virtually an invalid and his presence further taxed Fannie's already depleted mental and physical energies. In addition to nursing Lawrence, Fannie also had their two young children who needed her attention. Moreover, as a result of a visit before the minie ball struck at Petersburg, she was again pregnant. As noted earlier, Fannie's pregnancies had been unusually difficult, and she was now thirty-nine years old. Chamberlain's frustration at not being with his regiment in a position of command must have caused tensions between them, not only because of his agitation about being removed from the scene of action but also because the "habit of command" may indeed have become a habit that was unwelcome at home. And not insignificant was the nature of the wound. The combination of the minie ball and the subsequent surgeries that saved his life most assuredly damaged Chamberlain's sexual capabilities. For a man who had been so forthright about his sexual relationship with his wife, this presumably was a great loss to him, and it surely affected the way the Chamberlains interacted in their marriage.[55]

Five months after receiving the wound at Petersburg, Chamberlain returned to the field in November 1864 despite the objections of his family. George Adams assured him he could obtain a position at Bowdoin and his parents urged him to take a job as collector of customs at Bath, which he had been offered, but he believed his "prospects in the Army were never better." He was uncompromising, even when thinking of his "young + dependent family." And by this time his family included another member; Fannie gave birth to a daughter, Gertrude, on January 16, 1865. Chamberlain asserted, "I am so confident in the sincerity of my motives that I can trust my own life + the welfare of my family in the hands of Providence." It is doubtful that Fannie felt quite so sanguine. Once again,

Lawrence made a decision that affected his "dependent family" against the wishes of his wife. His dedication to the Union cause, and the satisfaction he received from soldiering, greatly tempered the influence over him that Fannie had enjoyed prior to the war.[56]

Chamberlain could not let go of the military. And in his opinion, his decision had its reward. After Generals Lee and Grant met at Appomattox Courthouse in April 1865, Grant chose Chamberlain to accept the formal surrender from the Army of Northern Virginia. The surrender, and Chamberlain's command ordering his Union troops to salute the surrendering Confederates, was undoubtedly his finest hour. But it signaled the end of a war that had both appalled and enthralled him. He had lost friends and acquaintances and had witnessed human behavior at its worst, but ironically, like so many soldiers who fought in the Civil War, the bloodiest event in American history had allowed him to travel, test his limits, gain national recognition, and form close bonds with other men. The war had been the defining experience in Lawrence Chamberlain's life, and his wife had not been a part of it.[57]

Chamberlain's discharge from the army in January 1866 left him in an emotional abyss. While his past deeds created a reputation that preceded him always, his days of heroics had come to an end. In the winter of 1866, Chamberlain reluctantly resumed teaching at Bowdoin, something he had resolved never to do. Without the distraction of imminent battles or postwar parades and speeches, Lawrence had to face a future rife with chronic pain caused by his wounds, a career that he now found unfulfilling, and a home life that fell short of the ideal he had imagined during lonely nights in camp.[58]

The year preceding Lawrence's discharge had been a particularly trying one for the Chamberlains. In January 1865 Lawrence underwent the first of a series of operations—the last one would be in 1883—to address the inflictions caused by the wound he received at Petersburg. And in August, Fannie and Lawrence endured the heartbreak of losing their seven-month-old daughter to a sudden illness. The cumulative effects of the war—the separation, the anxiety, and the lingering readjustments necessitated by Lawrence's wounds—as well as their personal losses surely took a toll on the Chamberlains both individually and as a couple.[59]

Immediately following the war, Fannie and Lawrence spent a good deal of time apart. Speaking engagements frequently drew Lawrence away from home in Brunswick. Fannie continued to travel, as she had begun to do during the war. She spent at least two months—from March to early May 1866—in New York City while the children stayed in Maine with Lawrence. It is unclear who in particular Fannie visited so frequently in New York, but her visits always included outings with Lawrence's brothers.[60]

During her extended absence in the spring of 1866, Fannie wrote Lawrence, "I cannot see or hear of anything beautiful without you, it all comes to that." But the letters also suggest deterioration in their ability to communicate. Unsure even of where to write to him, Fannie chided Lawrence, "Why don't you let me know more about things, dear? . . . Where are you and how are the children." Sensing the widening gulf between them, she ended the letter almost desperately, asking, "Dear, dear Lawrence write me one of the old letters. . . . I am as in the old times gone bye [*sic*] Your Fannie." Alluding to his health and his disabilities in his melancholic reply he lamented, "There is not much left in me to love. I feel that too well."[61]

This period was, in some ways, the incarnation of Lawrence's much earlier feverish dream during the first years of their marriage in which Fannie left her "poor Nonny" to "amuse" herself. But the postwar reality was that they were both pulling away from each other as they struggled to redefine their relationship as husband and wife, and they were both feeling the pain.

Following his brief and unsatisfying return to teaching, Chamberlain held several highly visible positions. Whereas his tenacity and obstinacy had elicited praise, admiration, and promotion on the battlefields, his unwavering adherence to his own strong convictions during his careers as a civilian leader often generated controversy.

Chamberlain's nomination in 1866 as the Republican party's gubernatorial candidate in Maine buoyed his flagging spirits and ultimately allowed him to leave his position at Bowdoin. He won the September election with an unprecedented majority and subsequently served four consecutive terms as governor. Yet early in his tenure, no doubt to the consternation of the Republicans, Chamberlain proved that he voted according to his own conscience, not necessarily those of the party; he both opposed the attempt to remove President Andrew Johnson from office in 1867 and expressed reservations to an amendment to the Constitution extending the vote to former slaves. But it was not until he confronted issues that directly affected his home state voters that he experienced opposition.[62]

In 1868 two issues in particular had engaged the passions of the citizens of Maine: temperance and capital punishment. Chamberlain engendered the ire of temperance advocates by opposing the establishment of auxiliary police to control prohibition violations. But his position on capital punishment prompted the more significant reaction. Forsaking recent Maine tradition, Chamberlain declared he would not sidestep the orders of the courts when they issued a death sentence. Not only did his theoretical stance in support of capital punishment unsettle many of his constituents, but the outcry against an impending execution in 1868 was exacerbated by the volatile issue of race. The first man Chamberlain ordered put to death was a former slave who had been convicted of rape and murder.[63]

Considering the Chamberlains' physical separation, Lawrence's penchant for the "habit of command," and his refusal to allow the Republican party platform to sway his decisions, it is doubtful that he debated political decisions with his wife. It was during these crises that the rift between Lawrence and Fannie, both spatially and emotionally, continued to widen. The governorship kept Lawrence busy, and it dictated that he spend a great deal of time in Augusta, the state capital. Fannie preferred to remain at home in Brunswick or to go visiting.[64] Feeling alienated from Fannie and defensive in the midst of this bleak period, Chamberlain received word that his wife was telling people that he had physically and emotionally abused her and that she intended to divorce him. He wrote her an angry letter in which he thundered, "I should think we had skill enough to adjust the terms of a separation without the wretchedness to all our family." Fannie's plan to divorce him may have been only a rumor, but his quickness to believe the report is significant. The text of the letter demonstrates that their marriage had suffered a great strain and that their estrangement by 1868 had left them vulnerable to hearsay and gossip.[65]

Despite Chamberlain's gubernatorial difficulties, his tenure in office had not been altogether unsuccessful or without support. His intellect and reputation continued to command respect, and in 1871 he was invited to become president of his alma mater. He accepted. Yet, once again, his forceful opinions as president of Bowdoin College unsettled both alumni and students alike, this time eliciting a near mutiny among the college's student body.[66]

While the alumni eventually capitulated to his efforts to expand the curriculum, Chamberlain's enthusiasm for the students' mandatory participation in military science classes and drills did not. The new president instituted the program with federal funding in the fall of 1872. By the following spring the student body had virtually shut down the institution by boycotting drills and subsequently earning themselves suspensions from the college. Ultimately most of the students returned to Bowdoin on the threat of expulsion, but in this instance Chamberlain had won the battle but lost the war. Drill was declared voluntary the following year.[67]

In January 1880, Maine politics embroiled Lawrence Chamberlain in yet another public upheaval. In the 1870s a national debate raged over the gold standard. Farmers, who increasingly found themselves in debt, led the cry to relax the gold standard and ease credit. By the end of the decade, Maine voters had established the Greenback-Labor party as a political force in the state. When the new party edged out the Republican nominee for governor in 1878, the Republicans in the state legislature joined the Democrats to elect their candidate, Alonzo Garcelon, rather than vote for the "upstart" party's nominee. But by 1879, the Republicans were once again in ascendance in the state legislature, and the Democrats were desperately trying to hold on to power. Garcelon, citing illegal voting and incorrect ballot counts, attempted to alter the outcome of the 1879 election, hoping to forestall the seating of a Republican governor. Republican leaders moved quickly to enlist a public outcry. They were successful;

Maine Republicans grabbed their weapons and headed to Augusta. Garcelon, still governor, surrounded himself in the capitol with a small army and prevailed upon Chamberlain, as "military commander of the state," to provide additional support. Chamberlain hurried to the capitol, but focused his energy on trying to dissuade angry mobs from engaging in the violence that seemed certain to erupt. His insistence on remaining neutral during the twelve-day ordeal incurred the wrath of all sides, and he even received death threats.[68]

By the time this affair occurred, Lawrence and Fanny had begun to resolve their personal differences and their letters reflect the respect and love that bound them together. In the midst of the struggle in Augusta, Chamberlain wrote a letter to Fannie likening the exigency to a battle and describing his position as "another Round Top." He even referred to the incendiaries in the crowd as "rebels." But in this letter he also confided in Fannie, expressed concern for her position, and sought to soothe her anxiety for their safety during this explosive event.[69]

In the 1870s, the Chamberlains seem to have begun directing their attention to renovating their home in Brunswick, a decision that included relocating the building a short distance from where it stood. Both Lawrence and Fannie took part in the building's new character: Lawrence designed the entrance hall and Fannie an elaborate crystal candelabrum. They both engaged in redecorating the interior of their "new" home. The successful renovation of the Chamberlain house symbolically parallels the rebuilding of their relationship, which appears to have occurred at the same time. In 1878, the entire family, including their children twenty-one-year-old Grace and nineteen-year-old Wyllys, enjoyed a relaxing but memorable trip to Europe that bound them all closer together.[70]

In their later years, the Chamberlains occasionally spent time apart from one another as Lawrence's business ventures drew him away. But Lawrence's letters to Fannie display their former tenderness. In the late 1890s he wrote, "I have your beautiful letter that quickens all my great love for you so that I am impatient of any conditions that seem to keep you away from me." Even when discussing Fannie with their daughter Grace he added, "I don't want to go any where or see anything without her."[71]

Notwithstanding the criticism Fannie received during the war for traveling away from her children, the Chamberlains were devoted parents and remained close to their children. Letters reveal that Lawrence felt particularly close to, and proud of, his daughter Grace. After her marriage in 1881 to Horace Allen, a financially successful lawyer, Grace settled in Boston, but she continued to see her parents often. In the 1890s, Grace and Horace had three daughters: Eleanor, Beatrice, and Rosamond. Lawrence and Fannie's frequent visits to the Allens allowed them to dote on their three grandchildren. Their son Wyllys graduated from Bowdoin in 1881 and eventually studied law at Boston University. He practiced law for a time—his father seemed to have been his most loyal client—but was apparently unable to achieve financial independence much to the concern of his father. Ultimately, though, it was his lack of success in a career and his perpetual bachelorhood that made it possible for Wyllys to attend to the increasing needs of his parents as they aged.[72]

By the late 1880s, both Fannie and Lawrence were experiencing poor health: Lawrence's wounds had never healed completely and Fannie, who had suffered an eye affliction since childhood, was losing her sight. It must have been heartbreaking to Fannie, who had spent so many happy hours painting and whose works graced the walls of the Chamberlain home, to be left in a world of darkness. As they grew older and more infirm, it was Lawrence who became Fannie's nurturer. He reverted to his habit of referring to Fannie in diminutive terms such as "our poor tired 'little one' " and " 'little Mama,' " conjuring up images of a fragile female who hardly resembled the independent young woman who had tried to steer her husband's career. Her diminishing eyesight deprived Fannie of her self-reliance and transformed her into a more submissive wife.[73]

Although many years had passed since Chamberlain had performed his military feats during the Civil War, those events continued to shape the lives of both Lawrence and Fannie. As Lawrence tried to explain to Fannie when he took part in Grant's funeral in 1885, "[Y]ou know I have had great + deep experiences + some of my very life has gone into the history of the days that are past." For his participation as a hero in those divisive and terrible days of the past, Chamberlain continued to be rewarded with powerful positions and public prominence. In 1893—thirty years after the event—he received the country's highest military honor, the Congressional Medal of Honor, for his bravery and success at Gettysburg. Fannie had nursed her husband back to health several times during the war and, despite her travels, cared for their two young children while facing an uncertain future. Yet society did not publicly recognize the heroics and struggles of the women whose "front" remained the home. Although Fannie no doubt received a great deal of attention for being the wife of a hero, her wartime sacrifices did not merit the postwar celebrity of her husband's military actions.[74]

Chamberlain never could let go of the war that initiated the breach in their relationship. Before the war, they had been the center of each other's lives. During the war, they had spent a great deal of time apart, and their separate experiences increased the differences between them. The war that had torn the nation apart had divided them as well. Their recollections of those terrible years were not the shared memories of times with their children and families in peace, but private memories of different horrors. Afterward, the Civil War became almost an obsession for Lawrence, and when the United States declared war on Spain in 1898,

Chamberlain—seventy years old and unable to walk without pain due to the wound he received at Petersburg—volunteered his services to the United States Army in an attempt to recapture the glories of the past. The memories of the camps and battlefields that impelled Chamberlain to focus so intently on his three years as a Union soldier, Fannie could not share with him.[75]

Yet Chamberlain and his wife remained ever the romantics they had been in their youth. In the 1890s, during a period when living arrangements precluded their living together, Lawrence wrote Fannie a letter that perhaps speaks to her loneliness during the war years as well. He consoled her, "Do not feel bitterly that others have of me what you cannot. I do not think that is ever so . . . all that is best—all that is most mine is kept for you + is most yours." The Civil War had separated them; it had wounded both Lawrence and their relationship. But in the end the spiritual, if not the physical, romance remained.[76]

Virtually unable to see and growing weaker, Fannie broke her hip in the summer of 1905. In October, shortly after reaching her eightieth birthday, Fannie passed away. Lawrence Chamberlain survived his wife by nine years. As a widower he spent time with his children, particularly with Grace and her daughters; continued to sit on the board of trustees of Bowdoin; and wrote extensively about the Civil War. His most ambitious work was published after his death as *The Passing of the Armies*. But Chamberlain continued to pay the price of his heroism at Petersburg; he suffered from recurrent pain and infections. On February 24, 1914, in the presence of his two children, Lawrence Chamberlain died of his wounds.[77]

Fanny and Lawrence Chamberlain's lives and marriage intersected with one of the most remarkable and horrible periods in America's history. The Civil War surely shattered many of the romantic visions of their youth and altered the path of their lives in ways they could not have imagined. The anxiety and terror—and even romance—of war took a toll on their intimacy, both emotionally and physically. Although changed by the war years, ultimately they recognized the value of their marriage and were able to rekindle their tenderness toward one another.

In some ways the Chamberlains were unique. Most soldiers did not become as famous as Joshua Lawrence Chamberlain, and many wounded veterans were not fortunate enough to be able to return to their jobs and careers. Moreover, both Lawrence and Fannie came from middle-class, educated backgrounds. They had the skills and the time to reflect on their relationship. However, the war transformed hundreds of thousands of American men, northern and southern, both physically and psychologically. Like Lawrence and Fannie Chamberlain, countless couples, with varying degrees of success, faced the challenge of adjusting to the wounds and emotional distances the war engendered.

_____

TEN

The Civil War Partnership of Elizabeth and George A. Custer

_____

SHIRLEY A. LECKIE

After graduating as valedictorian of the Young Ladies Female Seminary at Monroe, Michigan, in June 1862, twenty-year-old Elizabeth Bacon experienced intense frustration. With no alternatives to marriage save school teaching, she hoped somehow to escape the household drudgery matrimony had brought her closest friends.[1] Slender and blessed with abundant brown hair and alert grey eyes, she had attracted numerous beaux. A West Point cadet, a high school principal from nearby Toledo, Ohio, a widowed clergyman, and two lawyers represented a sampling of her recent conquests. None made a lasting impression.[2]

Libbie, as she was known to family and friends, met George Armstrong Custer in November 1862 at a seminary party. Although she later described him as almost six feet tall, according to West Point records, he was slightly under five feet, nine inches, with reddish-blonde hair and blue eyes as his most distinguishing features. Like most of Monroe's residents she knew that twenty-two-year-old Autie had risen quickly in the army, for she congratulated him on his "very rapid" promotions. Her father, retired Judge Daniel Bacon, kept abreast of war news and had undoubtedly commented on Armstrong's readiness to undertake dangerous reconnaissance missions and his ability to gather accurate intelligence. These qualities had catapulted young Custer to a position as aide to General George B. McClellan, commander of the Army of the Potomac. Unfortunately, President Abraham Lincoln had recently dismissed the overly cautious commander for the second time after he had allowed General Robert E. Lee's Army of Northern Virginia to escape across the Potomac following the

Battle of Antietam on September 17. Now young Custer was on furlough, awaiting further orders.[3]

Despite his admirable war record, the captain's background made him unacceptable as Libbie Bacon's suitor in more ways than one. His father, Emmanuel Custer, a blacksmith turned farmer, was a fervent Democrat and Methodist. Daniel Bacon, by contrast, was a former Whig turned staunch Republican and an elder in Monroe's First Presbyterian Church. Finally, he had first laid eyes on the young officer two years earlier when as a lieutenant he had careened drunkenly down the street after an evening of heavy drinking. It mattered little that Armstrong had since taken the temperance oath and kept it—Monroe fathers saw him as a threat to their daughters' virtue.

Monroe citizens may have heard the gossip stemming from young Custer's birthplace of New Rumley, Ohio. Some residents of this Harrison County town whispered that the trials of Alexander Holland, superintendent of a local infirmary accounted for Custer's appointment to West Point in the first place. While Armstrong had written Representative John Bingham, asking for assistance in entering the Academy, his appointment came, the story went, after Holland had intercepted a note from Armstrong to his daughter. As a schoolteacher boarding in the Holland household, Custer had asked Mollie (Mary) to meet him "at the trundle bed." Although Holland had summarily evicted the youth, the persistent suitor continued bombarding his loved one with letters and poems. Finally, in exasperation, the angry father prevailed on Bingham to give Custer the appointment he had earlier sought. At the Academy, the young man had distinguished himself as the class rogue, barely escaping dismissal for his numerous demerits. Thus, his strong military record during the war was offset by his reputation as a sower of wild oats.[4]

From the first, Autie Custer was smitten with Libbie. Learning her normal schedule, he appeared beside her as soon as she stepped outside her home. Elizabeth, pleased with her new conquest, relegated him to escort duty while she ran errands or traveled to and from church or singing school. When he called at her home, however, she refused to see him.[5]

Knowing intuitively that Monroe's most sought after young woman was highly competitive, Armstrong riveted her attention by appearing in public with her chief rival, the attractive and free-spirited Fannie Fifield. His strategy worked so well that when he arrived at the front early in April 1863 he carried Libbie's ambrotype with him.[6]

Armstrong and Elizabeth were now involved in an intricate game of courtship. Obviously by underscoring his attractiveness to others, Autie heightened his allure in Libbie's eyes. Libbie matched him in every way. Reflecting on his relationship with Miss Fifield, she noted in her diary, "He, like others, takes all she gives which I sometimes think is *everything*, but when a man has all he desires in one he rarely desires the girl for his

wife. And he has as exalted ideas about what a woman should be as anyone." As for herself, "I *know* the reason he loved me [was] because I
wouldn't let him kiss me and treat me as if we were engaged."[7] The young
woman who wrote these comments was neither as naive nor as sheltered
as she maintained in the numerous drafts of her never-completed Civil
War memoirs.[8] Although the prevailing double standard tolerated pre-
marital sexual activity in males, females lost value as prospective wives if
they were suspected of impurity before marriage.[9]

Returning to his regiment, the Fifth Cavalry, Armstrong learned that
changes were under way in the Army of the Potomac. General Joseph
Hooker had replaced McClellan's immediate successor General Ambrose
Burnside after the Union debacle at the Battle of Fredericksburg in December 1862, and he was transforming the northern cavalry. Relegated
earlier to picket and courier duty, it was becoming a true "mounted arm,"
similar to the hard-striking Confederate cavalry. Increasingly it was engaging in reconnaissance, counterreconnaissance, raiding, and military operations that supported infantry action. In this context, Custer displayed
not only his usual initiative and willingness to take chances but a growing
ability to inspire his men through bold and courageous leadership. He
soon attracted the attention of Brigadier General Alfred A. Pleasonton,
head of two cavalry divisions. Before long, Pleasonton, like McClellan earlier, chose Armstrong as his aide.

Lee's victory at Chancellorsville in early May 1863 cost Hooker his command. Afterward Lee invaded the North, seeking a decisive victory on
enemy soil. As his Army of Northern Virginia penetrated the passes of the
Blue Ridge Mountains, Pleasonton's cavalry, seeking to determine their
strength and direction, encountered the Confederate horse under Jeb
(James Ewell Brown) Stuart. Although Stuart forced Pleasonton to retreat
at Brandy Station on June 9, the Union cavalry acquitted itself so well that
for the first time the men in blue understood that Stuart's "Invincibles"
were not invulnerable. Among those winning commendations that day was
George A. Custer.

Thirteen days later, Pleasonton was promoted to major general and on
June 28, Custer received a startling letter. At twenty-three, he had become
the youngest general in the Union army. Pleasonton had sent his name,
along with those of twenty-five-year-old Elon Farnsworth and twenty-six-
year-old Wesley Merritt, to General George Meade, Hooker's replacement.
These youths were willing to risk all to transform the cavalry into a deadly
mobile force within the Union army.

Custer's command was the Michigan Brigade, which included the First,
Fifth, Sixth, and Seventh Michigan Cavalry regiments. Ironically, only a
few weeks earlier he had unsuccessfully sought the colonelcy of the Fifth
Michigan.[10]

On July 3, 1863, on the third day of the Battle of Gettysburg, Jeb
Stuart's forces, in a three-hour fight, came no closer than two and a half

miles from the Union rear. This was due largely to the headlong charges of the Michigan Brigade, led by Custer shouting: "Come on, you Wolverines."[11] Northern newspapers now hailed the "Boy General" as the newest hero in the war. Almost unnoticed in the acclaim, the Michigan Brigade sustained casualties exceeding 25 percent, a portent of things to come.[12]

Elizabeth, although of marriageable age, was an "obedient" daughter and would never have married without her father's consent. Armstrong's rising star was changing Daniel Bacon's views on his character, but the young general believed that more was needed. To assure his success as Libbie's suitor, he obtained testimonials from prominent men in Monroe, among them Judge Isaac Christiancy, a founder of the Republican party. (Armstrong had recently appointed the judge's son James to his staff despite the latter's drinking problem.) In November, Bacon gave Armstrong permission to correspond directly with his daughter.[13] By Christmas, the couple had selected February 9, 1864, as their wedding day.

Determined to escape the confines of a small Michigan town and lacking a public arena of her own, Libbie Bacon found the "splendid" attributes of her "own particular star" far more attractive than the staid predictability of her other admirers. Moreover, the physical attraction between the two had grown. Although Elizabeth feared the "solemn" responsibility wives assumed for improving their husband's character, she looked forward to becoming Armstrong's "little wife."[14]

Armstrong, in turn, was eager to escape bachelorhood. As one biographer has noted, within Custer, the boy and the man vied for dominance.[15] In Victorian America of the Civil War era, soldiers saw in combat a crucial test of their manliness. There was another test as well, however, and that was the assumption of marital duties.[16] For Armstrong, who had already seen horrendous carnage on the battlefield, becoming a husband undoubtedly presented a way of becoming the "man" in the "man and wife" proclaimed in the wedding ceremony. At some level, he may have felt that clothed in this new status, he would find the horrors of warfare easier to face.

Marriage answered another need. From the beginning of their relationship, Autie recognized and relied on Libbie's excellent judgment. He knew that her discernment would offset his tendency to act impulsively. While the latter contributed to his success as a cavalry officer, it led him to take chances such as speaking out inappropriately at times or becoming involved in heavy gambling.[17] Later, as he confessed in an 1867 letter, "merging upon manhood, my every thought was ambitious—not to be wealthy, not to be learned, but to be great."[18] Marrying the most attractive and sought-after young woman in Monroe was a promising start for an officer who seized every opportunity the war presented for advancement.

Shortly before his daughter's wedding, Daniel Bacon became alarmed. Recently Michigan senator, Jacob Howard, had questioned the advisability of confirming Custer's promotion to brigadier general. Armstrong wrote

Bacon, assuring him that Senator Howard was now perfectly satisfied as were other members of the Michigan delegation, especially Senator Zachariah Chandler and Representative F. W. Kellogg. Enemies, including Michigan's abolitionist governor, Austin Blair, and Brigadier General Joseph Copeland, former commander of the Michigan Brigade, had accused him of being a " 'Copperhead' and a strong opponent of the administration and the present war policy." Custer vehemently denied those charges.[19]

The young officer mentioned nothing about the hot-tempered and impolitic remarks he and other members of McClellan's staff had made following Lincoln's preliminary Emancipation Proclamation on September 22, which freed all slaves in states still in rebellion after January 1, 1863. Deeply opposed to transforming a war to restore the Union into a drive to end slavery in the South, they had talked of marching on Washington to depose the president and turn McClellan into a "dictator" to allow him to conduct warfare without interference.[20] Since his dismissal, moreover, McClellan had emerged as the likely Democratic candidate for the presidency. Many feared that if elected, he would make peace by allowing Southerners to retain their peculiar institution. In that context, as the former member of McClellan's staff who had helped the general write his final report after the second dismissal, young Custer was bound to arouse suspicions.[21]

The Senate had to approve Custer's promotion to brigadier, and the signs were unfavorable when a member from his own state was opposed. For the moment, Armstrong saw all charges as "completely refuted." (He had already written Senator Howard voicing his strong support for the Lincoln administration's war aims.) Assuring his future father-in-law that he had "no anxiety whatever in regard to my confirmation," he had avoided the topic earlier to spare Libbie "unnecessary anxiety and discomfort."[22]

Following an elaborate wedding in which Libbie, resplendent in white satin, exchanged vows with her brigadier before an overflow crowd at Monroe's First Presbyterian Church, the couple left on their honeymoon. After visiting Libbie's relatives at Onondaga County, New York, they arrived at West Point Military Academy. Armstrong, having graduated last in his class in 1861, was eager to show his former professors both the star on his shoulder and his attractive bride. Elizabeth, never having seen "so lovely a place in the United States," now understood why her husband said he wanted to be buried here.[23]

Nonetheless, the newlyweds experienced their first marital quarrel in this setting. When Armstrong learned that several cadets had escorted Libbie down Lovers' Walk and a professor had kissed her after Armstrong had left her alone, he fell into sullen silence. Libbie, after countering that the cadets were only boys and the professor a "Methuselah," then blurted out, "Well, you left me with them, Autie!"[24] Although her husband softened, she had endured the first of his many "silent seasons."

As Autie later explained, the "long, lonely beats that he walked, [and] the many solitary confinements of the guardhouse for misdemeanors" had caused him to retreat periodically into himself. Libbie, relieved that his withdrawal was not due to "my defects or his disappointments in me," maintained that she accepted these periods as his way of coping with difficulties, trying "not to mind them." She stated later, "Though I lived through a blaze of sunshine for twelve years, there were many silent seasons which I learned to understand and respect."[25]

In truth, such episodes haunted her. In writing her never-published memoirs of the Civil War, she reworked her drafts of the West Point quarrel repeatedly. Obviously, she wanted to please her husband, noting that any "sensitive and indulged girl with the humility of those who truly love would ascribe to any silence of a bridegroom that he had taken her own very humble estimate of herself."[26] Determined not to disappoint him, she sought to gain his approval by becoming an asset to his career. Later, after his death, she continued that pattern, sparing no effort to protect his reputation from detractors.

After a brief sojourn in New York City, the couple arrived in Washington where the young general introduced his wife to politicians, diplomats, dignitaries, and their families. During wartime, the practice of awarding rank by brevet or temporary title had made brigadiers almost commonplace, but the couple's attractiveness brought them extraordinary attention. Days after their arrival in the city, however, Armstrong was ordered to rejoin his brigade.[27] Libbie accompanied him when he returned to his command at Stevensburg, Virginia, south of Brandy Station on the extreme right flank of the Army of the Potomac.

There she met for the first time Eliza Brown (later Denison), a freedwoman who had joined the general as his cook the previous August. Libbie, having neither interest nor competency in cooking or domestic duties, left all household labor to Eliza. The latter also provided her with much needed mothering, for the bride found army life a "violent transition."[28]

While Armstrong was her boyish and often teasing husband in private, in public he was often a stern disciplinarian, barking orders to men older than himself. Sometimes, his officious manner with subalterns and soldiers spilled over into his relations with his wife. Libbie also discovered that without meaning to, she easily violated military protocol. Her efforts to intercede on behalf of members of the staff, who sought her womanly advice on problems with sweethearts or their inability to overcome drinking or gambling, brought swift reprimands from her husband. Seemingly innocent remarks, moreover, had unforeseen consequences. When she commented at a gathering on "the pleasant gentlemanly air" of career officers, Armstrong informed her later that such statements created hard feelings among volunteers, "and so," she wrote her parents, "I am improving."[29]

Worse was the horror of suspense when her husband undertook a dangerous mission. On February 28, 1864, Armstrong left on a diversionary raid. While Judson Kilpatrick, commander of the Third Division of the Cavalry Corps, and Colonel Ulric Dahlgren moved against Richmond to free imprisoned Union soldiers, Custer led 2,000 men into Albemarle County, Virginia. After destroying the Virginia Central Railroad, he planned to move toward Charlottesville, drawing troops away from the Confederate capital. As he said good-bye, Libbie hid her anxiety, but afterward, mistrusting the southern couple overseeing the farm where they resided, she returned to Washington.

The raid failed abysmally, claiming many lives, including Dahlgren's, while Custer barely eluded a Confederate ambush. Libbie never forgave Kilpatrick who, in her view, had instigated the raid to win glory.[30] More important, she now knew what it meant to be a soldier's wife. Apprehension tormented her until Pleasonton telegraphed her on March 1 that Armstrong had arrived safely at Madison Court House.[31]

Shortly after, Elizabeth, boarding at Hyatt's rooming house on Sixth Street, heard "the clank of a saber rattling on stairs. . . . In the middle of a wakeful night of suspense, the door burst open to welcome a mud besplattered but perfectly fresh and buoyant warrior, whooping with joy, having eluded with an inferior force, the pursuing foe."[32]

Resuming their honeymoon, the couple appeared in the centers of power in Washington. They were delighted when they saw artist Al Waud's drawing of Custer leading his Charlottesville raid on the cover of the March 19 issue of *Harper's Weekly*. Later Elizabeth beamed from the balcony of the House of Representatives as congressmen congratulated Armstrong on the floor. Afterward, he met Lincoln. "I find it very agreeable to be the wife of a man so generally known and respected," Libbie wrote her parents.[33]

Ulysses S. Grant, following his victories at Vicksburg, was since early March general-in-chief of the army, the first to hold that rank since George Washington. Though Meade remained nominal commander of the Army of the Potomac, Grant directed actions in the field. In a war that catapulted men of modest backgrounds into prominence, Major General Philip H. Sheridan, the son of Irish immigrants, replaced Pleasonton who, along with Kilpatrick, was sent to the western theater.

Armstrong was uneasy. Although he knew of Sheridan's contributions at Chattanooga and Missionary Ridge, he had no idea that the diminutive "Little Phil" wanted to engage Jeb Stuart's Invincibles in northern Virginia.[34] His first star confirmed, Custer wanted a second, specifically as commander of the Third Division, Kilpatrick's former position.

Elizabeth, attuned to her husband's desires, actively sought to advance his career. As a young woman in the anomalous position of living alone in Washington, she acted behind the scenes. She would never, for example, have visited the White House to intercede with Lincoln on behalf of her husband as had Jessie Benton Frémont, the wife of John C. Frémont. She knew that such action, which violated widespread ideals of appropriate female behavior, would have been counterproductive. When the daughter of the late Thomas Hart Benton had asked Lincoln to retain her husband as commander in Missouri after Frémont had decreed the slaves of residents still in rebellion to be free, the president had met Jessie Frémont's request with cold and humiliating disdain.[35]

Libbie's strategy was more subtle and similar to that pursued by Elizabeth Blair Lee. The latter, as adviser to her husband Samuel Phillips Lee, a naval officer, used her influence as the daughter of Francis Preston Blair, editor of the *Washington Globe* and adviser to presidents, to advance his career before the war began. During the war, she worked behind the scenes, helping her husband become acting rear admiral of the North Atlantic Blockading Squadron by keeping him informed of developments from their home in Silver Spring outside the capital. Elizabeth Blair Lee also relayed important messages to and from her influential father. By 1864, she was visiting the wives of politicians and dignitaries to help Samuel attain the position of permanent rear admiral, a prize that eluded him until 1870.[36]

Libbie Custer's method was to socialize with powerful Republicans. Whenever possible, she accompanied Senator Chandler and Representative Kellogg and their wives to dinner parties and other social events. Both members of the Michigan delegation, captivated by her charm and beauty, eagerly filled her dance books at capital "hops."[37] Years later in numerous drafts of her Civil War memoirs, Elizabeth described herself as a frightened, often awkward young woman who spent her time during the war years "mostly blushing." She noted the social blunders she committed with her husband at his headquarters, where she portrayed herself as the brunt of good-natured jokes. Later she claimed that she was unsure of herself in the capital city.[38] In truth, once she learned the finer points of military protocol, she displayed superb social skills in both settings.

Chandler and Kellogg, for example, called on her at times alone in her boardinghouse. Usually they brought her information or invited her to accompany them and their wives to a social event. Over time, however, both became flirtatious, especially when inebriated. Despite her youth and inexperience, Libbie expertly evaded their kisses without bruising their egos—no small feat for a twenty-two-year-old.[39] She proved her adaptiveness in other ways. When the Custers were reunited, either in the capital city or during the times she joined her husband for brief periods in camp, the two projected a romantic image.

As an adolescent, Armstrong had devoured the novels of Sir Walter Scott, especially those that celebrated the valor of chivalrous knights. He also relished the works of Charles Lever that extolled the exploits of Napoleonic-era cavaliers. During his years at West Point, moreover, he had formed friendships with Southerners, such as Thomas L. Rosser, presently commanding the Confederacy's Laurel Brigade, and Stephen Ramseur, who at twenty-seven would soon become the Army of Northern Virginia's youngest major general. Armstrong's associations with men from a region where the cavalier was the embodiment of ideal manhood left their mark on him as did his battlefield rivalry with Jeb Stuart, known as the "Knight of the Golden Spurs" in his homeland. Increasingly Custer sought to become the northern version of the South's preeminent cavalier.[40]

Armstrong's self-designed uniform underscored the image he sought to project. In his "D'Artagnan boots," his broad-brimmed hat rakishly askew over his flowing curls, and his gold braided pants and jacket, he placed himself at the front of battle. His red necktie attracted Confederate sharpshooters, but by constantly moving he evaded their bullets. His flamboyant dress and his devil-may-care attitude struck the desired note when a *New York Herald* correspondent described him as "a first-class hero" and "as gallant a cavalier as one would wish to see."[41] Elizabeth, who shared with her husband her fondness for the romantic poems of Alfred Lord Tennyson, fell instinctively into the role of the cavalier's lady. With her dark hair artfully arranged in elaborate curls and her wide satin or brocade hooped skirts, she seemed, as she described herself later, like one of "the tiny china dolls from the pincushions that pervade church fairs."[42]

Achieving that image demanded spending much of Armstrong's salary on clothes to the horror of Libbie's stepmother, Rhoda Pitts Bacon. Armstrong, on the other hand, although admonishing his wife to "practice economy," was more upset by her failure to call on an officer's wife. The lady's husband, he noted ominously "is one of my best friends, and feels the omission deeply."[43]

Nonetheless, Libbie's socializing soon paid dividends, as evidenced by the growing cordiality of the Kelloggs. Although command of the Third Division went to James H. Wilson, a friend of Grant's, the congressman's message of April 17 cheered Armstrong. "No true man like you can be killed by such gross favoritism on the part of the Chief of the Army."[44]

The friendship proved even more productive when the Michigan congressman and his wife asked Elizabeth to accompany them to a levee at the White House. As she was introduced to the president, Lincoln recognized her as the wife of the general who "goes into a charge with a whoop and a shout." "Well," he added, "I'm told he won't do so any more," implying that marriage had tamed the young warrior. When Elizabeth demurred, he replied: "Oh, then you want to be a widow, I see." That seemed so ludicrous that both laughed. Never bypassing a chance to create a favorable impression and reinforce the idea that her husband supported the administration's policies, Libbie directed a clerk "to tell Mr. Lincoln he would have gained a vote, if soldiers' wives were allowed one."[45]

Armstrong was overjoyed at Elizabeth's appearance at the White House and "proud" that she had been "honored by his Highness." As for the dance she had attended recently, he was "so much obliged to Mr. Chandler for inviting you. You did perfectly right in accepting; it is just what I urged you to do." She was to ignore "the idle opinions of those whose time is occupied with other people's business."[46] Although Armstrong had displayed jealousy at West Point, whatever misgivings he now harbored were secondary to the benefits he received from his wife's deft socializing.

In this partnership, in which both worked as a team to win the Boy General promotion despite lingering concerns that he remained a "McClellan man," the two assigned each other attributes and responsibilities based on their sex. It was a common belief among Americans in the nineteenth century that women were innately more virtuous than men. Thus, like other middle-class men—such as the Union cavalry leader in the western theater, Major General Benjamin H. Grierson in his letters to Alice Grierson, or the Confederate general, William Pender, in his correspondence with Fanny Pender—Autie in his letters to his wife, accorded her moral superiority and chronicled the ways in which her influence had already improved his character.[47] "Loving so fine a being truly and devotedly as I do, it seems impossible that I ever should or could be very wicked," he assured Elizabeth on April 23.[48] Libbie, who had undergone conversion at seventeen and was deeply religious, wanted her husband to become a professing Christian. Then if he died in combat she would know that he had at least achieved salvation in the hereafter. Autie refused, although he urged her to remain pious. "It may seem strange to you, dear girl, that I, a non-professing (tho not an unbeliever) Christian, should so ardently desire you to remain so."[49] Probably she was not alarmed. Despite the religious fervor of her mother, Eleanor Sophia Page Bacon, her father had not undergone conversion until 1856, two years after his wife had died. Thus there was hope for Armstrong; in the meantime at least he prayed before each battle. Afterward, he was confident "that my destiny is in the hands of the Almighty. This belief," he added, "more than any other fact or reason, makes me brave and fearless as I am."[50]

Elizabeth needed that assurance; perceptive and shrewd as she was, she read the ominous signs. "The silence in the papers shows that a great battle is expected," she wrote her parents on May 1, 1864. Numerous army wagons clattered over the pavement daily, and many veterans were returning to duty. She and a neighbor watched the troops from their windows "as just a block from here," to the strains of martial music, "they turn to cross the bridge—'into the jaws of death' it seems."[51]

For many men, it was an apt description as Union strategy changed significantly. Rather than targeting Richmond, Grant planned first to destroy Lee's army. Although he hoped to avert a war of attrition, especially one that could cost Lincoln the next election, he could replace his losses. The Confederacy could not. As the first step toward mounting an unrelenting offensive, Grant ordered his divisions across the Rapidan on the

night of May 4.[52] Armstrong, noting that all communications might cease
for several days, advised his wife not to "borrow trouble."[53]

Two days of fighting followed in dense underbrush and wooded areas
in the Battle of the Wilderness of May 5 and 6. When it was over, Union
forces had sustained casualties of 17,500 or two and a half times those of
the Confederacy. Grant, undeterred, moved southward. Sheridan's cavalry
assisted by raiding toward Lee's supply lines, destroying twenty miles of
railroads and three weeks worth of rations before confronting Jeb Stuart
at Yellow Tavern. On May 11, in the ensuing battle, the southern cavalier
was mortally wounded, but the news left Armstrong with mixed emotions.
Although his rival had fallen, he saw Stuart's successor, Wade Hampton,
as a more able general.[54]

Shortly after, a Washington newspaper carried the story that Custer also
had died in combat. Libbie was overcome with grief until John Bingham,
the Ohio congressman who had recommended Armstrong for West Point
eight years earlier, arrived at her boardinghouse to tell her that the report
was in error.[55]

Autie's death was now an ever-present possibility. His letters told her
that even "with the bullets whistling by me and shells bursting all around
me," his thoughts were of her, and "even death staring me in the face
only serves to render you more dear."[56] If he died he wanted to leave her
"a name which will be a source of pride to you in after life."[57] The Michigan Brigade, while "cover[ing] itself with undying glory," was enduring
losses that in May totaled 45 percent. Of the 1,700 men in Custer's brigade, 98 would be listed as killed, 330 as wounded, and 348 as missing
in action before the wilderness campaign ended.[58] Daniel Bacon, after
reading the reports in the Michigan newspapers, wrote his daughter, "Do
not fail to telegraph if anything happens to Armstrong. Be calm, submissive and composed is the wish and prayer of your Father."[59]

At Trevilian Station on June 11, the Michigan Brigade, "detached from
the main body, for the purpose of turning the enemy flank," encountered
Hampton's troopers. Battling alone in dense, tangled underbrush, the
Wolverines sustained 416 casualties, including 41 killed, the highest for
the cavalry in the entire war.[60] Armstrong's letter, describing the battle,
underscored the precariousness of his situation. At one point, surrounded
on three sides, his arm and shoulder bruised by spent bullets and his
cheek grazed by a sharpshooter's bullet, he barely escaped entrapment,
leaving behind a valise with his wife's letters.[61]

The loss of her letters mortified the young general. While he had "enjoyed every word" of her thinly veiled references to their uninhibited love-
making, he cautioned her to "be more careful hereafter in the use of
double entendu [*sic*]."[62] Libbie thought otherwise. "There can be nothing
low between man and wife if they love each other," she countered.[63] Then,
seeing his consternation over the thought that Confederates were amusing
themselves by reading their intimate letters and fearing he might think

less of her in his embarrassment, she reversed herself. Having confided her love and desire in letters that unfortunately have not survived, Elizabeth now promised to never "again offend my dear boy's sense of nicety by departing from that delicate propriety which, I believe, was born in me—the lady in me inherited from my mother." At his slightest vexation, she was "grieved and [would] try to do better."[64]

Another consideration was at work here. Armstrong might perish at any time, and with that in mind, Libbie set aside differences as they arose. As she noted years later, for many army wives, "with parting ever before them in that period of uncertainty, even the mildest tiff was avoided with the husband rushing constantly into action."[65]

Whatever lay ahead, Libbie wanted children. Someday in peace, "little children's voices will call to us. I can hardly wait for my little boy and girl," she wrote Armstrong in one letter.[66] In another, she told of praying for a child she could raise to become "a cornerstone in the great church of God—and Autie, if God gives me children I shall say to them: 'Emulate your Father! I can give you no higher earthly example.' But *then* I can say to them: 'Emulate him in his Christian as well as his moral character,' can I not?"[67] As was common among nineteenth-century women in the United States, she saw rearing children in a devout household as her primary purpose in life. Unfortunately her hopes for motherhood were never realized, and one Custer biographer surmises that Armstrong's treatment for gonorrhea at West Point may have left him incapable of fathering children.[68]

As was common among women of that era, Libbie blamed herself for failing to conceive. However, when she berated herself, Armstrong tried to reassure her.[69] By war's end, he counted their childlessness a blessing. At one point, encamped in Martinsburg, Virginia, he eagerly awaited Libbie's arrival for a brief reunion while another general's wife remained at home awaiting her second child. Autie rejoiced that his wife was "not so burdened yet, but is able to come and go," and time strengthened that feeling.[70] But Elizabeth regretted until her death that she had never borne a son to carry on her husband's "honored name."[71]

By mid-June 1864, Grant, after waging unceasing war against Lee's army, had brought his forces before the Confederate entrenchments at Petersburg. During the past six weeks, the Army of the Potomac had sustained casualties totaling over 65,000.[72] Living in Washington, Libbie saw the results of that carnage daily. Steamers, wagons, and trains brought the dead back to the rapidly proliferating embalming establishments and a continuing procession of military funerals.[73] Medical personnel, facing unprecedented demands, called for volunteers to attend the wounded and the dying.

Seeing the overburdened staff at Mount Pleasant Hospital, many of them women striving vainly to cope with the sick and mangled bodies, Elizabeth thought of volunteering as a nurse. She learned, however, that her duties would prevent her from joining her husband at a moment's notice, which would be especially important if he were wounded. Armstrong's brother, Tom Custer, who eventually left the Twenty-first Ohio Volunteers to become his brother's aide (an accepted practice in that era), recalled his sister-in-law in those days. She was so responsive to her husband's call to join him in the field that she slept, he was certain, with her boots on and buckled.[74]

Lieutenant James Christiancy, the son of Isaac Christiancy, had been among those wounded earlier at Harris's Shop, Virginia. Elizabeth arranged for the alcoholic rake to board at her rooming house. There, as she nursed him to health, she sought his "reformation" and conversion. Her actions, endearing her to Lieutenant Christiancy's influential father, Isaac Christiancy, strengthened her husband's standing with Michigan's Republican leaders.[75] While nursing the youth, Elizabeth maintained her contacts, visiting the capitol with a friend and the Radical Republican senator from New Hampshire, John Hale. In the House, Hale introduced Elizabeth to Speaker Schuyler Colfax who praised Custer enthusiastically. Outside, Representative Kellogg assured Libbie that Armstrong's promotion to major general was imminent. Returning home, she heard a similar report from her landlady; Radical Republican senator Benjamin Wade was her source.[76]

By late June, Sheridan's cavalry was encamped on the James River, below City Point, Virginia. When Libbie discovered that officials planned to visit the troops, she asked Kellogg for permission to accompany them and then "avoided his attempt to kiss me by moving aside and offering him a chair."[77] In early July, as the *Baltimore* docked at City Point, Armstrong, oblivious to all, leaped aboard the steamship and embraced his bride of five months before an admiring crowd of congressmen, senators, dignitaries, and their wives. Caroline Dana Howe later memorialized the scene in a poem, "Young Custer's Bride."[78]

For the most part, July and early August of the seemingly interminable summer of 1864 brought Elizabeth only sweltering heat and apprehension. At times, almost frantic with loneliness and anxiety, she escaped the oppressive heat of her boardinghouse by walking with a friend to a nearby park. Along the way they sometimes met female government workers dressed in black, "weary creatures who had lost their husbands or sons, in the war and were working for daily bread for themselves or their children." Seeing these women "hurrying home to cook dinner for their children," Libbie shuddered, hoping the day would never come when she would find herself a widow.[79]

As the summer wore on, the siege of Petersburg continued and casualties mounted. Growing numbers of Northerners, sickened by the carnage, called for an end to the war, and newspapers declared the Union cause lost. Many predicted that McClellan, whom the Democrats had nominated on a platform that termed the war a failure and called for peace, would win in November. If so, he would surely obtain an immediate armistice by offering to reverse the Emancipation Proclamation.[80]

When Atlanta, an industrial and transportation center for the Confederacy, fell on September 2, 1864, and Admiral David Farragut captured Mobile the next day, Lincoln's chance for reelection improved dramatically. Still McClellan's candidacy posed problems for Custer. Fearing that some Radical Republicans continued to doubt his dependability, he sent Isaac Christiancy a letter on September 16, voicing his strong support for the president's policies. To his father Emmanuel Custer's chagrin, he emphasized that the only peace he favored was one "forced by the points of our bayonets."[81]

Sheridan, after assuring Grant that the people of the Shenandoah Valley would be left with "nothing but their eyes to weep with over the war," instructed his subalterns to transform the Valley into "a barren waste." Custer proved a most reliable lieutenant, thereby gaining Little Phil's confidence. Whether burning farmhouses and fields outside Dayton, Virginia, or as he had done earlier in August, retaliating against John Mosby's rebel guerrillas by executing four of them "without trial," according to Grant's dictates, Custer acted decisively.[82] The Army of the Shenandoah, moving rapidly between October 6 and October 8, cut a swath of devastated fields and buildings between the Alleghenies and the Blue Ridge Mountains.[83]

When Senator Chandler visited Elizabeth at her boardinghouse, "tight as usual, and disgusting when he has taken too much," she moved her chair as tactfully as possible to "keep him from kissing me."[84] Staying on good terms with the Michigan senator, a member of the powerful Committee on the Conduct of the War, remained essential. In addition, her friendship with the Kelloggs was reaping other benefits. Since the congressman had offered to visit Monroe and deliver a speech in Custer's honor, the young wife wrote her father, suggesting he ask his friends to invite him. "But don't let anybody know you did so. For when he praises Autie they might think us proud. We have a right to be, but not to be 'set up.' "[85]

On Tuesday, October 25, Armstrong and Libbie stood together in the office of Edwin Stanton during a presentation ceremony of flags captured at Cedar Creek. Afterward, the secretary of war officially announced Custer's promotion to major general, noting "a good general, makes good men." Elated, Libbie wrote her parents: "People are beginning to call me Mrs. Major-General. But I have been too well-trained by you to be 'stuck up.' "[86]

Lincoln won the election that November by a landslide largely because of Atlanta's fall and events in the Shenandoah Valley. That winter, because Armstrong "still charged the enemy with the same impetuosity after as before marriage," Sheridan allowed Elizabeth to remain at Winchester, Virginia, headquarters after ordering the other wives to leave.[87] He was grateful that marriage had not ruined Custer's willingness to take chances.[88]

Early in 1865, a wave of religious enthusiasm swept through the eastern theater of the war. When Custer obtained a furlough the couple returned to Monroe. Facing the stress of the looming spring campaigns and influenced by his wife's constant entreaties, Armstrong attended a Monroe revival. On February 5, 1865, he "accepted Christ as my Saviour."[89] Overjoyed, Emmanuel Custer, aware that his younger son, as Armstrong's aide, was also prone to take risks, asked Libbie to "counsel Thomas" as well.[90]

As Custer returned to his division, Libbie, her parents, and a cousin, Rebecca Richmond, attended Lincoln's second inaugural. Afterward, the young women went to the ball, accompanied by Senator Chandler where Elizabeth "danced with him simply out of etiquette."[91] Armstrong, involved in fierce campaigning, hoped his now fabled "Custer's luck" would prevail. By war's end at least eleven and possibly twelve mounts were shot from under him, several of them as he contributed to further victories that spring at Waynesboro, Dinwiddie Courthouse, Five Forks, and Saylor's Creek.[92]

As a young woman living alone in the capital city, Libbie observed life in the Washington of her day, which she described to her father as "Sodom." From her earliest weeks at Mrs. Hyatt's boardinghouse she had met, she wrote Autie, "so many wives in name only idling around with other men."[93] Throughout the year, she noted that some women—a Mrs. K and the wife of Major G—were carrying on with other men. The latter flirted with Senator Chandler and then a doctor while her husband "sat quietly talking in the next room. . . . Autie," she noted, "it is rather the exception than the rule that married people here care for each other."[94]

By spring 1865, Libbie, fearing that her reputation would suffer by remaining at Mrs. Hyatt's, found other quarters with the help of former Vice-President Hannibal Hamlin.[95] Armstrong looked forward to their next meeting in her new dwelling. He was especially eager to try out the "soft place upon somebodys carpet because as that lady remarked in reference to piercing ears &c there are a great many ways of *doing things* some of which I believe are not generally known."[96] The physical bond between the couple, like their partnership to promote Autie's career, was now stronger and more intense than ever.

In Wilmer McLean's parlor at Appomattox Courthouse, Lee accepted Grant's terms of surrender on April 9, 1865. The Confederates were allowed to lay down their arms and return home for spring planting provided they observed their parole. Among those who purchased mementos, Sheridan exchanged twenty dollars in gold for a dark pine table with spool-shaped legs on which Grant had written the surrender terms and signed the peace document.[97]

Later he gave the table to Custer as a present for Libbie with an enclosed note. "My Dear Madam, I respectfully present to you the small writing table on which conditions for the surrender of the Confederate Army of Northern Virginia were written by Lt. General Grant—and permit me to say, Madam," Sheridan continued, "that there is scarcely an individual in our service who has contributed more to bring about this desirable result than your very gallant husband."[98] Libbie sent the table to her parents, admonishing them, "Don't give away a splinter even. They tell me I might sell it for a million dollars." Enclosed was a copy of Sheridan's letter, which she treasured even more.[99]

The Custers met for the first time after Lee's surrender in the White House of the now vanquished Confederacy. Libbie had accompanied the Committee on the Conduct of the War to Richmond after its fall, and since President Jefferson Davis and his wife Varina had fled the city, General Godfrey Weitzel and his wife had moved into the presidential mansion. Although they were called away, Elizabeth, as their guest, spent the first night in the former president's bed. The next night she moved to Varina's bed where Armstrong awoke her on the morning of April 12. His appearance stunned her. The last battles of the war had left him, as she wrote a friend, "tanned, but thin and worn."[100]

On May 23, 1865, after the Army of the Potomac participated in the Grand Review in Washington, D.C., a final victory parade, Armstrong bade his division farewell. Libbie was beside him, dressed in black velvet riding cap, tailored to match her husband's uniform and accented with a red feather that echoed his red cravat. Her apparel revealed not only her emotional affiliation with her husband but her ideal for herself as a wife. As she had written him earlier, "I cannot love as I do without my life blending with yours. I would not lose my individuality, but would be, as a wife should be, part of her husband, a life within a life."[101]

Despite the promise of that spring day, Armstrong found peace more traumatic than war. As one of his biographers notes, "He loved war. It nourished and energized him. It triggered those complex mechanisms of intellect and instinct that made his tactical decision nearly flawless" and provided "the environment in which a youth so endowed could gain the obedience and adulation of several thousand followers and inspire them to fight and die for him." It also served as "the catalyst that drove a young man hardly past the threshold of manhood to measure up to the stars that adorned his shoulder straps." Unfortunately, the new challenges ahead proved more formidable. At times in the decade of life remaining to him, "the boy who had been held in check for two years by the awesome demands of 'Glorious War'—not just the exuberant, fun-loving boy but the immature, foolish boy as well," often came to the fore.[102]

After a brief and frustrating stint of postwar duty in Louisiana and Texas, in which volunteer troops who had served in the western theater of the war almost mutinied from the mistreatment they received at Custer's hands, the tarnished hero's rank reverted to captain in the Fifth Cavalry. Failing to find a more remunerative career than the military, he accepted in July 1866 the lieutenant colonelcy in the Seventh Cavalry, one of the new regiments formed to police the developing regions of the Trans-Mississippi West.

In an area, once known as the "Great American Desert," the Plains Indians—the Cheyennes, Arapahoes, Kiowas, Kiowa-Apaches, Comanches, and Sioux—sought to defend their homeland against the growing encroachment of miners, ranchers, and farmers transported westward by the proliferating lines of the transcontinental railroad. In 1867, the vastly reduced postwar army was no longer composed largely of native-born citizen soldiers. Instead it drew its men from the poorer classes of Americans, such as Irish or German immigrants who faced severe discrimination and enjoyed few employment opportunities elsewhere. Given the recent experience of the Civil War in which massed armies had confronted each other using tactics drawn from the era of the Napoleonic Wars, the military proved at first inept in its campaigns. During the spring and summer of 1867, Custer served under General Winfield Scott Hancock (another hero of Gettysburg) on the Kansas Plains. In far-flung operations that attained nothing other than wearing out men and horses, Custer learned one lesson. The Plains tribes were expert guerrilla fighters. Once they eluded the army, they were almost impossible to intercept or recapture.

Frustrated by the lack of adequate supplies, the high desertion rates of soldiers far different from the loyal and often adulatory troops he had commanded during the war, and the boredom and monotony of serving in the "American Siberia," Armstrong summarily ordered the shooting of deserters. Then he left his post at Fort Wallace without authorization in July 1867 to visit his wife at Fort Riley. In the ensuing court-martial, he was sentenced to suspension from rank and pay for one year.[103] Nonetheless, when Lieutenant Colonel Alfred Sully, like General Hancock, proved incapable of fighting the Plains Indians, General Sheridan, turned to Custer to implement the same principles of total warfare against them that the Boy General had executed in the Shenandoah Valley. In November 1868, along the banks of the Washita River in Indian Territory, Custer struck the village of the Cheyenne peace chief, Black Kettle, unexpectedly at dawn. Afterward the Seventh Cavalry destroyed all tepees, food supplies, and ponies, leaving them to face starvation unless they moved to reservations.

Unfortunately for Custer, the divisions among Americans regarding Indian policy and the atrocities suffered by Black Kettle's band in 1864 at the hands of the Colorado militia at Sand Creek led many eastern humanitarians to characterize the Washita as a "massacre." This response was a disheartening contrast to the praise a northern public had heaped on the Boy General during the recent war.[104]

Nonetheless, despite the controversy that now dogged his career, Custer emerged in the public mind as his country's foremost Indian fighter.

He had learned to place the highest priority on cutting off the Indians' avenues of escape, and to accomplish that, he was willing to forgo reconnaissance to gain the advantage of a surprise attack.[105] From that standpoint, his celebrated luck was likely to give out eventually, a nerve-wracking possibility that haunted Elizabeth. On the banks of the Little Bighorn River in present-day Montana, Custer, knowing little about the terrain before him and certain that the Indian village ahead was fleeing, split his Seventh Cavalry into three battalions. Separated from the rest of his command, he and his entire battalion of five companies were wiped out on June 25, 1876, by the Sioux and their Northern Plains allies.

Following that battle, Custer's superiors—including the commander of the expedition, General Alfred Terry, and President Ulysses S. Grant—blamed him for the disaster. Terry accused him of failing to play his assigned role in a larger campaign of converging columns. Grant maintained that Custer had overmarched his men to win a victory single-handedly against the Sioux. Others, such as the novelist Charles King, Colonel Robert Hughes, and writer Cyrus T. Brady, repeated versions of those charges in the 1890s and early twentieth century.[106]

Despite the blame heaped upon Custer following the Little Bighorn, the partnership Elizabeth had forged with her husband in the Civil War held fast even after Armstrong's death. The Custer marriage in the postwar years had never been the unbroken idyll Elizabeth later described in her writings. Faced with the difficulties of frontier military service in the postwar era, Armstrong had resorted to heavy gambling as a way of countering his frustration, despite his wife's protestations. An even greater threat to the couple's relationship arose from Armstrong's dalliance with the well-known actress Maggie Mitchell and his long friendship with the opera singer Clara Kellogg. Worse yet, in 1869, he had entered into an intimate relationship with the Cheyenne woman Monahsetah.[107]

In the end, however, none of these women competed with Elizabeth. As Libbie basked in her husband's "reflected glory," so Armstrong increasingly depended on her for counsel and emotional support. Thus it was not surprising that in 1871, after a period of estrangement between the two, Armstrong wrote Elizabeth that she was "irrevocably my first, my present and my last love. All the women are," he added in a statement that said it all, "but as mere toys compared to you."[108]

Following Custer's death in 1876, Elizabeth spent her fifty-seven years of widowhood defending her husband's reputation and memorializing him in every way possible. By giving the dime novelist Frederick Whittaker access to her husband's personal papers, she enabled him to publish *The Complete Life of Gen. George A. Custer* less than six months after Armstrong's death. That 1876 work, while poorly written, became the basis of novels, paintings, and an epic poem by Ella Wilcox in 1896.[109]

Libbie did not stop there. In her three books, *"Boots and Saddles"*

(1885), *Tenting on the Plains* (1887), and *Following the Guidon* (1890), she transformed her husband into a devoted family man and exemplary commander.[110] Her books sold well enough to make her a popular figure on the well-paying lecture circuit where she described the sacrifices army officers and their families had made to advance the nation's expansion. Although she never mentioned her own widowhood, her presence in black on stage served as a constant reminder of her husband's death and her own personal loss. In 1901, Charles Scribner and Sons published Mary Burt's *The Boy General*, a condensation of Elizabeth Custer's three works, as a textbook for grammar school children that would teach patriotism and "lessons in manliness."[111] In part due to his wife's writing, George A. Custer now entered the pantheon of national heroes as a martyr to westward settlement and a model hero for boys.

When reporters interviewed Libbie on June 3, 1910, on the eve of the dedication of the Monroe statue of her husband, sculpted by Edward Potter and erected by the State of Michigan, she informed them that she was writing a fourth book. It would describe her life with Armstrong during the Civil War, and since she had no children to consider, it would be an "intimate work, a human document of the General's life and mine."[112]

Although she had been working on this project since 1890, the widow never finished this volume. Perhaps the Monroe monument, by depicting Custer on the third day of the Battle of Gettysburg as he was sighting Jeb Stuart's cavalry from behind Rummel's barn, captured in bronze her ideal image of him. Here is no rash foolhardy soldier, but instead a thoughtful observer, "alert, tense, his hat in hand," absorbing the scene quickly before moving on to glory.[113]

Another possibility exists. By promising "an intimate story" of her marriage during the Civil War, Elizabeth Custer may have set herself an impossible goal. To have related the entire account of how her astute socializing in Washington lessened the suspicions Radical Republicans in Congress harbored concerning her husband would have diminished the larger-than-life image of him she had crafted in her writings. Moreover, since she derived her public standing in large measure from Armstrong's magnified heroism, guarding his reputation took precedence over any personal objectives.

Finally, to have told the fuller story, would have been to admit that, even at twenty-two, she had proved herself enterprising, shrewd, and calculating in her efforts to advance her husband's career. Instead in her various rough drafts, which have been compiled by Arlene Reynolds and published in 1994 in their most polished form as *The Civil War Memories of Elizabeth Bacon Custer*, Elizabeth portrayed herself as naive and often awkward and embarrassed.[114] Such traits were seen as the natural attributes of middle-class Victorian women who entered marriage innocent of worldly experience and needing their husbands' guidance.

Certainly that portrayal of herself in her works brought high praise and a devoted following. Critics on both sides of the Atlantic were captivated by her depiction of herself as a timid woman, valiantly fighting her fears and looking to her husband for courage and protection. A reviewer for the *Chicago Dial* characterized Elizabeth as "the perfection of a wife," while another critic writing for *Current Literature* lauded her as a woman "entirely free from egotism."[115] More recently, a modern scholar attributes Libbie's success as a writer to "the contrast between a dependably heroic husband and a wife who epitomized the Victorian view of femininity, forthrightly confessing her own fear, vulnerability, and weakness."[116]

Elizabeth succeeded so well in her depiction of herself in all her writings, speeches, and public demeanor that Jacob Howard, the Michigan senator who had briefly obstructed Senate confirmation of Custer's promotion to brigadier in December 1863, was quoted in a 1907 work in a memorable way. He saw Elizabeth Custer as "one of America's model wives," who "unites in her charming personality all that goes to make a woman attractive to a manly, chivalric man."[117]

In 1927, John B. Kennedy interviewed the aged widow for an article in *Collier's*. He described her as a "benign character from Thackeray or Dickens" as she sat in her parlor at 72 Park Avenue in New York City.[118] She had arrived at that prestigious address in the last decades of her life through her earnings on the lecture circuit and shrewd investments in real estate, especially in Bronxville, a Westchester County suburb outside New York City; it has been described as "endlessly copied and never matched."[119] Surrounded by memorabilia of the past, she characterized herself as grateful that she had lived long enough to hear Theodore Roosevelt describe her husband "as a shining light to all the youth of America."

On April 4, 1933, one month after President Franklin Delano Roosevelt had initiated his New Deal, Elizabeth Custer died. She was four days short of her ninety-first birthday. A year later, Frederic Van de Water published *Glory-Hunter: A Life of General Custer*, the first iconoclastic biography of George A. Custer. The reassessment of the Boy General was under way, but even among Custer's detractors, the romance of the Custer marriage lived on. Of the alliance forged during the Civil War era between the D'Artagnan-like cavalier and the doll-like figure in her billowing hoop skirt, Van de Water wrote, "The love his wife bore him and he bore her may be George Armstrong Custer's most intrinsically sound fame."[120]

He was correct. The Custer marriage, for all its turmoil, was a genuine love story, but it never matched the picture Elizabeth Bacon Custer portrayed in her books. Instead, it was inherently more interesting. It was the union of two complicated and flawed individuals, filled with yearning ambition, a passion for life, and a compelling desire for sexual and romantic fulfillment. Both knew intuitively from the days of their courtship that together they were magical, a gestalt that was more than the sum of their parts.

If that was true during their lifetime, it remains even truer now that they are gone. No scholar ever has or ever will undertake a biography of George Armstrong Custer without due attention to his marriage and the character of his wife. In the end, bringing Elizabeth into the picture invariably softens, flatters, and casts a romantic aura over the Boy General who emerges. At the same time she appears as an ideal wife and the epitome of a loyal and steadfast widow. Thus, in a very real sense, the partnership forged between Elizabeth and George A. Custer during the Civil War continues to influence both our perceptions and our opinions of them to the present day. It is the attainment of their mutual objective and Elizabeth Custer's supreme and enduring achievement.

ELEVEN

Permutations of a Marriage

John Charles and Jessie Benton Frémont's Civil War Alliance

PAMELA HERR

When the Civil War began and the renowned western explorer John Charles Frémont was named commanding general of the Department of the West, with headquarters in St. Louis, he and his wife, Jessie, were thousands of miles apart—a situation commonplace in their long and complex marriage.[1] In early 1861, John Frémont, with both his lawyer and, evidence suggests, a mistress in tow,[2] had gone to Europe to raise capital for his California gold mines. At the same time, as the Republican party's 1856 presidential candidate, he was negotiating for a position in the new Lincoln administration, possibly an ambassadorship or cabinet post.[3] But as civil war broke out, he pushed for a military appointment. "My great desire is to serve the country in the most direct and effective way that possibly I can," he wrote his longtime supporter Francis Preston Blair.[4] "He is terribly in earnest," a Pennsylvania congressman described John Frémont at this decisive moment. "He says he is now to do the work of his life."[5]

While her mercurial husband journeyed to Europe, Jessie Benton Frémont remained behind in San Francisco with the couple's three children: Lily, eighteen; Charley, ten; and Frank, six. Although Jessie seems to have dismissed rumors of John's infidelities as politically motivated, she was nonetheless restless and lonely, and she welcomed the news of her husband's appointment. "I have not been so happy in years for him as now," she wrote an acquaintance. "An army of cares has been boring into our lives these few years past, and I thank heaven for this noble chance in a great cause, which has come to Mr. Frémont now."[6] While she characteristically claimed that her happiness was for her husband rather than herself, in reality, his appointment presented her with the tantalizing prospect of resuming a more active role in his career. Although this vigorous woman would scarcely admit it even to herself, the appointment also offered her the possibility of moving beyond the confines of woman's traditional sphere, to act, however indirectly and discreetly, in the public world beyond.

As Jessie Frémont set out to meet her husband in New York in June 1861, her expectations were high. She hoped to exercise her genuine idealism, expressed in her longtime opposition to slavery, as well as her ambition, in promoting her husband's career. More personally, she yearned to reestablish the intimacy and emotional closeness that had seeped out of her twenty-year marriage. To an acquaintance she wrote determinedly, "We go to join Mr. Frémont & I will be with him everywhere—I will."[7]

The Frémonts' marriage had begun in youthful passion when seventeen-year-old Jessie, the precocious, high-spirited daughter of powerful Senator Thomas Hart Benton of Missouri, defied her family to elope in 1841 with the dashing but impecunious John Charles, a twenty-eight-year-old army explorer who was born illegitimate.

A bold, adventurous child, Jessie had been her father's favorite, "given the place a son would have had."[8] Born in 1824 and raised mainly in Washington, D.C., she had acquired an intimate knowledge of politics under Thomas Benton's shrewd tutelage. Her mother's influence was less overt, for Elizabeth Benton was a gentle, domestic woman who embodied the pieties of nineteenth-century womanhood. Yet within the family, her voice had power, for it was she, raised on a prosperous Virginia estate with forty slaves, who convinced her husband and taught her children that slavery was wrong. Like many southern women, she stressed the domestic consequences of slavery to the slaveholder's family. "She urged upon us many reasons why we ought never to own them," Jessie explained in an 1856 letter to the abolitionist Lydia Maria Child. "She dwelt especially on the evil influence of slavery on the temper of children, making them domineering, passionate, and arbitrary. I would as soon place my children in the midst of small pox, as rear them under the influences of slavery."[9]

While Jessie was raised within a secure family circle, with the advantages provided by her father's political position and her mother's upper-class Virginia lineage, John grew up in precarious circumstances on the fringes of genteel southern society. His father was Charles Fremon,[10] a French émigré who taught dancing and language in Richmond, Virginia; his mother, Anne Whiting Pryor, descended from a patrician Virginia family fallen on hard times. Pressured into marriage with a wealthy old man, she had, after twelve childless years, run off with Fremon. "I have found," she explained, "that happiness consists not in riches."[11] Two years later, in 1813, John Charles was born in Savannah, Georgia; all his life he would bear the stigma of illegitimacy. When he was five, his father died, and the impoverished family, which by then included several younger children, settled in Charleston, South Carolina, where Anne took in boarders and struggled to educate her children. John grew up a loner—proud, reserved, cautious in sharing his feelings, skeptical of rules and authority, yet eager, at times to the point of recklessness, to prove himself. An outsider, alienated from the dominant white slave-holding class, he found it natural to oppose slavery. The author Rebecca Harding Davis, a friend and supporter of the Frémonts during the Civil War, shrewdly observed, "He made of Freedom a religion. I don't know that he had any especial liking for the negro—very few Abolitionists [had]. But the slavery of the black man—of any man—was abhorrent to him."[12]

By his mid-twenties, John had found work that suited his bold and restless temperament. Employed by the U.S. Army Corps of Topographical Engineers, he served as chief assistant to the eminent French scientist-explorer Joseph N. Nicollet on two successive wilderness surveys to the frontier midwest. Stationed temporarily in Washington, D.C., he met Jessie Ann Benton.

She was by then an ebullient young woman, dark-haired and dark-eyed, never precisely beautiful, but with an irreverent charm, a "wild strawberry flavor," as the young Charles Sumner described it, that captivated male admirers.[13] Sent during these years to Miss English's Female Academy in Georgetown, she was a rebellious pupil, actively protesting against the restrictions and snobbery of what she derisively called a "society" school.[14] But Victorian America offered few direct outlets for her incipient talents and ideals, and it was perhaps predictable that her energy, passion, and youthful rebellion would converge on the dashing figure of John Charles Frémont, a lithe and handsome man whose piercing grey-blue eyes conveyed a Byronic intensity. Years later, Jessie would remember with glee how "all Washington was horrorstruck" by her rash and forbidden marriage.[15]

Over the course of their long marriage, Jessie Frémont would play an active although often hidden role in her husband's controversial career: serving as adviser and aide, collaborating on writing projects, penning much of his correspondence, and defending him against critics. During the Civil War her role would expand to include the virtual management of the Western Department while John was in the field. For a variety of reasons, including John's impatience with the details of administration and the drudgery of writing, his own unconventional upbringing in a household headed by a woman, and the power that Jessie brought into the marriage through her father, John accepted her help and came to depend on it. In the Frémonts' numerous collaborations, it is often difficult to untangle Jessie's part. As a proper Victorian wife, she felt obligated to minimize her work, yet on a less conscious level, she was eager for the recognition and credit she deserved. Thus in an 1893 letter she characterized her role as "secretary and other self," an ambiguous phrase that at once reduced her work to the mere clerical and expanded it to full partnership.[16]

The Frémonts' marriage would be characterized by periods of intimacy and collaboration, inevitably followed by times of separation that seemed, in later years, as much psychological as geographical. The pattern began in the first years of their marriage, when John led a series of exploring expeditions to the frontier West, bold and arduous wilderness treks that would not only make him celebrated in his day but became the basis of his most enduring fame. Despite the hardship and danger, John himself would look back on these first expeditions as the most joyous and fulfilling work of his life. He was a natural leader to the mountain men and roving frontiersmen, outsiders like himself, who accompanied him. "I can never forget . . . how cheerfully he suffered with his men when undergoing the severest of hardships," his loyal chief scout, Kit Carson, remembered.[17]

During these years, Jessie, often pregnant or encumbered with small children, was left behind to wait. (She would ultimately bear five children, two of whom died in infancy.) She discovered what she later called her "most happy life work" when John returned from his first important expedition, which reached South Pass in the Rocky Mountains, and tried unsuccessfully to write the requisite government report. Jessie eagerly volunteered to help, for "second lieutenants cannot indulge in secretaries," as she justified her role.[18] It soon became a fuller collaboration as they paused to talk over issues and phrasing, "a form of discussion," John explained, "impossible except with a mind and purpose in harmony with one's own and on the same level." As they worked they grew so close that to him she seemed like his own "second mind."[19] Together they turned a routine geographical report into a vivid and readable account, published by Congress and excerpted in newspapers throughout the nation. However, it was the Frémonts' best-selling second report, written when John returned from a daring fourteen-month journey to Oregon and Mexican-held California in 1843–1844, that made him a national hero. Combining scientific accuracy with narrative verve, it has become a classic in the literature of exploration.

During his third expedition (1845–1847), John played a rash and still controversial role in the Bear Flag Revolt and conquest of California. Subsequently, when U.S. army and navy authorities tangled over supreme authority in California, he unwisely sided with the navy and was court-martialed. His sensational trial, conviction, and partial pardon by President James Polk only increased his fame, for the nation sympathized with the young explorer caught between quarreling military authorities. Nonetheless, John, embittered, resigned from the army. This episode created a lingering ill will between him and regular army officers that would compound his difficulties during the Civil War. It was the first in the series of at least partially self-inflicted defeats that would mark John Frémont's erratic career, reversals over which Jessie, as a woman, had little control.

In 1849, while John journeyed overland on a privately financed fourth expedition, Jessie and their six-year-old daughter crossed the Isthmus of Panama by dugout canoe and muleback to join him in California. There, in one of the startling reversals that punctuated their lives, their Las Mariposas mines brought them a sudden fortune in gold. In 1850 John was elected to the U.S. Senate; in 1856 the celebrated explorer was nominated for the presidency by the newly formed Republican party on a platform opposing the extension of slavery. "There is no name which can find such favor with the masses," proclaimed newspaperman Horace Greeley, acknowledging the political potency of John Frémont's heroic image.[20]

The Frémonts' partnership flourished again as Jessie became the first presidential candidate's wife to play an active, although necessarily discreet role in what became known as the "Frémont and Jessie" campaign. Behind the scenes, she supervised correspondence and public relations efforts, even writing sections of a campaign biography that artfully concealed her husband's illegitimacy. Meanwhile, the story of her elopement and her opposition to slavery were featured sympathetically in the Republican press, while at campaign rallies her name evoked rousing cheers. Inspired in part by her prominence, women attended political events in increasing numbers. "What a shame that *women* can't vote," declared the abolitionist Lydia Maria Child. "We'd carry 'our Jessie' into the White House on our shoulders."[21]

While John Frémont received the majority of northern votes, sweeping New England and New York, he was defeated nationwide by the Democrat's compromise candidate, James Buchanan. The loss of the election brought the first clear psychological break in the Frémonts' marriage. Jessie, suffering from a depression possibly augmented by her husband's rumored infidelity, took their children to Europe for an extended stay while John journeyed to California to supervise his gold mines. She soon discovered she missed her husband intensely: "Love me in memory of the old times when I was so dear to you," she wrote him poignantly from Paris. "I love you now much more than I did then."[22] In 1858, the reunited family settled in California, where a series of crises at their gold mines brought them closer. "Jessie as usual was my best ally," John wrote the Francis Preston Blair family in a rare burst of feeling.[23] To her longtime confidante, Elizabeth Blair Lee,[24] Jessie joyfully described her husband's new domesticity. "He takes part in & likes all the details of our household—the children's plays & witticisms & lessons—he looks after our comforts, & is in fact head of the house. No 'wild turkey' left. It's so easy to take care of children when two help. I feel now as if we were a complete & compact family. . . . Now we share & share and he is far the happier for it. As for me, you need no telling how satisfied my craving heart is."[25]

But the pattern of withdrawal returned, as it would throughout the Frémont marriage, for by now John seemed both to long for Jessie's devotion and the warmth of family life, yet feel engulfed and imprisoned by it. He was soon traveling restlessly about the state on mining business, and then, in January 1861, to Europe. Nonetheless, as the Civil War began and Jessie set out to meet her husband in New York, she hoped for a new intimacy created within a reestablished working partnership.

Accompanied by her three children and a maid, Jessie reached New York City on July 13, 1861, after a tense voyage from Panama, harassed by Confederate privateers.[26] John, dressed in uniform, was at the wharf to meet them. Over the next ten days, he would be fully occupied in buying arms and recruiting staff for his Western Department, which included Illinois and the entire region from the Mississippi River west to the Rocky Mountains. Eagerly, Jessie plunged into work beside him. "We have really had no chance to have a talk," she confided to a friend. "I haunt around taking my chances of a word—sometimes it is only a look—but after the hungry yearning of that far off blank life at Black Point [in San Francisco] it is enough." She herself was a whirlwind of activity, writing exuberantly of her maid's horror "at my pace and contempt for bonnet boxes & extra wraps & such like."[27] The crisis both released her energy and provided the rationale for action beyond the domestic sphere. "The restraints of ordinary time do not apply now," she would justify women's expanded role.[28]

As the Frémont family set out by train for St. Louis in late July 1861, the nation expected much from the "gallant and romantic Frémont," as a *New York Times* correspondent described him.[29] At forty-eight, his beard and hair were tinged with silver, but he was still a lean, handsome man, a dashing figure on horseback, lithe and elegant in his uniform. Proud and reserved, he was not an easy conversationalist, but at this point his reticence only enhanced his manly image. To writer Rebecca Harding Davis he seemed "the ideal soldier—simple, high-bred, courteous."[30] It was easy to picture him, as did a *New York Times* reporter, leading his troops down the Mississippi, "bearing the eagles of the Republic in triumph along either bank . . . to the Gulf of Mexico."[31] John himself seemed to envision as much: "My position in the west will embrace a really grand scope of operation and in consequence great responsibility," he wrote a young aide. "I realize the war . . . will be hard and sanguinary but the heads of our columns point to New Orleans and Charleston and we will plant the old flag on Sumter again."[32]

Jessie, at thirty-seven, was nearly as well known as her husband. Stout now, her dark hair pulled back and pinned at the nape of her neck, she cultivated a social charm almost southern in its appeal, yet cut through with a refreshing directness and wit. An admiring journalist noted her "broad comprehensive masculine intellect" and "quick feminine intuitions," and like many others, detected in her the mental strength, political shrewdness, and tenacity of her father.[33] Inevitably some believed she had more intellect and energy than her husband. "Have you met Mrs. Frémont?" the Reverend Thomas Starr King of San Francisco wrote Henry Bellows of the U.S. Sanitary Commission during this period. "I hope so. Her husband I am very little acquainted with, but she is sublime, and carries guns enough to be formidable to a whole Cabinet—a she-Merrimack, thoroughly sheathed, and carrying fire in the genuine Benton furnaces."[34]

When the Frémont family reached St. Louis on July 25, 1861, the city seemed tense and hostile. "I found myself in enemy country," John bluntly recalled.[35] Although Missouri was a slave state, men like Congressman Frank Blair of St. Louis, the Frémonts' longtime friend and political supporter, had thus far managed to keep it in the Union. But the situation was precarious. Confederate troops had invaded southern Missouri and were threatening nearby Cairo, Illinois, strategically located at the junction of the Ohio and Mississippi Rivers. While Unionists probably outnumbered secessionists, particularly among the large German-American population, the state's power structure and wealthy elite supported the southern cause. In St. Louis, tenuously held by a small Union force, Confederate soldiers were openly recruited at a St. Louis mansion, while "secesh belles" cursed Union soldiers who dared wear their uniforms in the street.[36]

Several crises demanded immediate attention. At Cairo, General Benjamin M. Prentiss urgently needed reinforcements, while General Nathaniel Lyon, situated at Springfield in southwestern Missouri, also begged for additional troops to combat approaching Confederate forces. Meanwhile, in the northern part of the state, marauding guerrilla bands were burning bridges, destroying railroad lines, and terrorizing Union sympathizers. Moreover, the federal government, alarmed after the recent defeat at Bull Run, was diverting arms shipments meant for Frémont's Western Department to the east and removing troops from his command to defend Washington, D.C.

Two days after their arrival, Jessie wrote her old friend Elizabeth Blair Lee about the desperate situation. The Western Department was in chaos; they had found "an arsenal without arms or ammunition—troops on paper and a thoroughly prepared and united enemy thick and unremitting as mosquitoes." Jessie found it irresistible to think she might relieve the situation by personal intervention. "The President is a western man and not grown in red tape. If he knew the true defenceless condition of the west it would not remain so. I have begged Mr. Frémont to let me go on & tell him how things are here. But he says I'm tired with the sea voyage—that I shan't expose my health any more & that he can't do without me." There was no time for pleasantries, for the "womanish" letters, as Jessie once described them, that she had long exchanged with Lizzie Blair Lee. "If I write of nothing else" except the war, Jessie concluded, "it is because nothing else is of moment compared with this."[37]

Over the next months, John Frémont, preoccupied and harassed, would turn over innumerable duties to his energetic and resourceful wife, whom he knew from long experience was utterly loyal, efficient, and dependable. As often in the past, his most confidential letters were in her hand, frequently written in her own words after only informal conversation. Thus on July 28, as John arranged for a flotilla of steamboats to relieve Cairo, Jessie wrote to her friend Lizzie Lee's brother, Montgomery Blair, Lincoln's postmaster general and their most important contact in the Lincoln administration. Explaining that the letter was based on her husband's "telling—not absolutely from dictation," she outlined the need for "money & arms without delay & by the *quickest conveyance.*" Three days later, she wrote Blair again, describing her husband's recent actions and repeating the need for aid. "I put down his own words as he talked & give them to you in unshaped sentences."[38] Meanwhile, on July 30, in Jessie's hand, John had written directly to Abraham Lincoln to inform him of the critical situation. "I will hazard everything for the defense of the department you have confided to me," he concluded, "and I trust to you for support."[39] By August 5, Jessie was writing Montgomery Blair that her husband could not even "make time to put his pen to paper except for necessary signatures. But he wishes you to know things in which your aid may be of vital importance & you understand I am a faithful reporter when he has not time to dictate."[40] On the same day, she also wrote to Lincoln on behalf of her husband: it was a routine response to a letter Lincoln had forwarded to John, and Jessie answered it succinctly, speaking of her husband in the third person, and leaving it unsigned.[41] In this way she avoided revealing, as she could to a family friend like Montgomery Blair, that John Frémont's wife was writing many of his letters.

During this charged period, Jessie constantly pushed the boundaries of her sphere. When John organized an eight-steamboat, 3,800-man flotilla to rescue beleaguered Cairo, she traveled with the flotilla, evidently without her husband's initial knowledge. According to a story Jessie told long afterward to a soldier who had been at Cairo, she concealed herself aboard one of the steamboats until it started downriver, when much to her husband's "surprise and apparent annoyance she made her appearance in the cabin, but her persuasive faculties proved sufficiently powerful to carry the point in sharing the danger."[42] In a letter to Montgomery Blair on her return, Jessie said nothing of this aspect, but she did describe the stirring scene at Cairo. "The sound of the shouts with which we were welcomed at Cairo stays in my memory," she wrote. "Only a weak & threatened garrison seeing aid coming could make such sounds. Gen'l Prentiss's voice as he said 'I shall sleep tonight' said volumes."[43]

The chaotic situation and distance from Washington allowed Jessie to assume an extraordinary role, but prudently, the Frémonts tried to camouflage the extent of her participation in the military affairs of the department. Such concealment was made easier because Jessie had arranged to rent a cousin's St. Louis mansion to serve as both their personal residence and military headquarters, allowing her to move easily and unobtrusively between home and office.

Despite her consuming activity, Jessie struggled to maintain a domestic intimacy with her three children. As a wealthy family, the Frémonts were, of course, well assisted by servants, freeing Jessie from both housework and, when she chose, child care. By all accounts she was a warm and affectionate mother, "overflowing with maternal instinct."[44] John was less closely involved in his children's lives, both because of his frequent absences and his reserved temperament. Nonetheless, all three children, echoing their mother, would remain devoted to him, and after his death, to his memory.

In St. Louis the war dominated family life. Daughter Lily, plain, sensible, and unadventurous, joined a Union women's sewing group and often copied dispatches for her mother.[45] Never a belle, Lily nonetheless received attention as General Frémont's daughter, when soldiers serenaded her or a military camp was named in her honor. The two Frémont boys, dressed in small army uniforms especially made for them, played constantly at war; and each in turn managed to injure himself, although not seriously, with exploding gunpowder. John was "charmed," Jessie reported, by six-year-old Frank's "coolness" when he was hurt. The two boys reveled in the attentions of the headquarters staff. "Frank is uncommonly good & handsome," she commented affectionately of her younger son, "getting a little priggish with too much admiration but I am not the one to put him on half rations."[46]

In these first tense weeks, Jessie developed a real camaraderie with her husband's staff; to her they became, as she said in a telling domestic metaphor, "as one household."[47] The Frémont staff was itself an unconventional mixture of regular army officers, dedicated abolitionists, former European revolutionaries, and California acquaintances eager to profit from the war. To many citizens of Missouri, however, the abolitionists would come to seem dangerously radical, the foreign officers flamboyant and impractical, and the Californians unscrupulous outsiders who used their friendship with John Frémont to gain lucrative contracts that would otherwise have gone to local merchants. The situation was made far worse when the chief quartermaster, a career army officer whom John stubbornly trusted, proved to be personally corrupt.

Despite such potential problems, during these first hectic weeks, John Frémont seemed a man of purposeful activity. He began defensive fortifications around St. Louis, organized a home guard of local citizens to protect Union-held towns, established an elite unit of cavalry troops to protect himself and his headquarters, and initiated the construction of a fleet of innovative iron-sheathed mortar and gun boats that would later become the core of the Union's victorious river fleet. His name inspired men to enlist, and he was soon struggling to arm, equip, and train thousands of new troops. Left virtually on his own by the federal government, he acted swiftly, often without competitive bidding. Although his carelessness would come back to haunt him, at this early stage the press and public watched with admiration. "His name is a tower of strength to

his friends and a terror to his foes," proclaimed the *New York Times* correspondent in St. Louis.[48]

Although John had moved quickly and effectively to relieve vital Cairo,
he concluded that he lacked the troops and transportation to aid General
Nathaniel Lyon at Springfield as well, and he instructed the outnumbered
officer to fight or retreat as he saw fit. Choosing to take the offensive,
Lyon was killed on August 10, 1861, at Wilson's Creek, near Springfield.
With more than a thousand casualties, the Union forces abandoned south-
western Missouri to the Confederates, and the first murmurs against John
Frémont's generalship were heard.[49]

As hundreds of wounded soldiers were brought to St. Louis, the need
for hospitals and nursing care became urgent. "For a week past or more
I have been investigating military hospital business," the Unitarian minister and civic leader William Greenleaf Eliot recorded in his notebook
on August 31, "have proposed a plan to Genl. Frémont, had several long
talks with Mrs. F., who has sent for Miss Dix, whom we expect tomorrow."[50]
Eliot's plan resulted a week later in the establishment of the Western
Sanitary Commission, in a document in Jessie's handwriting and signed
by John. Meanwhile Jessie prepared the way for the arrival of Dorothea
Dix, an old acquaintance who had become the army's controversial new
director of nursing, by writing in collaboration with Eliot a newspaper
article that praised Dix as "our American Florence Nightingale" and explained the advantages of women as professional nurses.[51]

During the Civil War, Dorothea Dix would often tangle with military
doctors and male members of the U.S. Sanitary Commission. "No one can
cooperate with her," complained commission official George Templeton
Strong.[52] Yet when she reached St. Louis on August 31, she and Jessie
quickly established a cordial and effective working relationship, suggesting
that Dix's problems may often have been gender-related, involving the
reluctance of male authorities to allow a woman to assume a managerial
role. Together the two women inspected hospitals and camps, and examined various buildings as potential sites for additional hospitals. Dix
also traveled to the garrison at Cairo, where many soldiers were sick with
fever. At the conclusion of her visit, she was eager to give General Frémont
her recommendations, but John, both preoccupied and habitually impatient with administrative specifics, instead provided Jessie with presigned
requisitions, which she and Dix filled out as they needed.[53] Within six
weeks, four hospitals with more than two thousand beds had been
established.[54]

Meanwhile, in mid-August, bold, hard-drinking, aggressive Congressman Frank Blair of St. Louis had reached the city. With his father, Francis
Preston Blair, who had been Thomas Benton's closest friend and political
ally, and his brother, Postmaster General Montgomery Blair, Frank had
been instrumental in persuading Lincoln to give John the western command. Now, however, Frank was barraged with complaints from local business and political leaders about inefficiency and favoritism at Frémont

headquarters, as well as the general's aloofness, inaccessibility, and ostentation. At the same time, Frank found his place as leader of the pro-Union forces usurped. While courteous, John seemed remote, reluctant to talk over the critical situation in Missouri with him. Moreover, when Frank suggested that John make himself more accessible by opening his offices to all callers for an hour a day, John curtly refused. He was also unwilling to give Frank the generalship of the state militia that he coveted. Writing to his brother Montgomery, Frank concluded that John "feared some sort of rivalry with me."[55]

Within two weeks, Frank Blair came to believe that John lacked the capacity and temperament to command the Western Department. "He talks of the vigor he is going to use, but I can see none of it," Frank wrote his brother Montgomery in one of several long, increasingly critical letters. As recently as August 24, Montgomery had remarked to a colleague, "I think Frémont is to be the real hero." But by early September, convinced by his brother's negative assessment, Montgomery concurred that John was "hopeless" and passed Frank's damning letters on to the president.[56]

To alienate Frank Blair and the St. Louis establishment was extraordinarily foolish. John was a thin-skinned and defensive man, uneasy with the rough give-and-take of politics and resentful of any authority not his own. Jessie did have political savvy and, through her father, a knowledge of Missouri men and issues. Moreover, she was, observers agreed, both practical and realistic. But her loyalty was above all to her husband, and it dangerously warped her judgment. In St. Louis she encouraged a tight circle of followers who bolstered John's tenuous sense of self. More and more, both she and John would come to judge men not on their abilities or honesty but on their personal loyalty.

At this crucial point, Confederate forces controlled half the state of Missouri, while marauding rebel bands plundered Union-held areas of the countryside with increasing boldness. On August 30, 1861, in a sudden, desperate move, John declared martial law and, most significantly, announced a limited emancipation decree, freeing the slaves of Missouri rebels. While he was no doubt influenced by his abolitionist sympathies, his specific purpose was strategic: to force Missourians in the rebel army to return to their homes or lose their slave property. "As a war measure," he believed "this . . . was equal to winning a deciding battle." Characteristically, he had consulted no one beforehand except Jessie and a Quaker abolitionist aide.[57]

John Frémont's unauthorized decree created a national sensation. It touched the moral impulse of the war, as yet unacknowledged by the Lincoln administration. In a stroke, he became the lightning rod for growing Union sentiment to make emancipation the purpose of the war. The decree has had an "electric effect upon all parts of the country," observed Maine senator William Fessenden. "Men feel now as if there was something tangible and real in this contest. F[rémont] is showing great qualities as a soldier, but this proclamation has shown him to be a statesman."[58]

But Abraham Lincoln, anxious to keep wavering border states like Kentucky in the Union, requested "in a spirit of caution and not of censure," that John rescind the decree "as of your own motion." Stubbornly, John refused and instead asked Lincoln to "openly direct" him to revoke it. "If I were to retract [it] of my own accord," John explained testily, "it would imply that I myself thought it wrong, and that I had acted without the reflection which the gravity of the point demanded. But I did not. I acted with full deliberation, and upon the certain conviction that it was a measure right and necessary, and I still think so."[59]

Jessie learned of her husband's response to the president only when he asked her to copy it for him. Proudly she saw there was "no faltering." At this crisis point, she related, "I was given my part." Bearing her husband's reply, she would go to Washington to see Abraham Lincoln, both to present the case for the emancipation decree and "to answer—as [John] knew I could—questions rising from it."[60]

Jessie confidently relied on her privileged position as the daughter of Benton and the wife of Frémont to provide access to the White House, but she counted on her own intelligence and thorough knowledge of the situation in the Western Department to make the president listen. Evidently neither she nor John recognized that her gender might complicate the situation: "General Frémont had no idea but that I, always in constant intimate friendship with my Father and himself and previous Presidents would not be accepted as qualified to speak and answer for him as formerly," she wrote many years later in a detailed account of her meeting with Lincoln. "Mr. Frémont judged women as he had been fortunate enough to know them, helping in council as well as home."[61]

Jessie reached Washington on September 10, 1861, after a hot, dusty, three-day train ride. The president received her coolly. Ordinarily courteous in such situations, Lincoln did not even ask her to sit down. Jessie handed him her husband's letter, "telling him General Frémont felt the subject to be of so much importance, that he had sent me to answer any points on which the President might want more information." While Lincoln read the letter, she found a seat and sat down, for "instinct told me the President intended to discourage me, and I did not intend to appear nervous." Lincoln drew up a chair beside her. "I have written to the General and he knows what I want done," he told her curtly. Jessie tried to explain her husband's view more fully. He believed, she said, that it would be "long and dreadful work to conquer by arms alone, that there must be other consideration to get us the support of foreign countries." England, France, and Spain were on the verge of recognizing the South; "they were anxious for a pretext to do so; England on account of her cotton interests, and France because the emperor dislikes us."[62] Emancipation of the slaves would at once give the North a powerful moral edge and deter European nations from aiding the Confederacy.

"You are quite a female politician," Lincoln replied. "I felt the sneering tone," Jessie recalled, "and saw there was a foregone decision against all listening." But Lincoln had more to say. "The General ought not to have done it," he continued rapidly, referring to the proclamation. "He never would have done it if he had consulted Frank Blair. . . . The General should never have dragged the negro into the war. It is a war for a great national object and the negro has nothing to do with it."[63]

No doubt Jessie was tired and tense, and she neglected to use her considerable charm. But she was also a clear and forceful speaker, with firsthand information about the Western Department as well as intelligent views on the politics of emancipation. Normally Abraham Lincoln was unusually tolerant as a listener, at least with men, able to hear opposing views with equanimity. Whether his dismissive response to Jessie reflected his own particular psychology and attitude toward women or more simply the conventional view of a patriarchal culture is difficult to determine. But the fact that she was a woman evidently prevented him from taking her mission seriously. Moreover, although Lincoln had already read Frank Blair's critical letters about John Frémont, discussed them with his cabinet, and instructed Montgomery Blair to go to St. Louis to investigate, he withheld this information from Jessie.

Civil War chroniclers have habitually treated this meeting as an amusing anecdote, the story of an overwrought and faintly ridiculous woman overstepping her gender boundaries to berate a bemused president. Lincoln, in describing the scene two years later to aide John Hay, set the tone for such accounts by casting himself as the innocent victim of a hysterical female: "She . . . taxed me so violently with so many things that I had to exercise all the awkward tact I have to avoid quarreling with her."[64] When she heard this story years later, Jessie is said to have replied, "Strange, isn't it, that when a man expresses a conviction fearlessly, he is reported as having made a trenchant and forceful statement, but when a woman speaks thus earnestly, she is reported as a lady who has lost her temper."[65] In their ten-volume biography of Lincoln, Hay and John G. Nicolay repeated the president's version. Except for this incident, Jessie Frémont's role in the Civil War would largely disappear from public view.[66]

The day after her meeting with Lincoln, the patriarch of the Blair family, Francis Preston Blair, came to see Jessie. The two had long been close, but Blair was now furious with John for defying the president and with Jessie for defending him. "Who would have expected you to do such a thing as this, to come here and find fault with the President," she recalled Blair's words. "Look what Frémont has done; made the President his enemy." Blair condemned her for her unwomanly role. "It is not fit for a woman to go with an army," he told her. "If you had stayed here in Washington you could have had anything you wanted."[67] In his anger, Blair revealed that his son Frank had written derogatory letters about her husband and that Montgomery, concurring, had passed them on to the president. To Jessie, this was betrayal. The two quarreled bitterly.

Francis Blair was now convinced that the Frémonts' vast ambitions were at the root of the problem. "In a word they hate & fear Frank & are also hostile to everybody in the administration who is supposed to stand between them & imperial power," he wrote angrily to his daughter, who was staying in Pennsylvania.[68] Lizzie Blair Lee was horrified. "A formal quarrel fills me with a terror I can't articulate," she replied. It is unfortunate that Lizzie Lee was away while Jessie was in Washington, for perhaps if the two longtime friends had been able to meet and talk, they might somehow have mediated the conflict. But no meeting occurred, nor did either attempt to correspond with the other. As the situation unraveled over the next weeks, Jessie sided with her husband and Lizzie with her brothers and father. "The more I think of that couple, the more bitterly I feel my disappointment in them—," Lizzie wrote her father in late September, "it is so humiliating to have bolstered up such unworthy people so long."[69]

Jessie herself saw the quarrel on two levels. On the personal level, she viewed Frank Blair's rivalry with her husband as crucial, evoked by John's refusal to give him the command he wanted or to grant military contracts to his friends; on the national level, she believed opposition was based on the emancipation decree. Before leaving Washington, she talked with sympathetic political leaders like Illinois senator Lyman Trumbull, who enthusiastically supported the decree. "Collateral issues and compromises will be attempted but the true contest is on the proclamation," she telegraphed her husband from Washington. "Some true active friends here and the heart of the country with you everywhere."[70]

The resulting feud made John Frémont's position in Missouri increasingly precarious. The Blair men marshaled their considerable influence in a concerted attack on John, both privately to Abraham Lincoln and publicly in the press. More covertly, they attacked Jessie as well, attributing many of John's actions to his "vixen of a wife," as Montgomery now described her.[71] In the Blair men's version of events, John was a courageous but dangerously incompetent man, flailing beyond his depth, while Jessie was a clever and vengeful woman who had stepped outside her proper sphere. "She is perfectly unscrupulous, you know," Montgomery now claimed.[72] Lizzie Blair Lee, however, blamed John far more than Jessie. "Jessie[']s part in this matter has disappointed me sorely," she wrote her husband Phil in mid-October. "Things which I had learnt to believe about her husband made me think him unreliable—but only added to my pity & affection for her—I am now convinced that in countenancing & covering his sins she has shared & been degraded by them—& yet I can see in her efforts to elevate him & excite his ambition a struggle to win him from his grovelling nature—"[73]

Stories about the Frémont partnership multiplied. One officer, seeing John on military business, was convinced that he had glimpsed Jessie standing behind a large pier glass mirror where she could hear every word. "I was afterwards told that she invariably observed that rule, without regard to who the visitor or visitors might be. I was further informed that the general never gave a decisive answer on any subject unless he had first consulted Mrs. Frémont."[74] When John twice had Frank Blair briefly arrested for insubordination, Montgomery Blair was convinced it "was as the phrase is 'Genl' Jessie's doing altogether."[75] Jessie was also blamed for the emancipation decree. "If the war is prosecuted with vigor the bayonet will free most of the niggers in this state," one Missourian wrote Montgomery Blair, "but Frémont has a very smart wife & must spread himself out in sensation dispatches for the newspapers."[76] To such critics, the result of this unnatural partnership was wholesale disaster. "Did you ever hear of such a superb jackass as 'John C. & Jessie Benton Frémont Major General Commanding,' " jeered a Blair partisan. "And poor Missouri has to suffer for their folly & crime."[77]

As the criticism grew, John retreated more into himself, narrowing the circle around him to only the most loyal. When Montgomery Blair arrived in St. Louis to assess the situation for the president, John received him so impassively that Montgomery suspected he had been using opium.[78] While her husband withdrew into a proud silence, Jessie fought back fiercely but covertly. She would call this expanded political work in defense of her husband her "silent activity."[79] She corresponded with sympathetic congressmen like Schuyler Colfax of Indiana and arranged for eastern supporters to write pro-Frémont articles and letters for the press.[80] She also cultivated journalists like Albert D. Richardson, the St. Louis correspondent of Horace Greeley's formidable *New York Tribune*, whose dispatches henceforth included material provided by Jessie.[81] Clearly dazzled, Richardson would later remember her as one of the "four or five great conversationalists" he had met in his lifetime, "if not queen of them all."[82]

Amid the war of words, the military situation deteriorated still further when on September 21, 1861, Union forces were decisively defeated at Lexington, near Kansas City. Determined to salvage the situation as well as his own reputation, John decided to take personal command of his troops in a concerted effort to defeat the rebel forces and drive them from the state.

John left for the field in late September. Under normal conditions, he might have relished the task ahead. By temperament the opposite of a general like George C. McClellan, John preferred to act, to risk his life even, rather than to talk, to prepare, or to ponder. During his western expeditions, he had shown himself to be brave to the point of recklessness. As Francis Preston Blair had once noted, "Frémont's genius is one for action."[83] Moreover, he clearly preferred the primitive conditions of camp life to the political conflicts and bureaucratic intrigue of St. Louis. "The General looks well, and I think enjoys himself much better than in Oriental St. Louis," an aide described him in early October.[84] His frontier experience served him well as he assembled and moved an army south through the autumn countryside, foraging for food and improvising transportation and equipment as he went. "The September rains were over; the fine weather of the Indian summer had come; the hay was gathered, and the corn was hardening, and we were about to carry out the great object of the campaign," John recalled long afterward.[85] His troops were in high spirits, cheering their leader as he galloped through camp, a dashing horseman on his magnificent gray charger.

Meanwhile, Jessie remained at their St. Louis headquarters, along with a skeleton staff of officers. "My dear chief has gone to do his hard unsustained duty. Mine is as hard—to stay behind & keep the truths collected in form for friends to use," she explained.[86] Yet as her husband's confidante and representative, she now assumed a range of duties that went far beyond public relations. A year later, writing in her characteristically disarming and discursive style, she revealed just how unusual a role she had played.

> Perhaps I should explain, that the frequent reference of official work to my care came not merely from Mr. Frémont's long habit of referring all manner of work and duties to me as acting principal in his absence, but because nearly all the General's reliable officers were with him. Of those remaining, his quartermaster became ill of fever, and was in a critically dangerous state from the time of the army's leaving. The adjutant, Captain [Chauncey] McKeever, who was very active and thorough in his attention to his duties, had his right arm disabled by a relapse of injuries received at Bull Run, causing several times so much fever and suffering as to leave actually no other head than myself; for Colonel [John T.] Fiala also became ill. . . . Knowing . . . that anything requiring attention would be sure to receive it, night or day, the General wrote to me for what was needed; and many a despatch was sent, and combination made at the bedside of invalids too worn to sit up.[87]

Over the next month, as John pursued the Confederate forces, Jessie labored to get him the troops, arms, and transportation he needed. In near-daily letters to his wife, John sent requests and instructions. "I am going on with formation of the plan I had indicated to you in my letter of yesterday," he wrote on October 10. "What the full plan is, I will let you know by sure hand, and will also inform _____, so that you and he may work together in aid of it." On October 15 he thanked her "for the sabres and guns; send any such things forward as best you can." On October 18 he told her to "ask Captain McKeever to do all that is humanly possible to get wagons, mules, harness, and drivers sent forward to Tipton." Two days later he instructed her to "send me forward all the regiments possible. Arm them with the Austrian musket as altered by Greenwood."[88]

At this point of greatest challenge, the Frémonts drew closer. John's letters from the field reveal his reliance on his wife, both emotionally and practically, as well as his own attempts to give her the support she also needed. "Be of good heart," he wrote on October 9, "we are fulfilling the task allotted to us, and we will try to do it bravely. . . . After a few weeks

in the field, this will be one of the finest armies in the world." Two days
later he was even more confident: "My plan is New Orleans straight. . . . I
think it can be done gloriously."[89] At other times, hampered by enemies
within the Lincoln administration, he professed a cool detachment: "Do
not be the least uneasy or discouraged," he wrote in mid-October, "it is
really now a matter of indifference whether I retire from this business or
not. It has become almost too disgusting to endure."[90] A day later, more
cheerfully, he told her she "need not be alarmed at my movements southward. They will be well considered, and you must just give me what aid
you can. . . . Keep your health good, and don't get agitated. . . . I want this
little note to go to you freighted only with pleasant thoughts, a harbinger
of success, and meetings soon to come."[91]

By now, however, the federal government seemed to thwart him at
every turn. In mid-October 1861, the war department froze funding for
all Western Department contracts until they could be reviewed in Washington, and in a decision aimed at John's controversial personal staff,
suspended pay for officers whose commissions had not been approved by
the president. It was widely rumored that John was to be replaced. Several
of his generals in the field disregarded his orders and publicly questioned
his competence, while members of a hostile congressional committee
holding hearings in St. Louis claimed to have uncovered "an organized
system of pillage right under the eye of Frémont."[92]

Jessie grew increasingly distraught at the "chilling influences of a hostile
administration and a doubting, if not blaming country." Moreover, she
had allowed John to take ten-year-old Charley with him to the field, and
she now morbidly contemplated her son's death. "The result of what I
have felt & seen is to make me more than willing that my children should
die young," she wrote a friend despondently. "Charley begged to go . . .
and in my heart if he should end his little life in his sincere belief that
he is helping defend the flag, I should be glad for him that he had not
lived to become changed into what men usually become. The loss to me
will not be long. I am wearing out with suspense & weariness of heart.
Such simple true patriotism as we both brought to the work—honestly we
thought it was the country to be served. But I am unworthy of my chief
who writes to me that I must keep well & full of faith for he will wring
success from all this yet."[93]

Meanwhile in Washington, the president grew more distrustful. Even
the daring recapture of Springfield, Missouri, on October 25 by Frémont's
elite bodyguard disturbed the Lincoln administration, who feared that the
guard's battle cry, "Frémont and Union," had unsettling political impli-
cations. Then, on November 2, 1861, as John Frémont's army chased the
Confederate forces to the southern Missouri border, he was removed from
his command by the president.

Hearing the news, his troops threatened to mutiny. A great wave of
protest swept across the North. When John returned to St. Louis, immense

crowds, shouting "Frémont and Union," escorted him through the streets in a torchlight procession. "I could not stand it," Jessie wrote. "I went far up to the top of the house, and, in the cold night air, tried to still [my] contending emotions."[94] Their mission in Missouri had failed, but her husband was now the hero of a growing portion of the North passionately opposed to slavery.

John Frémont was a careless administrator, and his neglect of the St. Louis establishment was politically foolish. Yet he had created a vast army from scratch in just a few months, inspired great enthusiasm among his troops, and by the time of his dismissal, virtually driven the rebel forces from the state. Over the next years, the corruption and inefficiency uncovered in Missouri would seem minor compared to later wartime scandals, while Lincoln himself would prove far more tolerant of a long series of blundering generals. Many shrewd observers, including Jessie Frémont, suspected that the dismissal of John Frémont was in part the act of a consummate politician not unwilling to oversee the downfall of a formidable political rival.

Bitterly, the Frémonts returned to New York City. While John remained largely silent, even in private letters, Jessie freely expressed her anger to sympathetic friends. By now her opposition to slavery and her defense of her husband had merged. To her, John was the leader of a great popular movement to free the slaves, a movement thwarted by petty politicians like Lincoln and the Blairs. "There is not much doubt that slavery has, as usual, found a Northern man to do her work," she said of Lincoln that winter.[95]

Jessie remained determined to defend and explain her husband's record to the public. "I'm savagely tired of injustice to my Chief," she wrote a friend, "& remembering I was never out of slave soil until after I was twenty-four, I've a right to rebel."[96] Within weeks, she had sketched out what would become *The Story of the Guard*, an account of the victory of the heroic Frémont bodyguard at Springfield and less directly, a subtle and persuasive defense of her husband's command. "Don't be frightened," she wrote her publisher, James T. Fields, "it's as soft as carded wool."[97] For the first time, she boldly put her own name on a title page and justified her decision by assigning the book's proceeds to a charitable fund for the benefit of the families of the men slain at Springfield. "For any personal object I should never use my name," she explained in the preface. "But I think my father also would more than approve, when it is to do justice and to aid the widow and the orphan."[98]

Jessie decided not to publish *The Story of the Guard* immediately, for she feared that her indirect yet powerful indictment of the Lincoln administration might jeopardize her husband's chances for another military command. When the book finally appeared a year later, reviews were favorable, although gender issues were consistently raised in indirect ways. The *Atlantic Monthly* reviewer, for example, seemed eager to stress Jessie's womanliness and to contradict rumors that she was a more talented writer than her husband. The reviewer differentiated Jessie's prose from John's more "manly" style: "Mrs. Frémont is a true woman, and has written a true woman's book. . . . We cannot be mistaken. The hand that penned the 'Story of the Guard' could not hold the pen of [Frémont's Emancipation] Proclamation or . . . the narrative of the Rocky-Mountain Expedition."[99] *The Hesperian*, a woman's magazine, also emphasized her femininity: "instead of being a labored and exhaustive defence of General Frémont by the fair Jessie, while her Benton blood was up, it is as mild and gentle as the heart of a woman."[100]

In January 1862, encouraged by growing public support, the Frémonts took their case to Washington, where they conducted a skillful lobbying campaign. Their goal now was not only to clear John's name but to force Abraham Lincoln to give him a new military command. "She has scarcely slept or rested," the wife of a Republican official observed of Jessie. "To see her Husband vindicated, is the restless burning of her soul, and she is mistress of every statistic, every item, that can weigh for or against him."[101] Together the Frémonts prepared an elaborately documented defense of John's Missouri command for the powerful Committee on the Conduct of the War, dominated by sympathetic Radical Republicans who, like the Frémonts, advocated immediate emancipation. After extensive hearings, a majority of the committee would conclude that John's administration of the Western Department "was eminently characterized by earnestness, ability and most unquestionable loyalty."[102]

As the Republican party split into bitter factions over the issue of immediate emancipation, Jessie Frémont came to represent, for many antislavery Northerners, the newly active woman, released from ordinary restraints by the national crisis and dedicated both to serving her country and to the abolition of slavery. To abolitionist Elizabeth M. Davis, the wife of a Pennsylvania congressman, Jessie was "a whole-souled splendid woman—fully her husband's equal great as he is."[103] In contrast, Kentucky-born Mary Lincoln, whose extravagant shopping sprees and presumed southern sympathies had been well publicized, seemed a "vulgar doll," as Lydia Maria Child condemned her, pursuing an outmoded role as a domestic ornament in time of national crisis. The president's wife, to such women, seemed unable to comprehend the seriousness of the war, the moral issues involved, or women's potential role in the war effort. "I reckon the presence of 'our Jessie' in Washington will make her a little uncomfortable," Child wrote a friend that winter.[104]

In March 1862, Abraham Lincoln conceded this political battle to the Frémonts. Bowing to popular and congressional pressure, he named John commanding general of the recently created Mountain Department with headquarters in Wheeling, West Virginia. "General Frémont has a strong hold on the hearts of the people and of the soldiers. We all feel enthusiasm and admiration for him," a young soldier (and future president), Rutherford B. Hayes, recorded in his diary that month.[105] Again, Jessie chose to accompany her husband to his post, but this time only six-year-old Frank, whom his parents now affectionately called "the Corporal," was with them, for they had sent Lily to Quebec for a long stay with Jessie's sister and placed Charley in a Connecticut boarding school populated, Jessie noted approvingly, by the children of politically compatible abolitionists, including a "little Beecher and others of the faithful sort."[106] Though over the years John had frequently been absent from home for long periods, Jessie, a devoted mother, had never been separated from any of her children before. Now, however, all family life would be subordinated to the exigencies of war.

In Wheeling, John reassembled much of his controversial staff of foreign-born officers, young idealists, and California cronies, and again Jessie had her place at headquarters. At first both were optimistic. "Mr. Frémont is so well again," Jessie reported happily to a friend.[107] As in St. Louis, she found the wealthy elite were secessionist but "the working & middle class all for emancipation." While John focused on military strategy, she attended to the political front. Corresponding with congressional allies, she worked to secure additional arms and troops. "*Don't let troops be withdrawn from this Dept.,*" she wrote Congressman George Julian of Indiana. "They are trying to take away the Blenker Division & that leaves nothing." She was also eager to defeat antiemancipationist candidates in the summer congressional elections. "I can take care of Mr. [Moses Fowler] Odell & will attend to his defeat next week," she wrote Julian bluntly, "but I think a man or two might be found to attend to the West & prevent the next House from being crammed with men whose speeches are like editorials in the N.Y. *Herald* or like the arguments used in Cincinnati against Wendell Phillips."[108]

When John took the field in early May 1862, Jessie returned to New York. "I left him at a camp in the mountains deep down in Virginia, with the advance guard of the Blenker Division fine soldiers & filling the air first with shouts of welcome," she reported to a friend. "A happier (or handsomer) man never headed a column than the one I left at New Creek. Each day he makes about 20 miles & you will hear of results."[109]

Renting a house at Little Neck, Long Island, she retrieved her children and continued her "silent activity" on behalf of her husband. "I enclose you copies of the two last dispatches from the General," she wrote Sydney Howard Gay of the *New York Tribune* on June 21. "As I get my dispatches by favor," she added pointedly, "I dare not make the information known except to a few useful friends who will give all the help possible without telling why."[110]

But for the most part, Jessie was forced to wait while her husband fought his own battles, both with the Confederate enemy and northern opponents. For her it seemed the most difficult task of all. "It is so hard to have one's body in one place when all one's heart & soul & strength are in another," she wrote Annie Fields, her publisher's wife.[111] "If I could only see him—he has no one with him to whom he can rest his mind, & laying off that burthen start again," she told Gay.[112]

She watched helplessly as her husband, along with Generals Nathaniel Banks and Irvin McDowell, were brilliantly outmaneuvered by Stonewall Jackson in the Shenandoah Valley. John's own feelings swung from hope to bitterness at what he perceived as lack of support from the Lincoln administration. "At any hour I may have another severe battle with Jackson," he wrote a business associate, "and as the usual detractions and unaccountable deficiencies exist here that embarrassed me in Missouri, I have my hands and head full."[113] At times he expressed what was either modesty or passivity. "Dear Jes," he wrote his wife on May 26, 1862, as he set out with orders to cut off Jackson. "I have a moment to send you my love—all is going . . . well here. We march Eastward tomorrow, but already there are indications that Jackson is [in] retreat. Maybe we can catch him."[114]

As Jackson continued to strike and elude the Union forces, the administration concluded that Frémont had failed to act vigorously and promptly. By now, many observers saw him as a man of gesture rather than action. A *New York Times* correspondent who met him in West Virginia found him appealing but only because he looked "so splendidly on horseback,"[115] while the German-American reformer Carl Schurz, asked by Lincoln to see and assess Frémont, pronounced his "whole personality . . . rather attractive—and yet one did not feel quite sure."[116] In late June, after persistent difficulties in coordinating the actions of his three floundering generals in the Shenandoah region, Lincoln decided to merge their commands under a single man. Convinced, rightly or wrongly, of Frémont's incompetence, he chose General John Pope, a blustering West Point graduate who had been publicly hostile to John while under his command in Missouri. Rather than serve under a man he distrusted, and whom he also outranked, John resigned his command. Angry and humiliated, he went home to Jessie. When the writer Rebecca Harding Davis saw him the next day, he had already retreated into his habitual courteous reserve.[117]

Thus John Frémont's military career ended in late June 1862, when the war itself was little more than a year old. His own mistakes and the Blair smear campaign had done their work. Although he was permitted to retain a small staff in the expectation of a new assignment, Abraham Lincoln would never give him another command. A month later the Quaker suffragist Lucretia Mott, who had long supported the Frémonts, reported on their anger at the president. Jessie "calls Lincoln an Ass— Frémont says [Lincoln] is sold to the Border states—& that we shall never succeed until universal Emancipation is proclaimed."[118] It was thus with mixed emotions that in January 1863, the Frémonts welcomed Lincoln's Emancipation Proclamation, feeling with many Northerners that it should have come far sooner.

Settling in New York City, they turned more and more to their own separate interests. John resumed active management of his gold mining company and began to dabble in railroads as well. While he habitually repressed the bitterness he felt at the failure of his hopes and ambition, he was now a far more cynical man, increasingly willing to engage in dubious schemes to advance his own interests.

Meanwhile, Jessie, who vented her own anger more directly in conversations and correspondence, threw herself into a frenzy of charitable and other war-related activities. With her usual managerial skill, she superintended the publication of a series of war letters and memoirs that were sold at the New York Sanitary Fair, and raised several thousand dollars for the Sanitary Commission by staging a series of concerts and a lavish children's production of *Cinderella*.

As the war dragged on and one inept Union general replaced another, Jessie joked mordantly that the administration changed generals "nearly as often as a bad housekeeper changes servants."[119] In 1864, John Frémont, supported by a dwindling group of followers who included Wendell Phillips and Elizabeth Cady Stanton, challenged Lincoln for the presidency, but Sherman's victory at Atlanta made Lincoln's candidacy inevitable and John withdrew from the contest.[120]

As the war drew to a close, the Frémonts felt profoundly ambivalent. While their cause had triumphed, they had lost a bruising personal struggle. The pro-Lincoln *New York Times* now called the once "gallant and romantic" John Frémont "the lost leader . . . a political adventurer of the most dangerous kind."[121]

The Frémonts' Civil War experiences were in many ways unique. Instead of separating them, as it did many military couples, the conflict initially brought them together in renewed intimacy and partnership. Eager both to attain personal glory and to carry out their antislavery ideals, John Frémont and his clever and energetic wife had seemed a formidable force as they set out so hopefully for St. Louis in July 1861. The Missouri command shattered their dreams. Although John's military capabilities were never truly tested in Missouri or, arguably, later in West Virginia, he lacked the political and administrative skills his position demanded. In the end, despite her strenuous efforts, Jessie, as a woman, could do little to change either her husband's temperament or the course of events. Nonetheless, she suffered the repercussions of venturing so conspicuously beyond woman's traditional sphere. Collaborating earlier with John on his expedition reports or working behind the scenes on his presidential campaign, she had escaped public censure largely because her role was less known. During the Civil War, however, in working at army headquarters, in writing *The Story of the Guard* under her own name, and in her wide-ranging political and press manipulations, she moved far beyond her previous forays into the public world and, predictably, gained attention and often disapproval. The Blair men, who had long known of her intimate involvement in her husband's work, now painted her as a brazen woman, a camp follower who boldly interfered in the male world. Her visit to Abraham Lincoln became a minor scandal. Ultimately, her alliance with her husband was branded "a superb jackass"—a ridiculous and unseemly union. Although the antislavery North at first admired her activity, when her husband's reputation was tarnished, she, as his wife, shared the stain.

The Frémonts emerged from the Civil War bruised and chastened. In 1865, drawing on their still considerable gold-rush fortune, they purchased a lavish Hudson River estate, where Jessie withdrew into a luxurious domesticity centered on her three children and a conservative upperclass social world. At last, she seemed the true Victorian wife, devoted exclusively to her family and home. When Elizabeth Cady Stanton asked her to sign a women's suffrage petition, she refused, yet in a striking show of inner ambivalence, nonetheless sent money for the cause.[122]

John, cynical and embittered after his Civil War experiences, turned to new and questionable business schemes, mining and railroad ventures that further sullied his reputation and gradually drained the family's gold-rush fortune. Following an old pattern, he was often away during these years, ostensibly tending his far-flung business interests but also, rumor had it, pursuing occasional romantic liaisons.[123] Meanwhile, the Frémonts' two boys, Charley and Frank, encouraged by their mother and doubtless influenced by their own Civil War experiences, attended Annapolis and West Point, respectively, and then pursued military careers.[124] The boys would remain close to their mother and loyal to their more remote father, but Jessie's greatest comfort was now her daughter, the quiet and unassuming Lily, who never married and over the years remained doggedly faithful. The two women, united in their devotion to the mercurial John Frémont, provided each other with the emotional support they seldom received from him.

Within a decade, however, the family's fortune had slipped away, hastened both by the financial panic of 1873 and John's personal failings as a businessman. The Frémonts were forced to sell their Hudson River estate and, in a humiliating public auction, their furniture, books, and many paintings. They would spend their remaining years in genteel poverty.

Reinvigorated by their need, Jessie began to write professionally, penning reminiscences and children's stories that became the family's most stable source of income. Her work was deliberately bland and uncontroversial, for both her Civil War experiences and her need to please a conventional public made her cautious. Only occasionally, as in the antislavery story "The Deck Hand," did she express her political convictions.[125] Her energy was now devoted to earning a living and, indirectly, defending her husband's name, for like Elizabeth Bacon Custer, she used her writing to promote and protect her husband's heroic image and to present her complex marriage as a simple romantic idyll.

In 1878, when John obtained an appointment as territorial governor of Arizona from an old supporter, President Rutherford B. Hayes,[126] he, with Jessie serving as his financial agent in New York, scrambled unsuccessfully to regain some financial security through investments in western land and mines.[127] In 1885–86, noting the spectacular success of Ulysses S. Grant's memoirs, the Frémonts collaborated hopefully on the first volume of John's life, but the exploits of a questionable hero evoked little interest and few copies were sold.

During these years, Jessie continued to defend her husband, fiercely in private, with more subtlety in her public writing. Never acknowledging his alleged infidelities, if indeed she heard the rumors, and rarely his business incapacities, she remained devoted. To her he had become "more great in his silent acceptance of undeserved calamity than in the days men praised him."[128] And although she scrupulously preserved the outward forms of obeisance to "the General," as she referred to him, their adversity made her strong as it weakened him. When she arranged for the artist Gutzon Borglum to paint her husband in his Civil War uniform, "Frémont always came in on the arm of his wife who seemed the one person he wanted to please," an observer reported. "She brought with her a military coat adorned with gold fringe and epaulets, a garment [he] wore with dignity."[129]

Sad, aloof, tarnished, John seemed a beaten man. No longer able to support his family, he retreated further into himself. In a poem written during these years, he recalled the careless joy and freedom he had felt during his early western expeditions. Since then his hopes had ended in "hateful strife and thwarted aim." He compared the "lonesome gloom" of his innermost feelings to the "dreary wastes of frozen plain."[130]

To Jessie the poem seemed a "de profundis cry," evoking her deepest maternal feelings of pity and tenderness.[131] Yet John, while he depended on Jessie's love and devotion, must have found it hard at times to face this still strong and resourceful woman, who seemed to believe in him more than he did in himself. Beneath the surface forms and courtesies, Jessie seemed the dominant force. Yet it was not that simple. She had always needed his love more than he needed hers, and so in a deeper sense, it was he who ultimately controlled their relationship. Elusive, fleeing, just out of reach, he held her fast.

In the summer of 1883, while living in New York City, Jessie received an unexpected visit from an old friend, Elizabeth Blair Lee, whom she had not seen since the Civil War feud between the Blairs and Frémonts severed their friendship. The two women had nonetheless kept in contact indirectly, through Lizzie's husband, Samuel Phillips Lee, who had maintained his own friendship with the Frémonts, perhaps in part because of his long-standing antagonism toward Lizzie's brother, Montgomery Blair. Over the years, Jessie Frémont and Phil Lee had corresponded sporadically but cordially, often about the Frémonts' son Charley, for whom Phil, as his godfather, helped obtain an appointment to the Naval Academy.

Lizzie Lee's 1883 visit was evidently prompted by disturbing reports about the Frémonts she had heard from a mutual friend, who told her that Jessie looked "hungry—they are so poor," and added that "Jessie's infatuation about Frémont, his power over her is still in full force." Lizzie herself had long viewed John as morally corrupt and financially careless, a man who would "gamble away his own & her children's bread over & over again . . . and he too faithless even to pretend to live with her." To Lizzie and other old friends, Jessie's loyalty seemed excessive: "She belongs to him body & soul," Lizzie wrote Phil, "& he does with [her] as much as he pleases as he does with his own right hand—& this better hand right has done a vast deal of hard work for him."[132]

When Lizzie called on Jessie that summer, however, the two women—now sixty-five and fifty-nine, respectively—seem to have skirted around such dangerous topics and talked instead of their children. Yet both women were deeply moved by their meeting. Writing afterward to thank Lizzie for her visit, Jessie was overwhelmed by memories of a happier, more hopeful time. "It was so good of you to come and see me—every way. . . . there is no need to put such feelings in words—not in written words which are so feeble after all. Life narrows and grows chill when one is as transplanted as I have been time after time—it was more to me than you who have 'lived among your own people' can realize, to have the earlier time of unbroken home and friends brought livingly to me." Poignantly, she recalled Lizzie's tender concern more than thirty years before, when the two women had watched through the night as Jessie's five-month-old daughter died in Jessie's arms. Remembering that time, Jessie added bitterly, "I knew it, dimly, then—I know it surely now, that for the death of a baby girl there should be no sorrow for life is hard on women."

Jessie ended her letter with a promise to visit Lizzie whenever she was in Washington, to "tell you better than a letter can . . . that I am always your old friend."[133] But far too much lay mutely between the two women to rekindle their friendship on the old basis. Jessie had cast her lot with John long before, and her loyalty remained with him. She knew the inner man, proud and insecure, as Lizzie and others could not. Moreover, she had wrapped her own identity so tightly around the heroic image she had helped him create that although it might be tarnished in others' eyes, in hers it would always remain intact.

In 1888, the Frémonts moved to Los Angeles, naively hoping to profit from the southern California real estate boom. Though money remained a constant problem, the bitterness of lost battles faded. "Here on this far shore where the serene climate gentles hard memories," Jessie wrote to the poet John Greenleaf Whittier in November 1889, "I seem to look back into another life—its strifes ended—only its results in good cherished."[134] The Frémonts had come to see their opposition to slavery as their most important and lasting contribution to the Civil War. John's rash and unauthorized emancipation order, limited though it was to the slaves of

Missouri rebels, had evoked an enthusiasm in the North that continued to swell until Abraham Lincoln had at last issued a fuller emancipation decree.

The Frémonts remained strapped for money, however, and following the pattern of their marriage, John soon journeyed east on an extended trip to petition Congress for a pension for his military service during the Civil War and to pursue assorted business ventures; except for a six-week return visit in the summer of 1889, he remained in the east for the next two years. Then suddenly and unexpectedly, in July 1890, seventy-seven-year-old John Frémont died of peritonitis in a New York City boarding house.

Jessie suffered intensely from her husband's death; as a cure she threw herself into a final defense of his career. She and her son Frank, now an army officer, completed a 400-page second volume of John's memoirs, including a lengthy account of his Civil War generalship in Missouri and West Virginia. Tedious and one-sided, the volume was never published, but the writing itself seemed to relieve Jessie. Gradually she recovered in the benign California climate, cosseted by a warm and lively circle of reform-minded women who offered her friendship and much-needed financial support.

Jessie Frémont's twelve years of widowhood were a time of growing serenity, although until her death in December 1902 at age seventy-eight, she, like the widows Julia Grant and Elizabeth Bacon Custer, remained a proud and spirited defender of her husband's record. Borglum's "noble . . . knightly" portrait of John in his Civil War uniform now hung above her desk. In death, her elusive husband had at last become the unchanging and faithful hero she had always wanted him to be. "It is our true shrine," Jessie wrote the artist, "we keep flowers there always."[135]

TWELVE

"A Good Wife, the Best Friend in the World"

The Marriage of Elizabeth Blair and S. Phillips Lee

VIRGINIA JEANS LAAS

The marriage of Elizabeth Blair and Samuel Phillips Lee in the spring of 1843 began a mutually satisfying life together that lasted until his death, fifty-four years later. Although not without tribulations, it was a solid union that withstood separation, war, and family conflict. Superficially, it appeared to be a most conventional marriage: a strong-willed, patriarchal naval officer and his submissive, most ladylike wife. Their relationship, however, was (as are most marriages) much more complicated. They were, to a remarkable degree, partners in marriage, even best friends. That they could attain near equality was due in large measure to her family. It was the Blair family that gave Phillips Lee a home, a place to belong; it was the Blair family that gave Elizabeth a strong sense of self-worth. That larger circle of parents, siblings, aunts, uncles, cousins, and child provided the underlying stability that nurtured each of them throughout their long life together.

It was not always so. In August 1839, Lizzie and Phil first met in the romantic setting of White Sulphur Springs in western Virginia. They quickly fell in love and just as quickly encountered family opposition, which led to a four-year tumultuous on-again, off-again courtship. Because of his deep attachment to his daughter, Francis Preston Blair had never encouraged Elizabeth to marry at a young age. Now when she was twenty-one, he had to face the possibility that his daughter might leave him. Beyond his reluctance to give up his daughter were his strong objections to Phillips Lee—to the young man himself, to his family background, to his profession, and to his prospects for the future.[1]

What was wrong with this young man? He was handsome, intelligent, polite, sincere, and had an air of seriousness that other young men seemed to lack. On the surface, his heritage seemed stellar. Born in Fairfax County, Virginia, in 1812, he was the grandson of Richard Henry Lee, a signer of the Declaration of Independence. His branch of the Lee family, however, had not prospered. His mother had died when he was four years old; his father, Francis Lightfoot Lee, had suffered a nervous breakdown when Phillips was only eight. The five Lee children had then been placed under the care of a court-appointed committee. The second child and oldest son, Phillips became the head of a poor and struggling branch of the otherwise illustrious Lees of Virginia. He had joined the navy when he was fourteen.

Knowing Lee's background, Preston Blair could reasonably suspect Lee of being a fortune-hunting sailor bent on moving up in the world. In addition, marriage to a naval officer meant long separations of husband and wife, not the sort of life Preston Blair envisioned for his beloved daughter. Worse, it entailed separation of wife from her family, a prospect too painful for him to consider. Then there was simply a father's love for his only daughter; as he admitted to her, "I cannot bring myself to resign my rights in you to anyone & to confess a truth I never saw the man I was willing you should marry."[2]

In every way, Phillips was pursuing a woman well above his station. Born on June 20, 1818, the exceptionally attractive, slender, intelligent, and vivacious, twenty-one-year-old Elizabeth had been educated by tutors at home and at Mrs. Sigoigne's exclusive private school in Philadelphia. Her father had come to Washington in 1830 at the request of President Andrew Jackson to edit the Democratic newspaper, the *Globe*, and he remained a nationally powerful political figure. Lizzie, his only and precious daughter, had two brothers who showed great promise. Montgomery, who had been graduated from West Point in 1836, was embarked on a law career in St. Louis; young Frank would graduate from Princeton in 1841, and attend law school at his father's alma mater, Transylvania University in Lexington, Kentucky. The mother of these children, Eliza, traced her ancestry to colonial Virginia and her grandfather Christopher Gist who had fought with George Washington and Edward Braddock at Fort Duquesne; her father, Nathaniel, had gained fame in both the French and Indian War and the American Revolution. Thus, on both sides of her house, Elizabeth could claim kinship to innumerable distinguished families of America, including Gists, Breckinridges, McDowells, and Prestons.[3] She was part of a stable, cohesive, and relatively prosperous family.

At the time of their meeting, Phillips was indeed unimpressive. Deeply in debt and broken in health, Lee had recently been sent home by the erratic Charles Wilkes from his exploring expedition.[4] Disagreements with his commander, both significant and petty, had culminated in the promotion of junior officers over him. Although Lee was justified in his dissatisfaction with his treatment, his detachment from the service was nevertheless humiliating. Lee's recent history did not make him a pleasing choice to a doting father for his only daughter. So strong was Preston Blair's opposition to the marriage that he forced a one-year separation.

At first, Lizzie obeyed her father, breaking off the relationship. A cycle of reconciliations following separations ensued for nearly four years.[5] The climax came in December 1842 when Lizzie thought that she had finally rejected this "hard stern man."[6] In a desperate effort to overcome her rejection of him, Phillips let down his reserve and spoke from his heart, explaining his vision of their marriage: "My sentiment is to respect, esteem, & love for life the woman I wed, to make her affections mine, to put all the tenderness of my heart upon her . . . to repose all confidence in her, & then I shd hope to find in one so loved & so honored—a good wife, the best friend in the world."[7] His eloquence so moved her, she confronted her parents and asserted her determination to marry Phillips Lee. Her parents reluctantly acquiesced, but they withheld any real approval. Preston Blair could not bring himself to attend the wedding, fleeing to the St. Louis home of his son Montgomery who had also strongly disapproved of the match. No longer the docile daughter, the nearly twenty-five-year-old Elizabeth defied her family, even in the face of her father's refusal to give her away. In the presence of the rest of her family, she married Phillips Lee on April 27, 1843, after four troubled years of courtship.

The Blair family relatively quickly embraced Phillips Lee. Only six months after the wedding, Lizzie's mother thought of Phil as another son and judged him a "fond true hearted husband."[8] While it took a little longer for her father to come around, her mother's comments marked the beginning of reconciliation. Although Blair had not attended her wedding, he had promised his daughter conditional acceptance: if her husband's feelings remained "as constant & as kind as they have . . . been . . . I shall give him gratitude in proportion to the kindness he shows you."[9]

Within a year, Francis Preston Blair was satisfied with the union. His daughter, after all, never really left home. Because Lee was so often away on active service, Elizabeth made her home with her parents most of the time. In the late 1840s, she joined her husband for the summer months on Coast Survey duty at Lewes, Delaware, and at Pensacola, Florida, but during the winters the couple lived in Washington with the Blairs. During the summer of 1847, when Lee saw service in the Mexican War, his wife remained in Washington. Their longest separation came in the fall of 1851, when Lee commanded *Dolphin*, surveying in the Atlantic Ocean along the coasts of Africa and South America. After his return in July 1852, he was stationed in Washington to work with Matthew Maury at the National Observatory and to complete the report of his survey, published in 1854.[10] All the while, he and Lizzie lived with her parents in Blair House (now the President's Guest House) on Pennsylvania Avenue or at their Silver Spring country home. Phil had married into a close, affectionate, and loyal family; he was encircled by a warmth that he had never had in his own family.

So, too, in his relationship with Lizzie, he found a love and devotion unlike anything he had ever experienced. Her letters to him suggest their passion. She referred to one of his ships as her rival, the Miss *Vanderbilt*, and wrote provocatively, "I am sure I could creep in that little berth. The weather is very cool you know—dear me. I wish it so much, don't be surprised if my spirit should be seen in little berth pulling the whiskers or curling somebody's hair, or—but I won't say what."[11] Although less comfortable with expressing his longings, Phil was "love sick if ever man was." Occasionally his letters hint at his desire for his wife, as when he wrote, "I shall dream of you to night. Would to God I could feel your little arm under my neck. What a happiness that would be!"[12]

Sometimes his love was almost chivalrous. While off the coast of Mexico in time of war, he honored his fourth wedding anniversary in 1847 by sharing a bottle of wine with his mess, offering the toast, "Sweethearts and Wives." When some of his officers wanted to reverse the words, he replied, "my wife is my sweetheart—began so, continues so and I hope will end so."[13] Despite their separation (and perhaps because of it), the couple established a firm and solid union. Through their letters, they nurtured their love for each other and were contented in their marriage.

Into this contented relationship came relatively few instances of discord. Even when Lee was not on active sea duty, he was still absent a good deal of the time. Although he had a steady income from the navy, he felt driven to provide a better livelihood for his family.[14] He could never forget the poverty and instability of his childhood. Early in life he had accepted the burden of providing for his younger siblings, and making money had always been a compelling motivation for him. To increase his wealth, he had invested in western lands, mainly in St. Louis, and whenever he had the opportunity, he traveled west to improve his investments.[15] All the while, Lizzie was comfortably and contentedly surrounded by kin.

In the fall of 1855, during one of Lee's "runaway trips" to the West, Elizabeth inadvertently precipitated their first marital crisis. In a letter to her husband, she explained a "money talk" she had had with her father. When Preston Blair had offered her $10,000 (the amount he had given each of her brothers) she had refused. Because she lived with her parents, she felt she was an added expense for them, which her brothers were not. She did, however, wish to share in any inheritance equally with her brothers. In reply, her father had hinted that he did not wish any of his estate to pass to the Lees.[16]

Sensitive and proud, Phillips Lee took mortal offense and wrote his wife a scathing letter. She in turn wrote back that she had burned that letter and coldly signed her terse note, "E. Blair Lee."[17] Because his letter went up in flames, we cannot know what it was that he found most infuriating, but several possibilities are readily apparent. The thought that his wife was a burden upon her parents must have been galling to him, struggling as he was to provide a suitable patrimony; that she had turned down

$10,000 in cold cash without consulting him could easily have angered any poor boy from Virginia. The suggestion that his Lee relatives could be money-grubbing leeches stung his sense of honor and pride in his family. Perhaps, too, the implication that he had not sired an heir could have been the most hurtful blow of all. Whatever his motivation, he ceased writing to his wife.

The very act of stopping correspondence indicates the seriousness of the breach. When they married in 1843, they had promised to write each other every day. Although Phil had not been totally faithful to the promise, Lizzie had. For three long weeks he subjected his wife to the silent treatment; she finally broke the impasse.

In her attitude toward marriage, Elizabeth Lee adhered quite closely to conventional standards of the day.[18] She acquiesced to the male prerogative and her own subordination in most matters. She never associated with any feminist organizations. She was comfortable within her sphere of husband, home, and family; her greatest pleasures and fulfillment came from her roles as wife, daughter, and sister. She expected, without defining it, something of a companionate marriage, but she also accepted her husband as her "Lord and Master." Their reconciliation, therefore, is remarkable for the manner in which she accomplished it. She smoothed the matter over, but she did not submit to her husband's will or admit to being in the wrong. By an adroit amalgam of personal independence and wifely deference, she steadfastly preserved her self-respect within the confines of her role as dutiful wife.

Elizabeth Lee sought her husband's forgiveness not because she thought she had been wrong, but because it was Communion Day, "& those who take part in that holy service must not according to the rules of the church do so without 'making amends' to all those whom they have 'offended.' " Distressed but unbowed, she admitted, "It is the first time I have felt compelled to seek forgiveness from any but my Creator before partaking of the Sacrament." Although she confessed that she had succumbed to tears and a "half broken heart" and she accepted the duties imposed by her role as wife, she refused to admit to any wrong: "My conscience that [that] which I have done was meant for the best & as much for your sake as my own, supports me—I have not sunk as I should have done if I were obliged to bring home to myself that I had ever been wanting to you in duty, in respect or most devoted love—no you have had all—& still have all that the fond heart of a wife can give." Her firmly rooted sense of self did not permit her to submit: "I have set it down as a religious duty to perserve [sic] my own self respect."

Regardless of the conventions of society, Elizabeth Blair Lee demonstrated a consciousness of her own self-esteem and was determined to protect it. Proud but ever-devoted, she entreated him: "Now my own dear Phil write me an affectionate letter—forgive me my offences & trust to my fixed purpose my fond feelings & good intentions."[19] Within a week,

Phil was home, and their crisis had passed. The couple evidently reconciled satisfactorily: within a year Lizzie astounded and delighted her family by announcing her pregnancy after fourteen childless years of marriage. Francis Preston Blair Lee was born on August 9, 1857.

The birth of little Blair, however, could not eradicate all family discord. Lizzie's brother Montgomery had always disliked Phil, and over the years the two men had developed a deep antipathy for each other. The occasion for the ultimate rift between them was minor yet decisive. In 1858, when brother Frank brought his children, suffering from whooping cough, to Silver Spring, Montgomery invited only his sister, not Phil, to escape to his home. That slight was too much for Phillips Lee. The two men ceased to speak. The rupture was so serious that Montgomery would not even speak *of* Phil to Lizzie until April 1862.

On the heels of this serious breach in relations with her family, Lee precipitated another marital crisis. His solution to family disharmony was to get away from them. With considerable investments in St. Louis, he announced his desire to move to Missouri. Elizabeth demurred. Her lack of enthusiasm evidently angered her husband, and she countered with a mild rebuke: "I cannot account for your harsh impatience today save by thinking you may think me too selfish to go to St. Louis."

Never mentioning how much she might regret leaving her own family, she rested her objection on the health of their baby. For Lizzie, the hot and humid summers of St. Louis were too great a danger to her child's health.[20] Lee then countered with the suggestion that he go alone to St. Louis to look after his investments and spend the rest of the winter in Texas. That suggestion brought rebellion and a lecture: "You are my Lord & Master & can do as you please but you will never go to Texas without me with my consent. . . . I am perfectly insensible to any argument about economy. We are not poor enough to make it a duty to ourselves—& our child needs no such sacrifice & if he did I am not willing to make it at such expense." Her position on the matter perfectly clear, she then chastised him for his lack of consideration: "Nothing in life so breaks my heart & so wounds & mortifies my spirit as this absolute indifference—& this willingness to be away from me."

She rightly saw his suggestions as a ploy to test where her devotion lay—to the Blair family or to him. She responded with her own hurt feelings and her refusal to be separated from him: "I'll be submissive in all things but this—& in this I've ever been rebelling humbling to my pride as it is to reiterate it when so cast off but you think I've the comforts & the happiness of a home which I relinquish reluctantly—but tis not the first time you have wronged the loyalty of my affection for you."[21] They remained that winter in Washington.

Preston Blair, aware of his son-in-law's unhappiness, offered a solution. Since his return from the *Dolphin* cruise in 1852, Lee had been stationed primarily in Washington with a variety of duties at the Observatory and on examining and court-martial boards; sea service did not seem to be part of his foreseeable future. Blair determined to build a house for his daughter and her husband. He had given his home in Washington to his son Montgomery in 1851 and felt that it was his paternal duty to provide similarly for his daughter. He liked Phil, treating him as another son, and he could not bear the thought of separation from his grandson. He had another reason. His wife, Eliza, had never been on good terms with Montgomery's wife, Minna, and by 1859, they were barely speaking to each other. Lizzie Lee called Minna "Mrs. No. 6," referring to the latter's Pennsylvania Avenue address. Because Eliza, too, was fond of Phil, and Lizzie was the apple of her father's eye, a Lee home could, and did, provide a congenial city headquarters for the elder Blairs. Blair's property abutted Montgomery's home, and by August 1859 he had constructed a three-story house that shared a common wall with his son's residence.

Despite frosty relations with Minna and Montgomery, the Lees enjoyed a large measure of domestic harmony. Little Blair Lee, the darling of his parents, quickly became the favorite of his grandparents. As ferociously competitive as Preston Blair was in the political realm, he was sensitive, affectionate, warm, and delightful in his personal relations. Through the years, Phil had proved himself to the older man, and Blair, true to his word, developed a trusting camaraderie with Phil.

This happy home circle ended in the fall of 1860 when Lee was ordered to take command of the sloop of war *Vandalia* with orders to join the East India Squadron. It was a disturbing assignment on several counts. For his family, it meant a two-year separation, but Lee was a sailor, and active sea service was what he always wanted. More upsetting was the thought of leaving U.S. waters when his nation was in turmoil. The sectional division that had become increasingly severe during the 1850s, coupled with Abraham Lincoln's election to the presidency and South Carolina's threat to secede from the Union, made civil war seem a distinct possibility.

Despite his misgivings, Lee sailed from New York on December 7, 1860, headed for the China Sea.[22] On February 27, 1861, he anchored his ship in Table Bay, Cape of Good Hope, Africa. Although it is not certain, Lee probably learned of the secession of South Carolina and the resignation of some southern senators. He faced his most momentous decision: should he return to his troubled country or obey his orders? After he weighed anchor on March 18, he sailed indecisively in the South Atlantic for a full week. Finally, on March 25, he set *Vandalia*'s course firmly for home. Not until May 4 when he encountered an American schooner east of Cuba did Lee have any possibility of learning that war had indeed begun.

Unlike his third cousin Robert E. Lee, Phillips never doubted where his allegiance lay. In later years, he maintained that he had taken an oath to defend the United States and when he read over his commission, he could not find any reference to the state of Virginia. That devotion to the

Union was deeply felt by Lee and all the Blairs. Their roots in Virginia and Kentucky, however, left them sympathetic to their southern cousins. Lizzie aptly described the family attitude when she remarked that she could never "feel alien to the Rebels." She clung to them, maintaining, "they are my people, my countrymen, mad men as they are, my heart aches for them."[23] The only Southerner for whom she had no sympathy was her husband's third cousin Robert E. Lee to whom Preston Blair had tendered Lincoln's offer of command of the Union army. His refusal elicited her disdain: "No vain woman was ever more easily lured from honor and duty by flattery than was this weak man by the overtures of wily politicians."[24]

After bringing his ship home, Lee reported to the navy department with some trepidation. His concern, however, was quickly put to rest. Since Lincoln's proclamation of the blockade of southern ports, Secretary of the Navy Gideon Welles was desperate for men and ships and thus overlooked Lee's disobedience of orders. Welles immediately posted him to duty off Charleston, his first Civil War assignment. Thereafter Lee compiled a solid record of service to the United States Navy: he saw action with Admiral David D. Farragut in the capture of New Orleans in April 1862; he commanded the North Atlantic Blockading Squadron from September 1862 to October 1864; his last wartime command was the Mississippi Squadron from November 1864 to August 1865.

Throughout the war, Lizzie and Phil rarely saw each other. Even at times when it would have been possible for her to join him, he refused, thinking it improper for a wife to follow her husband into war. Married eighteen years, the forty-three-year-old Lizzie had abundant experience in lengthy separations from her naval husband. She had also had long training in writing the kinds of letters her absent husband expected.[25] He wanted the latest news from Washington, and she was perfectly situated to give it to him. "I have," she told him, "seen the inside view."[26] She frequently mentioned that "Father went to see the P," meaning that Preston Blair had crossed Pennsylvania Avenue to consult with the president at the White House. Her father, a founder of the Republican party, was an intimate adviser to Lincoln; brother Montgomery was postmaster general; brother Frank was a congressman from Missouri who also served in the Union army as a major general. Nearly everyone of any importance in Washington appeared at the Blair-Lee door. Not unusual was the day she reported that at dinner time, there had been "12 hats on the rack."[27]

More important, Lizzie was her husband's closest adviser. Lee had been raised in "the hard school" of the navy and had not only a strong sense of duty but also a highly developed sensitivity to slights, which made him quick to take offense.[28] His penchant for bluntness and his innate confidence in his own opinions often brought him to the brink of insubordination. It was Lizzie who smoothed his sharp edges, providing sound and reasonable advice.

The habit of turning to her for counsel had begun early in their marriage when the young Lieutenant Lee had become involved in an unpleasant dispute in 1844 with his superiors on the Coast Survey. When he submitted to her a draft of a letter he intended for the superintendent of the survey, Alexander Dallas Bache, she pointed out its abrasiveness, sensibly stating its probable effect: "Now it strikes me that without Mr. Bache is extremely good natured, he will take mortal offense at this same letter & make it good cause for having you discontinued on the service."[29]

While she was quite frank in her advice, Elizabeth Lee, knowing her husband was easily offended, almost always couched her counsel in gentle terms. Allowing for his prickly nature, she acquiesced to the superficial forms expected of a nineteenth-century wife. She was a fascinating combination of her father, a thoroughly political animal, and her mother, whose nickname was "the Lioness." Eliza Blair had been a strong model for her daughter. She had ignored her family's advice when she married Francis Preston Blair. An equal partner in her own marriage, Eliza had been an active participant in her husband's newspaper, contributing articles and special features. Accustomed to heeding her advice, Blair had always appreciated his wife's intelligence and need for personal expression; "the Lioness" was no idle nickname.[30] Elizabeth had grown up with the example of a woman who understood public affairs and was never shy in offering her opinions to her husband. The daughter followed her mother's lead, modifying and softening the approach. As Elizabeth wrote Phil, "I think there is no wrong in giving utterance to honest feelings . . . I always shall think it my right to speak out to you . . . & I expect always will—Then the responsibility of action rests with you & whatever it is I'll try to be content."[31]

The political prominence of her own family made it possible for Elizabeth to try to advance her husband's career.[32] From the time she first moved to Washington in 1830, she had been surrounded by politics. Her father maintained that she had been "brought up in caucus." In her childhood she had copied documents for Andrew Jackson and as an adult had assisted her father and brothers in their political activities. Elizabeth knew how to use her political experience for her husband's benefit; as she told him, "I know the ropes for I've seen them well pulled."[33] She used the traditional methods employed by military wives to help their husbands: she wrote letters, arranged casual encounters with the secretary of the navy, enlisted the aid of her father and brothers, used the socially expected calls on the wives of important congressmen and senators, and gave political dinners for influential government officials. Typical is her reassurance to her husband that she was energetically pulling the ropes: "Whilst we in family circle were talking—Mr. Cameron arrived—said he had no family— no dinner—& knew where he wanted to come & enjoy both—The table was consequently enlarged—it was hardly fixed when Fremont drove up—& ere fixing was quite done—Govr Sprague & a Rhode Island reinforcement came—now the whole table was cleared off & enlarged."[34]

Although Lee had had remarkable success in capturing a blockade runner off Charleston with his sloop, Lizzie realized the superiority of steam power over sail. Knowing that success and promotion for her husband would come only when he had exchanged *Vandalia* for a steamer, she marshaled her considerable forces to that object, telling Phil in the first summer of the war that she was "hot after a steamer for you."[35] Enlisting her father's and brothers' help, she focused her efforts on navy secretary Gideon Welles, Silas Stringham, commander of the Atlantic Blockading Squadron, and Hiram Paulding, commander of the New York yard where steamers were under construction. She vowed to "jog-jog" officialdom until Lee had what he wanted.[36] Her persistence paid off: Welles assigned Lee to *Oneida* with orders to join David G. Farragut, commanding the Gulf Blockading Squadron.[37]

Arriving at the Southwest Pass of the Mississippi River on March 26, Lee proved himself to be a cooperative hard worker. He was cool under fire when Farragut's squadron came under intense bombardment from the Confederate forts guarding the approach to New Orleans. The hypercritical David Porter had high praise for his fellow officer: "I never saw a ship more beautifully fought and managed. He was under fire more than anyone else. . . . His ship was a good deal cut up. He had much more than his share of killed and wounded and said less about it than those who did not take the bull so closely by the horns. I admire Lee very much for his cool calm bravery, the highest quality an officer can possess."[38] Lizzie, on the other hand, found "these dark days of anxiety" nearly unbearable. For weeks she did not know if he was alive; for a time, she was so distraught that she could not even speak his name.[39]

Lee remained with Farragut's flotilla after the capture of New Orleans, moving up the Mississippi to the blockade of Vicksburg. In July, Welles recalled him to Washington and to everyone's surprise, appointed Lee to command the North Atlantic Blockading Squadron. In this instance, there is no evidence that the Blair family had influenced Welles's decision. While Lee had proved his courage under fire, the navy secretary had appointed him over others with greater seniority for other qualities: his honesty, dedication to hard work, business acumen, steady attention to detail, and his knowledge of the seacoast from his past Coast Survey duty.[40] The responsibilities of command included enforcement of the blockade, regulation of internal trade on the rivers, and cooperation with the army in reconnaissance and raids. Not requiring bold, aggressive leadership, the job demanded organizational and administrative skills in addition to meticulous record keeping of captured ships and cargoes and strict adherence to rules regarding trade permits.

On September 4, 1862, Captain Lee assumed command of the North Atlantic Blockading Squadron with the rank of acting rear admiral.[41] Lee was ideally suited for the position. During his tenure of command, he devised the blockading strategy that was used for the rest of the war. While never complete, the blockade became increasingly effective under Lee's guidance. To the extent that his resources allowed him, he cooperated with the army in raids into the interior.

As she had done so often during their marriage, Lizzie acted as her husband's best friend, giving him the benefit of her sound advice from her vantage point in Washington. As commander of the North Atlantic Blockading Squadron, Lee faced grumbling from both the navy department and the public. The blockade was not perfect, and the South delighted in publishing accounts of successful blockade runners. To counter the impression that his blockading efforts were ineffective, Elizabeth offered specific suggestions: that each captain should report every "fruitless chasing" every day; that Lee should "pile & file them in the Dept as a part of your official record." Because of her "inside view," she informed her husband that she had "reason to believe that Mr. W[elles] does *not* understand" the difficulties of maintaining a blockade. Her advice to her husband was subtle: "I think you might write him a *private* synopsis of the state of things based upon these reports." Knowing his penchant for bluntness, she urged, "Make this in a kindest respectful tone—*in a private letter* to Mr. W."[42]

Normally, Elizabeth's advice echoed her father's opinions or at least benefited from them, but occasionally she acted alone. When in July 1864 Lee's rash and impetuous dash up the Potomac to rescue the capital from Jubal Early's raid had brought censure from the navy department, Elizabeth suggested the proper course: "After a sober night of thought & without any chance of consulting with father, my own conclusion is—drop the discussion."[43]

Unlike Jesse Frémont who personally challenged President Lincoln, Elizabeth Blair never overstepped the bounds of propriety. Only once did she contemplate direct confrontation. In 1863, to fulfill her husband's wishes, she became particularly intent upon seeing that Lee's acting rank was made permanent. She threatened to call by herself on President Lincoln and Secretary Welles. It was an empty threat. Knowing that such direct action on her part would anger the males of her family, including her husband, she depended upon her father and brothers to make those official calls on her husband's behalf.[44] Knowing that promotion required a vote of thanks from Congress, Elizabeth set to work with a will in her pursuit of an admiralship for Phil. She validated her claim that he had support in Congress by telling him, "I have felt that pulse industriously for 6 weeks."[45] Between her father's calls and her own, she was optimistic: "I have a thousand fair promises both from Senators—Reps & Secretaries."[46] It was not for lack of his wife's efforts that Lee remained only acting rear admiral until well after the war.

Through her letters, Elizabeth Lee maintained and nurtured the marital bond. She was the linchpin of a large and extended family, writing regularly to innumerable aunts, uncles, cousins, brothers, and sisters-in-

law. Calling her letters "a family institution," she developed great skill as
a correspondent.[47] Always optimistic, always loving, she gave Phil intelligent reports of public people and events; at the same time, she assured
him of her constant love and affection. She thought of her letters as her
"thinking aloud" with him, and her unaffected style kept her loving nature
alive in his memory.[48] Political and military intelligence interspersed with
routine family detail bound Phil tightly to the family.

Nearly always optimistic, Lizzie filled her letters with words of encouragement and cheerful buoyancy. Knowing that Phil's attention needed to
be focused on the tasks of war and that her letters could affect his morale,
she was careful not to complain too much. She limited her expressions
of anxiety to her concern for him and refrained from burdening him with
anything that would stir his solicitude for her.

Near the end of the war, however, she felt compelled to share her fears.
In late March 1865, she found a lump in her breast. Although she tried
to reassure Phil that she did not think surgery would be necessary, her
mother upbraided her for telling him about it until they knew the seriousness of her condition. Not until April 14 did she again mention the
tumor. She told Phil how frightened she had been when the doctor suspected cancer and insisted on surgery. Unaccountably, the tumor disappeared and she did not then have the operation. Nevertheless, she could
not refrain from unburdening herself to her husband, telling him, "I
could not shake off the feeling that morning that I would die under that
knife & chloroform & to leave the world without seeing you again seemed
worse than death."[49]

In June 1865, she did have the surgery. Without mentioning her ailment again to her husband and without telling even her parents, she
submitted to "knife and chloroform," attended only by two women friends.
She recovered quickly and by mid-month had resumed limited public
activities.[50]

During the war, Elizabeth's primary diversion, aside from her family
concerns, was her work for the Washington City Orphan Asylum. Since
1849 she had been a member of its governing board and in 1862 was
elected first directress, a position she held until her death in 1906. A
traditional nineteenth-century women's benevolent society, it served, as
did similar institutions for innumerable upper-class women, as an outlet
for their managerial and organizational skills.[51] Elizabeth Lee devoted
endless hours during the Civil War to this philanthropic effort: fund raising, purchasing supplies, hiring and firing employees—in short, she ran
a business. An efficient administrator, she reorganized the board, instituted a Sunday School, and oversaw the construction of a new building
for the asylum.[52] Not wishing to step outside her prescribed sphere, she
justified this public work by claiming that it assuaged her loneliness. As
the war was coming to an end, she explained: "I took it to get rid of myself
when pining into sickness for my husband—[It] gave me work for head,

heart & hands—& a refuge ever ready for me when my life was too lonesome to be happy."[53]

In her husband's absence, however, the focus of Lizzie's life was their son Blair. Her daily running commentary in her letters to her husband on the boy's development from age three to eight detailed his antics, always emphasizing his love for his absent father. Elizabeth shared her concerns for their son, her theories of child rearing, and her hopes for his future.

Blair also proved a solace to the mother. With her husband exposed to danger, she relied on her child to help her endure the long and anxious separation, as she explained on Blair's birthday: "I sometimes wonder what would have become of me in these last three years of separation from you & bitter miseries of the War—I have how many times felt most gratefully that he was an endless source of occupation, comfort & joy to me."[54] When Lee was engaged in the capture of New Orleans, his wife was desperately worried about him and described her efforts to keep occupied: "My bread is as chips & no labor attracts or interests me & I hang about my child for quietness—& I can watch his plays with pleasure—& little does he know how much he really does take care of his Mama for his Papa."[55]

Little Blair, moreover, provided his share of childhood preciousness that his mother faithfully rendered in touching vignettes, incidents that bind parents together in treasured memories: "He talks about you & I try to do so cheerfully—he has fine plans for tying you in bed next time we get you home to keep you from going away. 'I'll bring him every thing good to eat & wont starve him ' & so he prattles & comforts me with his sympathy."[56] After Phil had been home for a brief visit in 1864, Lizzie reported that Blair had picked up many of his father's mannerisms, including calling her "Lizzie." She had responded rather sharply, she told Phil: "I told him if he did not want me for a *Mama* he ought call me Mrs. Lee—He was very cut—& has never since called me Lizzie."[57]

Like every good mother, she wished to shape her child's character, and her discussions of Blair's development and her hopes for him formed a crucial connection with her husband. Reveling in the little tasks he did for her or his grandparents—whether it was bringing in wood or spading in the garden—she tried to nurture his good qualities, explaining to Phil, "I think I am honest & earnest in my desire to make our boy a good boy and man as far as it is in my power." Her goal was to find the right balance between discipline and affection: "not to spoil him by too much care, notice or money, but still to let him see & believe in the devoted love which I think we both feel for him."[58]

The possibility that their son could be spoiled by wealth became a particular concern for the Lees as Phil began to accumulate prize money for the capture of blockade runners. As commander of the North Atlantic Blockading Squadron, he was entitled to one-twentieth of his squadron's share.[59] As soon as he had captured his first prize in the summer of 1861, Phil and Lizzie began to consider the consequences for their son. As Lizzie explained to Phil: "I never want Blair to own a cent in his own right until he makes it—I think boys get too soon out of the guidance of Parents—I want Blair taught the use of money but dont spoil him with it—that is my great fear for our child—in our tenderness we may not develop his really fine nature."[60]

That prize money, along with his Blair family connection, cost Lee professionally. As commander of the largest Union naval squadron for two years, Lee garnered more prize money during the Civil War than any other officer.[61] All that money brought jealousy; many thought Lee had received ample monetary compensation for his services and should not receive additional reward through promotion. Although he had held acting rank since assuming command of the North Atlantic Blockading Squadron, he was not promoted to rear admiral until 1870.[62]

Two events in 1864 marred his stellar record: in May, his association with Benjamin Butler's move up the James River, which ended in the debacle of the army's being bottled up by the Confederates only eight miles from Richmond; and in July, his unauthorized movement to counter Early's raid on Washington. The first proved to Ulysses Grant that Lee was not a bold commander; the second convinced Welles that Lee could panic under pressure.[63] The result was that in the fall of 1864, Welles removed Lee from command of the North Atlantic Blockading Squadron and reassigned him to the Mississippi Squadron. Welles justified the change by claiming that Lee was "destitute of heroic daring." While Lee had "administered the affairs of his squadron safely," the secretary thought that his acting rear admiral had "failed to devise and execute any important act." In a word, he was too cautious.[64] It seemed not to matter that neither the army nor the navy had given Lee's theater priority for offensive operations, treating it as a backwater and never allocating sufficient men or materiel for aggressive action. It was only after Sherman's Atlanta campaign had begun that the North Atlantic command assumed importance. Butler and Lee had failed to take Richmond, and Grant wanted more aggressive leadership to close Wilmington, the only remaining Confederate port in North Carolina. Grant preferred David Porter, an officer with whom he had previously worked.

As important to Lee's reassignment was the political climate. Although Preston Blair had been a founder of the Republican party, he had not gravitated, as many in his party had, to radicalism. Indeed, by 1863, he and his sons were the leaders of the conservative faction. Supporting Lincoln's cautious approach to emancipation, the Blairs had favored colonization and compensation to border state slaveholders in 1861 and had backed the president's moderate and conciliatory approach to Reconstruction in 1863. They had consistently differed with Radicals over military appointments, remaining advocates for McClellan for far too long and opposing Radical favorites John Pope, John Frémont, Joseph Hooker, and Benjamin Butler. The Blair men, loyal to Lincoln, relished a good fight and sacrificed their own political fortunes for Lincoln who used them as "lightning rods" to deflect opposition from himself. Aggressive and confrontational, the Blairs allowed their political conflicts with Radicals to degenerate into personal rancor. By mid-1864 the Blairs had become anathema to Radical Republicans who were in no mood to reward Preston Blair's "other son." In June, Frank had been forced out of Congress; in September Montgomery had been forced out of the cabinet.[65] Likewise, Lee was removed from command of the North Atlantic Squadron.

Indeed, Preston Blair treated Phil like another son. Neither hard talk nor gentle pleading with Secretary Welles could change his orders, and Blair offered fatherly advice: "Now let me entreat you to take the physic as Monty does. It will operate well notwithstanding the nausea. We are all honest & have done our duty—there all the honor lies."[66] Lee followed Blair's advice and served nearly another year as commander of the Mississippi Squadron. His most important duty in the West was to cooperate with General George H. Thomas at Nashville in repulsing the Confederate army of John Bell Hood in December 1864. Both cautious and methodical in their preparations, Thomas and Lee exasperated their superiors, but the near total destruction of Hood's army deflected further criticism. At war's end, Lee remained in the West to oversee the reduction of his squadron, returning home finally in August 1865.

In the years following the Civil War, Lizzie and Phil continued to share homes with her family—either at the Lee's Pennsylvania Avenue home or at the Blair's Silver Spring farm. All bent to the oar with a will for two goals: keeping Phil near home and gaining his promotion to admiral. For a few years, Lee saw duty ashore, serving as president of the Board of Examiners of volunteer officers, on court-martial boards, as an inspector of navy yards, and as chief signal officer of the navy. His promotion to admiral in the spring of 1870, however, meant that he once again went to sea.

Early in the war, Lizzie had vowed: "Well we will know how to appreciate a home together in peaceful times even more than ever."[67] And they did. While the Civil War did not fundamentally alter the Lee relationship, it did deepen the bond through shared memories of danger, anxiety, and participation in a common cause. Lee reveled in his family life after the Civil War and when he sailed once again, admitted that he was "very home sick."[68] He sent loving messages through his wife to his son: "Tell him I do want a hug badly & to take him a playing on my back."[69] Impressing upon his wife and son the need "to make the old people happy," he frequently expressed his "respect, devotion & gratitude" to the elder Blairs: "We, who have shared their hospitable home so long, must now make life easy & pleasant for them to the utmost extent of our capacity."[70]

Lizzie missed her Admiral-husband and, as she always had, made sure to tell him: "All my joy has gone away with you."[71] The passage of years since their marriage in 1843 had not dimmed her ardor, and she reminded him that too many couples drifted apart in middle age because they neglected each other and "husbands are no longer lovers." She demurely suggested that passion was still a part of their marriage: "It is lonesome when I go to bed."[72]

During his final cruise, Lee entrusted their affairs completely to his wife, telling her "you have power and responsibility." Reviewing their financial situation and admonishing economy, he was confident that her management "will exceed mine."[73] Although she had many years' experience supervising their affairs, she accepted his orders casually: "It was delightful to get your letter—homily & all."[74] His confidence in Lizzie extended beyond her fiscal skills to the more important task of parenting their son. His letters to Blair are filled with his own good advice, but always he urged his son to turn to his mother "because I have unfailing faith in her capacity to rear you right."[75] Cautioning against "bad boys, bad habits, and bad women" (in addition to cards, tobacco, and alcohol), he counseled fourteen-year-old Blair to "keep confidence with your mother who is and will be your best friend."[76]

At last, after forty-five years of continuous military service, Lee's naval career ended. He came home from the Caribbean in August 1872 and retired from the navy on his sixty-first birthday, February 13, 1873. The eighty-two-year-old Preston Blair turned over management of the Silver Spring farm to his son-in-law, who ran it as he had so many ships, keeping a daily log of plantings, weather, chores, projects, and expenses. After the death of her father in 1876 and her mother in 1877, Lizzie inherited Silver Spring, and the Lees owned two residences, the farm and their home in Washington.[77]

Never able to shake free of the memories of his childhood poverty, Lee fretted about expenses. He began a campaign to move his family permanently to the Silver Spring farm and rent the city house. At age sixty, Lizzie was unalterably opposed to that plan, contending that her parents' mode of spending the summers at Silver Spring and the winters in the city had prolonged their lives.[78] Year after year, Lee doggedly pushed for the more economical arrangement; he argued with his wife to no avail. On February 13, 1885, he complained in his farm log: "I was born February 13, 1812, and am 73 years old to-day. I gave to-day solid reasons to my son & wife for stopping the expense of two establishments. . . . My good purpose was not appreciated, or respected even."[79] By 1888 he was finished with pleading; retired Rear Admiral Samuel Phillips Lee moved permanently to Silver Spring farm.

Elizabeth Blair Lee, although distressed by her husband's decision, continued to move from the city to the country as the seasons dictated. Both partners remained obdurate. When spring arrived the following year, Lee stiffly noted in his farm log on March 7: "Told Mrs. Lee I wished her to return home by the 15th inst. . . . She replied 'I will not come before the first of April.' " Neither ever gave in. Until his death in 1897 at the age of 85, he lived on the farm and she moved from the city to the country with the changing seasons. They saw each other almost every day; the farm was, after all, only six miles from their city home. Despite their disagreement over living arrangements, they sustained their abiding love for each other. Every year Lee faithfully noted in his log the anniversary of his marriage, commenting in 1877, "My wife has made me happy, & so has my son."[80] When Lizzie wrote to her husband from Hot Springs, Virginia, in 1894, she closed her letter with the admonition, "Take good care of yourself my first best love."[81]

After Lee's death on June 5, 1897, Lizzie made her home with their son Blair and his wife Anne in the two homes that the Lees owned. During the Civil War, she had expressed her hope that Blair would become "a prop to our old age."[82] The young man more than fulfilled his mother's fondest wish. Blair graduated from Princeton and began his legal career in 1883. Following the Blair tradition, he became involved in politics and was Maryland's first popularly elected United States senator. An exemplary son in every way, he tenderly and conscientiously cared for his aging mother until her death on September 13, 1906.

The patterns and tenor of the marriage of Elizabeth Blair and Phillips Lee were well established by the time of the Civil War. In 1861 they had been married eighteen years, and their life together had been shaped by his military career. Letters, particularly hers, often formed the nexus of their relationship. Through their correspondence, they worked out their differences, explained their hopes and dreams for the future, and reiterated their devotion to each other. By the time of the war, Lizzie had become an adept letter writer, and her skillful presentation of political and military matters, interspersed with intimate domesticities, linked Phil all the more tightly to his family. Her devotion to the Union cause, his cause, bolstered his confidence and reinforced his commitment to duty. More important, perhaps, he recognized his wife's ability to soften his rough edges and blunt his abrasiveness. He had wanted a wife who could be his best friend, and he was grateful that he had found a companion whose opinion he valued and advice he trusted. And always, her expressions of love for him kept their bond intact.

The Blair family provided the larger home circle, fostering connection to an extended family. After their initial opposition to the marriage, Preston and Eliza Blair became Phillips Lee's strong supporters, welcoming him as another son and giving him a sense of belonging. Their acceptance (reinforced by the birth of their grandson) fostered gratitude and loyalty in their son-in-law, and he repaid them with tender care in their old age. Lizzie's brother Frank had been an ally from the beginning, and his affable good nature broke through Phil's natural reticence. When Frank faced straitened circumstances in his later years, it was Phil who sent him money. Even Montgomery helped bind Phillips Lee to his wife and the Blairs. Although Montgomery's animus toward Lee abated after the Civil War, it did not end. Lizzie never wavered in her loyalty, standing with her husband against her eldest brother, a situation that gave Phil great satisfaction. At every turn, the Blairs tried to use their political influence to advance Phil's career. His attachment to the Blair clan was both a boon and a burden to Lee; he probably lost as much as he gained from the connection. Nevertheless, it was important to Lee that they rallied to his cause whenever he needed help with the navy department or Congress.

For Lizzie, marriage to a career naval officer gave her the best of both worlds: she found fulfillment through marriage to a man she loved while retaining her close connection to her own kin. As the only daughter and only sister in her family, she was especially beloved. Her parents nurtured her intelligence and fostered her strong sense of self-worth. Her parents' marriage provided her with a vivid example of shared authority, loyal devotion, and respect for women. When she and Phil disagreed, Lizzie was able to resist submission to her husband's will because a lifetime of family support had given her self-respect and individual identity. Although she accepted many of the tenets of what has been called "the cult of true womanhood" and genuinely believed that wives should be submissive to their husbands, she found ways to assert her will, make independent judgments, shape the direction of their mutual life, and even defy her husband.

The Civil War had intensified their mutual appreciation of each other and their family. Those four years of turmoil brought home to them the fragility of existence and inspired their determination to cherish their life together. Tested by the calamity of war, their marriage was not without vicissitudes, but it remained a strong and stable union, sustained by their enduring love for each other.

NOTES

EDITORS' INTRODUCTION

1. Examples include John Rozier, ed., *The Granite Farm Letters* (Athens: University of Georgia Press, 1988); Reid Mitchell, *The Vacant Chair: The Northern Soldier Leaves Home* (New York: Oxford University Press, 1993); James M. McPherson, *For Cause and Comrades: Why Men Fought in the Civil War* (New York: Oxford University Press, 1997); Drew Gilpin Faust, *Mothers of Invention: Women of the Slaveholding South in the American Civil War* (Chapel Hill: University of North Carolina Press, 1997).
2. James L. Roark, "Behind the Lines: Confederate Economy and Society," in *Writing the Civil War: The Quest to Understand*, ed. James M. McPherson and William J. Cooper, Jr. (Columbia: University of South Carolina Press, 1998), 222.
3. Philip Shaw Paludan, "What Did the Winners Win? The Social and Economic History of the North during the Civil War," in *Writing the Civil War*, ed. McPherson and Cooper, 196.
4. Emory M. Thomas, *Robert E. Lee: A Biography* (New York: W. W. Norton, 1995), 190.
5. Thomas J. Jackson to Mary Anna Jackson, July 23 [1861], quoted in *The Blue and Gray*, 2 vols. ed. Henry Steele Commager (Indianapolis: Bobbs-Merrill, 1950), I, 115.
6. John Y. Simon, ed. *The Personal Memoirs of Julia Dent Grant* (New York: G. P. Putnam's Sons, 1975), 104.
7. For readers seeking additional and recent publications related to the couples in our book, see William J. Cooper, Jr., *Jefferson Davis, American* (New York: Alfred A. Knopf, 2000); Michael Fellman, *The Making of Robert E. Lee* (New York: Random House, 2000); John M. Taylor, *Duty Faithfully Performed: Robert E. Lee and His Critics* (Dulles, VA: Brasseys, 1999); Emory Thomas, *Robert E. Lee: An Album* (New York: W. W. Norton, 2000); Gerard A. Patterson, *Justice or Atrocity: General George E. Pickett and the Kinston, N.C. Hangings* (Gettysburg, PA: Thomas Publications, 1998); Richard F. Selcer, *Lee vs. Pickett: Two Divided by War* (Gettysburg, PA: Thomas Publications, 1998); Harry Maihafer, *The General and the Journalists: Ulysses S. Grant, Horace Greeley, and Charles Dana.* (Washington: Brasseys, 1998); Geoffrey Perret, *Ulysses S. Grant: Soldier & President* (New York: Random House, 1997); Brooks D. Simpson, *Ulysses S. Grant: Triumph over Adversity, 1822–1865* (Boston: Houghton Mifflin, 2000); Stanley P. Hirshson, *The White Tecumseh: A Biography of General William T. Sherman* (New York: Wiley, 1997); Brooks Simpson, and Jean V. Berlin, eds., *Sherman's Civil War: Selected Correspondence of William T. Sherman, 1860–1865* (Chapel Hill: University of North Carolina Press, 1999); David Roberts, *A Newer World: Kit Carson, John C. Frémont and the Claiming of the American West* (New York: Simon and Schuster, 2000).
    See also Lesley J. Gordon, " 'To Comfort, to Counsel, to Cure': Davis, Wives and Generals," in *Jefferson Davis's Generals*, ed. Gabor Boritt (New York: Oxford University Press, 1999), 104–28, for a slightly different look at the Lees and Davises, in addition

to discussions of the Beauregards, Braggs, and Johnstons. A just published study that examines the broader issue of marriage in U.S. history is Nancy Cott, *Public Vows: A History of Marriage and the Nation* (Cambridge, MA: Harvard University Press, 2000).

CHAPTER ONE

This article has been expanded and revised for this collection. It appeared in an earlier version as "The Marriage of Varina Howell and Jefferson Davis: 'I gave the best and all my life to a girdled tree,' " in *The Journal of Southern History*, 65 (February 1999): 3–40.

1. There are many valuable biographies of Jefferson Davis as well as of Varina Howell Davis. The most recent biography of Jefferson Davis is by William J. Cooper, Jr., and of Varina Davis by Gerry Van der Heuval. I look forward to the upcoming biography of Varina Davis by Joan E. Cashin. Because the perspective of this study is not on the lives but rather on the marriage of Varina and Jefferson Davis, I have for the most part relied on the abundant Davis correspondence exchanged primarily between husband and wife that is on deposit in the following manuscript repositories: University of Alabama, Tuscaloosa; the Museum of the Confederacy; Duke University; Emory University; Library of Congress; Mississippi Department of Archives and History; New York Public Library; University of North Carolina, Chapel Hill; Pierpont Morgan Library; Rice University; Tennessee State Library and Archives; Transylvania University; Tulane University; the University of Virginia; and the Virginia Historical Society. *The Papers of Jefferson Davis*, being published under the skillful stewardship of Lynda Lasswell Crist, Mary Seaton Dix, and Kenneth H. Williams, has proved to be of inestimable assistance to me. Lynda Crist and Elaine Thompson, a graduate student at Rice University, have also immeasurably assisted me in my research in the Davis papers held by the Jefferson Davis Association at Rice. To date, nine volumes of the papers of Jefferson Davis have been published by Louisiana State University Press and supported in part by the National Historical Publications and Records Commission. I wish also to thank Professor Frederick Heath for his many contributions to this project.
2. Varina Davis, Autobiographical Sketch, Jefferson Davis Papers (University of Alabama, Tuscaloosa); Varina to Constance Cary Harrison, April 5, 1880, Harrison Family Papers (University of Virginia, Charlottesville); Varina Davis to Jefferson Addison Hayes, [May] 20, 1894, Davis Papers (Mississippi Department of Archives and History, Jackson); Ishbel Ross, *First Lady of the South: The Life of Mrs. Jefferson Davis* (New York: Harper, 1958), 13–17; and Eron Rowland, *Varina Howell, Wife of Jefferson Davis*, 2 vols. (New York: Macmillan, 1927), I, 18–25 and 42–45. See also Joan E. Cashin, "Varina Howell Davis (1826–1906)," in *Portraits of American Women*, ed. G. J. Barker-Benfield and Catherine Clinton (New York: St. Martin's Press, 1991), 258–77.
3. Jefferson Davis, "Autobiographical Sketch," in *The Papers of Jefferson Davis*, 9 vols. to date, ed. Haskell M. Monroe, Jr., James T. McIntosh, Lynda Lasswell Crist, Mary Seaton Dix, and Kenneth H. Williams (Baton Rouge: Louisiana State University Press, 1971–), I, lxxii–lxxiii. See also William Allen Shelton, *The Young Jefferson Davis, 1808–1846* (New York, 1982). Clement Eaton, *Jefferson Davis* (New York: The Free Press, 1977), includes a chapter on the women in Davis's life (pp. 21–32). The three-volume biography by Hudson Strode, *Jefferson Davis: American Patriot, 1808–1861*; *Jefferson Davis: Confederate President*; and *Jefferson Davis, Tragic Hero: The Last Twenty-Five Years, 1864–1889* (New York: Harcourt, Brace, 1955, 1959, 1964), is based on wide research but is in many instances uncritical. The most recent biography, and very important to Davis scholars, is that of William C. Davis, *Jefferson Davis: The Man and His Hour* (New York: HarperCollins, 1991). For Davis at Transylvania see Margaret Newnan Wagers, *The Education of a Gentleman: Jefferson Davis at Transylvania, 1821–1842* (Lexington: University of Kentucky Press, 1943). The documents in Monroe et al., eds., *Papers of Jefferson Davis*, I, 10–105, cover the West Point years.
4. For Davis's first marriage see the following footnotes in Monroe et al., eds., *Papers of Jefferson Davis*, I, 250–51, n. 3, 347–48, n. 2, 408, n. 4–5; and Sarah Knox Taylor to

Margaret M. S. Taylor, June 17, 1835, ibid., 406–7. See also Walter L. Fleming, "Jefferson Davis' First Marriage," *Publications of the Mississippi Historical Society*, 12 (1912): 21–36; and Holman Hamilton, *Zachary Taylor: Soldier of the Republic* (Indianapolis: Bobbs-Merrill, 1941), 100–109.

5. Varina Howell to Margaret Howell [December 19, 1843], Monroe et al., eds., *Papers of Jefferson Davis*, II, 52–53.

6. Ibid.; and Varina Davis to Jefferson Davis, February 8, 1866, Davis Papers (University of Alabama) (quotation); Rowland, *Varina Howell*, I, 44; and Frank E. Everett, Jr., *Brierfield: Plantation Home of Jefferson Davis* (Hattiesburg, MS, 1971), 8.

7. Jefferson Davis to Varina Howell, November 22, 1844, Monroe et al., eds., *Papers of Jefferson Davis*, II, 226. For political affiliations see ibid., 57, n. 9 and 58.

8. Varina Davis, *Jefferson Davis, Ex-President of the Confederate States of America: A Memoir by His Wife*, 2 vols. (New York: Belford Company, 1890), I, 200; and Accession No. 73.3, Clothing, Outwear, Catalogue (Mississippi Historical Museum, Jackson).

9. Varina Davis to Major W. H. Morgan, n.d. [1889], Jefferson Davis and Family Papers (Manuscript Division, Library of Congress, Washington). During the Civil War, the wife of a Union general who had known Jefferson during his courtship of Sarah told an acquaintance that Varina, though "a woman of fine looks and very smart and ambitious, with great influence," was "strange to say, without the affections of her husband [who] . . . thinks of nothing but his first wife." John D. Hayes, ed., *Samuel Francis Du Pont: A Selection from His Civil War Letters*. Vol. II: *The Blockade, 1862–1863* (Ithaca, NY: Cornell University Press, 1969), 118.

10. Monroe et al., eds., *Papers of Jefferson Davis*, I, liv, lxiv–lxv (quotation), and lxvi, n. 10.

11. Varina Davis to Margaret Howell, January 30, 1846, ibid., II, 419–20.

12. Varina Davis, *Jefferson Davis*, I, 206.

13. Varina Davis to Margaret Howell, June 6, 1846, Monroe et al., eds., *Papers of Jefferson Davis*, II, 641–42.

14. Jefferson Davis to Lucinda Farrar [Davis Davis] Stamps, July 8, 1846, ibid., 695.

15. For these troubles among the Davises see the testimony in the trial record, *Jefferson Davis v. Joseph H. D. Bowmar, et al.*, Warren County, Mississippi, Chancery Court, July 3, 1874–January 8, 1876, 346–47, 354–58, 364, 366–68 (Mississippi Department of Archives and History). See also Everett, *Brierfield*, 31–41.

16. Jefferson to Varina, December 10, 1846, Monroe et al., eds., *Papers of Jefferson Davis*, III, 94–95 (first and third quotations on p. 94; second on p. 95) and 96, n. 11.

17. Ibid., xxxiv–xxxv, 96, n. 11 and 122; and *Davis v. Bowmar*, 349–51 and 357–58.

18. Jefferson Davis to Varina Davis, January 3 and 4, 1848, extract printed in Paul C. Richards, *The American Scene: A Panorama of Autographs, 1504–1980*, [January 1983], 66, item 230 (copy in the offices of the Jefferson Davis Association, Fondren Library, Rice University, Houston).

19. Jefferson to Varina, April 18, 1848, Monroe et al., eds., *Papers of Jefferson Davis*, III, 302–3.

20. Ibid., 303.

21. Varina Davis to Margaret Howell, November 14, 1845 (Old Court House Museum, Vicksburg, MS).

22. Varina Davis to Jefferson Davis, in Monroe et al., eds., *Papers of Jefferson Davis*, IV, 7.

23. Sarah S. Ellis, *The Guide to Social Happiness* (New York, 1847).

24. Varina to Jefferson, January 25 [1850], Monroe et al., eds., *Papers of Jefferson Davis*, IV, 62.

25. Lady Charlotte Campbell Bury, *The Wilfulness of Woman*, 3 vols. (London, 1844); and Library of Congress Loan Record of Jefferson Davis, in Monroe et al., eds., *Papers of Jefferson Davis*, IV, 173.

26. Varina Davis to Margaret and William Howell, August 3, 1850, Davis Papers (University of Alabama); and Margaret Howell to Varina Davis, April 7, 1851, William Burr Howell Papers (Mississippi Department of Archives and History).

27. Varina Davis to Margaret Howell, March 4, 1852, Davis Papers (University of Alabama).

28. Margaret Howell to William Howell, August 20, 1852, ibid.

29. Jefferson Davis, *The Rise and Fall of the Confederate Government*, 2 vols. (New York: D. Appleton, 1881), I, 22–23. Varina recorded in her memoir that she hoped following the inauguration "to be at home again [at Brierfield] and dwell in happy obscurity" but that Jefferson's friends "over-persuaded" him to return to Washington. Varina Davis, *Jefferson Davis*, I, 477.

30. Monroe et al., eds., *Papers of Jefferson Davis*, V, 42, n. 16.

31. Varina Davis to Margaret Howell, March 26, 1854, in Hudson Strode, ed., *Jefferson Davis: Private Letters, 1823–1889* (New York: Harcourt, Brace, and World, 1966), 76–77.

32. For a convenient listing and discussion of the birth and death dates of the Davis children, see Monroe et al., eds., *Papers of Jefferson Davis*, I, 522–23.

33. Varina Davis to William B. Howell, November 14, 1858, and Varina Davis to Margaret Howell, November 21, 1858, Davis Papers (University of Alabama).

34. Jefferson to Varina, August 23, 1857, ibid.

35. Varina to Jefferson, April 19, 1859, ibid.

36. Jefferson to Clement Clay, May 17, 1859, Clement C. Clay Papers (Perkins Library, Duke University, Durham, NC); Varina Davis, *Jefferson Davis*, I, 570–82; Jefferson Davis to Franklin Pierce, April 4, 1858, Franklin Pierce Papers (Manuscript Division, Library of Congress); and Varina Davis to C. Bland Payne, February 25, 1898, Jefferson Davis Papers (Perkins Library, Duke University).

37. Margaret Howell to Varina Davis, January 27, 1852, Howell Papers; Varina Davis to Margaret Howell, May 25, 1852, Davis Papers (University of Alabama); Eliza Davis to Jefferson Davis, n. d., Howell Papers; *Davis v. Bowmar*, 348–50; and Monroe et al., eds., *Papers of Jefferson Davis*, IV, 301, n. 2.

38. Varina to Margaret Howell, April 25, 1859, in Strode, ed., *Private Letters*, 108–9.

39. Paul D. Escott, *After Secession: Jefferson Davis and the Failure of Confederate Nationalism* (Baton Rouge: Louisiana State University Press, 1978), 1–15, explains Davis's sectionalism and nationalism before 1860.

40. Janet Sharp Hermann, *The Pursuit of a Dream* (New York: Oxford University Press, 1981).

41. Varina to Jefferson, November 15, 1860, Davis Papers (University of Alabama). For the Davises' relationships with Northerners in the period, see, for example, Varina's comments on William Henry Seward in her *Jefferson Davis*, I, 579–83.

42. Varina Davis, *Jefferson Davis*, I, 686–99.

43. Davis to Alexander M. Clayton, January 30, 1861, in Monroe et al., eds., *Papers of Jefferson Davis*, VII, 28 (quoted phrase); and Varina Davis, *Jefferson Davis*, II, 12 (quotation), 18–19. See also John H. Reagan, *Memoirs with Special Reference to Secession and the Civil War* (New York: Neale Publishing Co., 1906), 109.

44. Jefferson Davis to Varina, February 20, 1861, *Papers of Jefferson Davis*, VII, 53–54.

45. Interview by Frederick Heath with Tucker Hill, White House of the Confederacy, August 7, 1985 (notes in my possession); Varina Davis, *Jefferson Davis*, II, 34–36 and 198–201; and Ross, *First Lady of the South*, 134–35.

46. Varina H. Davis to Francis Lawley, April 8, 1898, Pierce Butler Collection, Tulane University. See also Varina Davis to John S. Preston, April 1, 1865, Davis Papers (Museum of the Confederacy, Richmond).

47. Gerry Van der Heuvel, *Crowns of Thorns and Glory: Mary Todd Lincoln and Varina Howell Davis: The Two First Ladies of the Civil War* (New York: Dutton, 1988), 113. See also Eli N. Evans, *Judah P. Benjamin: The Jewish Confederate* (New York: Free Press, 1988), esp. 137–58.

48. Ross, *First Lady of the South*, 139–41; Varina Davis, *Jefferson Davis*, II, 301–2; and Van der Heuvel, *Crowns of Thorns and Glory*, 115.

49. Varina Davis to Jefferson Davis, April 7, 1865, in *Jefferson Davis Constitutionalist: His Letters, Papers, and Speeches*, 10 vols., ed. Dunbar Rowland (Jackson: Mississippi Dept. of Archives and History, 1923), VI, 537–39. Edward A. Pollard, *Life of Jefferson Davis, with a Secret History of the Southern Confederacy Gathered "Behind the Scenes in Richmond"* (Philadelphia: National Publishing Co., 1869), 157, claims that Jefferson "was as wax in the hands of his wife." Bell Irvin Wiley, *Confederate Women* (Westport, CT: Greenwood Press, 1975), in his chapter on Varina (pp. 82–139), presents a more balanced summary of the role of the first lady. See also Evans, *Judah P. Benjamin*, passim.

50. Varina Davis, *Jefferson Davis*, II, 160–62 and 204 (quotation).

51. Ibid., 163.

52. Jefferson to Varina, May 16, 1862, Davis Papers (Museum of the Confederacy). Numerous historians and biographers have blamed Davis's personality in part for Confederate failure. See, for example, David M. Potter, "Jefferson Davis and the Political Factors in Confederate Defeat," in *Why the North Won the Civil War*, ed. David Donald (Baton Rouge: Louisiana State University Press, 1960), 101–2 and 91–114; and Escott, *After Secession*.

53. Varina recalled in her memoir that her husband had been "a nervous dyspeptic by habit, and if he was forced to eat under any excitement, was ill after it for days. He said he could do either one duty or the other—give entertainments or administer the Government—and he fancied he was expected to perform the latter service in preference; and so we ceased to entertain except at formal receptions or informal dinners and breakfasts given to as many as Mr. Davis's health permitted us to invite." Varina Davis, *Jefferson Davis*, II, 161. See also Harris D. Riley, Jr., "Jefferson Davis and His Health," Part I, *Journal of Mississippi History*, 49 (August 1987): 179–202, and Part II, ibid., (November 1987): 261–87.

54. *Papers of Jefferson Davis*, VIII, viii.

55. Ibid.

56. Francis W. Smith to Anna Maria Smith, July 24, 1862, Smith Family Papers (Virginia Historical Society, Richmond). A perceptive Richmond woman, favorable to Varina, described her during the war as "a tall, commanding figure, with dark hair, eyes and complexion, and strongly marked expression, which lies chiefly in the mouth. With firmly set yet flexible lips, there is indicated much energy of purpose and will, but beautifully softened by the usually sad expression of her dark, earnest eyes. She may justly be considered a handsome woman, of noble mien and bearing, but by no means coming under the description of the feminine adjective 'pretty'." [Sallie A. Putnam] *Richmond during the War: Four Years of Personal Observation by a Richmond Lady* (New York: G. W. Carleton and Co., 1867), 38.

57. Van der Heuvel, *Crowns of Thorns and Glory*, 114; and C. Vann Woodward, ed., *Mary Chesnut's Civil War* (New Haven, CT: Yale University Press, 1981), 437 and 609. This famous work contains good detail on the Davises' relations with the Johnstons, on Varina's attitude toward Richmond society, and on Jefferson's health. Although aware of their faults, Chesnut liked and admired both Davises. See, for example, her comment on April 5, 1865: "At this late day and as things stand now, not for worlds would I fail in any outward show of my deep reverence and respect for the president and Mrs. Davis. In the days of their power they were so kind to me" (p. 779). Negative rumors about Varina, as well as about Jefferson, apparently circulated throughout the Confederacy. A North Carolina woman, for example, reported hearing that Varina was "a Philadelphia woman" who "is not worthy of her husband, for I learn that she is neither neat or Ladylike in her dress, travels in old finery with bare arms covered with bracelets." Beth G. Crabtree and James W. Patton, eds., *"Journal of a Secesh Lady": The Diary of Catherine Ann Devereux Edmonston, 1860–1866* (Raleigh, NC: Division of Archives and History, Dept. of Cultural Resources, 1979), 180. See also J. B. Jones, *A Rebel War Clerk's Diary at the Confederate States Capital*, 2 vols. (Philadelphia: Lippincott, 1866), I, 165–66, and II, 288, 357, 453; Harry Simonhoff, *Jewish Participants in the Civil War* (New York: Arco Publishing Co., 1963), 188; and William C. Davis, *Jefferson Davis*, 537–39.

58. Eli N. Evans, *Judah P. Benjamin*, 152–53.

59. Ibid., 215.

60. *Papers of Jefferson Davis*, IX, xli–xliii.

61. Eli N. Evans, *Judah P. Benjamin*, 228.

62. John W. Burgess, *Reminiscences of an American Scholar* (New York: Columbia University Press, 1934), 291–92.

63. V. Jefferson Davis to E. Leslie Williams, Esq., February 17, 1890, Jefferson Davis Papers (Manuscript Division, Library of Congress).

64. Dealer's Catalogue—*Collector*, #850, 1977, p. 18, Item K–142.

65. J. B. Jones, *A Rebel War Clerk's Diary at the Confederate States Capital*, II, 357.

66. Varina Davis, *Jefferson Davis*, II, 496–97.

67. Woodward, ed., *Mary Chesnut's Civil War*, 609.

68. Ross, *First Lady of the South*, 203.

69. Celeste Clay to her sisters, January 17, 1865, Clement Clay Letters, "Confederate Notables" File, Miscellaneous Records, War Department Collection of Confederate Records, Record Group 109 (National Archives, Washington, DC).

70. Jefferson Davis to Varina Davis, April 5, 6, 14, 22, 23, 1865, and Varina Davis to Jefferson Davis, April 7, 13, 19, 22, 28, May 3, 1865, all in Davis Papers (Museum of the Confederacy). For the Davises' escape from Richmond and capture by federal troops in May, see also Alfred J. Hanna, *Flight into Oblivion* (Richmond: Johnson Publishing Co., 1938), 3–101; and Burke Davis, *The Long Surrender* (New York: Random House, 1985), 5–148.

71. Varina Davis to Jefferson Davis, November 13, 1865, Davis Papers (University of Alabama). See also Varina Davis to Joseph Davis, September 5, 1865, Mary Stamps Papers (Southern Historical Collection, Wilson Library, University of North Carolina, Chapel Hill).

72. Jefferson Davis to Varina Davis, September 26, 1865, Davis Papers (Transylvania University, Lexington, Kentucky). See also other letters to Varina from Jefferson in prison in the Davis Papers at Transylvania and in Strode, ed., *Private Letters*, 165–275.

73. Paul H. Bergeron, ed., *The Papers of Andrew Johnson* (Knoxville: University of Tennessee Press, 1989), VIII, 672.

74. Jonathan Truman Dorris, *Pardon and Amnesty under Lincoln and Johnson: The Restoration of the Confederates to Their Rights and Privileges, 1861–1898* (Chapel Hill: University of North Carolina Press, 1953), 278–312. A printed copy of his bail bond, May 13, 1867, is in the Davis Papers (Manuscript Division, Library of Congress).

75. Francis Fessenden, *Life and Public Services of William Pitt Fessenden*, 2 vols. (Boston, 1907), II, 57. See also Varina Davis to Horace Greeley, June 22, 1865, Davis Papers (Museum of the Confederacy); Varina Davis to William Henry Seward, July 10, 1865, Blair-Lee Papers (Princeton University); Varina Davis to U. S. Grant, December 18, 1865, Frederick M. Dearborn Collection (Houghton Library, Harvard University); and Varina Davis, *Jefferson Davis*, II, 775–82.

76. Jefferson Davis to Burton Harrison, July 7, 1867, Harrison Family Papers (Manuscript Division, Library of Congress); Varina Davis to Lise Mitchell, April 20, 1869, Lise Mitchell Papers (Tulane University, New Orleans); Jefferson Davis to Maggie Davis, May 10, 1869, Jefferson Davis to Varina Davis, September 25, 1869, Davis Papers (University of Alabama); Varina Davis, *Jefferson Davis*, II, 797–811; and Strode, *Jefferson Davis, Tragic Hero*, 326–54.

77. Surviving evidence provides only an incomplete view of the sources and amounts of the Davises' income after the war. Former Confederate cabinet officer Judah P. Benjamin wrote Varina from Europe that at least $12,500 was available for their use from Confederate funds in England. Benjamin soon invested some of this money for her in English government securities. Judah Benjamin to Varina Davis, September 1, November 16, December 6, 1865, and January 25, 1866, all in Davis Papers (Transylvania University). See also Varina Davis to William Preston Johnston, August 29, 1866, Johnston Papers (Tulane University); and Varina Davis, *Jefferson Davis*, II, 796.

78. For a study of the Davis Bend experiment, see Janet Sharp Hermann, *The Pursuit of a Dream.*

79. Jefferson Davis to Varina Davis, November 23, 1869, Davis Papers (University of Alabama). See also Jefferson Davis to Varina Davis, November 9 and December 4, 1869, ibid.; Jefferson Davis to Lise Mitchell, November 30, 1869, Mitchell Papers; and Varina Davis, *Jefferson Davis*, II, 811–12.

80. Varina Davis to Jefferson Davis, undated [January 22, 1870], fragment, Davis Papers (University of Alabama).

81. Jefferson to J. Addison Hayes, October 18, 1878, Davis Papers (University of Alabama). See also Varina Davis to Jefferson Davis, undated [January 22, 1870], Mary Custis Lee to Varina Davis, November 18, 1872, Jefferson Davis to Varina Davis, November 6, 1873,

and February 26, 1877, J. Addison Hayes to Jefferson Davis, January 5, 1877, all in Davis Papers (University of Alabama); Jefferson Davis to Jefferson Davis, Jr., July 21, 1874, and Jefferson Davis to William Preston Johnston, August 22, 1874, Johnston Papers; Francis H. Smith to Jefferson Davis, August 26, 1874, in Rowland, ed., *Jefferson Davis Constitutionalist*, VII, 397–98.

82. The Hayes children were Jefferson Davis, who died soon after his birth in 1877; Varina Howell Davis, born 1878; Lucy White, born 1882; Jefferson Addison, born 1884; and William Davis, born 1889. Monroe et al., eds., *Papers of Jefferson Davis*, IV, 415–16. See also Strode, *Jefferson Davis: Tragic Hero*, 410, 417, 449–50.

83. Jefferson Davis to Mary Stamps, October 16, 1873, Mary Stamps Papers. See also Jefferson Davis to Mary Stamps, September 20 and November 23, 1873, ibid.; Jefferson Davis to Varina Davis, August 26, 28, and September 7, 10, 1873, Davis Papers (University of Alabama); and Morton Keller, *The Life Insurance Enterprise, 1855–1910: A Study in the Limits of Corporate Power* (Cambridge, MA: Belknap Press of Harvard University Press, 1963), 8.

84. Jefferson Davis to Varina Davis, January 5, 1874, Davis Papers (University of Alabama). See also Varina Davis to Jefferson Davis, January 1, 1874, and Jefferson Davis to Varina Davis, December 29, 31, 1873, and January 8, 16, 18, 21, 26, 1874, ibid.

85. See especially Davis Papers, 1874 to 1888, ibid.

86. Jefferson to Virginia Clay, May 18, 1870, Clay Papers; an abundance of letters from Jefferson to Virginia are in this collection. See also Carol Bleser and Frederick M. Heath, "The Clays of Alabama: The Impact of the Civil War on a Southern Marriage," in *In Joy and in Sorrow: Women, Family, and Marriage in the Victorian South, 1830–1900*, ed. Carol Bleser (New York: Oxford University Press, 1991), 135–53.

87. Jefferson to Mary Stamps, April 16, 1875, and October 11, 1881, Mary Stamps Papers. See also other letters from Jefferson to Mary in this collection.

88. Varina Davis, *Jefferson Davis*, I, 1.

89. J. B. Smallwood, "Sarah Anne Ellis Dorsey," in *Lives of Mississippi Authors, 1817–1967*, ed. James B. Lloyd (Jackson: University Press of Mississippi, 1981), 137–40; W. A. Evans, "Sarah Ann Ellis Dorsey, Donor of Beauvoir," *Journal of Mississippi History*, 6 (April 1944): 89–102; Varina Davis, *Jefferson Davis*, II, 825–26; and Bertram Wyatt-Brown, "A Family Tradition of Letters: The Female Percys and the Brontëan Mode," in *In Joy and in Sorrow*, ed. Bleser, 192–95. For fuller documentation on Sarah Dorsey's life and work see Bertram Wyatt-Brown, *The House of Percy: Honor, Melancholy, and Imagination in a Southern Family* (New York: Oxford University Press, 1994), 116–69.

90. Jefferson Davis to Varina Davis, May 1, 1877, undated fragment [June 11, 1877], July 15, 1877, Davis Papers (University of Alabama); Jefferson to J. Addison Hayes, June 29, 1877, Davis Papers (Mississippi Department of Archives and History); Varina Davis to Jefferson Davis, September 9, 1877, Davis Papers (University of Alabama).

91. Varina to Jefferson, April 18, 1878, Davis Papers (Tulane University). See also Jefferson to A. D. Mann, January 1, 1878, Jefferson Davis Shrine (Beauvoir, Mississippi). Although Varina stayed in Memphis to avoid Mrs. Dorsey, she also remained there to care for Maggie, who gave birth to a child in March. See Varina to Jefferson, March 3, April 7, 1878, and Jefferson to Varina, February 16, April 10, 1878, Davis Papers (University of Alabama); and Jefferson to Varina, March 15, 187[8], Davis Papers (Mississippi Department of Archives and History).

92. Wiley, *Confederate Women*, 131.

93. Strode, *Jefferson Davis, Tragic Hero*, 430.

94. William C. Davis, *Jefferson Davis*, 672. Since this book went to press, William J. Cooper, Jr., has published his magisterial biography of Jefferson Davis, *Jefferson Davis, American* (New York: Alfred A. Knopf, 2000). However, Cooper does not present evidence that shows how much Davis hurt Varina and how culpable he was in manipulating both his wife and Sarah Dorsey.

95. Varina to Jefferson, April 18, 1878, Davis Papers (Tulane University); and Jefferson to Pollie, November 8, 1878, Davis Papers (University of Alabama).

96. Sarah Dorsey to Jefferson Davis, March 28, 1879, Davis Papers (University of Alabama);

Jefferson to Varina, July 2, 4 (second quotation), 1879, Davis Papers (Transylvania University); and Varina to the Reverend J. Owen Dorsey, October 14, 1894, Davis Papers (Mississippi Department of Archives and History).

97. Promissory Note, Jefferson Davis to Sarah Dorsey, February 20, 1879, Gilder-Lehrman Collection (Pierpont Morgan Library, New York). Also, Sarah Dorsey to Jefferson, March 28, 1879, Davis Papers (University of Alabama).

98. "Will of Mrs. Sarah A. Dorsey," January 4, 1878, typescript copy (Southern Historical Collection); and Varina Davis, *Jefferson Davis*, II, 828–29.

99. Jefferson Davis to J. D. S. Newell, January 11, 29, February 21, 1883, January 5, September 21, December 25, 1884, and May 5, 1885, Newell Papers (Tennessee State Library and Archives); Jefferson Davis to J. Addison Hayes, June 4, 1877, Davis Papers (Transylvania University); Hermann, *Pursuit of a Dream*, 201–4, 206–7, 211; and Everett, *Brierfield*, 96–111.

100. Varina to "My Precious Baby" (Varina Anne Davis), January 28, 1886, Davis Papers (University of Alabama).

101. Jefferson to Margaret Hayes, August 7, 1882, Davis Papers (University of Alabama); Varina to Constance Cary Harrison, December 20, 1886, Harrison Family Papers (University of Virginia). See also Varina to Gaston Robbins, July 15, 1886, William McKendree Robbins Papers (Southern Historical Collection). On raising flowers and foods, see Varina to Winnie, February 16, 1880, and Varina to Margaret Hayes, April 11, 1884, Davis Papers (University of Alabama).

102. Varina to Constance Cary Harrison, December 20, 1886, Harrison Family Papers (University of Virginia).

103. Varina to Jubal A. Early, May 7, 1888, Jubal A. Early Papers (Manuscript Division, Library of Congress).

104. Varina to Constance Cary Harrison, April 5, 1880, Harrison Family Papers (University of Virginia).

105. Davis's two-volume *Rise and Fall of the Confederate Government* was published in 1881 in New York by D. Appleton and Company.

106. William C. Davis, *Jefferson Davis*, 676. This view is similar to the one expressed by the seventeen-year-old Varina when she first met Jefferson, as quoted above in the material cited in foonote 5.

107. Not all Southerners approved of Davis's public appearances in the mid-1880s. Some considered him a troublesome symbol who spoke rashly and revived sectional animosities. For instance, the Pinckneys of Charleston did "not approve of President Davis coming out and making speeches." They preferred "for Davis to remain in seclusion." Mrs. Poppenheim to Mary and Louisa Poppenheim, May 4, 1886, Louisa Boatwright and Mary Barnett Poppenheim Papers (Perkins Library, Duke University).

108. Varina to Jefferson, June 3, 1875, Davis Papers (University of Alabama).

109. Varina to Miss Hartley Graham, Jan. 22, 1887, ibid.

110. Strode, *Jefferson Davis, Tragic Hero*, 512.

111. William C. Davis, *Jefferson Davis*, 705.

112. Varina to Mrs. Merrick, [February 26, 1890], Davis Papers (Mississippi Department of Archives and History).

113. On Varina's widowhood, see Suzanne T. Dolensky, "Varina Howell Davis, 1889 to 1906: The Years Alone," *Journal of Mississippi History*, 47 (May 1985): 90–109.

114. Ibid.; and Varina Davis, *Jefferson Davis*. See also Varina to "My Dear Friend," February 19, 1880, Davis Papers (University of Alabama); and Varina to Constance Cary Harrison, October 19, 1890, Harrison Family Papers (University of Virginia).

115. Varina to William Preston Johnston, June 21, 1891, Johnston Papers; Varina to Mary Hunter Kimbrough, typescripts, October 16, November 12, 1894, Davis Papers (Manuscript Division, Library of Congress); Varina to Margaret Sprague, March 25, 1895, Davis Papers (Mississippi Department of Archives and History). Suzanne Dolensky stresses the independence demonstrated by Varina's living in the North, becoming a professional writer, and making such controversial decisions as deciding that Jefferson's remains would be buried in Virginia rather than in competing southern states.

116. Varina to Major W. H. Morgan, n. d. [1889], Davis Papers (Manuscript Division, Library of Congress).

117. Mrs. Jefferson Davis, *The Grasshopper War* (Buffalo, NY, 1903); and Dolensky, "Varina Howell Davis," 95–96.

118. Varina Davis, *Jefferson Davis*, I: 1.

119. Varina to Mary Hunter and Judge Kimbrough, July 8, 1902, Kimbrough Collection (Mississippi Department of Archives and History). See also Varina to Margaret Hayes, June 21, 1899, Davis Papers (University of Alabama); Varina to Burton Harrison, February 19, 1904, Harrison Family Papers (University of Virginia); and Varina to "Dear Sir," n. d., Davis Papers (Emory University).

120. Varina to Mary Craig Kimbrough, n. d. [June, 1903], Mrs. M. C. K. Sinclair Collection (Indiana University, Bloomington).

121. Varina to W. B. Smith, March 15, 1901, Joseph Davis Smith Papers (Louisiana State University); Varina to Judge and Mary Hunter Kimbrough, April 23, 1902, and Varina to Judge Kimbrough, November 6, 1902, August 18, 1906, Davis Papers (Manuscript Division, Library of Congress) (transcripts). See also Dolensky, "Varina Howell Davis," 97–101.

122. Ima Hogg to Ernesto Caldeira, June 13, 1973 (Jefferson Davis Association, Rice University).

123. Varina to Mrs. W. J. Charleton, May 1905, Davis Papers (Emory University).

124. Ross, *First Lady of the South*, 417.

125. Varina to Margaret Davis, February 25, 1872, Davis Papers (Mississippi Department of Archives and History).

126. Varina to James Redpath, October 1, 1888, Davis Papers (Mississippi Department of Archives and History).

127. John J. Craven, *Prison Life of Jefferson Davis* (New York: Carleton, 1866), 271. These were almost certainly not Davis's exact words. Craven's book was actually composed by a ghostwriter, Charles G. Walpine. The account was, however, based on Craven's notes and diaries. See Chester D. Bradley, "Dr. Craven and the Prison Life of Jefferson Davis," *Virginia Magazine of History and Biography*, 62 (January 1954): 50–94.

CHAPTER TWO

1. This account of the Lees' wedding depends upon Emory M. Thomas, *Robert E. Lee: A Biography* (New York: W. W. Norton, 1995), 63–66. Indeed, this entire essay is an outgrowth of the biography. This interpretation of the Lees' marriage differs somewhat from that in the biography, thanks in part to the critiques of Mary P. Coulling and Frances Taliaferro Thomas. Also important to the topic is Douglas S. Freeman, *R. E. Lee: A Biography*, 4 vols. (New York: Charles Scribner's Sons, 1934–35).

2. Thomas, *Lee*, 23–46; and Paul C. Nagel, *The Lees of Virginia: Seven Generations of an American Family* (New York: Oxford University Press, 1990), 161–85.

3. Thomas, *Lee*, 34–37, 61–64.

4. Ibid., 64–65; Lee to Andrew Talcott, Ravensworth, July 13, 1831, Robert Edward Lee Papers (Virginia Historical Society); Lee to Carter Lee, June 15, 1831, Robert E. Lee Papers (University of Virginia); Freeman, *Lee*, I, 105–110; Rose Mortimer Ellzey MacDonald, *Mrs. Robert E. Lee* (Boston, Ginn and Company, 1939), 31–35.

5. George Washington Custis (Boo): 1832–1913; Mary Custis (daughter): 1835–1918; William Henry Fitzhugh (Rooney): 1837–1891; Anne Carter (Annie): 1839–1862; Eleanor Agnes (Wigs): 1841–1873; Robert Edward, Jr. (Rob): 1843–1914; Mildred Childe (Precious Life): 1846–1904. This information is in Thomas, *Lee*; a good genealogical chart is on the end papers of Nagel, *Lees*.

6. Thomas, *Lee*, 81–82.

7. Ibid., 82–83; Lee to Mary Lee, Detroit, August 21, 1835, in Norma B. Cuthbert, "To Molly: Five Early Letters from Robert E. Lee to His Wife," *Huntington Library Quarterly*, (May, 1952): 271.

8. Lee to Andrew Talcott, Washington, October 12, 1835, Talcott Papers (Virginia

Historical Society); Lee to Andrew Talcott, Washington, October 21, 1835, Talcott Papers (Virginia Historical Society); Lee to Andrew Talcott, Washington, November 9, 1835, in George Green Shackelford, ed., "From the Society's Collections: Lieutenant Lee Reports to Captain Talcott on Fort Calhoun's Construction on Rip Raps," *Virginia Magazine of History and Biography*, 60 (July, 1952): 472; Lee to Andrew Talcott, Washington, November 18, 1835, Talcott Papers (Virginia Historical Society); Lee to Andrew Talcott, Washington, November 25, 1835, Talcott Papers (Virginia Historical Society); Lee to Andrew Talcott, February, 1836, Talcott Papers (Virginia Historical Society); and Lee to Andrew Talcott, June 22, 1836, in Shackelford, "Lee Reports to Captain Talcott," 483.

9. Thomas, *Lee*, 84–85.
10. MacDonald, *Mrs. Lee*, 125–26; Thomas, *Lee*, 313.
11. Thomas, *Lee*, 277–79.
12. Ibid., 175–83; the quotation is from Lee to Albert Sidney Johnston, San Antonio, October 25, 1857, Mrs. Mason Barret Collection (Howard-Tilton Library, Tulane University).
13. Thomas, *Lee*, 66.
14. Lee to Mary Lee, Richmond, June 10, 1862, Clifford Dowdey and Louis H. Manarin, eds., *The Wartime Papers of R. E. Lee* (New York: Bramhall House, 1961), 189; and Lee to Chass, Dabb's Farm, June 22, 1862, ibid., 197.
15. Thomas, *Lee*, 318; Dowdey and Manarin, eds., *Wartime Papers*, 649–717; Lee to Mary Lee, Camp, April 21, 1864, Lee Family Papers (Virginia Historical Society); and Lee to Mary Lee, Camp, April 22, 1864, Lee Family Papers (Virginia Historical Society).
16. Robert and Mary Lee to Mrs. M. F. Custis, [August 28–31, 1831], Lee Family Papers (Virginia Historical Society).
17. Lee to Mary Lee, St. Louis, August 5, 1837, Lee Family Papers (Virginia Historical Society); Lee to Andrew Talcott, Fort Monroe, April 10, 1834, Lee Family Papers (Virginia Historical Society).
18. The quotation is from Robert and Mary Lee to Mrs. M. F. Custis, [August 28–31, 1831], Lee Family Papers (Virginia Historical Society); Thomas, *Lee*, 71; Nagel, *Lees*, 239–40.
19. Lee to Andrew Talcott, Fort Monroe, July 3, 1833, in Shackelford, "Lee Reports to Captain Talcott," 469.
20. Sara B. Bearss, "The Farmer of Arlington: George W. P. Custis and the Arlington Sheep Shearings," *Virginia Cavalcade*, 38 (Winter, 1989): 124–33; Freeman, *Lee*, I, 129–31; Nagel, *Lees*, 234–35; Thomas, *Lee*, 60–62.
21. Lee to Carter Lee, Washington, May 2, 1836, Robert E. Lee Papers (University of Virginia).
22. Mary Custis to Mary Lee, Arlington, October 6, 1831, Custis Family Papers (Virginia Historical Society); Thomas, *Lee*, 76–77, 164–65.
23. Lee's letter to his mother-in-law is quoted in Nagel, *Lees*, 242; Lee to Mary Lee, Fort Hamilton, May 19, 1846, Lee Family Papers (Virginia Historical Society).
24. Robert E. Lee, Jr., *Recollections and Letters of General Robert E. Lee* (New York: Doubleday, Page & Co., 1904), 3–4.
25. Lee to Anne Lee, San Antonio, August 27, 1860, Lee Family Papers (Virginia Historical Society).
26. Thomas L. Connelly, *The Marble Man: Robert E. Lee and His Image in American Society* (New York: Knopf, 1977), xiv, 172, 180.
27. See Thomas, *Lee*, 84–85, 120, 316.
28. See Douglas Freeman, "Lee & the Ladies: Unpublished Letters of Robert E. Lee," *Scribner's Magazine*, 78 (October, 1952).
29. This letter is quoted in Freeman, *Lee*, I, 113–14.
30. Lee to Tasy Beaumont, Arlington, January 21, 1840, Robert Edward Lee Papers (Virginia Historical Society); and Lee to Tasy Beaumont, Fort Hamilton, March 11, 1843, Robert Edward Lee Papers (Virginia Historical Society).
31. Lee to Andrew Talcott, Washington, February 21, 1833, Lee Family Papers (Virginia Historical Society).
32. Lee to Markie (Martha Custis Williams), Baltimore, May 10, 1851, in *"To Markie":*

The Letters of Robert E. Lee to Martha Custis Williams, ed. Avery Craven (Cambridge, MA: Harvard University Press, 1933), 24–27, 81.

33. Thomas, *Lee*, 106–107.
34. MacDonald, *Mrs. Lee*, 75–76; Thomas, *Lee*, 65–66.
35. Robert E. Lee, Diary (Virginia Historical Society).
36. Lee to G. W. Custis Lee, Fort Hamilton, November 30, 1845, Lee Family Papers (Virginia Historical Society).
37. See Thomas, *Lee*, 170 and n 17.
38. Lee to Custis Lee, Baltimore, March 28, 1852, Robert Edward Lee Papers (Virginia Historical Society).
39. Lee, Jr., *Recollections*, 9.
40. Lee to Mildred Lee, Lexington, January 8, 1870, in ibid., 380–81.
41. MacDonald, *Mrs. Lee*, 45 (letter quoted on p. 50).
42. See Thomas, *Lee*, 230–31, 313, 317.
43. See Dowdey and Manarin, eds., *Wartime Papers*, for samples.
44. Letters quoted in MacDonald, *Mrs. Lee*, 141, 194, and 231.
45. Thomas, *Lee*, 402, 411–15.
46. Letter quoted in MacDonald, *Mrs. Lee*, 230.
47. Marvin Rozear et al., "R. E. Lee's Stroke," *Virginia Magazine of History and Biography*, 98 (April, 1990): 291–308.
48. Quoted in MacDonald, *Mrs. Lee*, 295.

CHAPTER THREE

1. For the historiography of the lemon-sucking myth, see James I. Robertson, Jr., *Stonewall Jackson: The Man, the Soldier, the Legend* (New York: Macmillan, 1997), x–xi. Popular Civil War historian Robertson's recent biography is an exhaustive, largely descriptive chronicle of Jackson's life and military exploits. For Mary Anna Jackson's denunciation of unfavorable characterizations of her husband, see, for example, M[ary] A[nna] Jackson to Mrs. Thomas Baxter Gresham, Charlotte, North Carolina, October 17, 1911, in the Mary Anna Jackson Papers (Virginia Military Institute, Lexington, Virginia); Mary Anna Jackson, "Mrs. 'Stonewall' Jackson Denounces 'The Long Roll,' " *New York Times*, Sunday Magazine, October 29, 1911, 6–7; "Mrs. Jackson Writes of the 'Long Roll,' " *Confederate Veteran*, 19, no. 12 (December 1911): 591.
2. ["Stonewall" to Mary Anna Jackson], April 18, 1863; ["Stonewall" Jackson to Mary Anna Jackson], October 20, 1862, letters reprinted in Mary Anna Jackson, *Life and Letters of General Thomas J. Jackson* (with an introduction by Henry M. Field) (New York: Harper and Brothers, 1892), 412–22, 363–65.
3. For biographical information on Mary Anna Morrison Jackson, see Jackson, *Life and Letters of General Jackson*, especially 89–95 (quotation appears on p. 91), and Robertson, *Stonewall Jackson*, chapter 7, especially 175.
4. Thomas Jonathan Jackson does not lack biographers. The following list should by no means be considered exhaustive: Thomas Jackson Arnold, *Early Life and Letters of General Thomas J. Jackson* (New York: Fleming H. Revell, 1916); William C. Chase, *Story of Stonewall Jackson* (Atlanta: D. E. Luther, 1901); John Esten Cooke, *The Life of Stonewall Jackson* (New York: C. B. Richardson, 1863); Robert Lewis Dabney, *Life and Campaigns of the Lieut.-Gen. Thomas H. Jackson (Stonewall Jackson)* (Richmond, VA: Blelock, 1866); Daniel John Warwick, *The Life of Stonewall Jackson, from Official Papers, Contemporary Narratives, and Personal Acquaintance, by a Virginian* (New York: Charles B. Richardson, 1863); Bryon Farwell, *Stonewall, a Biography of General Thomas J. Jackson* (New York: W. W. Norton, 1992); George Francis Robert Henderson, *Stonewall Jackson and the American Civil War*, 2 vols. (London: Longman, Green, 1898); Mary Anna Jackson, *Life and Letters*; Robertson, *Stonewall Jackson*; Allen Tate, *Stonewall Jackson, the Good Soldier: A Narrative* (New York: Minton, Balch & Company, 1928); Frank Everson Vandiver, *Mighty Stonewall* (New York: McGraw Hill, 1957). Quotation from Henderson, I: 19.
5. Henderson, *Stonewall Jackson and the American Civil War*, I, 35.
6. Robertson, *Stonewall Jackson*, 78.

7. Mary Anna Jackson, *Life and Letters*, 96–97.

8. For a brief account of the Jackson-Junkin courtship, clandestine engagement, and secret marriage, see Robertson, *Stonewall Jackson*, 144–47. Mary Anna Jackson remarked in her 1892 biography of her late husband that Jackson and Junkin "had both kept their secret so well guarded that, when their marriage was announced, it took the town by surprise." Mary Anna Jackson, *Life and Letters*, 97–98.

9. Robertson, *Stonewall Jackson*, 149. Certainly Jackson was not alone in his desire for a "family atmosphere." In a study of courtship in America, Ellen Rothman notes that "the most sought-after circle of middle class life" during the antebellum era was the home. Although Rothman focused her study on antebellum Northerners, her pronouncements on this score seem applicable to Jackson. See Ellen Rothman, *Hands and Hearts: A History of Courtship in America* (Cambridge: Harvard University Press, 1984), 107, and chapter 5, passim.

10. Thomas Jackson Arnold, *Early Life*, 218.

11. Ibid., 219–20; quoted in Robertson, *Stonewall Jackson*, 160. Historian Anne C. Rose has observed that "Victorian" men, "whose attitudes were less divided than women's," seemed especially susceptible to anguish over the loss of a spouse and expressed their sense of bereavement openly. See Anne C. Rose, *Victorian America and the Civil War* (Cambridge: Cambridge University Press, 1992), 152.

12. Elizabeth Preston Allen, *The Life and Letters of Margaret Junkin Preston* (Boston: Houghton, Mifflin, 1903), 71–72.

13. Ibid., 72–73.

14. Thomas [J. Jackson] to "My Dear Sister" [Margaret Junkin], Lexington, Virginia, February 14, 1855, in the Margaret Junkin Preston Papers (Manuscript Collection #1543, Southern Historical Collection, University of North Carolina, Chapel Hill).

15. Thomas [J. Jackson] to "My Dear Sister Maggie" [Junkin]. Neale's Island, Wood County, Virginia, August 16, 1855, Preston Papers (Southern Historical Collection). Historian Karen Lystra has observed that nineteenth-century "lovers constantly urged each other to 'write freely.' Love was often seen as both the cause and the effect of unfettered communication." See Lystra, *Searching the Heart: Women, Men, and Romantic Love in Nineteenth-Century America* (New York: Oxford University Press, 1989), 21.

16. Robertson, *Stonewall Jackson*, 175. Rose notes that "Victorian" men remarried with a sense of great urgency. "Second marriages for men with young children were in part a necessity," she writes, "yet most formed new families with an enthusiasm generated by mating's appeal." Genuine feelings of grief and loss notwithstanding, the prospects of a new marriage seemed for many overwhelming. See Rose, *Victorian America*, 153.

17. Mary Anna Jackson, *Life and Letters*, 100. It is important to note here that Mary Anna Jackson was referring not to Major Jackson's inability to marry Maggie Preston but to his overwhelming grief over the loss of his wife. Mary Anna Jackson consistently avoided any mention of her husband's emotionally intimate relationship with his sister-in-law.

18. Letter dated April 25, 1857 reprinted in ibid., 101–2.

19. Thomas J. Jackson to Margaret Junkin, Lexington, Virginia, May 25, 1857, in the Preston Papers, (Southern Historical Collection). For the growing importance of engagement rings to the betrothal ritual, see Rothman, *Hands and Hearts*, 161–62.

20. Lexington [Virginia] *Gazette*, August 6, 1857, 2.

21. Mary Anna Jackson, *Life and Letters*, 108. Rothman notes that, by mid-century, women could assume that "the men they loved could deviate from prescribed sex roles. . . . The more intimate the relationship, the more a person tended to see his or her mate as an exception to the negative and an embodiment of the positive aspects of the sexual stereotypes." Surely Mary Anna Jackson did not consider her husband's military image a "negative" embodiment of the sexual stereotype. She nevertheless sought to supplement that image with a "softer," seemingly contradictory, or at the very least unexpected, image of the general. Rothman, *Hands and Hearts*, 98. Robert Lewis Dabney echoed Anna Jackson's sentiments in his "authorized" biography of the general. "In no man was the domestic affections ever more tender and noble," he wrote in 1866. "He who only saw the stern self-denying soldier in his quarters, amidst the details of the commander's duties, or on the field of battle, could scarcely comprehend the gently sweetness of his home life. . . . He was intensely fond of his home, where all his happiness

and every recreation centered. As his foot crossed its threshold, care lifted itself from his brow, his presence brought cheerfulness, and by his example of childlike gaiety he allured its inmates to every innocent enjoyment. . . . In his household, the law of love reigned." See *Dabney, Life and Campaigns,* p. 117.

22. Anna Jackson, *Life and Letters,* 145–46. See also Robertson, *Stonewall Jackson,* 189–216.

23. Anna Jackson, *Life and Letters,* 146–47. Drew Faust has pointed out that most Confederate women had to adjust to reconfigured households, noting that this process was difficult indeed. For the anxiety Confederate women experienced when their menfolk left for the war, see Drew Faust, *Mothers of Invention: Women of the Slaveholding South in the American Civil War* (Chapel Hill: University of North Carolina Press, 1996), chapter 2.

24. Anna Jackson, *Life and Letters,* 152–53. For a discussion of antebellum southern households, see Elizabeth Fox-Genovese, *Within the Plantation Household: Black and White Women of the Old South* (Chapel Hill: University of North Carolina Press, 1988), chapter 1. For the disruption of those households during the Civil War, see Faust, *Mothers of Invention,* chapter 2, passim, especially 331–32.

25. Ellen Rothman has observed in her study of courtship in America that correspondence represented "more than the artifacts of a relationship; in many cases they were, for a time, the relationship itself." This observation seems especially valid in cases of physical separation. Rothman, *Hands and Hearts,* 9. Karen Lystra reached a similar conclusion in her study of romantic love in the nineteenth century. "With almost no other means of voicing themselves across even the smallest distance," she observed, "nineteenth-century lovers bridged the silence with ink and pencil." See Lystra, *Searching the Heart,* 12. Drew Faust offered a different reading, suggesting that correspondence of separated husbands and wives served only as the detritus of a sundered relationship. "Women of the Confederate South confronted a changed emotional landscape in which the most fundamental personal attachments became as elusive as dreams," Faust wrote, "only as tangible as the letters that served as the residual substance of these ruptured ties." See Faust, *Mothers of Invention,* 115.

26. Letter dated June 4, 1861, reprinted in Mary Anna Jackson, *Life and Letters,* 159.

27. Ibid., 205–6.

28. See Robertson, *Stonewall Jackson,* 264. For a fuller account of Jackson's nickname, see, for example, James M. McPherson, *Battle Cry of Freedom: The Civil War Era* (New York: Oxford University Press, 1988), 342.

29. Letters dated July 22 and 29, 1861, reprinted in Dabney, *Life and Campaigns,* 229. Anna Jackson, of course, did her part to ensure that "truth" would prevail. Her biography of her late husband serves not only as a paean to the general but also as a vehicle to remake her own image as the general's wife. Writing more than thirty years after the battle of Manassas, she seemingly accepted both the general's reluctance to boast of his achievements and the praise he received. "Though he was so reticent of his own part in the battle," she wrote, "it was well known that his brigade saved the day, the credit of which was justly given to its commander." See Anna Jackson, *Life and Letters,* 178–79.

30. Lexington [Virginia] *Gazette,* August 1, 1861. Later editions hardly offered more thorough commentary on Jackson. See, for example, reports printed August 8 and August 15, 1861.

31. Letter dated August 5, 1861, reprinted in Anna Jackson, *Life and Letters,* 179–80. A member of the Stonewall Brigade recalled: "There was not a newspaper reporter, 'war-correspondent,' in our army . . . certainly none in Jackson's brigade. . . . I never saw but one reporter in Jackson's army and he lasted about twenty-four hours. In this may be found the secret of his secrecy and the thunderbolt swiftness of his surprises." Douglas later noted that there was "little intimacy between the General and the press." See Henry Kyd Douglas, *I Rode with Stonewall: Being Chiefly the War Experiences of the Youngest Member of Jackson's Staff from the John Brown Raid to the Hanging of Mrs. Surratt* (Chapel Hill: University of North Carolina Press, 1940), 17, 35. Karen Lystra has observed that in mid-nineteenth-century American culture, romantic love "contributed to the displacement of God by the lover as the central symbol of ultimate significance." Although Anna Jackson may not have abandoned her faith in a Christian God, her husband's warnings that she refrain from engaging in near idol-worship suggest that he considered her efforts to magnify his image dangerous indeed.

32. Anna Jackson, *Life and Letters*, xv.
33. Anna Jackson, *Life and Letters*, 209–10; Rose, *Victorian America*, 184.
34. Anna Jackson, *Life and Letters*, 149, 158.
35. Rose, *Victorian America*, 185. For antebellum southern gender conventions, see Elizabeth Fox-Genovese, *Within the Plantation Household: Black and White Women of the Old South* (Chapel Hill: University of North Carolina Press, 1988), chapter 4.
36. General Jackson also noted that his wife should make the trip only if a proper escort were available. Moreover, she was to spare no expense "in making your trip comfortable." Anna Jackson, *Life and Letters*, 186–187. Drew Faust has pointed out that the "safety and purity of young white girls was a particular concern in the wartime South, for they were seen as especially vulnerable in case of enemy invasion or slave uprising." See Faust, *Mothers of Invention*, 39. General Jackson seemed concerned for his wife's safety and comfort in the presence of Confederate soldiers. His anxiety over his wife's traveling unescorted to meet him suggests the unease he, and doubtless many other Confederate men, felt about the war's disruption of antebellum southern gender conventions.
37. Anna Jackson, *Life and Letters*, 187–89.
38. Anne C. Rose has noted that although a modern transportation system made it possible for families to visit husbands and fathers away at war, they did not have to do so, suggesting to her that their decision to "take advantage of possible mobility must have been rooted in their cultural attitudes." See Rose, *Victorian America*, 185.
39. Anna Jackson, *Life and Letters*, 190–91.
40. Ibid., 199–200, 205, 210, 212–13. Cornelia McDonald, who lived in the Shenandoah Valley during the war, supported Anna Jackson's account. According to McDonald, the town of Winchester warmly embraced Jackson during his stay there. See Cornelia McDonald, *A Diary with Reminiscences of the War and Refugee Life in the Shenandoah Valley, 1860–1865*, annotated and supplemented by Hunter McDonald (Nashville: Cullon and Ghertner, 1934), passim, especially 37, 161–62.
41. The Reverend James R. Graham, "Reminiscences of Gen. T. J. ("Stonewall") Jackson," reprinted in Anna Jackson, *Life and Letters*, 485–507 (quotation from 488). Quotation from Anna Jackson from *Life and Letters*, 237.
42. See James I. Robertson, *The Stonewall Brigade* (Baton Rouge: Louisiana State University Press, 1991), 57–67.
43. For an account of the Bath-Romney campaign suggesting that Jackson's men questioned their leader, see John B. Imboden, "Stonewall Jackson in the Shenandoah," *Battles and Leaders of the Civil War. Being for the Most Part Contributions by Union and Confederate Officers. Based upon "The Century War Series,"* ed. Robert Underwood Johnson and Clarence Clough Buel of the editorial staff of "the Century Magazine," new introduction by Roy F. Nichols (New York: Thomas Yoseloff, 1956), II, 282–98. Anna Jackson, *Life and Letters*, 240, 223–24. (The reminiscences are reprinted on 466–647.)
44. Dabney, *Life and Campaigns*, 635. Dabney also noted that so concerned was Jackson over the absenteeism that he proposed a plan by which a monetary reward would be paid by the delinquent soldier to the person who apprehended and delivered the absentee soldier (see 633–34).
45. Douglas, *I Rode with Stonewall*, 13. Robertson reminds his readers to read Douglas critically, for his account is far from flawless.
46. Faust, *Mothers of Invention*, 126. Anna Jackson, *Life and Letters*, 373–74, 375–76. For Victorians' attitudes toward children see Anne C. Rose, *Victorian Americans and the Civil War*, chapter 4, passim, especially 162–77.
47. Anna Jackson, *Life and Letters*, 411–12, 426–27.
48. Robertson, *Stonewall Jackson*, 754.
49. Daniel W. Stowell, "Stonewall Jackson and the Providence of God," in *Religion and the American Civil War*, ed. Randall M. Miller, Harry S. Stout, and Charles Reagan Wilson (New York: Oxford University Press, 1998), 187–207.
50. Ibid., 450–51.
51. Ibid., 465.
52. See Robertson, *Stonewall Jackson*, 759, 923, n. 28. For more on Julia Jackson, see Robin Veder, "'Julia, Daughter of Stonewall': Julia Thomas Jackson," *Virginia Cavalcade*, 46 (Summer 1996): 4–19.

53. Mary Anna Jackson to Margaret Junkin Preston, Cottage Home, North Carolina, June 16, 1866, in the Preston Papers (Southern Historical Collection).

54. Gaines M. Foster, *Ghosts of the Confederacy: Defeat, the Lost Cause, and the Emergence of the New South, 1865–1913* (New York: Oxford University Press, 1987), 42.

55. Mary Anna Jackson to Mrs. Tegmeyer, Charlotte, North Carolina, March 31, 1898; Mary Anna Jackson to Mrs. Gresham, Charlotte, North Carolina, December 3, 1900; Mary Anna Jackson to Mrs. Gresham, Charlotte, North Carolina, February 11, 1904, all in the Gresham Family Papers (Virginia Polytechnic Institute and State University Libraries Special Collections Department, Blacksburg, Virginia).

56. Dabney, *Life and Campaigns*, v–vi. The degree to which Anna Jackson relied on Dabney's account of her late husband to write her own biography of "Stonewall" Jackson suggests her approval of Dabney's portrayal of General Jackson.

57. Undated correspondence, reprinted in William C. Chase, *The Story of Stonewall Jackson: A Narrative of the Career of Thomas Jonathan (Stonewall) Jackson, from Written and Verbal Accounts of His Life, Approved by His Widow, Mary Anna Jackson* (Atlanta: D. E. Luther, 1901), 36.

58. The series ran from 1884 through 1887, nearly doubled the sales of the magazine in the first year of its publication alone, prompted the Century Company to issue a four-volume companion set that sold over 75,000 copies, and ultimately garnered over one million dollars for the entire project. For information on the Battles and Leaders series, see, for example, Stephen Davis, "A Matter of Sensational Interest: The Century 'Battles and Leaders' Series," *Civil War History*, 27 (December, 1981): 338–49; Arthur John, *The Best Years of the Century: Richard Watson Gilder, Scribner's Monthly, and Century Magazine, 1870–1909* (Urbana: University of Illinois Press, 1981), especially 125–80; Robert Underwood Johnson, *Remembered Yesterdays* (Boston: Little, Brown, 1923), 189–237; and Preface to *Battles and Leaders of the Civil War. Being for the Most Part Contributions by Union and Confederate Officers. Based upon "The Century War Series,"* ed. Robert Underwood Johnson and Clarence Clough Buel of the editorial staff of "the Century Magazine," new introduction by Roy F. Nichols (New York: Thomas Yoseloff, 1956), I, ix–xi.

59. Robert Johnson, *Remembered Yesterdays*, 191.

60. Margaret Junkin Preston, "Personal Reminiscences of Stonewall Jackson," *Century*, 32 (October 6, 1886): 927, 936.

61. Mary Anna Jackson, *Life and Letters*, especially 56–88. The second printing of the biography bears this apology from the publisher: "On pages 56–88 there appear frequent and extended extracts from an interesting article by Mrs. Margaret J. Preston. . . . The appropriate credit for the use of these extracts was inadvertently omitted from the first edition of this work, and the Publishers are glad of the opportunity to make this acknowledgment to the author of the article referred to." Harper and Brothers apologized personally to Preston, continuing to maintain that the slight was purely accidental. See Harper and Brothers to Mrs. Margaret J. Preston, New York, March 11, 1892, in the correspondence files of the Preston Papers (Southern Historical Collection).

62. Margaret Junkin Preston to editors of the *Century*, Lexington, Virginia, February 23, 1892, in the Century Company Records (Rare Books and Manuscripts Reading Room, New York Public Library, New York).

63. Mary Anna Jackson, *Life and Letters*, 65–66.

64. Ibid., 67. It is not surprising that Anna Jackson named Dabney as her source but not Preston. In claiming his authority for writing his work, Dabney explained that "the widow and family of General Jackson" entrusted him with the task. Moreover, he noted his position as Jackson's chief of staff during the Valley and Chickahominy campaigns, claiming he possessed "personal knowledge of the events on which the structure of his military fame was first reared." That Anna Jackson was so careful to respect Dabney's personal knowledge of her late husband but not Margaret Preston's is telling, indeed. Perhaps even she recognized the near impossibility of inserting herself into the military narrative while realizing the possibilities of claiming the "personal" narrative of her late husband. See Dabney, *Life and Campaigns*, v–vi.

65. Margaret Junkin Preston to the editors of the *Century*, Lexington, Virginia, February 23, 1892, in the Century Company Records (New York Public Library). Mary Anna Jackson was a bit more forthright in a biographical sketch she wrote of her late husband for

Hearst Magazine. Describing her return to Lexington as a new bridge, she wrote that "the General's sister-in-law ... greeted me in the sweetest manner. 'You are taking the place that my sister had,' she said, 'and so you shall be a sister to me.' This was Margaret Junkin Preston, whose influence left such a strong impress upon the General." It is important to note that this sketch appeared nearly twenty years after the book-length biography was published. See Mary Anna Jackson, "With 'Stonewall' Jackson in Camp: More Confederate Memories," *Hearst Magazine,* 24 (1913): 386.

66. Henry M. Field, who wrote the introduction to *Life and Letters of General Thomas J. Jackson,* perpetuated this fiction that Anna Jackson held a proprietary claim to the general's lifestory. "Knowing, as she only can know, all his worth ... she is right to let him speak for himself [in letters] in these gentle words that are whispered from the dust. And sure we are that those who have read all the great histories of the war will turn with fresh interest to this simple story, written out of a woman's heart." Anna Jackson, *Life and Letters,* xvii.

67. Ibid., v–vi, 89.

68. Mary Johnston, *The Long Roll* (Boston: Houghton Mifflin, 1911), 163–64. Not surprisingly, Anna Jackson offered a different interpretation of the soldiers' assessment of their leader. Quoting an unnamed source, Anna Jackson included in her biography the following testimony for a soldier who served under General Jackson: "Wherever the voice of our brave and beloved general is heard, we are ready to follow. I have read of the devotion of soldiers to their commanders, but history contains no parallel case of devotion and affection equal to that of the Stonewall Brigade for Major-General Jackson. We do not look upon him merely as our commander—do not regard him as a severe disciplinarian, as a politician, as a man seeking popularity—but as a Christian; a brave man who appreciates the condition of a common soldier; as a fatherly protector; as one who endures all hardships in common with his followers; who never commands others to face danger without putting himself in the van. The confidence and esteem of the soldiers are always made known in exulting shouts whenever he makes his appearance." See Anna Jackson, *Life and Letters,* 203.

69. Mary Anna Jackson to Mrs. Gresham, Charlotte, North Carolina, October 17, 1911, in the correspondence files of the Mary Anna Jackson Papers (Virginia Military Institute).

70. Mary Anna Jackson, "Mrs. 'Stonewall' Jackson Denounces 'The Long Roll,'" *New York Times Sunday Magazine,* October 29, 1911, 6–7; see also "Mrs. Jackson Writes of 'The Long Roll,'" *Confederate Veteran,* 19 (December 12, 1911), 591.

71. Captain J. P. Smith, "Stonewall Jackson: His Character," *Confederate Veteran,* 19 (October 10, 1911), 497–98. Smith later expanded his review of *The Long Roll* in "Jackson in The Long Roll," *Southern Historical Society Papers,* 43 (1920): 76–82.

72. Mary Johnston, "Mary Johnston Defends 'The Long Roll,'" *Confederate Veteran,* 19 (November 11, 1911): 548.

73. Joseph Ames to Mary Johnston, Baltimore, [Maryland], October 29, 1911, in the correspondence files of the Mary Johnston Papers, MS#3588 (Special Collections Department, Alderman Library, University of Virginia, Charlottesville).

74. William Clayton Terrence, "General Stonewall Jackson and 'The Long Roll': A Reply to Miss Johnston's Critics," Richmond *Times-Dispatch,* November 19, 1911, in the clippings files of the Mary Johnston Papers, MS# 3588 (University of Virginia).

75. Ferris Greenslet to Mary Johnston, Boston, [Massachusetts], October 31, 1911, in the correspondence files of the Mary Johnston papers, MS# 3588 (University of Virginia).

76. Eugenia Hill Arnold, "Sketch of the Life of Mary Ann Jackson," reprinted in the *Southern Historical Society Papers* (Richmond: Southern Historical Society, 1920), XLIII, 89.

CHAPTER FOUR

1. LaSalle Corbell Pickett, *What Happened to Me* (New York: Brentano's, 1917), 34–35. This essay is drawn especially from Lesley J. Gordon, *General George E. Pickett in Life and Legend* (Chapel Hill: University of North Carolina Press, 1998).

2. Biographical details from Gordon, *General George E. Pickett.*

3. Pickett, *What Happened to Me,* 35, 37–38.

4. LaSalle Corbell Pickett, "My Soldier," *McClure's Magazine,* 30 (March 1908): 563.
5. Pickett, *What Happened to Me,* 38.
6. Ibid., 30.
7. This essay will use available sources, some clearly fictional, some more obviously factual, to describe and evaluate the Pickett marriage, both actual and idealized.
8. Pickett, *What Happened to Me,* 1–5.
9. Gordon, *General George E. Pickett,* 35–36; 196, n. 25.
10. LaSalle Corbell Pickett, "My Soldier," 564; Gordon, *General George E. Pickett,* 53.
11. Gordon, *General George E. Pickett,* 42–67.
12. Pickett, *What Happened to Me,* 110–11.
13. Ibid., 121.
14. Quoted in William A. Young, Jr., and Patricia C. Young, *56th Virginia Infantry* (Lynchburg, VA: H. E. Howard, 1990), 74.
15. G. Moxley Sorrel, *Recollections of a Confederate Staff Officer* (1905, reprint, Dayton, OH: Morningside, 1978), 153.
16. LaSalle Corbell Pickett, *The Bugles of Gettysburg* (Chicago: F. G. Browne, 1913), 66; also Sorrel, *Recollections,* 153.
17. Gary Gallagher, "A Widow and Her Soldier: LaSalle Corbell Pickett as Author of the George E. Pickett Letters," *Virginia Magazine of History and Biography,* 94 (July 1986): 329–44.
18. Pickett, ed., *The Heart of a Soldier,* 66.
19. Examples of Pickett's less than admirable behavior on the battlefield include John Cheeves Haskell, *The Haskell Memoirs,* ed. Gilbert E. Govan and James W. Livingood (New York: G. P. Putnam's Sons, 1960), 32, 51–52; Eppa Hunton, *Autobiography of Eppa Hunton* (Richmond: William Byrd Press, 1933), 81, 85; Clayton Coleman to John W. Daniel, July 1, 1904, John W. Daniel Papers (Alderman Library, University of Virginia, Charlottesville).
20. Hunton, *Autobiography,* 127.
21. E. P. Alexander, *Fighting for the Confederacy: The Personal Recollections of General Edward Porter Alexander,* ed. Gary W. Gallagher (Chapel Hill: University of North Carolina Press, 1989), 255.
22. Robert A. Bright, "Pickett's Charge," *Southern Historical Society Papers,* 31 (1903): 234; also Gordon, *General George E. Pickett,* 110–12.
23. George E. Pickett to LaSalle Corbell, July 23, 1863, in Inman Papers (John Hay Library, Brown University, Providence, Rhode Island); letter also reprinted in Arthur Crew Inman, ed., *Soldier of the South: General Pickett's War Letters to His Wife* (Boston: Houghton Mifflin, 1928), 78.
24. Gordon, *General George E. Pickett,* 106–20.
25. Pickett, ed., *The Heart of a Soldier,* 68; Pickett, *Pickett and His Men,* 408.
26. Pickett, ed., *The Heart of a Soldier,* 8.
27. LaSalle Corbell Pickett, *The Bugles of Gettysburg* (Chicago: F. G. Browne, 1913), 139.
28. Pickett, *Bugles of Gettysburg,* 126, also 120; Gordon, *General George E. Pickett,* 118.
29. LaSalle Corbell Pickett, *Pickett and His Men* (Atlanta: Foote and Davies, 1899), 318.
30. Pickett, *What Happened to Me,* 124.
31. Wedding details gathered from Pickett, "The Wartime Story of General Pickett," *Cosmopolitan,* 56 (May 1914): 764; *Pickett and His Men,* 320–21; Heather Palmer, "The Civil War Wedding of LaSalle Corbell," *Lady's Gallery,* 1, no. 6 (n.d.): 53–54; Pickett, *What Happened to Me,* 126–29; Arthur Crew Inman, *The Inman Diary: A Public and Private Confession,* ed. Daniel Aaron, 2 vols. (Cambridge, MA: Harvard University Press, 1985), I: 328.
32. *Richmond Dispatch,* September 22, 1863.
33. Pickett, *Pickett and His Men,* 318.
34. Her obituary called her the "child bride" of the Confederacy. For example, see "Obituary," *Confederate Veteran,* 39 (April 1931): 151; and *Washington Post,* March 23, 1931; see also Pickett, *Pickett and His Men,* 318, and Rable, *Civil Wars,* 51. LaSalle Corbell Pickett, "My Soldier," *McClure's Magazine,* 30, no. 5 (March 1908): 568. Her "childish" traits especially come through in her autobiography, *What Happened to Me,* 143–45, 191–

99, 207–16. David G. Pugh, *Sons of Liberty: The Masculine Mind in Nineteenth Century America* (Westport, CT: Greenwood Press, 1983), 65–68; Carroll Smith-Rosenberg, "The Hysterical Woman: Sex Roles and Role Conflict in 19th-Century America," *Social Research*, 39 (Winter 1972): 655–56; Elizabeth Fox-Genovese, *Within the Plantation Household: Black and White Women of the Old South* (Chapel Hill: University of North Carolina Press, 1988), 109; Bertram Wyatt-Brown, *Southern Honor: Ethics and Behavior in the Old South* (New York: Oxford University Press, 1982), 201–2.

35. Pickett, *What Happened to Me*, 136; also Pickett, *Pickett and His Men*, 326; Rable, *Civil Wars*, 72; Shirley A. Leckie, *Elizabeth Bacon Custer and the Making of a Myth* (Norman: University of Oklahoma Press, 1993), 36, 45.

36. Pickett, *What Happened to Me*, 141; Faust, *Mothers of Invention*, 9–29.

37. Gordon, *General George E. Pickett*, 124–27.

38. Pickett, quoted in *Executive Document No. 98*, House of Representatives, 39th Congress, 1st Session, 80.

39. Gordon, *General George E. Pickett*, 137–41; George E. Pickett to Samuel Cooper, May 17, 1864, Letters Received, Adjutant Inspector General's Office, Record Group 109, (National Archives, Washington, DC); Josiah Gorgas, *The Civil War Diary of General Josiah Gorgas*, ed. Frank Vandiver (University: University of Alabama Press, 1947), 100. P. G. T. Beauregard to Braxton Bragg, May 11, 1864, U.S. War Department, *War of the Rebellion: Official Records*, Series I, Vol. 51, pt. 2, 920; Clifford Dowdey, *Lee's Last Campaign: The Story of Lee and His Men against Grant, 1864* (Boston: Little, Brown, 1960), 238; William Glenn Robertson, *Back Door to Richmond: The Bermuda Campaign, April–June 1864* (Newark: University of Delaware Press, 1987), 112; see also Gordon, *General George E. Pickett*, 127–34.

40. Pickett, *Pickett and His Men*, 340.

41. Pickett, *What Happened to Me*, 138.

42. LaSalle Corbell Pickett, ed., *The Heart of a Soldier as Revealed in the Intimate Letters of Genl. George E. Pickett, CSA* (New York: Seth Moyle, 1913), 123. As with all of the published Pickett letters, it is unclear whether these were entirely LaSalle's words or his. Given George's earlier concern with protecting the inhabitants of the Northern Neck, particularly the women, it is entirely plausible that he expressed such worries. She may have rephrased his thoughts to make them more dramatic to her readers.

43. Pickett, *Pickett and His Men*, 341.

44. Pickett, *What Happened to Me*, 139.

45. Pickett, ed., *The Heart of a Soldier*, 125. Italics from original.

46. Gordon, *General George E. Pickett*, 141–43.

47. Pickett, *Pickett and His Men*, 357; Pickett, *What Happened to Me*, 141.

48. Pickett, *Pickett and His Men*, 362–64

49. Pickett, *What Happened to Me*, 143.

50. Pickett, *Pickett and His Men*, 361.

51. Pickett, *What Happened to Me*, 144–45. An abbreviated form of this story is included in *Pickett and His Men*, 360–61, but LaSalle left out any mention of her picking up the head.

52. Pickett, *Pickett and His Men*, 343. For more on LaSalle Corbell Pickett and the Lost Cause, see Lesley J. Gordon, "Let the People See the Old Life as It Was: LaSalle Corbell Pickett and the Myth of the Lost Cause," in *The Lost Cause*, ed. Alan T. Nolan (Champaign: University of Illinois Press, 2000), 170–84.

53. Robert E. Lee to James Longstreet, January 19, 1865, Fairfax Papers (Virginia Historical Society, Richmond).

54. Gordon, *General George E. Pickett*, 145–46; Douglas Southall Freeman, *Lee's Lieutenants: A Study in Command*, 3 vols. (New York: Charles Scribner's Sons, 1944), III, 627; Douglas Southall Freeman, *R. E. Lee: A Biography*, 4 vols. (New York: Charles Scribner's Sons, 1935), IV, 25–26; Walter Harrison to George E. Pickett, November 14, 1864, Fairfax Papers (Virginia Historical Society).

55. Gordon, *General George E. Pickett*, 146–53; John S. Mosby, *Memoirs of Colonel John S. Mosby*, ed. Charles W. Russel (Boston: Little, Brown, 1917), 381–82; Freeman, *R. E. Lee*, IV, 112.

56. LaSalle Corbell Pickett, "The First United States Flag Raised in Richmond after the War," in *The Fourth Massachusetts Cavalry in the Closing Scenes of the War for the Maintenance of the Union*, ed. William B. Arnold (Boston: n.p., n.d.), 19–22 (quotation from p. 21).

57. Pickett, *What Happened to Me*, 164–65. See also Pickett, "My Soldier," 567.

58. Gallagher, "A Widow and Her Soldier," 337; Merrill D. Peterson, *Lincoln in American Memory* (New York: Oxford University Press, 1994), 92; Carl Landrum, "General Who Studied Law in Quincy," *Quincy Herald-Whig*, March 24, 1991.

59. Pickett, *What Happened to Me*, 185.

60. Ibid., 200–203; Gordon, *General George E. Pickett*, 156–58.

61. Pickett, *What Happened to Me*, 261–70; Inman, *The Inman Diary*, II, 328.

62. George E. Pickett to Ulysses S. Grant, March 12, 1865, "Amnesty Papers," Record Group 94, (National Archives); Ulysses Grant to Andrew Johnston, March 16, 1866, *The Papers of Ulysses S. Grant*, ed. John Simon (Carbondale: Southern Illinois University Press, 1988), XVI, 120–22.

63. Patricia Faust, ed. *Historical Times Illustrated Encyclopedia of the Civil War* (New York: Harper and Row, 1986), 12; editors' notes included with George E. Pickett to Andrew Johnston, June 1, 1865, *Papers of Andrew Johnston*, ed. Paul N. Bergeron et al. (Knoxville: University of Tennessee Press, 1989), VIII, 165, n. 3.

64. Gordon, *General George E. Pickett*, 161–63.

65. George E. Pickett to "My Dear Friend," December 14, 18—, Pickett Family Typescript Notebook (Virginia Historical Society).

66. George E. Pickett to Benjamin Starke, March 16, 1866, Pickett-Starke Letters, Oregon Historical Society (Portland, OR).

67. W. Heth to George E. Pickett, March 23, 1869, Pickett Family Typescript Notebook (Virginia Historical Society).

68. Pickett, ed., *Heart of a Soldier*, 208–9; Pickett, *What Happened to Me*, 340–51.

69. Gordon, *General George E. Pickett*, 166–67; Pickett, *What Happened to Me*, 340–51; Pickett, "My Soldier," 569–70 (quotation on p. 570); "Obituary," Richmond *Dispatch*, July 31, 1875.

70. LaSalle Corbell Pickett to James T. Pickett, February 9, 1878, Edmond Meany Papers (University of Washington Libraries, Manuscripts and Archives Division, Seattle).

71. Pickett, *What Happened to Me*, 363.

72. Ibid., 150; Francis E. Willard and Mary A. Livermore, eds., *A Woman of the Century: Fourteen Hundred-Seventy Biographical Sketches Accompanied by Portraits of Leading American Women in All Walks of Life* (Chicago: Charles Wells Moulton, 1893), 571; Gordon, *George E. Pickett*, 168–69;

73. For example, LaSalle Corbell Pickett to James Tilton Pickett, February 9, 1878, Edmond Meany Papers (University of Washington Libraries); H.C. McReavy to Jessie K. Girsdale, August 19, 1933, Pickett Collection (Washington State Capital Museum, Olympia). See also LaSalle Corbell Pickett, *Literary Hearthstones of Dixie* (Philadelphia: J. B. Lippincott, 1912), 253; Gordon, *George E. Pickett*, 169–70.

74. *New York Times*, July 5, 1887. Also Gordon, *General George E. Pickett*, 171–81.

75. Pickett, *Pickett and His Men*, 29–30.

76. Ibid., 89; Gallagher, "A Widow and Her Soldier," 329–44.

77. Pickett, *Pickett and His Men*, v.

78. Some of these women included Julia Ward Howe, Fannie Kemble, and Sara Evans Wilson. See LaSalle Corbell Pickett, *Literary Hearthstones of Dixie* (Philadelphia: J.B. Lippincott, 1912), and LaSalle Corbell Pickett, *Across My Path: Memories of People I Have Known* (1916; reprint, Freeport, NY: Books for Libraries Press, 1970). Standard references for Lost Cause mythology include Charles Reagan Wilson, *Baptized in Blood: The Religion of the Lost Cause, 1865–1920* (Athens: University of Georgia Press, 1980); Gaines M. Foster, *Ghosts of the Confederacy: Defeat, the Lost Cause, and the Emergence of the New South* (New York: Oxford University Press, 1987); Rollin G. Osterweis, *The Myth of the Lost Cause, 1865–1900* (Hamden, CT: Archon Books, 1973). See also Gordon, "Let the People See the Old Life as It Was."

79. John C. Waugh, *The Class of 1846: From West Point to Appomattox. Stonewall Jackson, George McClellan and Their Brothers* (New York: Warner Brothers Books, 1994), 577, n. 14.

80. Reference to LaSalle as "Mother Pickett," in undated obituary, United Daughters of the Confederacy, Virginia Division, Boydton, Mecklenburg Co., Chapter No. 157, Scrapbook, 1913–1957 (Virginia Historical Society); details of burial controversy from *Washington Post*, March 29, 1931, *New York Times*, March 29, 1931; Mary H. Mitchell, *Hollywood Cemetery: The History of a Southern Shrine* (Richmond: Virginia State Library, 1985), 137–38.

81. Quoted in Deborah Fitts, "Pickett's Wife to Be Reburied & His Grave Rededicated in March," *The Civil War News* (February/March 1998): 1, 27.

CHAPTER FIVE

The author would like to acknowledge the assistance of Donald C. Pfanz in the preparation of this article.

1. Anonymous obituary of George Washington Campbell, Polk-Ewell-Brown Papers, (Southern Historical Collection, University of North Carolina at Chapel Hill); obituary of Elizabeth Campbell Brown Ewell, January 23, 1872, in the *Nashville Union and American*, Brown Ewell Papers, 1803–1919 (Tennessee State Library and Archives, Nashville).

2. Elizabeth Stoddert Ewell to Benjamin Ewell, March 11, 1850, Benjamin Stoddert Ewell Papers (College of William and Mary, Williamsburg, Virginia). Lewis Baker, *The Percys of Mississippi: Politics and Literature in the New South* (Baton Rouge: Louisiana State University Press, 1983).

3. Typed copy of James Percy Brown's will, November 6, 1842, in Packet #27 (Bolivar County, Mississippi, Court Files, Rosedale).

4. Rebecca Ewell to [?], January 1, 1854, Ewell Papers (Library of Congress, Washington D.C.)

5. Rebecca Ewell to Benjamin Ewell, December 12, 1845, Benjamin Stoddert Ewell Papers (College of William and Mary); Thomas T. Gantt to Elizabeth Campbell Brown, Brown-Ewell Papers (Tennessee State Library).

6. On the centrality of family and children to southern women, see Elizabeth Fox-Genovese, "Family and Female Identity in the Antebellum South: Sarah Gayle and Her Family," in *In Joy and in Sorrow: Women, Family, and Marriage in the Victorian South, 1830–1900*, ed. Carol Bleser (New York: Oxford University Press, 1991), 15–31.

7. For one example of Lizinka's shrewd business dealings, see Elizabeth Campbell Brown to David Hubbard, January 10, 18[56], David Hubbard Papers (Tennessee State Library).

8. Herman Hattaway and Archer Jones, *How the North Won: A Military History of the Civil War* (Urbana: University of Illinois Press, 1983), 405; see also Richard Taylor, *Destruction and Reconstruction: Personal Experiences of the Late War* (1879; reprint, New York: Longmans, Green, 1955), 36–37. For the definitive biography of Richard S. Ewell, see Donald C. Pfanz, *Richard S. Ewell: A Soldier's Life* (Chapel Hill: University of North Carolina Press, 1998). This is a superb study based on extensive manuscript research. A less rigorous study of Ewell but one that includes some of his antebellum and wartime correspondence can be found in Percy Gatling Hamlin, *Richard Stoddert Ewell: "Old Bald Head" (General R. S. Ewell), The Portrait of a Soldier and the Making of a Soldier: Letters of General R. S. Ewell* (1935, 1940; reprint, Gaithersburg, MD: Combined by Ron R. Van Sickle Military Books, 1988).

9. Pfanz, *Richard S. Ewell*, 11–12.

10. Jill K. Garrett, *"Hither and Yon:" The Best of the Writings of Jill K. Garrett* (Columbia, TN: [n. p.], 1986), 64; Elizabeth [?] to Lucuis [?], February 5, 1935, Brown-Ewell Papers (Tennessee State Library).

11. Hamlin, *Old Bald Head.*

12. Ibid., 39.

13. Elizabeth Campbell Brown to David Hubbard, December 23, 1855, David Hubbard Papers (Tennessee State Library).

14. Thomas Gantt to Elizabeth Campbell Brown, December 26, 1855, Brown-Ewell Papers (Tennessee State Library).

15. Thomas Gantt to Elizabeth Campbell Brown, November 2, 1855, Brown-Ewell Papers

(Tennessee State Library). Before Ewell made his final decision in December, the reasons he gave to Gantt the previous month kept him from accepting Lizinka's offer.

16. On the relationship between southern masculinity and patriarchy, see Elizabeth Fox-Genovese, *Within the Plantation Household: Black and White Women of the Old South* (Chapel Hill: University of North Carolina Press, 1988), 38–39, 63–64.

17. Campbell Brown memoir in Ewell letter book, Campbell Brown–Richard S. Ewell Papers (Tennessee State Library).

18. Hamlin, *Richard Stoddert Ewell*, 78.

19. Ibid., 73–75.

20. On the wartime challenges to Confederate women's identity, see George Rable, *Civil Wars: Women and the Crisis of Southern Nationalism* (Urbana: University of Illinois Press, 1989), especially chapter 6; Drew Gilpin Faust, *Mothers of Invention: Women of the Slaveholding South in the American Civil War* (Chapel Hill: University of North Carolina Press, 1996), especially chapters 4 and the epilogue.

21. Hamlin, *Richard Stoddert Ewell*, 84. For Ewell's actions in Jackson's valley campaign, see Robert Gaither Tanner, *Stonewall in the Valley, Thomas J. "Stonewall" Jackson's Shenandoah Valley Campaign, Spring, 1862* (Garden City, NY: Doubleday, 1976).

22. Richard S. Ewell to James E. B. Stuart, May 14, 1862, Stuart Collection, Box One, item SA-17 (Huntington Library, San Marino, California).

23. On the wounding of Ewell, see John Hennessy, *Return to Bull Run: The Campaign and Battle of Second Manassas* (New York: Simon & Schuster, 1993), 182, 189–90.

24. Hamlin, *Richard Stoddert Ewell*, 129–33.

25. Campbell Brown memoir in Ewell letter book, Campbell Brown–Richard S. Ewell Papers (Tennessee State Library).

26. Elizabeth Campbell Brown to Richard S. Ewell, September 9, 1862, Brown-Ewell Papers (Tennessee State Library).

27. Hamlin, *Richard Stoddert Ewell*, 136.

28. On the Confederate debates surrounding Gettysburg and the Lost Cause interpretation of Richard S. Ewell in Pennsylvania, see J. William Jones and others, eds., *Southern Historical Society Papers*, 52 vols. (1876–1959); reprint with 2-vol. index (Millwood, NY: Kraus, 1977–80), esp. vols. 4–6; and Thomas L. Connelly and Barbara L. Bellows, *God and General Longstreet: The Lost Cause and the Southern Mind* (Baton Rouge: Louisiana State University Press, 1982), 30–31. Ewell has particularly suffered at the hands of modern historians. For recent scholarship on Jackson that indicts Ewell for failing to seize Cemetery Hill, see Bevin Alexander, *Lost Victories: The Military Genius of Stonewall Jackson* (New York: Henry Holt, 1992), 330; Paul D. Casdorph, *Lee and Jackson: Confederate Chieftains* (New York: Paragon House, 1992), 396; and John Bowers, *Stonewall Jackson: Portrait of a Soldier* (New York: William Morrow, 1989), 356. For other critical assessments of Ewell, see Glenn Tucker, *High Tide at Gettysburg: The Campaign Pennsylvania* (Indianapolis: Bobbs-Merrill, 1958), 189; Douglas Southall Freeman, *Lee's Lieutenants: A Study in Command* (New York: Scribner's, 1942–44), III, 93; Clifford Dowdey, *Death of a Nation: The Story of Lee and His Men at Gettysburg* (New York: Knopf, 1958), 142; and Herman Hattaway, *Shades of Blue and Gray: An Introductory Military History of the Civil War* (Columbia: University of Missouri Press, 1997), 143.

29. Jubal Early believed that additional support from A. P. Hill would have resulted in the capture of Cemetery Hill. He wrote in his official report: "Meeting with an officer of Major-General Pender's staff, I sent word by him to General Hill that if he would send up a division, we could take the hill to which the enemy had retreated." See his Gettysburg report in the U.S. War Department, *The War of the Rebellion: A Compilation of the Official Records of the Union and Confederate Armies*, 127 vols., index, and atlas (Washington, DC: U.S. Government Printing Office, 1880–1901), 27(2): 830 (hereafter cited as Official Records; all references are to series 1). Sandie Pendleton agreed that A. P. Hill should have supported Ewell in an attack against Cemetery Hill. See Alexander S. Pendleton, letter, July [?], 1863, Ellinor Porcher Gadsden Papers (University Library of Washington and Lee University, Lexington, Virginia). Of late there has been a noticeable shift in the Gettysburg historiography toward Ewell, including Alan T. Nolan, "R. E. Lee and July 1 at Gettysburg," in *The First Day at Gettysburg: Essays on Confederate and*

Union Leadership, ed. Gary W. Gallagher (Kent, OH: Kent State University Press, 1992), 22–29; Gary W. Gallagher, "Confederate Corps Leadership on the First Day at Gettysburg: A. P. Hill and Richard S. Ewell in a Difficult Debut," in *First Day at Gettysburg*, ed. Gallagher, 30–56; and Harry W. Pfanz, *Gettysburg: Culp's Hill and Cemetery Hill* (Chapel Hill: University of North Carolina Press, 1993), 72.

30. For historians who have fantasized about Jackson clinching victory at Gettysburg, see Alexander, *Lost Victories*; Casdorph, *Lee and Jackson: Confederate Chieftains*; and Bowers, *Stonewall Jackson: Portrait of a Soldier*.

31. Alexander S. Pendleton, letter, July [?], 1863, Ellinor Porcher Gadsden Papers (Washington and Lee).

32. James Conner, *The Letters of General James Conner, C.S.A.* (Columbia, SC: The State Co., 1933), 114–15.

33. Eppa Hunton, *Autobiography of Eppa Hunton* (Richmond: William Byrd Press, 1935), 127.

34. For a useful discussion of how Confederate women used the "privileges of gender" to engage in political action, see Faust, *Mothers of Invention*, 198–202.

35. Jedediah Hotchkiss to his wife, November 22, 1863, Jedediah Hotchkiss Papers, Reel 4 (Library of Congress).

36. "To the Editors of the Enquirer," Richmond *Enquirer*, November 18, 1863, p. 2.

37. Everard H. Smith, ed., "The Civil War Diary of Peter W. Hairston, Volunteer Aide to Major General Jubal Early, November 7–December 4, 1863," *The North Carolina Historical Review*, 67 (January 1990): 6; on the relationship between the Ewells and Early, see Freeman, *Lee's Lieutenants*, III: 332–33.

38. Pendleton refused to bring his wife to visit winter quarters and welcomed the letters in the Richmond *Enquirer* and the Richmond *Examiner* that called for a prohibition of women in camp. See Alexander S. Pendleton to Mary Pendleton, November 25, 1863, William Nelson Pendleton Papers (Southern Historical Collection).

39. Alexander S. Pendleton to his mother, November 25, 1863, William Nelson Pendleton Papers (Southern Historical Collection).

40. Richard S. Ewell to Elizabeth Campbell Brown Ewell, December 20, 1863, Polk-Brown-Ewell Papers (Southern Historical Collection). Sandie Pendleton initially welcomed Ewell as Jackson's replacement. By the fall of 1863, he had become disillusioned with the new commander of the Second Corps. He wrote to his mother on October 16, 1863, that Ewell "has quick military perception & is a splendid executive officer, [but] lacks decision and is too irresolute for so large & independent command as he has." See Alexander S. Pendleton to his mother, October 16, 1863, William Nelson Pendleton Papers (Southern Historical Collection).

41. Conner, *Letters of General James Conner*, 114–15.

42. James B. Sheeran, *Confederate Chaplain: A War Journal of Rev. James B. Sheeran, c.ss.r 14th Louisiana, C.S.A.*, ed. Joseph T. Durkin, S.J. (Milwaukee: Bruce Publishing Company, 1960), 75.

43. Campbell Brown to Elizabeth Campbell Brown Ewell, May 20, 1864, Polk-Brown-Ewell Papers (Southern Historical Collection); Jedediah Hotchkiss to his wife, May 19, 1864, Hotchkiss Papers, Reel 4 (Library of Congress).

44. Conner, *The Letters of General James Conner*, 115.

45. Ibid.

46. The Reverend B. T. Lacy and Ware Recollections, November 11, 1892, from roll 39, Containers 38–39, "Jackson's Staff," Hotchkiss Papers (Library of Congress); Smith, ed., "The Civil War Diary of Peter W. Hairston," 76; Jedediah Hotchkiss to his wife, April 26, 1864, Jedediah Hotchkiss Papers, Reel 4 (Library of Congress); Jedediah Hotchkiss to his wife, April 24, 1864, Jedediah Hotchkiss Papers, Reel 4 (Library of Congress).

47. For a critical assessment of Ewell at the Wilderness, see Freeman, *Lee's Lieutenants*, III, 442; Dowdey, *Lee's Last Campaign: The Story of Lee and His Men against Grant, 1864* (1960; reprint, New York: Barnes & Noble, 1994), 170; Edward Steere, *The Wilderness Campaign* (New York: Bonanza, 1960), 448; Gary W. Gallagher, "The Army of Northern Virginia in May 1864: A Crisis of High Command," *Civil War History*, 36 (June 1990): 115; Gordon C. Rhea, *The Battle of the Wilderness: May 5–6, 1864* (Baton Rouge: Louisiana

State University Press, 1994), 444–45. For a more favorable interpretation, see Carmichael, "Escaping the Shadow of Gettysburg," 136–156.

48. Quoted from Gordon C. Rhea, *The Battles for Spotsylvania Court House and the Road to Yellow Tavern, May 7–12, 1864* (Baton Rouge: Louisiana State University Press, 1997), 255–56; William Allan, "Memoranda of Conversations with General Robert E. Lee," in *Lee: The Soldier*, ed. Gary W. Gallagher (Lincoln: University of Nebraska Press, 1996), 11.

49. Allan, "Memoranda of Conversations with General Robert E. Lee," 11–12.

50. On Ewell's capture at Sayler's Creek, see Chris Calkins, *The Appomattox Campaign: March 29–April 9, 1865* (Conshohocken, PA: Combined Books, 1997).

51. Hamlin, *Richard Stoddert Ewell*, 194.

52. Elizabeth Campbell Brown Ewell to Richard Stoddert Ewell, June 13, 1865, Filson Club, Louisville, Kentucky.

53. Elizabeth Campbell Brown Ewell to Richard S. Ewell, [undated], Polk-Brown-Ewell Papers (Southern Historical Collection).

54. Elizabeth Campbell Brown Ewell to Andrew Johnson, July 9, 1865, Polk-Brown-Ewell Papers (Southern Historical Collection).

55. Elizabeth Campbell Brown Ewell to Richard S. Ewell, July 9, 1865, Polk-Brown-Ewell Papers (Southern Historical Collection).

56. Elizabeth Campbell Brown Ewell to Richard S. Ewell, [undated], Ewell-Brown Papers (Tennessee State Library). Also see letters of May 28, 1868, and January 1, 1870, in the same collection.

57. Elizabeth Campbell Brown Ewell to Campbell Brown, June 13, 1868, Ewell-Brown Papers, (Tennessee State Library).

58. Elizabeth Campbell Brown Ewell to Richard S. Ewell, [undated], Ewell-Brown Papers, (Tennessee State Library). This letter was probably written after 1868.

59. Elizabeth Campbell Brown Ewell to Richard Ewell, December 31, 1869, Polk-Brown-Ewell Papers (Southern Historical Collection).

60. Elizabeth Campbell Brown Ewell to Richard S. Ewell, [undated], Ewell-Brown Papers (Tennessee State Library). This letter was probably written after 1868.

61. Quoted from, Pfanz, *Richard Ewell*, 484.

62. Lizinka Campbell Brown Ewell to Cambell Brown, December 29, 1870, Ewell-Brown Papers (Tennessee State Library).

63. Quoted from Pfanz, *Richard Ewell*, 495; Nashville *Republican Banner*, January 1, 1872, 4.

CHAPTER SIX

1. Josiah Gorgas to Amelia Gorgas, July 1, [1858], Gorgas Family Papers (Hoole Special Collections Library, University of Alabama, Tuscaloosa). Letters cited are located in the Gorgas Family Papers unless they are noted from another manuscript collection. Many letters in this collection are undated, partially dated, or incorrectly dated. Each date cited in a note represents a separate letter.

2. Information on Sarah Gayle may be found in Elizabeth Fox-Genovese, "Family and Female Identity in the Antebellum South: Sarah Gayle and Her Family," in *In Joy and in Sorrow: Women, Family, and Marriage in the Victorian South, 1830–1900*, ed. Carol Bleser (New York: Oxford University Press, 1991), 15–31, 268–72, and Fox-Genovese, *Within the Plantation Household: Black and White Women of the Old South* (Chapel Hill: University of North Carolina Press, 1988), 1–28. Information on John Gayle may be found in John Garraty and Mark C. Carnes, eds., *American National Biography*, 24 vols. (New York: Oxford University Press, 1999), VIII, 811–12; Thomas McAdory Owen, *History of Alabama and Dictionary of Alabama Biography*, 4 vols. (Chicago: S. J. Clarke Publishing Co., 1921), III, 646–47.

3. For biographical information on Amelia see Mary Tabb Johnston, *Amelia Gayle Gorgas: A Biography* (University: University of Alabama Press, 1978), and Sarah Woolfolk Wiggins, "Amelia Gayle Gorgas, A Victorian Mother," in *Stepping Out of the Shadows: Alabama*

Women, 1819–1900, ed. Mary Martha Thomas (Tuscaloosa: University of Alabama Press, 1995), 57–74, 200–205.

4.   For biographical information on Josiah, see Frank E. Vandiver, *Ploughshares into Swords: Josiah Gorgas and Confederate Ordnance* (Austin; University of Texas Press, 1952), and Sarah Woolfolk Wiggins, ed., *The Journals of Josiah Gorgas 1857–1878* (Tuscaloosa: University of Alabama Press, 1995).

5   Wiggins, *Journals of Josiah Gorgas,* xxxv–xxxvii. Josiah and Amelia were older than most couples in first marriages among upper-class Alabama families. See Ann Williams Boucher, "Wealthy Planter Families in Nineteenth-Century Alabama" (Ph.D. dissertation, University of Connecticut, 1978), 41–42, and Kenneth R. Johnson, "White Married Women in Antebellum Alabama," *Alabama Review,* 43 (January 1990): 8. For a discussion of Amelia and Josiah's child-rearing patterns, see Wiggins, "Amelia," 57–74, and "A Victorian Father: Josiah Gorgas and His Family," in *In Joy and in Sorrow,* 233–52, 321–26. Amelia as a middle child in the birth order of the Gayle children and Josiah as the youngest of the Gorgas children fit the profile of recommended birth order for couples in successful marriages, as detailed in Monica McGoldrick and Randy Gerson, *Genograms in Family Assessment* (New York: W. W. Norton, 1985), 46–58.

6.   James M. McPherson, *Ordeal by Fire: The Civil War and Reconstruction* (New York: Alfred A. Knopf, 1982), 197–98; Wiggins, ed., *Journals of Josiah Gorgas,* 97–98; Marie D. Gorgas and Burton J. Hendrick, *William Crawford Gorgas: His Life and Work* (Garden City, NY: Garden City Publishing Co., 1924), 36; Vandiver, *Ploughshares into Swords,* 84–127, 148–270; Johnston, *Amelia Gayle Gorgas,* 50–68.

7.   Johnston, *Amelia Gayle Gorgas,* 69–102.

8.   Josiah Gorgas to Amelia Gorgas, [1858]. For a discussion of the relationship between intimacy and power in marriage, see Steven M. Stowe, *Intimacy and Power in the Old South: Ritual in the Lives of the Planters* (Baltimore: The Johns Hopkins University Press, 1987).

9.   Josiah Gorgas to Amelia Gorgas, six letters, [1858].

10. Ibid., [July] 10, [1858], [1858], December 15, [1854].

11. Josiah Gorgas to Amelia Gorgas, [1858], May 30, June 2, 6, July 6, 1858.

12. Ibid., n.d., October 11, 1862, Saturday [1862], September [1862], Saturday [1862].

13. Amelia Gorgas to Josiah Gorgas, June 27, [1858], July 23, 1858.

14. Amelia to "My dear Sister" [Sarah Crawford], March 29, 1848.

15. [Josiah Gorgas], "Epistolary Gossipings of Travel, and Its Reminiscences," *Russell's Magazine,* 5 (May 1859): 134; Gorgas and Hendrick, *William Crawford Gorgas,* 34–35.

16. Gorgas and Hendrick, *William Crawford Gorgas,* 35; Wiggins, ed., *Journals of Josiah Gorgas,* 37.

17. Vandiver, *Ploughshares into Swords,* 10–14.

18. Ibid., 44–54; Wiggins, ed., *Journals of Josiah Gorgas,* 37. Gorgas probably thought he could gain a fresh start in the new southern army without realizing that many of his former fellow army officers, including Benjamin Huger, also would join the Confederacy.

19. Only one letter survives from one of Josiah's siblings after 1861. Other than a single reference to a sister of Josiah, the Gorgas correspondence mentions his family only relative to efforts to collect money owed to Josiah by his siblings.

20. Amelia Gorgas to Josiah Gorgas, July 29, August 13, 1865, [1866]; Josiah to Amelia, May 4, 5, [1865], June 4, 14, July 7, 9, 29, August 14, 20, September 11, October 4, 1865.

21. Amelia to [Josiah], [June 30, 1865]; Amelia to Josiah, n.d., in Richard H. Gayle to "My dear General" [Josiah Gorgas], July 7, 1865; Josiah to Amelia, July 7, September 11, 1865.

22. Josiah Gorgas to Amelia Gorgas, July 1865, July 7, 1865; Josiah to "Sister" [Sarah Crawford], September 20, 1865.

23. Amelia Gorgas to Josiah Gorgas, June 26, July 29, [1865]; Josiah to Amelia, April 10, 1865, July [1865]; Josiah to "Sister" [Sarah Crawford], [June] 1865; Richard H. Gayle to "My dear General" [Josiah Gorgas], July 7, 1865. For discussion of how the watershed of wartime changed many southern women, see Mary Elizabeth Massey, *Women in the Civil War* (1966; reprint, Lincoln: University of Nebraska Press, 1994); George C. Rable, *Civil Wars: Women and the Crisis of Southern Nationalism* (Urbana: University of Illinois

Press, 1989); Anne Firor Scott, *The Southern Lady: From Pedestal to Politics, 1830–1930* (1970; reprint, Charlottesville: University of Virginia Press, 1995), 81–102; Drew Gilpin Faust, *Mothers of Invention: Women of the Slaveholding South in the American Civil War* (Chapel Hill: University of North Carolina Press, 1996); Edward D. C. Campbell, Jr., and Kym S. Rice, eds., *A Woman's War: Southern Women, Civil War, and the Confederate Legacy* (Charlottesville: University of Virginia Press, 1996).

24. Josiah Gorgas to Amelia Gorgas, May 4, 5, [1865], July 29, September 11, October 4, 1865, July 1865. See also Amelia to Josiah, [July 1865].

25. Amelia Gorgas to Josiah Gorgas, June 26, July 29, [1865], September 5, 22, 1865.

26. Amelia to Josiah, January [1866].

27. Josiah to Amelia, August 14, 1865.

28. Amelia Gorgas to Josiah Gorgas, June 26, 30, [1865]; [Amelia to Josiah, 1865]; Amelia to Josiah, n.d., in Richard H. Gayle to "My dear General" [Josiah Gorgas], July 7, 1865.

29. Josiah Gorgas to Amelia Gorgas, July 1865, July 7, August 20, September 11, 1865, [1865], January 1, 1866; Amelia to Josiah, January 7, 1866.

30. Josiah Gorgas to Amelia Gorgas, August 20, September 4, 1865.

31. Ibid., September, 29, [1865].

32. Ibid.

33. Amelia Gorgas to Josiah Gorgas, October 1, 1865, January 7, 1866.

34. Ibid., August 23, 1865. For a discussion of the parents' relationship to W. C. Gorgas, see Wiggins, "Amelia" and "A Victorian Father."

35. Amelia Gorgas to Josiah Gorgas, September 5, 22, 1865.

36. Josiah Gorgas to Amelia Gorgas, January 23, [March] 16, [1866], January 16, February 22, March 7, 9, 20, 1866.

37. Amelia Gorgas to Josiah Gorgas, January 23, February 18, 1866, March 18, 20, [1866].

38. Ibid., March 20, [1866], March 28, 1866.

39. Josiah Gorgas to "my dear daughter" [Jessie Gorgas], July 3, [1867]. For a discussion of this stream of visitors, see Wiggins, "Amelia," 61–68.

40. Wiggins, ed., *Journals of Josiah Gorgas*, 200, 201, 203.

41. Josiah Gorgas to Amelia Gorgas, March 6, 25, [1869], March 19, April 4, 6, 1870; Amelia to Josiah, March 16, 1869, August 4, [1869]; Amelia to Josiah in Thomas Alvis to Josiah Gorgas, May 11, 1870.

42. Ibid., March 16, Sunday, April 3, Wed[nesday], August 4, 13, 1869, [October 1869]; Josiah to Amelia, Sunday 1860, Sunday eve 1869, [Summer 1869], Tuesday eve [1869], July 13, October 14, 22, 24, 26, 29, 1869, November 5, [1869], February 17, 18, March 4, 1870.

43. Amelia Gorgas to Josiah Gorgas, October 14, [1869]; Vandiver, *Ploughshares into Swords*, 292.

44. Josiah Gorgas to Amelia Gorgas, July 31, August 26, 30, September 6, 11, 1869, Thursday [1869], 1869, Sunday 1869, September 15, [1869], March 13, 19, 23, 25, 29, April 2, June 1, 1870; Amelia to Josiah, August 4, 13, 1869, 1869; Josiah to Amelia, n.d., in William Crawford Gorgas to Amelia Gorgas, August 15, 1869, William Crawford Gorgas Papers (Hoole Special Collections Library, University of Alabama, Tuscaloosa).

45. Josiah Gorgas to Amelia Gorgas, August 11, 1869, March 6, 25, [1869], March 19, April 4, 6, 1870; Amelia to Josiah, March 16, 1869, August 4, [1869], Wednesday 1869; Amelia to Josiah, n.d., in Thomas Alvis to Josiah Gorgas, May 11, 1870.

46. Josiah Gorgas to Amelia Gorgas, September 6, 1869, Monday [1869]; Wiggins, ed., *Journal of Josiah Gorgas*, 138. At no time did Amelia express dissatisfaction with her fate as Bertram Wyatt-Brown, *Southern Honor: Ethics and Behavior in the Old South* (New York: Oxford University Press, 1982), 126, suggests was a common attitude among southern white mothers.

47. Josiah Gorgas to Amelia Gorgas, Tuesday; Josiah to Amelia, n.d.

48. Josiah Gorgas to William Crawford Gorgas, February 10, 1876. For the background of this career choice, see Wiggins, "A Victorian Father," 246–50, 325. W. C. Gorgas distinguished himself first during the Spanish-American War when he applied Dr. Walter Reed's discovery of the cause of yellow fever. From 1904 through 1914, Gorgas served as chief sanitation officer for the U.S effort to build the Panama Canal. His success in

eliminating yellow fever and malaria made possible the completion of the canal with a minimum loss of life among the workmen. In 1915 he became U.S. Surgeon General, a post he retained until his retirement in 1918. He died July 4, 1920, in London.

49. Josiah Gorgas to Amelia Gorgas, January 25, [1872], February 2, 1872.
50. Ibid., January 25, February 6, 1872; George R. Fairbanks, *History of the University of the South, at Sewanee, Tennessee* (Jacksonville, FL: The H. & W.B. Drew Company, 1905), 145; Vandiver, *Ploughshares into Swords*, 297.
51. Fairbanks, *History of the University of the South*, 170–71; Vandiver, *Ploughshares into Swords*, 299–300.
52. Josiah Gorgas to Amelia Gorgas, [January 9, 1876], January 17, 1876; Josiah Gorgas to William Crawford Gorgas, March 9, 1877.
53. Josiah Gorgas to Amelia Gorgas, [January 9, 1876], January 17, 1876; Josiah Gorgas to William Crawford Gorgas, March 9, 1877.
53. Josiah Gorgas to William Crawford Gorgas, August 8, 1877; Amelia Gorgas to William Crawford Gorgas, October 14, 1877, December 2, [1877], April 28, [1878], [1878].
54. Josiah Gorgas, to Amelia Gorgas, January 25, 1876.
55. Vandiver, *Ploughshares into Swords*, 302–3.
56. Josiah Gorgas to Amelia Gorgas, [February 1878], [February 1878].
57. Ibid., [February 1878].
58. Ibid., [February 1878], February 8, 22, 1878, February 9, 10, [1878], nine letters [February 1878] with no day of month, February 25, [1878].
59. Josiah Gorgas to Amelia Gorgas, June 29, 1878; N. H. R. Dawson to Josiah Gorgas, July 5, 1878; Josiah Gorgas to William Crawford Gorgas, July 8, 1878; "Trustees Minutes, 1872–1880," University of Alabama, July 1878, 99–103 (microfilm) (Hoole Special Collections Library, University of Alabama, Tuscaloosa).
60. Amelia Gorgas to William Crawford Gorgas, July 15, 1878; Josiah Gorgas to Amelia Gorgas, February 2, 1879; Josiah Gorgas to George R. Fairbanks, November 25, 1878, George R. Fairbanks Papers (University of the South Archives, Sewanee, Tennessee); Vandiver, *Ploughshares into Swords*, 305–7.
61. Josiah Gorgas to Amelia Gorgas, June 16, [1878], August 2, 1878.
62. Josiah Gorgas to William Crawford Gorgas, September 13, 15, 19, 1878; Josiah Gorgas to Amelia Gorgas, September 15, 1878, [October 21, 1878]; Tuscaloosa *Gazette*, July 25, 1878.
63. Josiah Gorgas to Amelia Gorgas, October 15, December 21, 1878, [November 14, 1878].
64. Ibid., September 10, 19, 24, 25, 26, 30, October 6, 18, 23, 26, 31, November 5, 14, 19, 20, December 2, 3, 15, 23, 24, 27, 1878.
65. Amelia Gorgas to William Crawford Gorgas, January 16, February 11, 1879; Josiah Gorgas to Amelia Gorgas, January 30, February 2, 11, 17, 18, 20, 22, 1879.
66. Amelia Gorgas to William Crawford Gorgas, February 27, March 12, [1879], December 28, 1879.
67. Ibid., March 8, 19, May 6, 1879, March 12, [1879]; William Crawford Gorgas to Jessie Gorgas, June 1, 1879, William Crawford Gorgas Papers.
68. [Richard H. Gorgas] to William Crawford Gorgas, October 2, 1879; Amelia Gorgas to William Crawford Gorgas, October 3, 1879.
69. Amelia Gorgas to Sarah [Crawford], May 17, 1883.
70. *Crimson-White*, undated clippings, Gorgas Family Papers.
71. Jessie Gorgas to William Crawford Gorgas, September 30, 1916, William Crawford Gorgas Papers.
72. *Mothers of Invention*, xii, 247, 235.
73. William Crawford Gorgas to Jessie Gorgas, December 24, 1813; William Crawford Gorgas to Richard H. Gorgas, January 4, 1913; William Crawford Gorgas to Minnie Palfrey, December 18, 1914, William Crawford Gorgas Papers.
74. William Crawford Gorgas to Jessie Gorgas, April 4, 1913, October 19, 1914; William Crawford Gorgas to Richard H. Gorgas, January 4, 1913, William Crawford Gorgas Papers.
75. Josiah Gorgas to Amelia Gorgas, [1858].

CHAPTER SEVEN

1. *The Personal Memoirs of Julia Dent Grant*, ed. John Y. Simon (New York: G. P. Putnam's Sons, 1975). Hereafter cited as Julia Grant, *Memoirs*.
2. For more on the Davis and Lee marriages, see chapters one and two in this volume. For more on the Lincoln marriage, see Ruth Painter Randall, *Mary Lincoln: Biography of a Marriage* (Boston: Little, Brown, 1953), and especially Jean H. Baker, *Mary Todd Lincoln: A Biography* (New York: W. W. Norton, 1987).
3. Julia Grant, *Memoirs*, 38.
4. *Personal Memoirs of U. S. Grant*, 2 vols. (New York: Charles L. Webster, 1885–86), I, 32. Hereafter cited as Grant, *Memoirs*.
5. Ibid., I, 38.
6. Edward Chauncey Marshall, *The Ancestry of General Grant and Their Contemporaries* (New York: Sheldon, 1869), 72; Walter B. Stevens, *Grant in Saint Louis* (St. Louis: Franklin Club, 1916), 60–61; Lloyd Lewis, *Captain Sam Grant* (Boston: Little, Brown, 1950), 295, 333–34.
7. Julia Grant, *Memoirs*, 59–60.
8. Ibid., 76.
9. Grant, *Memoirs*, I, 247–48; Julia Grant, *Memoirs*, 92; *The Papers of Ulysses S. Grant*, 24 vols., ed. John Y. Simon (Carbondale and Edwardsville: Southern Illinois University Press, 1967–), II, 70, 83. Hereafter cited as Grant, *Papers*.
10. To Julia Grant, April 30, 1863, Grant, *Papers*, V, 103.
11. Ibid., IV, 119.
12. Julia Grant, *Memoirs*, 106.
13. Frederick Dent Grant, "At the Front with Dad," *Civil War Times Illustrated*, 35, no. 6 (December 1996): 16–31 passim, 99–116.
14. Julia Grant, *Memoirs*, 125–26; Grant, *Memoirs*, II, 110–12.
15. Horace Porter, *Campaigning with Grant* (New York: The Century Company, 1897), 22.
16. Albert D. Richardson, *A Personal History of Ulysses S. Grant* (Hartford: American Publishing Company, 1868), 388.
17. Julia Grant, *Memoirs*, 130.
18. Ibid., 130–31.
19. John A. Rawlins to Mary Emma Rawlins, April 25, 1864, in *The Life of John A. Rawlins*, ed. James Harrison Wilson (New York: Neale Publishing Company, 1916), 425.
20. To Julia Dent Grant, April 27, 1864, Grant, *Papers*, X, 363.
21. Porter, *Campaigning with Grant*, 283.
22. Julia Grant to Mrs. Charles Rogers, February 7, 1865, Grant Papers (Library of Congress).
23. Grant to Lincoln, January 31, 1865, Grant, *Papers*, XIII, 333.
24. Lincoln to Grant, February 1, 1865, *The Collected Works of Abraham Lincoln*, 9 vols., ed. Roy P. Basler et al. (New Brunswick: Rutgers University Press, 1953–55), VIII, 252. Hereafter cited as Lincoln, *Works*.
25. Grant to Stanton, February 1, 1865, Grant, *Papers*, XIII, 345.
26. Lincoln to Seward, February 2, 1865, Lincoln, *Works*, VIII, 256.
27. Julia Grant, *Memoirs*, 141.
28. Grant, *Papers*, XIV, 64.
29. Ibid., XIV, 91.
30. March 3, 1865, ibid., XIII, 281–82.
31. Adam Badeau, *Grant in Peace: From Appomattox to Mount McGregor* (Hartford: S. S. Scranton & Company, 1887), 362.
32. Ibid., 356–58.
33. Ibid., 358–59.
34. Wilson, *Rawlins*, 285–92, 303.
35. Grant, *Papers*, XIV, 366.
36. Julia Grant, *Memoirs*, 157; John Russell Young, *Around the World with General Grant*, 2 vols. (New York: American News Company, 1879), II, 356.
37. Julia Grant, *Memoirs*, 125.

CHAPTER EIGHT

1. Eleanor Sherman Fitch, undated notes, and Marie Sherman Fitch, "Tribute to Ellen Ewing Sherman," unpublished 1892 manuscript, Sherman Family Papers (Archives of the University of Notre Dame).
2. John J. Patrick, "John Sherman: The Early Years, 1823–1865" (Ph.D. dissertation, Kent State University, 1982), 6–7.
3. The most comprehensive information on Thomas Ewing is found in Paul I. Miller, "Thomas Ewing, Last of the Whigs" (Ph.D. dissertation, Ohio State University, 1933); Silvia T. Zsoldos, "The Political Career of Thomas Ewing, Sr." (Ph.D. dissertation, University of Delaware, 1977); Clement L. Martzloff, ed., "Autobiography of Thomas Ewing," Ohio Archaeological and Historical Society, *Publications*, 22 (1913): 126–204.
4. Ellen Sherman, "Recollections for My Children," unpublished manuscript, October 28, 1880, William T. Sherman Papers (Ohio Historical Society), Ellie Ewing Brown, "Notes on the Boyhood of Philemon Beecher Ewing and William Tecumseh Sherman," unpublished manuscript, c.1932, Sherman Family Papers (Archives of the University of Notre Dame).
5. John F. Marszalek, *Sherman: A Soldier's Passion for Order* (New York: The Free Press, 1993), 2–3.
6. Ibid, 12.
7. August 10, 1838, invitation, signed by William Tecumseh Sherman, William T. Sherman Papers (United States Military Academy); William Tecumseh Sherman to Ellen Sherman, May 4, 1839, Sherman Family Papers (Archives of the University of Notre Dame); Anna S. McAllister, *Ellen Ewing, Wife of General Sherman* (New York: Benziger, 1936), 17–18.
8. Anna S. McAllister, *Flame in the Wilderness* (Notre Dame, IN: Sisters of the Holy Cross, 1944), 25–27.
9. William Tecumseh Sherman to Ellen Sherman, April 7, 1842, Sherman Family Papers (Archives of the University of Notre Dame).
10. Marszalek, *Soldier's Passion*, 48–49. In his study of Victorian marriage, Steven Mintz points out that marriage was "viewed by contemporaries as an instrument of satisfaction and as a means to holiness," the latter certainly Ellen's particular hope. Mintz, *A Prison of Expectations, the Family in Victorian Culture* (New York: New York University Press, 1983), 128.
11. Ellen Sherman to W. T. Sherman, July 2, 1844, in McAllister, *Ellen Ewing*, 41; W. T. Sherman to Ellen Sherman, February 8, September 17, 1844, Sherman Family Papers (Archives of the University of Notre Dame).
12. W. T. Sherman to Ellen Sherman, June 30, 1846, Sherman Family Papers (Archives of the University of Notre Dame).
13. Marszalek, *Soldier's Passion*, 52–76; Ellen Sherman to W. T. Sherman, January 19, February 5, May 22, 1849; W. T. Sherman to Ellen Sherman, March 5, 1849, Sherman Family Papers (Archives of the University of Notre Dame). A standard study of nineteenth-century women's health concerns is John S. Haller and Robin M. Haller, *The Physician and Sexuality in Victorian America* (Urbana: University of Illinois Press, 1974).
14. William Tecumseh Sherman, *Memoirs of William T. Sherman* (New York: New American Library, 1990), I, 104–105; McAllister, *Ellen Ewing*, 62–65; Marszalek, *Soldier's Passion*, 81.
15. Marszalek, *Soldier's Passion*, 81–82. The literature on Victorian marriage is a part of the burgeoning number of studies on women, families, and gender. To cite even a small percentage of these works is beyond the scope of this essay. Several that proved helpful in this work include Carl Degler, *At Odds: Women and the Family in America from the Revolution to the Present* (New York: Oxford University Press, 1980); Phyllis Rose, *Parallel Lives: Five Victorian Marriages* (New York: Knopf, 1984); Steven Mintz and Susan Kellogg, *Domestic Revolutions, a Social History of American Family Life* (New York: The Free Press, 1988; Virginia Jeans Laas, *Love and Power in the Nineteenth Century: the Marriage of Violet Blair* (Fayetteville: University of Arkansas Press, 1998).
16. W. T. Sherman to Ellen Sherman, November 1, 1850, Sherman Family Papers (Archives

of the University of Notre Dame); Ellen Sherman to Hugh Boyle Ewing, February 22, 1851, William T. Sherman Papers (Ohio Historical Society).

17. W. T. Sherman to Hugh Boyle Ewing, May 6, December 8, 1851, William T. Sherman Papers (Ohio Historical Society).

18. W. T. Sherman to Thomas Ewing, Jr., August 30, 1852, Thomas Ewing Papers (Library of Congress).

19. Marszalek, *Soldier's Passion*, 90–92.

20. W. T. Sherman to Thomas Ewing, August 22, 1853, Thomas Ewing Papers (Library of Congress).

21. Ellen Sherman to Maria Boyle Ewing, December 1853, in McAllister, *Ellen Ewing*, 98; W. T. Sherman to Thomas Ewing, September 29, 1853, Thomas Ewing Papers (Library of Congress).

22. Marszalek, *Soldier's Passion*, 98–104. Contemporary perception viewed a Victorian wife's role as the bulwark of home and hearth, committed to husband and family. For a discussion of a wife who separated herself from her husband and then even wrote him of her flirtations, see Laas, *Love and Power*, chapters 5 and 6. Ellen Sherman seemingly violated societal mores by leaving her husband and children, but since she spent the time with her parents and one of her children, she could convince herself that she was still demonstrating family loyalty and duty.

23. Ellen Sherman to Maria Boyle Ewing, March 16, 1856, copy, January 4, 1857, copy, Sherman Family Papers (Archives of the University of Notre Dame).

24. W. T. Sherman to Henry S. Turner, July 3, 1856, William T. Sherman Papers (Ohio Historical Society).

25. W. T. Sherman to Ellen Sherman, October 6, 1857, Sherman Family Papers (Archives of the University of Notre Dame).

26. W. T. Sherman to Thomas Ewing, April 2, 15, 1858, Thomas Ewing Papers (Library of Congress).

27. For an extended description of Cump, see John F. Marszalek, *Sherman's Other War: The General and the Civil War Press* (Kent, OH: Kent State University Press, 1999), 30–33.

28. For a discussion of the husband-wife responsibility in the model early nineteenth-century family, see Mintz and Kellogg, *Domestic Revolutions*, 53. Degler, *At Odds*, 31, says, "The supportive qualities and dependence of the 19th-century wife were often matched by similar qualities in her husband."

29. W. T. Sherman to Ellen Sherman, July 28, 1861, Sherman Family Papers (Archives of the University of Notre Dame); McAllister, *Ellen Ewing*, 192.

30. McAllister, *Ellen Ewing*, 198–99; A. K. McClure, *Colonel Alexander K. McClure's Recollections of Half a Century* (Philadelphia: A. T. Hubbard, 1902), 332–33.

31. Marszalek, *Soldier's Passion*, 193–95.

32. Marszalek, *Sherman's Other War*, 71–74.

33. Ellen Sherman to W. T. Sherman, June 9, 1862, Sherman Family Papers (Archives of the University of Notre Dame).

34. Ellen Sherman to W. T. Sherman, March 7, 1862; W. T. Sherman to Ellen Sherman, March 1, 1862, Sherman Family Papers (Archives of the University of Notre Dame).

35. Marszalek, *Soldier's Passion*, 232–34.

36. Ibid., 237–38.

37. Ellen Sherman to W. T. Sherman, July 25, 1864, Sherman Family Papers (Archives of the University of Notre Dame).

38. Ellen Sherman to W. T. Sherman, August 16, 1864; W. T. Sherman to Ellen Sherman, August 9, 1864; Ellen Sherman to John Sherman, August 20, 1864, Sherman Family Papers (Archives of the University of Notre Dame).

39. John F. Marszalek, "The Inventor of Total Warfare," *Notre Dame Magazine*, 18 (Summer, 1989): 28–31; Ellen Sherman to W. T. Sherman, December 30, 1864, Sherman Family Papers (Archives of the University of Notre Dame); W. T. Sherman to Ellen Sherman, January 4, 1865, Sherman Family Papers (Archives of the University of Notre Dame); W. T. Sherman to Thomas Ewing, December 31, 1864, Thomas Ewing Papers (Library of Congress).

40. McAllister, *Ellen Ewing*, 294–98.

41. John F. Marszalek, "The Stanton-Sherman Controversy," *Civil War Times Illustrated*, 9 (October 1970): 4–12; Ellen Sherman to W. T. Sherman, April 26, May 17, 1865, Sherman Family Papers (Archives of the University of Notre Dame).

42. Marszalek, *Soldier's Passion*, 355–57.

43. Maria Sherman Fitch, "Recollections of Ellen Ewing Sherman," William T. Sherman Papers (Ohio Historical Society); Bessie Smith, typed 1914 manuscript concerning the wedding, Sherman Family Papers (Archives of the University of Notre Dame).

44. W. T. Sherman to Philip H. Sheridan, May 5, 1875, Philip H. Sheridan Papers (Library of Congress).

45. Marszalek, *Soldier's Passion*, 409–14.

46. Ellen Sherman to W. T. Sherman, May 27, 1868, Sherman Family Papers (Archives of the University of Notre Dame).

47. See Emory M. Thomas, *Robert E. Lee, a Biography* (New York, W. W. Norton, 1995); Michael Fellman, in his book *Citizen Sherman, a Life of William Tecumseh Sherman* (New York, Random House, 1995), leaves no doubt that he believes Sherman had affairs with Ream and Audenreid. He believes Sherman was a serious womanizer, but at least one reviewer joins this essayist in questioning Fellman's interpretation of the available documentation. James M. McPherson, "Gotterdammerung," *New York Review of Books*, 42 (December 21, 1995): 14–15.

48. Thomas Ewing, III, to B. H. Liddell-Hart, March 5, 1930, Thomas Ewing Papers (Library of Congress); W. T. Sherman to John E. Tourtelotte, December 6, 1888, Sherman Family Papers (Archives of the University of Notre Dame).

CHAPTER NINE

1. The author would like to thank the staff at the Pejepscot Historical Society for a delightful research experience, particularly Julia Oehmig for her assistance and insights, and Jarrod Diels-Roll for his help with photographs. Also my gratitude to the Reverend Dr. William Iams, pastor of the First Parish Church in Brunswick, Maine, for allowing me access to George Adams's diaries, and for our discussions on Adams and his family. This essay has benefited immensely from the exhaustive research done by Alice Rains Trulock and from her biography of Chamberlain. Trulock offers a sympathetic and insightful portrait of the man she unquestionably views as one of America's true heroes. See Alice Rains Trulock, *In the Hands of Providence: Joshua L. Chamberlain and the American Civil War* (Chapel Hill: University of North Carolina Press, 1992), 8–9; Fannie Chamberlain to Lawrence Chamberlain, November 27, 1862, Chamberlain-Adams Family Correspondence (Arthur and Elizabeth Schlesinger Library, Radcliffe College, Harvard University, Cambridge, Massachusetts). Recent works have addressed the relationships between southern husbands and wives during and after the war, such as Carol Bleser and Frederick M. Heath, "The Impact of the Civil War on a Southern Marriage: Clement and Virginia Tunstall Clay of Alabama," *Civil War History* (September 1984): 197–220, and Joan Cashin, " 'Since the War Broke Out': The Marriage of Kate and William McLure," in *Divided Houses: Gender and the Civil War*, ed. Catherine Clinton and Nina Silber (New York: Oxford University Press, 1992), 200–212. Victoria Bynum has done research on postbellum divorce in "Reshaping the Bonds of Womanhood: Divorce in Reconstruction North Carolina," also in Clinton and Silber, eds., *Divided Houses*.

2. Trulock, *In the Hands of Providence*, 43.

3. Adams Family Genealogy, Trulock Collection (Pejepscot Historical Society, Brunswick, Maine); Ashur Adams to Mr. Emmons, June 27, [no year] (Special Collections Room, Hawthorne-Longfellow Library, Bowdoin College, Brunswick, Maine); Charlotte Adams to Fannie Adams, March 12, 1833, Chamberlain-Adams Family Correspondence; Trulock, *In the Hands of Providence*, 43.

4. Thompson Eldridge Ashby, D.D., *A History of the First Parish Church in Brunswick, Maine* (Brunswick, ME: J. H. French and Son, 1969), 156–57.

5. Ibid. 157, n.

6. Charlotte Adams to Fannie Adams, March 12, 1833; Emilia Adams to Fannie Adams, April 3, [1838], both from Chamberlain-Adams Family Correspondence.

7. Charlotte Adams to Fannie Adams, March 12, 1833; Emilia Adams to Fannie Adams, April 3, 1838, both from Chamberlain-Adams Family Correspondence. These admonitions would continue until Fannie was an adult. In a letter vilifying Helen Root Adams in 1853, the always outspoken Cousin D. nevertheless warned Fannie that she must "remain kind and affectionate" with her father [George Adams] and that Fannie could "never cancel the debt of gratitude" she owed him. [Deborah Folsom] to Fannie Adams, February 17, 1853, Joshua Lawrence Chamberlain Papers (Maine Historical Society, Portland).

8. Fannie Adams to [George Adams], August 13, 1838, Chamberlain-Adams Family Correspondence.

9. "Mrs. Chamberlain's Funeral," *Brunswick Record*, October 27, 1905.

10. Fannie Adams to Joshua Chamberlain, June 14, 1851; Fannie Chamberlain to Joshua Chamberlain, [February 1857], both from Chamberlain-Adams Family Correspondence; Charlotte Adams to Fannie Adams, [November 25], 1847 (Bowdoin College).

11. Fannie Adams to [George Adams], August 31, 1838; Emilia Adams to [Fannie Adams], February 19, 1844, both from Chamberlain-Adams Family Correspondence; Charlotte Adams to Fannie Adams, [November 25], 1847 (Bowdoin College); Dr. Adams's diaries frequently mention Fannie's organ lessons. See particularly January–February 1844, Diaries of Dr. George E. Adams (First Parish Church, Brunswick, Maine).

12. Trulock, *In the Hands of Providence*, 43.

13. Ibid., 225–26, 33; Willard M. Wallace, *Soul of the Lion: A Biography of General Joshua L. Chamberlain* (New York: Thomas Nelson and Sons, 1960; reprint, Gettysburg: Stan Clark Military Books, 1991), 20 (page references are to reprint edition).

14. Trulock, *In the Hands of Providence*, 34.

15. Ibid., 34–35.

16. Ibid., 38–43.

17. Trulock, *In the Hands of Providence*, 44–45; Ellen M. Bacon to Fannie Adams, September 28, 1849, Joshua Lawrence Chamberlain papers; Diaries of Dr. George E. Adams, particularly February–May, 1850.

18. Trulock, *In the Hands of Providence*, 45; [Cousin D.] to Fannie Adams, February 17, 1853, Joshua Lawrence Chamberlain Papers; Diaries of Dr. George E. Adams, September 29, 1852, October 13, 1852, November 14, 1852, December 22, 1852, February 5, 6, 17, 1853; Abby A. Orme to Miss Adams, December 9, 1852, Chamberlain-Adams Family Correspondence.

19. Fannie Adams to Lawrence Chamberlain, June 14, 1851, Chamberlain-Adams Family Correspondence.

20. S. M. Allen to Fannie Adams, January 9, 1852, Chamberlain-Adams Family Correspondence; Anna Davis to Fannie Adams, March 10, 1852, Joshua Lawrence Chamberlain Papers.

21. S. M. Allen to Fannie Adams, January 9, 1852, Chamberlain-Adams Family Correspondence; Allen remained a friend to Fannie throughout her life and eventually reconciled himself to her relationship with Lawrence. Allen and Chamberlain later engaged in business ventures together, and his son Horace married Fannie and Lawrence's daughter Grace in 1881. Trulock, *In the Hands of Providence*, 361, 521, n. 79.

22. Joshua Lawrence Chamberlain to Fannie Adams, May 16, 1852, Chamberlain-Adams Family Correspondence.

23. Diaries of Dr. George E. Adams, February 24, 1852, March 29, 1852.

24. Fannie Adams to Charlotte, Milledgeville, January 10, 1853, Joshua Lawrence Chamberlain Papers; Abby A. Orme to Miss Adams, Milledgeville, December 9, 1852, Chamberlain-Adams Family Correspondence.

25. Trulock, *In the Hands of Providence*, 42.

26. Fanny to Charlotte, Milledgeville, January 10, 1853, Joshua Lawrence Chamberlain Papers.

27. Ellen K. Rothman, *Hands and Hearts: A History of Courtship in America* (New York: Basic Books, 1984), 22–23, 249; Richard A. Easterlin, George Alter, and Grechen A. Condran's demographic study of families in the North in 1860 focuses on farm families, but the writers found that on average husbands were three to six years older than their

wives. See Richard A. Easterlin, George Alter, and Grechen A. Condran's "Farms and Farm Families in Old and New Areas: The Northern States in 1860," in *Family and Population in Nineteenth-Century America*, ed. Tamara K. Hareven and Maris A. Vinovskis (Princeton, NJ: Princeton University Press, 1978), 40.

28. Joshua Lawrence Chamberlain to Fannie Adams [undated, probably 1853 or 1854], Chamberlain-Adams Family Correspondence.

29. Rothman's *Hands and Hearts* and Karen Lystra's *Searching the Heart: Women, Men and Romantic Love in Nineteenth-Century America* (New York: Oxford University Press, 1989) both examine courtship practices and find a great deal of discussion about sexuality among middle-class nineteenth-century Americans.

30. Lawrence Chamberlain to Fannie Adams [no date, probably 1853]; Lawrence Chamberlain to Fannie Adams, September 28, 1854, all in Chamberlain-Adams Family Correspondence.

31. Fannie Adams to Joshua Lawrence Chamberlain, June 23, 1865; Lawrence Chamberlain to Fannie Adams, September 28, 1854; Fannie Adams to Lawrence Chamberlain [no date, probably October 1854]; Lawrence Chamberlain to Fannie Adams, November 6, 1854, all in Chamberlain-Adams Family Correspondence.

32. Fannie Adams to Joshua Lawrence Chamberlain, Milledgeville, June 23, 1853.

33. Ashur Adams to "My dear Sir" [Lawrence Chamberlain], October 14, 1854; J. Lawrence Chamberlain to Fannie Adams, October 17, 1854, both in Chamberlain-Adams Family Correspondence.

34. Deborah Folsom to Fannie Adams, December 3, 1855, Joshua Lawrence Chamberlain Papers; Diaries of Dr. George E. Adams, November 29, 1855, December 2, 5, 7, 1855.

35. Joshua Lawrence Chamberlain to Fannie Chamberlain, February 1, 1857, Chamberlain-Adams Family Correspondence.

36. Joshua Lawrence Chamberlain to Fannie Adams Chamberlain, February 1, 1856 [contents suggest it was 1857], Chamberlain-Adams Family Correspondence; Diaries of Dr. George E. Adams, December 7, 1855; Trulock, *In the Hands of Providence*, 53–54; Fannie Adams to Lawrence Chamberlain, February 22, 1854, Chamberlain-Adams Family Correspondence.

37. Joshua Lawrence Chamberlain to Fannie Adams Chamberlain, February 1, 1857; Fannie Adams Chamberlain to Joshua Lawrence Chamberlain, February 8, 1857, both in Chamberlain-Adams Family Correspondence.

38. Fannie Adams Chamberlain to Joshua Lawrence Chamberlain, [February 1857], Chamberlain-Adams Family Correspondence.

39. Joshua Lawrence Chamberlain to Fannie Adams Chamberlain, May 20, 1857, Joshua Lawrence Chamberlain Papers; Fannie Adams Chamberlain to Joshua Lawrence Chamberlain, December 8, 1861, Chamberlain-Adams Family Correspondence.

40. Fannie Adams to Joshua Lawrence Chamberlain, February 22, 1854; Fannie Adams Chamberlain to Joshua Lawrence Chamberlain, January 31, [1857]; A. Nappy to [Lawrence Chamberlain], [February 1857], all in Chamberlain-Adams Family Correspondence; Diaries of Dr. George E. Adams, September 26, 1860, January 16, 1865; Trulock, *In the Hands of Providence*, 56, 57, 331.

41. Trulock, *In the Hands of Providence*, 57, 414, n.; Joshua Lawrence Chamberlain to "Dear Sae," February 19, 1860 (Library of Congress, Washington, D. C.). The letter contains a chilling and heart-rending description of what must have been Anna Davis Atkinson's death.

42. Trulock, *In the Hands of Providence*, 9, 57.

43. Lawrence Chamberlain to Fannie Chamberlain, October 10, 1862 (Library of Congress); for a discussion of the soldier's alienation from those at home, see Reid Mitchell, *The Vacant Chair: The Northern Soldier Leaves Home* (New York: Oxford University Press, 1993), particularly chapter 1, "Soldiering, Manhood, and Coming of Age," and chapter 2, "The Northern Soldier and His Community." Also, Gerald F. Linderman, *Embattled Courage: The Experience of Combat in the American Civil War* (New York: The Free Press, 1987).

44. Joshua Lawrence Chamberlain to Fannie Adams Chamberlain, October 10, 1862 (Library of Congress).

45. Joshua Lawrence Chamberlain to Fannie Adams Chamberlain, April 24, 1863 (Library of Congress).

46. Trulock, *In the Hands of Providence*, 73, 89–103, 111–12. The casualty estimates, which vary slightly among sources, are taken from Stephen W. Sears, *Landscape Turned Red: The Battle of Antietam* (New York: Warner Books, Popular Library, 1983), 327.

47. Trulock, *In the Hands of Providence*, 120–21, 173–74; report of John Benson, Surgeon, Twentieth Maine vols., July 27, 1863, Joshua Lawrence Chamberlain Military Service Records (National Archives, Washington, DC)

48. Trulock, *In the Hands of Providence*, 126–33.

49. John J. Pullen, *The Twentieth Maine: A Volunteer Regiment in the Civil War* (1957; reprint, Dayton, Ohio: Press of Morningside Bookshop, 1984), 111.

50. Trulock, *In the Hands of Providence*, 188, 130–50; Pullen, *The Twentieth Maine*, 104–24; Wallace, *Soul of the Lion*, 89–104; Mark Perry's *Conceived in Liberty: Joshua Lawrence Chamberlain, William Oates, and the American Civil War* (New York: Viking Press, 1997) offers a comparison of these two officers and a detailed look at the events of July 2, 1863.

51. Lawrence Chamberlain to Fanny Chamberlain, July 4, 1863 (Library of Congress).

52. Trulock, *In the Hands of Providence*, 120; Helen [Root Adams] to "My Dear Mother," February 19, 1864 (First Parish Church, Brunswick, Maine); Lawrence Chamberlain to Fanny Chamberlain, July 17, 1863 (Library of Congress). For a description of women's war work, largely in their own words, see Marilyn Mayer Culpepper, *Trials and Triumphs: Women of the American Civil War* (East Lansing: Michigan State University Press, 1991). For an analysis of the complex meanings of war work, see Jeanie Attie, "Warwork and the Crisis of Domesticity in the North," in Clinton and Silber, eds., *Divided Houses*. As to Fannie's participation in women's groups, she seems never to have gotten involved in the organizations available to women. Dr. Adams's diaries frequently mention the women of the parish gathering for temperance and other meetings, but there is never any mention of Fannie attending these meetings.

53. Joshua Lawrence Chamberlain Military Service Records; Fannie Chamberlain to Cousin D., April 14, 1865, Joshua Lawrence Chamberlain Papers; Trulock, *In the Hands of Providence*, 174.

54. Joshua Lawrence Chamberlain to Fannie Adams Chamberlain, June 19, 1864 (Bowdoin College); Trulock, *In the Hands of Providence*, 203–9, 214–15.

55. Trulock, *In the Hands of Providence*, 188, 203–9, 218–19; William H. Annesley, Jr., Wauwatosa, Wisconsin, to John Mulldy, M.D., September 29, 1986, Trulock Collection.

56. [George E. Adams] to Lawrence Chamberlain, September 6, 1864, Chamberlain-Adams Family Correspondence; Lawrence Chamberlain to Joshua Chamberlain, Esq., February 20, 1865 (Bowdoin College); Diaries of Dr. George E. Adams, January 16, 1865.

57. Lawrence Chamberlain to Sae Chamberlain, April 13, 1865 (Library of Congress).

58. Trulock, *In the Hands of Providence*, 334.

59. Ibid., 224, 331, 362.

60. Sara Chamberlain to Joshua Lawrence Chamberlain, Fast Day, 1866; Fannie Chamberlain to Joshua Lawrence Chamberlain, March 8, 19, 1866; Joshua Lawrence Chamberlain to Fannie Chamberlain, April 7, 1866; Fannie Chamberlain to Joshua Lawrence Chamberlain, April 15, May 1, 1866, all in Chamberlain-Adams Family Correspondence.

61. Fannie Chamberlain to Lawrence Chamberlain, March 8, 19, 1866; Lawrence Chamberlain to Fannie Chamberlain, March 23, 1866, all in Chamberlain-Adams Family Correspondence.

62. Trulock, *In the Hands of Providence*, 335–38.

63. Ibid., 339–41

64. Ibid., 337, 340.

65. Ibid., 337–41; Lawrence Chamberlain to Fannie Chamberlain, November 20, 1868, Joshua Lawrence Chamberlain Papers.

66. Trulock, *In the Hands of Providence*, 342–43.

67. Ibid., 345–47.

68. Ibid., 335–59.

69. Joshua Lawrence Chamberlain to Fannie Chamberlain, January 15, [1880] (Bowdoin College).

70. Trulock, *In the Hands of Providence*, 348–49, 354–55.

71. Joshua Lawrence Chamberlain to Fannie Chamberlain, [1891 or 1892], Joshua Lawrence Chamberlain Papers; Joshua Lawrence Chamberlain to "My dear Gracie," February 15, 1887, Bowdoin College.

72. Trulock, *In the Hands of Providence*, 361, 372; Wyllys to "My dear Daise," August 9, 1886 (Bowdoin College); Joshua Lawrence Chamberlain to Frances Adams Chamberlain, [no date, 1891?, 1892?], Joshua Lawrence Chamberlain Papers.

73. Joshua Lawrence Chamberlain to "My dear Grace," December 13, 1886; Grace to Fannie Chamberlain, April 19, 1883 (both in Bowdoin College); Joshua Lawrence Chamberlain to Sae, April 4, 1899 (Library of Congress).

74. Joshua Lawrence Chamberlain to Fannie Chamberlain, August 8, 1885, Joshua Lawrence Chamberlain Papers; Trulock, *In the Hands of Providence*, 367.

75. Trulock, *In the Hands of Providence*, 369.

76. Joshua Lawrence Chamberlain to Frances Adams Chamberlain, [no date, 1891?, 1892?], Joshua Lawrence Chamberlain Papers.

77. Trulock, *In the Hands of Providence*, 363, 372–76; Wallace, *Soul of the Lion*, 309–10.

CHAPTER TEN

1. Shirley A. Leckie, *Elizabeth Bacon Custer and the Making of a Myth* (Norman: University of Oklahoma Press, 1993; Paperback edition, 1998), 1–22. This essay builds on this earlier work and also information gained from *The Civil War Memories of Elizabeth Bacon Custer*. Reconstructed from the diaries and notes by Arlene Reynolds (Austin: University of Texas Press, 1994). Like many others, I am also indebted to the insights on gender relations during the Civil War that are provided in Catherine Clinton and Nina Silber, eds., *Divided Houses: Gender and the Civil War*, introduction by James M. McPherson (New York: Oxford University Press, 1992). Excellent material on Elizabeth and George Armstrong Custer during the Civil War is also found in Marguerite Merington, ed., *The Custer Story: The Life and Intimate Letters of General George A. Custer and His Wife Elizabeth* (Lincoln: University of Nebraska Press, 1987; reprint, New York: Devon-Adair Company, 1950).

2. Lawrence A. Frost, *General Custer's Libbie* (Seattle: Superior Publishing Company, 1976), 35–42; Louise K. Barnett, *Touched by Fire: The Life, Death, and Mythic Afterlife of George Armstrong Custer* (New York: Henry Holt, 1996), 21.

3. Merington, *The Custer Story*, 47, 51–52; Kent Steckmesser, *The Western Hero in History and Legend* (Norman: University of Oklahoma Press, 1965), 202; Robert Utley, *Cavalier in Buckskin: George Armstrong Custer and the Western Military Frontier* (Norman: University of Oklahoma Press, Oklahoma Western Biographies, 1988), 18–19; Jeffry D. Wert, *Custer: The Controversial Life of George Armstrong Custer* (New York: Simon & Schuster, 1996), 101–10.

4. Wert, *Custer*, 22; Merington, *The Custer Story*, 48–49; Utley, *Cavalier in Buckskin*, 14; Charles B. Wallace, *Custer's Ohio Boyhood* (Freeport, OH: Freeport Press, 1978), 23–24; Jay Monaghan, *Custer: The Life of General George Armstrong Custer* (Boston: Little, Brown, 1957), 10–11; Wert, *Custer*, 22–40.

5. Frost, *General Custer's Libbie*, 51–59; Barnett, *Touched by Fire*, 23.

6. Frost, *General Custer's Libbie*, 62.

7. Ibid.

8. Reynolds, ed., *Civil War Memories*, 3–8.

9. Karen Lystra, *Searching the Heart: Women, Men, and Romantic Love in Nineteenth-Century America* (New York: Oxford University Press, 1989), 79.

10. Wert, *Custer*, 71–86. Wert presents evidence that Custer may have learned of his promotion before he opened the letter on June 28.

11. Utley, *Cavalier in Buckskin*, 22–23; James M. McPherson, *Ordeal by Fire: The Civil War and Reconstruction* (New York: Oxford University Press, 1982), 330.

12. Utley, *Cavalier in Buckskin*, 24–25; Stephen E. Ambrose, "Custer's Civil War," *Timeline*, 7 (August–September 1990): 28.

13. Isaac P. Christiancy served intermittently as associate justice on the Michigan Supreme

Court and United States senator from 1875 to 1879. Talcott E. Wing, ed., *History of Monroe County, Michigan* (New York: Munsell and Company, 1890), 247; Ronald P. Formisano, *The Birth of Mass Political Parties* (Princeton, NJ: Princeton University Press, 1971), 214, 253; Frost, *General Custer's Libbie*, 81, 83; Wert, *Custer*, 106; Daniel Bacon to Armstrong, December 12, 1863, Lawrence A. Frost Collection of Custeriana (Monroe County Historical Commission Archives).

14. Frost, *General Custer's Libbie*, 76–82; Barnett, *Touched by Fire*, 42; Libbie to Autie, [November] 1863, January 1864, Merington, *The Custer Story*, 74, 78, 80.

15. Utley, *Cavalier in Buckskin*, 36.

16. Gerald Linderman explores the connection between one's response to combat and manliness in *Embattled Courage: The Experience of Combat in the Civil War* (New York: The Free Press, 1987). Two essays that look at combat from the perspective of male gender roles are Reid Mitchell, "Soldiering, Manhood, and Coming of Age: A Northern Volunteer," *Divided Houses*, 43–54, and David W. Blight, "No Desperate Hero: Manhood and Freedom in a Union Soldier's Experience," in Clinton and Silber, eds., *Divided Houses*, 55–75.

17. Autie to Libbie, January 8, 1869, Marguerite Merington Papers (Rare Books and Manuscript Division, New York Public Library, Astor, Lenox and Tilden Foundations, New York City); Autie to Libbie, November 22, 1863, Brice Custer Calhoun Collection, a Private Collection.

18. Autie to Libbie, April 10, 1867, Elizabeth B. Custer, *Tenting on the Plains; or, General Custer in Kansas and Texas* (New York: Charles L. Webster, 1887), 552–53.

19. Autie to Daniel Bacon, January 19, 1864, Marguerita Merington Papers. See Merington, *The Custer Story*, 80, for an altered and heavily edited version.

20. Gregory J. W. Urwin, *Custer Victorious: The Civil War Battles of General George Armstrong Custer* (East Brunswick, NJ: Associated University Presses, 1983), 51–52; James M. McPherson, *Battle Cry of Freedom: The Civil War Era* (New York: Oxford University Press, 1988), 559–60; Frederick Whittaker, *The Complete Life of Gen. George A. Custer* (New York: Sheldon & Company, 1876), 132–33. During the last year of his life, Custer began writing his Civil War memoirs for *Galaxy Magazine*, which published the first four installments in March, April, May, and June, 1876. Portions of another installment appeared in October 1876, ending with events in May 1862. In these Custer depicts President Lincoln as interfering with McClellan's strategy and preventing a speedy and honorable end to the war. See *Custer in the Civil War: His Unfinished Memoirs*, compiled and edited by John M. Carroll (San Rafael, CA: Presidio Press, 1977), 112–14, 136–43.

21. Richard Slotkin, *The Fatal Environment: The Myth of the Frontier in the Age of Industrialization, 1800–1890* (New York: Atheneum, 1985), 381–82.

22. Autie to Daniel Bacon, January 19, 1864, Marguerite Merington Papers. See also Merington, *The Custer Story*, 80, for an altered and edited version. G. A. Custer to Honorable J. M. Howard, January 4, 1864, January 19, 1864, in Hamilton G. Howard, *Civil War Echoes: Character Sketches and State Secrets* (Washington, DC: Howard Publishing Company, 1907), 304–13.

23. Libbie to Daniel Bacon, February 1864, Merington, *The Custer Story*, 84.

24. Ibid., 84–85.

25. Reynolds, ed., *Civil War Memories*, 38. See also Elizabeth B. Custer, "Writings of West Point," Microfilm Roll 5, Frames 5128 and 5199, Elizabeth B. Custer Collection (Little Bighorn Battlefield National Monument, Crow Agency, Montana).

26. Ibid.

27. Frost, *General Custer's Libbie*, 94.

28. E. B. Custer, "Manuscript with Some Corrections," Elizabeth B. Custer Collection, Roll 5, Frame 4174.

29. Libbie to parents, March 20, 1864, Marguerite Merington Papers.

30. Reynolds, ed., *Civil War Memories*, 44–52.

31. Frost, *General Custer's Libbie*, 100.

32. E. B. Custer, "Stevensburg," Elizabeth B. Custer Collection, Roll 5, Frame 4460.

33. *Harper's Weekly* (March 19, 1864), (March 26, 1864); Frost, *General Custer's Libbie*, 103; Libbie to parents, April 1864; Merington, *The Custer Story*, 87–89.

34. Paul A. Hutton, *Phil Sheridan and His Army* (Lincoln: University of Nebraska Press, 1985), 14; Jay Monaghan, *The Life of General George A. Custer* (Boston: Little, Brown, 1957), 187–88.

35. Pamela Herr, *Jessie Benton Frémont* (Norman: University of Oklahoma Press, 1987; originally published by Franklin Watts, 1987), 333–39.

36. *Wartime Washington: The Civil War Letters of Elizabeth Blair Lee*, ed. Virginia Jeans Laas (Urbana: University of Illinois Press, 1991), 164–75, 347–50; Dudley T. Cornish and Virginia Laas, *Lincoln's Lee: The Life of Samuel Phillips Lee, United States Navy, 1812–1897* (Lawrence: University of Kansas Press, 1986), 162–63. The ladylike but very effective ways that these women advanced their husbands' careers are discussed in separate chapters in this volume.

37. Mary Karl George, *Zachariah Chandler: A Political Biography* (East Lansing: Michigan State University Press, 1969), 63–67; Libbie to Parents, Merington, *The Custer Story*, 89–91.

38. Reynolds, ed., *Civil War Memories*, 72–73, 108–9.

39. Autie to Libbie, April 1864; Libbie to Autie, July 1864, October 1864, Merington, *The Custer Story*, 93, 113, 122–23.

40. Monaghan, *Custer*, 8; Frost, *General Custer's Libbie*, 299; Slotkin, *The Fatal Environment*, 376; Emory M. Thomas, *Bold Dragoon: The Life of J.E.B. Stuart* (New York: Harper & Row, 1986), 181; Brian W. Dippie, "George A. Custer," *Soldiers West: Biographies from the Military Frontier* (Lincoln: University of Nebraska Press, 1987), 101.

41. Cited by Frost, *General Custer's Libbie*, 114.

42. Reynolds, ed. *Civil War Memories*, 132.

43. Merington, *The Custer Story*, 100–101, 115–16, 120–21, 124, 99. (The quotation is on page 99.)

44. Representative F. W. Kellogg to George A. Custer, April 17, 1864, Elizabeth B. Custer Collection, Roll 2.

45. Merington, *The Custer Story*, 91.

46. Ibid., 93.

47. Colonel Benjamin Grierson described his ongoing improvements as a result of the influence of his wife, Alice Kirk Grierson, during the Civil War. William H. Leckie and Shirley A. Leckie, *Unlikely Warriors: General Benjamin H. Grierson and His Family* (Norman: University of Oklahoma Press, 1984), 28–29. See also William W. Hassler, ed., *The General to His Lady: The Civil War Letters of William Dorsey Pender to Fanny Pender* (Chapel Hill: University of North Carolina Press, 1966), 57–58.

48. Merington, *The Custer Story*, 92.

49. Ibid.

50. Autie to Libbie, May 1, 1864, Merington, *The Custer Story*, 95.

51. Libbie to parents, May 1, 1864, Merington, *The Custer Story*, 94.

52. McPherson, *Ordeal by Fire*, 410–24.

53. Custer to Elizabeth, May 4, 1864, Merington, *The Custer Story*, 95.

54. James M. McPherson, *Battle Cry of Freedom: The Civil War Era* (New York: Oxford University Press, 1988), 728; Libbie to parents, May 22, 1864, Merington, *The Custer Story*, 98.

55. Merington, *The Custer Story*, 109.

56. Autie to Libbie, May 16, 1864, Merington, *The Custer Story*, 97–98; Autie to Libbie, May 17, 1864, Marguerite Merington Papers.

57. Autie to Libbie, 17 May 1864, Marguerite Merington Papers.

58. Ambrose, "Custer's Civil War," 29.

59. Daniel Bacon to Libbie, June 1864, Merington, *The Custer Story*, 103.

60. Wert, *Custer*, 156–65; Urwin, *Custer Victorious*, 163–64.

61. Autie to Libbie, June 21, 1864, Merington, *The Custer Story*, 103–105.

62. Ibid., 105.

63. Libbie to Autie, June 1864, Merington, *The Custer Story*, 105–6.

64. Libbie to Autie, June 1864, ibid., 112.

65. Reynolds, ed., *Civil War Memories*, 7.

66. Libbie to Autie, June 10, 1864, Merington, *The Custer Story*, 102.

67. Libbie to Autie, October 30, 1864, cited by Frost, *General Custer's Libbie*, 121.

68. Wert, *Custer*, 34–35.

69. Merington, *The Custer Story*, 102.
70. Autie to Libbie, October 28, 1864, Merington, *The Custer Story*, 129; Autie to Libbie, October 31, 1868, cited by Frost, *Custer's Libbie*, 177.
71. Autie to Libbie, October 28, 1864, Merington, *The Custer Story*, 129; Autie to Libbie, October 31, 1868, cited by Frost, *General Custer's Libbie*, 177; John B. Kennedy, "A Soldier's Widow," *Collier's* (January 29, 1927), 10, 41.
72. McPherson, *Battle Cry of Freedom*, 732.
73. Libbie to parents, June, 1864, Merington, *The Custer Story*, 108–109; Margaret Leech, *Reveille in Washington, 1860–1865* (New York: Harper's, 1941), 326.
74. Elizabeth B. Custer, "Civil War," rough draft notes, Microfilm Roll 5, Elizabeth B. Custer Collection. See also Reynolds, ed., *Civil War Memories*, 90–91; Barnett, *Touched by Fire*, 37.
75. Libbie to Autie, June 1864, Merington, *The Custer Story*, 100.
76. Libbie to Autie, early June 1864, ibid., 101.
77. Libbie to Autie, July 1864, ibid., 113.
78. Caroline Dana Howe's poem is reprinted in Reynolds, ed., *Civil War Memories*, 173–75.
79. Merington, *The Custer Story*, 114; Frost, *General Custer's Libbie*, 112; Reynolds, ed., *Civil War Memories*, 93; Elizabeth Custer Questionnaire, April 3, 1870, Topeka, Kansas, Frank Mericante, Grand Rapids, Michigan. Typescript copy in Elizabeth Custer File in George Armstrong Custer Collection of the Monroe County Library System, Ellis Reference and Information Center, Monroe, Michigan.
80. McPherson, *Battle Cry of Freedom*, 758–73.
81. Bruce Catton, *The Civil War* (New York: Fairfax Press, 1980; reprint, American Heritage, 1960), 229–30; George A. Custer to Isaac Christiancy, September 16, 1864; Wert, *Custer*, 178–79.
82. Wert, *Custer*, 188; McPherson, *Ordeal by Fire*, 190.
83. Wert, *Custer*, 189.
84. Libbie to Autie, October 1864, Merington, *The Custer Story*, 122–23.
85. Libbie to Daniel Bacon, October 1864, ibid., 120.
86. Monaghan, *Custer*, 218–19; Libbie to parents, October 1864, Merington, *The Custer Story*, 127–28.
87. Elizabeth to parents, December 4, 1864, Merington, *The Custer Story*, 134–35; see also Reynolds, ed., *Civil War Memories*, 79.
88. E. B. Custer, "Stevensburg Series," Elizabeth B. Custer Collection, Roll 5, Frames 4030–34; Elizabeth to parents, December 4, 1864, Merington, *The Custer Story*, 134–35; see also Reynolds, ed., *Civil War Memories*, 79.
89. Gerald H. Shattuck, Jr., *A Shield and a Hiding Place: The Religious Life of the Civil War Armies* (Macon, GA: Mercer University Press, 1987), 89; Frost, *General Custer's Libbie*, 124; Daniel Bacon to Autie, February 8, 1865, Frost Collection.
90. Emmanuel Custer to Libbie, March 1865, Merington, *The Custer Story*, 144.
91. Libbie to Autie, March 8, 1865, ibid., 136–37.
92. Autie to Libbie, 16 March 1865, ibid., 141; Ambrose estimates twelve horses. "Custer's Civil War," 31.
93. Libbie to Autie, June 1864, Merington, *The Custer Story*, 101.
94. Libbie to Autie, September 6, 1864, ibid., 115.
95. Reynolds, ed., *Civil War Memories*, 96.
96. Autie to Libbie, March 30, 1865, Marguerite Merington Papers.
97. McPherson, *Battle Cry*, 849; Elizabeth B. Custer, "Where Grant Wrote Peace," *Harper's Weekly* (June 24, 1911), 6–7.
98. Philip Sheridan to Libbie, April 10, 1865; Custer, "Where Grant Wrote Peace," 7.
99. Libbie to parents, April, 1865, Merington, *The Custer Story*, 165. See also Elizabeth Custer, "Where Grant Wrote Peace," 6–7. The Appomattox table was given to the Smithsonian Institution after Elizabeth Custer's death. As a national treasure its value is beyond price.
100. Libbie to Laura Noble, April 1865, Merington, *The Custer Story*, 164.
101. Libbie to Autie, October 1864, ibid., 121.
102. Utley, *Cavalier in Buckskin*, 36.
103. Ibid., 36–56; Minnie Dubbs Millbrook, "The Boy General and How He Grew: George

Custer after Appomattox," *Montana: The Magazine of Western History*, 23 (Spring 1973): 34–43 and "The West Breaks in General Custer," *Kansas Historical Quarterly*, 36 (Summer 1970): 113–48.

104. Utley, *Cavalier in Buckskin*, 57–77.

105. Ibid.; Wert, *Custer*, 169–76, 267–71.

106. *Philadelphia Inquirer*, July 7, 1876; *New York Herald*, September 2, 1876; Charles King, "Custer's Last Battle," *Harper's New Monthly Magazine* (August 1890): 378–87; Robert Hughes, "The Campaign against the Sioux in 1876," *Journal of the Military Service Institution of the United States*, 79 (January 1896): 1–44; Cyrus T. Brady, *Indian Fights and Fighters: The Soldier and the Sioux* (New York: McClure, Phillips, 1904).

107. Utley, *Cavalier in Buckskin*, 107; Autie to Libbie, March 29, 1866, April 1, 1866, April 3, 1866, undated [Spring, 1871], Merington, *The Custer Story*, 180–81, 232, 234, 236, 237; Autie to Libbie, April 8, 1866, Brice Custer Calhoun Collection; Ben Clark, interviewed by W. M. Camp, Ben Clark Field Notes, Box 2, Folder F, Walter Camp Manuscript (Lilly Library, Indiana University, Bloomington).

108. Autie to Libbie, May 1, 1871, cited by Frost, *General Custer's Libbie*, 193–94.

109. Michael Tate, " 'The Girl He Left Behind': Elizabeth Custer and the Making of a Legend," *Red River Valley Historical Review*, 5 (Winter 1980): 5–23; Leckie, *Elizabeth Bacon Custer and the Making of a Myth*, 209–12. Whittaker's book was published by Sheldon and Company of New York City in 1876. For information on the impact Whittaker's book had on imaginative and artistic works, see Robert Utley, *Custer and the Great Controversy: The Origin and Development of a Legend* (Pasadena, CA: Westernlore Press, 1980), 121; Don Russell, *Custer's Last* (Fort Worth: Amon Carter Museum of Western Art, 1968); Ella Wilcox, *Custer and Other Poems* (Chicago: W. B. Conkey, 1886). For an excellent, more recent analysis of the Battle of the Little Bighorn paintings, see Brian W. Dippie, " 'What Valor Is': Artists and the Mythic Moment," *Montana: The Magazine of Western History*, 46 (Autumn 1996): 40–55.

110. Harper and Brothers published the first (the full title is *"Boots and Saddles"; or, Life in Dakota with General Custer*) and the third. Charles L. Webster published the second (the full title is *Tenting on the Plains; or, General Custer in Kansas and Texas*.

111. "Opinions of the press on *The Boy General*," promotional brochure for Scribner Series of School Reading, Brice Custer Calhoun Collection.

112. Frost, *General Custer's Libbie*, 292; unidentified newspaper, June [3], 1910, Elizabeth B. Custer Collection, Roll 6, Frame 6326.

113. Unidentified newspaper, June [3], 1910, Elizabeth B. Custer Collection, Roll 6, Frame 6326.

114. As noted in earlier endnotes, this work was published by the University of Texas Press.

115. *Chicago Dial*, May 1888; *Current Literature*, August 1888, Custer Collection, *Tenting on the Plains* Scrapbook, Box 7 (Monroe County Historical Commission Archives).

116. Barnett, *Touched by Fire*, 367.

117. Howard, *Civil War Echoes*, 241.

118. John B. Kennedy, "A Soldier's Widow," 10, 41.

119. Leckie, *Elizabeth Bacon Custer and the Making of a Myth*, 263–65; Kenneth T. Jackson, *Crabgrass Frontier: The Suburbanization of America* (New York: Oxford University Press, 1985), 95–96.

120. Frederic Van de Water, *Glory-Hunter: A Life of General Custer* (Indianapolis: Bobbs-Merrill, 1934), 123.

CHAPTER ELEVEN

1.   This essay, while focusing more directly on the Frémonts' marriage during the Civil War, draws upon material in Pamela Herr, *Jessie Benton Frémont* (New York: Franklin Watts, 1987) and Pamela Herr and Mary Lee Spence, eds., *The Letters of Jessie Benton Frémont* (Urbana: University of Illinois Press, 1993). Allan Nevins, *Frémont: Pathmaker of the West* (1955; reprint, Lincoln: University of Nebraska Press, 1992) remains the most comprehensive biography of John Charles Frémont, particularly in its treatment of the Civil War period, while Mary Lee Spence and Donald Jackson, eds., *The Expeditions of*

John Charles Frémont, vols. 1–3 (Urbana: University of Illinois Press, 1970–84), is an invaluable source not only on the expeditions but on the Frémonts in general. Jessie Benton Frémont and her son Francis Preston ("Frank") Frémont defended John Charles Frémont's Civil War record at length in an unpublished 1891 ms., "Great Events during the Life of Major General John C. Frémont . . . and of Jessie Benton Frémont," 217–381, Frémont Papers (Bancroft Library, University of California, Berkeley).

Particularly useful to me as I examined the Frémonts' marriage during the Civil War period were Catherine Clinton and Nina Silber, eds., *Divided Houses: Gender and the Civil War* (New York: Oxford University Press, 1992) and Elizabeth D. Leonard, *Yankee Women: Gender Battles in the Civil War* (New York: W. W. Norton, 1994). Several other works, while focusing on southern women, were also helpful: Carol Bleser, ed., *In Joy and in Sorrow: Women, Family, and Marriage in the Victorian South, 1830–1890* (New York: Oxford University Press, 1991); Catherine Clinton, *Tara Revisited: Women, War, & the Plantation Legend* (New York: Abbeville Press, 1995); and Drew Gilpin Faust, *Mothers of Invention: Women of the Slaveholding South in the American Civil War* (Chapel Hill: University of North Carolina Press, 1996).

2. A reliable witness, lawyer Frederick Billings, who traveled with John Frémont from San Francisco to Europe, mentioned his "woman," a Margaret Corbett, as well as her child, as also on board (to Trenor W. Park, January 14, February 22, 1861, Billings Mansion Archives, Woodstock, VT). For a somewhat dubious denial of this story, see George W. Wright to Montgomery Blair, March 12, [1861], Blair Papers (Library of Congress, Washington, D.C.). An earlier rumor about John Frémont arose after the 1856 presidential election, when campaign biographer John Bigelow became convinced that Frémont had "debauched" a servant girl in the Frémont household; the story is discussed in Preston King to Gideon Welles, March 3, April 9, 21, 1860, Welles Papers (Library of Congress); and Welles to Francis Preston Blair, April 9, 1860, Blair Papers.

3. For Frémont's negotiations, see Frederick Billings to Trenor W. Park, February 4, 6, 11, 22, and April 12, 1861; John Frémont to Billings, March 16, [1861], Billings Mansion Archives.

4. John Frémont to Francis Preston Blair, May 24, 1861, quoted in Nevins, *Frémont*, 474.

5. William M. Davis to Henry Kirke Brown, July 1, 1861, typescript, 1339, Henry Kirke Brown Papers (Library of Congress).

6. Jessie Benton Frémont to John C. Hopper, [May 1861], quoted in Nevins, *Frémont*, 473.

7. Jessie Frémont to the Reverend John A. Anderson, May [June] 11, [1861], Kansas Historical Society (Topeka).

8. Jessie Frémont, *A Year of American Travel* (1878; new ed., San Francisco: Book Club of California, 1960), 25.

9. Jessie Frémont to Lydia Maria Child, [late July/August 1856], Herr and Spence, *Letters*, 122–23.

10. In early adulthood, John Frémont added both a "t" and an accent to his surname.

11. Anna [Anne] Pryor to John Lowry, August 28, 1811, copy in Pryor ms. divorce petition (Virginia State Library, Richmond). John Pryor, with Anne's concurrence, applied to the Virginia legislature for a divorce but it was denied. Thus John Frémont's parents were apparently never able to marry.

12. Rebecca Harding Davis, *Bits of Gossip* (Boston: Houghton Mifflin, 1904), 175.

13. Charles Sumner to George Bancroft, April 22, 1846, Bancroft Papers (Massachusetts Historical Society, Boston).

14. On Jessie Frémont's various protests, see Herr, *Jessie Benton Frémont*, 47–50.

15. Jessie Frémont, quoted in Thomas Starr King to Randolph Ryers, October 19, 1860, King Papers (Bancroft Library).

16. Jessie Frémont to Samuel T. Pickard, April 1893, Samuel T. Pickard, *Life and Letters of John Greenleaf Whittier*, 2 vols. (Boston: Houghton Mifflin, 1895), II, 462.

17. Harvey Lewis Carter, *'Dear Old Kit': The Historical Christopher Carson* (Norman: University of Oklahoma Press, 1968), 122. It was most probably Jessie Frémont herself, in an unsigned June 15, 1847, article in the Washington *Union*, who first brought Carson to national attention; subsequently, the Frémonts' reports made him famous.

18. Jessie Frémont, typescript "Memoirs," 41, Frémont Papers (Bancroft Library).

19. John C. Frémont, *Memoirs of My Life . . .* (Chicago: Belford, Clark, 1887), 163.

20. *New York Tribune*, June 12, 1856. It was John C. Frémont's name and gallant image, rather than his actual presence, that the Republican campaign required. As was customary for presidential candidates during this period, both Frémont, who spoke with a slight stutter, and his opponent, the lackluster James Buchanan, remained at home during the campaign, receiving visitors and issuing occasional public letters, while their supporters spoke on their behalf. Thus even Abraham Lincoln, who spoke actively for Frémont in 1856, remained at home when he himself ran for president four years later.

21. Lydia Maria Child to Sarah Shaw, August 3, 1856, Milton Meltzer and Patricia G. Holland, eds., *Lydia Maria Child: Selected Letters, 1817–1880* (Amherst: University of Massachusetts Press, 1982), 291.

22. Jessie Frémont to John Frémont, July 29, [1857], Herr and Spence, *Letters*, 167.

23. John Frémont to Francis Preston Blair, July 16, 1858, Blair Papers.

24. For more about Elizabeth Blair Lee, see Virginia Jeans Laas's chapter on Elizabeth Blair and S. Phillips Lee in this volume as well as Laas, ed., *Wartime Washington: The Civil War Letters of Elizabeth Blair Lee* (Urbana: University of Illinois Press, 1991). On the friendship between Jessie Frémont and Lizzie, see Pamela Herr and Mary Lee Spence, " 'I Really Had Something Like the Blues': Letters from Jessie Benton Frémont to Elizabeth Blair Lee, 1847–1883," *Montana: The Magazine of Western History*, 41 (Spring 1991): 16–31.

25. Jessie Frémont to Elizabeth Blair Lee, June 2, 1860, Herr and Spence, *Letters*, 227–28.

26. *New York Times*, July 14, 1861.

27. Jessie Frémont to Thomas Starr King, July 20, [1861], Herr and Spence, *Letters*, 253.

28. Jessie Frémont, *The Story of the Guard* (Boston: Ticknor and Fields, 1863), 223.

29. *New York Times*, August 11, 1861.

30. Davis, *Bits*, 175.

31. *New York Times*, August 11, 1861.

32. John Frémont to Frederick Billings, July 1, 1861, Billings Mansion Archives.

33. *New York Tribune*, October 11, 1861.

34. Thomas Starr King to Henry Bellows, March 18, 1862, Bellows Papers (Massachusetts Historical Society, Boston; photocopy, Bancroft Library).

35. John Frémont, "In Command in Missouri," in *Battles and Leaders of the Civil War*, ed. Robert Underwood Johnson and Clarence Clough Buel, 4 vols. (New York: Century, 1887), I, 279.

36. Jessie Frémont and F. P. Frémont, "Great Events," 224; *New York Times*, July 19, 1861.

37. Jessie Benton Frémont to Elizabeth Blair Lee, July 27, [1861] and [December] 14, [1855], Herr and Spence, *Letters*, 255–56; 82. Jessie Frémont wrote at least eighty-five letters to Lizzie Lee between 1847 and 1861. While much of their contents, dealing with family and domestic matters, might be called "womanish," during the 1856 Frémont presidential campaign, when Lizzie's father, Francis Preston Blair, was one of John's most active supporters, politics was also a frequent topic. Unfortunately, Lizzie's return letters have been lost.

38. Jessie Frémont to Montgomery Blair, [July 28, 1861] and July 31, [1861], Herr and Spence, *Letters*, 256–57.

39. John C. Frémont to Abraham Lincoln, July 30, 1861, in *The War of the Rebellion: A Compilation of the Official Records of the Union and Confederate Armies*, 129 vols. (Washington, DC: U.S. Government Printing Office, 1880–1902), ser. 1, III, 416–17.

40. Jessie Frémont to Montgomery Blair, August 5, [1861], Herr and Spence, *Letters*, 260.

41. [Jessie Frémont] to Abraham Lincoln, August 5, 1861, Herr and Spence, *Letters*, 262.

42. Francis Grierson, "The Lights and Shadows of Life," typescript, 91 (Illinois State Historical Society, Springfield).

43. Jessie Frémont to Montgomery Blair, August 5, [1861], Herr and Spence, *Letters*, 261.

44. John Raymond Howard, *Remembrance of Things Past* (New York: Thomas Y. Crowell, 1925), 82.

45. Elizabeth Benton Frémont, *Recollections. . . . ,* compiled by I. T. Martin (New York: F. H. Hitchcock, 1912), 126.

46. Jessie Frémont to Frederick Billings, November 18, [1861], Billings Mansion Archives; Jessie Frémont to Billings, November 4, 1861, Herr and Spence, *Letters*, 295–96.

47. Jessie Frémont, *Guard*, x.
48. *New York Times*, August 18, 1861.
49. On the Wilson's Creek battle and Lyon's death, see Jessie Frémont and F. P. Frémont, "Great Events," 238; Nevins, *Frémont*, 485–88.
50. Notebook 6, Eliot Papers (Washington University, St. Louis). Eliot, incidentally, was the grandfather of the poet T. S. Eliot.
51. *St. Louis Democrat*, August 27, 1861, clipping in Notebook 6, Eliot Papers. It was most likely Jessie Frémont who saw to it that Dix's mission was also favorably reported in other newspapers. See, for example, the *New York Tribune*, September 6, 1861.
52. Allan Nevins and Milton Halsey Thomas, eds., *The Diary of George Templeton Strong*, 4 vols. (New York: Macmillan, 1952), III, 174.
53. Jessie Frémont and F. P. Frémont, "Great Events," 208.
54. Eliot describes the work of the Western Sanitary Commission in "Loyal Work in Missouri," *North American Review*, 98 (April 1864): 519–30.
55. Frank Blair to Montgomery Blair, August 29, 1861, Blair Papers.
56. Frank Blair to Montgomery Blair, August 29, September 1, 1861; Montgomery Blair to W. O. Bartlett, August 24, 1861; Montgomery Blair to Abraham Lincoln, September 2, 1861, all in Blair Papers.
57. John Frémont, "In Command in Missouri," 286. Jessie gave John full credit for the emancipation decree. According to her account in "Great Events," 252, he had "thought out and written" the decree in the early morning hours of August 30, 1861, but before publishing it, read it to her and aide Edward Davis, a Philadelphia Quaker who was the son-in-law of Lucretia Mott.
58. Charles A. Jellison, *Fessenden of Maine* (Syracuse: Syracuse University Press, 1962), 138.
59. For the text of John Frémont's decree, Lincoln's September 2 response, and Frémont's September 8 reply, see *Official Records*, ser. 1, III, 466–67, 469–70, 477–79.
60. Jessie Frémont and F. P. Frémont, "Great Events," 269.
61. Ibid. Jessie Frémont wrote three essentially similar accounts of the Lincoln meeting: a brief account in June 1888; a second fuller version dated April 10, 1890; and a third comprehensive account, written in 1891 as part of "Great Events," 269–72. All three accounts are in the Frémont Papers (Bancroft Library). The third account also appears in Herr and Spence, *Letters*, 264–69.
62. Herr and Spence, *Letters*, 265–66.
63. Ibid., 266.
64. Quoted in John Hay, *Lincoln and the Civil War in the Diaries and Letters of John Hay*, ed. Tyler Dennett (New York: Dodd, Mead, 1939), 133.
65. Quoted in Catherine Coffin Phillips, *Jessie Benton Frémont: A Woman Who Made History* (San Francisco: John Henry Nash, 1935), 253.
66. See John G. Nicolay and John Hay, *Abraham Lincoln: A History*, 10 vols. (New York: Century, 1890), IV, 415; and also, for example, Mary Elizabeth Massey, *Bonnet Brigades* (New York: Alfred A. Knopf, 1966), 167; Nevins, *Frémont*, 515–20; James G. Randall, *Lincoln the President*, 4 vols. (New York: Dodd, Mead, 1945–55), II, 20; and T. Harry Williams, *Lincoln and His Generals* (New York: Alfred A. Knopf, 1952), 37–38.
67. Jessie Frémont and F. P. Frémont, "Great Events," 272.
68. Blair's words quoted by Elizabeth Blair Lee to S. Phillips Lee, September 17, 1861, in Laas, *Wartime Washington*, 79.
69. Elizabeth Blair Lee to Francis Preston Blair, September 15, 27, 1861, Blair Papers.
70. Jessie Frémont to John Frémont, [September 11? 1861], Herr and Spence, *Letters*, 269.
71. Montgomery Blair to Frank Blair, September 27, 1861, Blair Papers.
72. Montgomery Blair to W. O. Bartlett, September 26, 1861, Blair Papers.
73. Elizabeth Blair Lee to S. Phillips Lee, October 14, 1861, Laas, *Wartime Washington*, 85.
74. Julian Kune, *Reminiscences of an Octogenarian Hungarian Exile* (Chicago: privately printed, 1911), 111.
75. Montgomery Blair to W. O. Bartlett, September 26, 1861, Blair Papers.
76. [S. S.?] to Montgomery Blair, September 3, 1861, Blair Papers.
77. Barton Bates to Edward Bates, October 10, 1861, Bates Papers (Missouri Historical Society, St. Louis).

78. John Frémont may well have been using opium at this time. Certainly the rumor had spread among the Blair set, for it is mentioned by Elizabeth Blair Lee as well as Blair associate Barton Bates, who called Frémont an "opium eater," and is implied by Governor Hamilton Gamble of Missouri, who found Frémont oddly "silent and apparently abstracted" during this period. See Laas, *Wartime Washington*, 88, 90, n.; Bates Diary, 217, Bates Papers; Wilbert Henry Rosin, *Hamilton Rowan Gamble, Missouri's Civil War Governor* (Ph.D. dissertation, University of Missouri, 1960 [Ann Arbor: University Microfilms, 1969]), 215–16. Opium was used by soldiers during the Civil War to steady their nerves and control their bowels; see David W. Blight, "No Desperate Hero: Manhood and Freedom in a Union Soldier's Experience," in Clinton and Silber, eds., *Divided Houses*, 66.

There is no evidence, however, that Frémont used opium after this period; he was also, throughout his life, a moderate drinker.

79. Jessie Frémont to Sydney Howard Gay, June 21, [1862], Herr and Spence, *Letters*, 329.
80. See especially her letters to Frederick Billings and Isaac Sherman in Herr and Spence, *Letters*, 272–83, 293–97.
81. See, for example, *New York Tribune*, October 17, 1861, which repeats Jessie Frémont's mid-October complaints to political operative Isaac Sherman.
82. Albert D. Richardson, *The Secret Service, the Field, the Dungeon, and the Escape* (Hartford: American Publishing, 1865), 195.
83. Francis Preston Blair to Isaac Sherman, February 7, 1861, Blair Papers.
84. "R" to Jessie Frémont, October 10, 1861, quoted in Jessie Frémont, *Guard*, 83.
85. John Frémont, "In Command in Missouri," 287.
86. Jessie Frémont to Frederick Billings, October 15, [1861], Billings Mansion Archives.
87. Jessie Frémont, *The Story of the Guard*, 88–89.
88. John Frémont's letters are quoted in Jessie Frémont, *The Story of the Guard*, 75, 88, 91, 110.
89. Jessie Frémont, *The Story of the Guard*, 74–75, 85.
90. John Frémont to Jessie Frémont, October [14?], 1861, author's copy.
91. Jessie Frémont, *The Story of the Guard*, 87–88.
92. Ruhl J. Bartlett, *John C. Frémont and the Republican Party* (1930; reprint, New York: Da Capo Press, 1970), 79.
93. Jessie Frémont to Frederick Billings, October 18, [1861], Herr and Spence, *Letters*, 282.
94. Jessie Frémont, *The Story of the Guard*, 202.
95. Jessie Frémont to James T. Fields, January 19, 1862, Fields Papers (Huntington Library, San Marino, California).
96. Ibid.
97. Jessie Frémont to James T. Fields, [October 8, 1862], Herr and Spence, *Letters*, 334.
98. Jessie Frémont, *The Story of the Guard*, xii.
99. *Atlantic Monthly*, 11 (1863): 143. Of course, it had been Jessie Frémont who held the pen when the Frémonts collaborated on the narrative of the Rocky Mountain expedition (the first report).
100. *Hesperian*, 9 (1863): 636.
101. Mrs. John A. Kasson, "An Iowa Woman in Washington, D.C., 1861–65," *Iowa Journal of History*, 52 (1954): 65.
102. U.S. Congress, House, *Report of the Joint Committee on the Conduct of the War*, 37th Cong. 3d sess., pt. 3 (Washington, DC: U.S. Government Printing Office, 1863), 6.
103. Elizabeth M. Davis to Lydia Brown, November 5, 1861, typescript, 1390, Henry Kirke Brown Papers.
104. Lydia Maria Child to Lucy Searle, October 11, 1861; and to Mary Stearns, December 15, 1861, Meltzer and Holland, *Lydia Maria Child*, 396, 400.
105. Rutherford B. Hayes, *Diary and Letters of Rutherford Birchard Hayes*, ed. Charles R. Williams, 2 vols. (Columbus: Ohio State Archaeological and Historical Society, 1922), II, 206.
106. Jessie Frémont to Thomas Starr King, March 10, [1862], King Papers (Society of California Pioneers, San Francisco).
107. Jessie Frémont to Frederick Billings, April 18, 1862, Herr and Spence, *Letters*, 317.
108. Jessie Frémont to George Julian, May 1, 1862, Herr and Spence, *Letters*, 320. Despite

Jessie's threat, New York Congressman Moses Fowler Odell, an antagonistic member of the Committee on the Conduct of the War, was reelected. The *New York Herald* strongly opposed emancipation; in a recent speech in Cincinnati, Wendell Phillips had been threatened by an antiabolitionist mob.

109. Jessie Frémont to Frederick Billings, May 7, [1862]. Herr and Spence, *Letters*, 323.
110. Jessie Frémont to Sydney Howard Gay, June 21, [1862], Herr and Spence, *Letters*, 328.
111. Jessie Frémont to Annie Adams Fields, May 29, [1862], Herr and Spence, *Letters*, 325.
112. Jessie Frémont to Sydney Howard Gay, June 21, [1862], Herr and Spence, *Letters*, 329.
113. John Frémont to Frederick Billings, June 13, 1862, Billings Mansion Archives.
114. Note to Jessie Frémont in John Frémont to Frank Frémont, May 26, 1862, Frémont Papers (Huntington Library).
115. J. Cutler Andrews, *The North Reports the Civil War* (Pittsburgh: University of Pittsburgh Press, 1955), 259.
116. Carl Schurz, *Reminiscences*, II, 344.
117. Davis, *Bits*, 180.
118. Lucretia Mott to Martha Wright et al., August 1, 1862, Osborne Family Papers, Syracuse.
119. Jessie Frémont to John T. Fiala, July 10, [1863], Herr and Spence, *Letters*, 354.
120. The day after John Frémont's withdrawal, Lincoln removed Montgomery Blair from the cabinet. The deal had been arranged by intermediaries between Lincoln and the Radical Republicans, who opposed Blair because of his softness toward slavery, including opposition in the cabinet to Lincoln's Emancipation Proclamation. John Frémont never admitted involvement, stating that he had resigned for the good of the party and to prevent the election of George B. McClellan, but clearly Blair's removal satisfied the Frémonts personally as well. See Nevins, *Frémont*, 578–82, 659–61; and Jessie Frémont's account of the arrangement in Herr and Spence, *Letters*, 487–89, 548–50.
121. *New York Times*, July 2, 1864.
122. See Jessie Frémont to Susan B. Anthony, April 22, [1866], Herr and Spence, *Letters*, 395–96.
123. Gossip and some evidence suggest that John Frémont was involved in extramarital affairs after the Civil War. In 1869, in Paris, for example, Frémont conducted a serious flirtation, if not clearly a sexual affair, with the young, unmarried American sculptor, Vinnie Ream. See Herr *Jessie Benton Frémont*, 388–90.
124. Charley eventually achieved the rank of admiral and served as commander of Boston Navy Yard. Frank, who left West Point before graduation due to illness, nonetheless pursued an army career; however, after his parents' deaths, he was court-martialed three times for financial irregularities and ultimately dismissed from the army for insubordination. On Frank's difficulties, see *New York Times*, January 4 and March 25, 1909.
125. Jessie Frémont, "The Deck Hand," in *The Will and the Way Stories* (Boston: D. Lothrop, 1891).
126. Hayes, who had supported John Frémont ardently in 1856 and served briefly under him in the Civil War, was responsive to the Frémonts' appeal for a federal appointment for John Frémont and to the urging of Republicans like Senator Zachariah Chandler of Michigan, who believed that Frémont deserved some compensation for his 1864 withdrawal as a presidential candidate opposing Lincoln, "for the good of the party." For details, see John Frémont to Zachariah Chandler, May 23, 1878, Chandler Papers (Library of Congress); and Herr, *Jessie Benton Frémont*, 400–401.
127. For details of the Frémonts' Arizona period, and particularly their financial activities, see Herr and Spence, *Letters*, 437–92.
128. Jessie Frémont to John Greenleaf Whittier, [January 21–22, 1880], Herr and Spence, *Letters*, 481.
129. Howard Shaff and Audrey Karl Shaff, *Six Wars at a Time: The Life and Times of Gutzon Borglum, Sculptor of Mount Rushmore* (Sioux Falls, SD: Center for Western Studies, Augustana College, 1985), 33–34.
130. John Frémont, "Recrossing the Rocky Mountains, After Many Years," typescript, Frémont Papers (Bancroft Library).
131. Jessie Frémont describes her reactions to the poem in a letter to John Greenleaf Whittier, [January 21–22, 1880], Herr and Spence, *Letters*, 479–82.

132. Elizabeth Blair Lee to Samual Phillips Lee, July 21, 1883, Blair-Lee Papers (Princeton). This revealing unpublished letter about the Frémonts' relationship was generously brought to my attention by Virginia Jeans Laas in 1986.

133. Jessie Frémont to Elizabeth Blair Lee, July 29, [1883], Herr and Spence, *Letters*, 498.

134. Jessie Frémont to John Greenleaf Whittier, November 19, 1889, New-York Historical Society.

135. Jessie Frémont to John Gutzon Borglum, January 17, 1891 [92], Herr and Spence, *Letters*, 545.

CHAPTER TWELVE

1. For details of their courtship, see chapter 5 of Dudley Taylor Cornish and Virginia Jeans Laas, *Lincoln's Lee: The Life of Samuel Phillips Lee, United States Navy, 1812–1897* (Lawrence: University Press of Kansas, 1986), 39–53; and Virginia J. Laas, "The Courtship and Marriage of Elizabeth Blair and Samuel Phillips Lee: A Problem in Historical Detection," *The Midwest Quarterly*, 27 (Autumn, 1985): 13–29.

2. Quoted in Elizabeth Blair to S. P. Lee, April 20, 1843. The family correspondence is part of the rich collection of Blair-Lee Papers located in Harvey Firestone Library, Princeton University.

3. For Blair family history, see E. B. Smith, *Francis Preston Blair* (New York: The Free Press, 1980), and William E. Smith, *The Francis Preston Blair Family in Politics*, 2 vols. (New York: Macmillan, 1933).

4. Charles Wilkes (1798–1877) led the United States Exploring Expedition of six vessels that explored the coast of Antarctica, islands in the Pacific, and the northwest coast of America from August 1838 to July 1842. The expedition was fraught with dissension and on its return, a court-martial board publicly reprimanded Wilkes for his illegal punishment of some of his men. For a thorough discussion of Wilkes's command difficulties, see William Stanton, *The Great United States Exploring Expedition of 1838–1842* (Berkeley: University of California Press, 1975), 96ff.

5. Long courtships filled with conflict and turmoil were not uncommon in the period. See Karen Lystra, *Searching the Heart: Women, Men, and Romantic Love in Nineteenth-Century America* (New York: Oxford University Press, 1989) and Ellen Rothman, *Hands and Hearts: A History of Courtship in America* (New York: Basic Books, 1984).

6. Elizabeth Blair to Samuel Phillips Lee, Christmas Day 1842.

7. S. P. Lee to Elizabeth Blair, December 26–27, 1842.

8. Quoted in E. B. Lee to S. P. Lee, October 7, 18, 1843.

9. Repeated in undated letter, E. Blair to S. P. Lee, received April 20, 1843.

10. Naval scientist Matthew Maury (1806–1873) was superintendent of the Depot of Charts and Instruments of the Navy Department, a position that included the superintendency of the Naval Observatory. His work on wind and current charts of both the Atlantic and Pacific oceans dramatically improved sailing times from New York to San Francisco. In 1855 he published the first modern text on oceanography. See Francis Leigh Williams, *Matthew Fontaine Maury: Scientist of the Seas* (New Brunswick, NJ: Rutgers University Press, 1963). S. P. Lee's account of his work was *Reports and Charts of the Cruise of the U.S. Brig Dolphin, Made under Direction of the Navy Department* (Washington, DC: Beverly Tucker, Printer to the Senate, 1854).

11. Elizabeth Blair Lee to Samuel Phillips Lee, July 12, 1844.

12. S. P. Lee to E. B. Lee, October 31, 1843; June 26, 1844.

13. Ibid., April 27, 1847.

14. For an excellent discussion of the importance to nineteenth-century men of providing for their families, see E. Anthony Rotundo, *American Manhood: Transformations in Masculinity from the Revolution to the Modern Era* (New York: Basic Books, 1993), especially 174–178.

15. In 1849, Lee began to buy property in St. Louis: houses, lots, and warehouses along the river. By 1859, he had purchased twenty-nine pieces of property in the city. He also owned property in Morgan County, Ohio, and Henry County, Kentucky, along with

various railroad and bank stocks. Lee business papers and John F. Lee to S. P. Lee, October 29, 1858, Blair-Lee Papers (Princeton University Library). Lee's prolonged absences were not uncommon for nineteenth-century men. See Rotundo, *American Manhood*, 146–50.

16. Elizabeth Blair Lee to Samuel Phillips Lee, October 31, 1855.

17. Ibid., November 13, 1855.

18. For an excellent discussion of the marital expectations of Victorian men and women, see Anne C. Rose, *Victorian America and the Civil War* (London and New York: Cambridge University Press, 1992), 145–192. For analysis of the idea of domesticity, see Barbara Welter, "The Cult of True Womanhood, 1820–1860," *American Quarterly* (Summer 1966): 151–74; Nancy Cott, *The Bonds of Womanhood: "Woman's Sphere" in New England, 1780–1835* (New Haven: Yale University Press, 1977); Carroll Smith-Rosenberg, *Disorderly Conduct: Visions of Gender in Victorian America* (New York: Oxford University Press, 1985); Mary Ryan, *Cradle of the Middle Class: The Family in Oneida County, New York, 1790–1865* (Cambridge: Cambridge University Press, 1981); and Ann Douglas, *The Feminization of American Culture* (New York: Avon Books, 1978).

19. Elizabeth Blair Lee to Samuel Phillips Lee, December 2, 13, 1855.

20. Ibid., September 23, 1858.

21. Ibid., November 18, 1858.

22. Log of *Vandalia*, Record Group 24: Records of the Bureau of Naval Personnel, National Archives, Washington, D.C.

23. Elizabeth Blair Lee to Samuel Phillips Lee, April 10, 1862, *Wartime Washington: The Civil War Letters of Elizabeth Blair Lee*, ed. Virginia Jeans Laas (Urbana: University of Illinois Press, 1991), 126. After the war, Lee gave money to many of his southern relatives. Family lore maintains that he gave half of his prize money to them. Cornish and Laas, *Lincoln's Lee*, 164–65.

24. E. B. Lee to S. P. Lee, May 18, 1862, in Laas, *Wartime Washington*, 148.

25. Her letters are essential to the reconstruction of their life; unfortunately, very few of his letters from the war period have survived.

26. Elizabeth Blair Lee to Samuel Phillips Lee, September 16, 1862, in Laas, *Wartime Washington*, 182.

27. Ibid., December 29, 1860, in Laas, *Wartime Washington*, 24n.8.

28. In his hypersensitivity, Lee was typical of naval officers of the period. See David F. Long, "The Navy under the Board of Navy Commissioners, 1815–1842," in *In Peace and War: Interpretations of American Naval History, 1775–1978*, ed. Kenneth J. Hagan, *Contributions in Military History* no. 16 (Westport, CT: Greenwood Press, 1978), 63–78.

29. Elizabeth Blair Lee to Samuel Phillips Lee, August 2, 1844.

30. For evidence of Eliza's strong character, see E. B. Smith, *Francis Preston Blair*, 8, 50, 310.

31. Ibid., November 28, 1858.

32. Her efforts in attempting to advance her husband's career were part of a well-established tradition for upper-class women, both North and South. Other examples can be found in Jean Baker, *Mary Todd Lincoln: A Biography* (New York: W. W. Norton, 1987); Pamela Herr, *Jessie Benton Frémont: A Biography* (New York: Franklin Watts, 1987); and C. Vann Woodward, ed., *Mary Chesnut's Civil War* (New Haven: Yale University Press, 1981).

33. Elizabeth Blair Lee to Samuel Phillips Lee, August 10, 1861.

34. E. B. Lee to S. P. Lee, June 28, 1861, in Laas, *Wartime Washington*, 54. Pennsylvanian Simon Cameron was Lincoln's secretary of war. William Sprague was Republican governor of Rhode Island. Major General John C. Frémont, son-in-law of Blair's friend Thomas Hart Benton, was in town to confer with Lincoln before assuming his command in Missouri.

35. Ibid., June 10, 1861, 45.

36. Ibid., July 6, 1861, 58.

37. Gideon Welles to S. P. Lee, January 20 and February 10, 1862, Blair-Lee Papers.

38. D. D. Porter to G. V. Fox, June 2, 1862, in Gustavus Vasa Fox, *Confidential Correspondence of Gustavus Vasa Fox, Assistant Secretary of the Navy, 1861–1865*, ed. Robert Means Thompson and Richard Wainwright, 2 vols. (New York: Devinne Press, for the Naval History Society, 1918), II, 114–15.

39. Elizabeth Blair Lee to Samuel Phillips Lee, April 15 and 24, 1862, in Laas, *Wartime Washington*, 128, 132.

40. Gideon Welles, *Diary of Gideon Welles, Secretary of the Navy under Lincoln and Johnson*, ed. Howard K. Beale, 3 vols. (New York: W. W. Norton & Co., 1960), May 16, 1866, II, 504.

41. Log of USS *Minnesota*, *Official Records of the Union and Confederate Navies in the War of the Rebellion*, 30 vols., series 1 (Washington, DC: U.S. Government Printing Office, 1894–1922), VIII, 3.

42. Elizabeth Blair Lee to Samuel Phillips Lee, August 23, 1864, in Laas, *Wartime Washington*, 410.

43. Ibid., July 26, 1864, 410.

44. Ibid., March 5, 1863, 249. For Jessie Frémont's confrontation with Lincoln, see Herr, *Jessie Benton Frémont*, 337–341.

45. Elizabeth Blair Lee to Samuel Phillips Lee, February 1, 1865, in Laas, *Wartime Washington*, 471.

46. Ibid., February 11, 1865, 475. Among those she had talked to were President Lincoln; Secretary of the Navy Welles; Montgomery's brother-in-law, Assistant Secretary of the Navy Gustavus Fox; Secretary of State William Seward; Secretary of War Edwin Stanton; Postmaster General William Dennison, who had replaced Montgomery in that position; Senators John Sherman of Ohio, Charles Sumner of Massachusetts; Preston Ken of New York, James Doolittle of Wisconsin, and Lyman Trumbull of Illinois; and Congressmen Moses Odell of New York, Dwight Townsend of New York, and James Brown of Wisconsin.

47. Ibid., August 12, 1863, 299.

48. Ibid., February 12, 1864, 348.

49. Ibid., March 27, April 14, 15, 1865, 488, 494, 495.

50. Evy Alexander to S. P. Lee, June 1, 1865; Dr. John F. Clary to S. P. Lee, June 3, 1865, Blair-Lee Papers; E. B. Lee to S. P. Lee, June 5, 9, 13, 14, 1865. Although Phil had applied for leave, his request had been denied. Percival Drayton to S. P. Lee, June 17, 1865, *Official Record of the Navies*, XVII, 27.

51. For a discussion of the role of benevolent work in women's lives, see Anne M. Boylan, "Women in Groups: An Analysis of Women's Benevolent Organizations in New York and Boston, 1797–1840," *Journal of American History*, 71 (December 1984): 497–523, and Lori Ginzberg, *Women and the Work of Benevolence: Morality, Politics, and Class in the Nineteenth-Century United States* (New Haven: Yale University Press, 1990).

52. On her Orphan Asylum activities, see, for example, Elizabeth Blair Lee to Samuel Phillips Lee, April 11, May 6, October 10, 1862; April 14, 1863; September 9, 1864. See Laas, *Wartime Washington*, 127, 138, 190, 258n.2, 427.

53. Ibid., February 7, 1865, 474.

54. Ibid., August 9, 1863, 296.

55. Ibid., May 1, 1862, 129n.2.

56. Ibid., January 29, 1862, 97.

57. Ibid., March 31, [1864], 361–62.

58. Ibid., March 5, 1863, 249.

59. For explanation of blockading practices and prize court procedures, see Virginia J. Laas, " 'Sleepless Sentinels': The North Atlantic Blockading Squadron, 1862–1864," *Civil War History*, 31 (March 1985): 24–38.

60. Elizabeth Blair Lee to Samuel Phillips Lee, June 25, 1861, in Laas, *Wartime Washington*, 52.

61. Lee received at least $126,000 in prize money. For an explanation of the intricacies of prize money payment, see Cornish and Laas, *Lincoln's Lee*, 123, and note 87, page 215.

62. "Documents of His Official Appointments in the United States Navy," Blair-Lee Papers.

63. Welles to S. P. Lee, July 19, 1864, *Official Records of the Navies*, X, 284.

64. Gideon Welles Diary, 2:161.

65. E. B. Smith, *Francis Preston Blair*, 331–349.

66. Francis Preston Blair to S. P. Lee, September 27, 1864.

67. Elizabeth Blair Lee to Samuel Phillips Lee, August 9, 1861, in Laas, *Wartime Washington*, 73n.7.
68. S. P. Lee to E. B. Lee, February 6, 1872.
69. Ibid., March 21, 1871.
70. Ibid., December 3, 1870, and August 11, 1871.
71. E. B. Lee to S. P. Lee, November 14, 1870.
72. Ibid., May 26, 1871.
73. S. P. Lee to E. B. Lee, February 29 and 2, 1872.
74. E. B. Lee to S. P. Lee, February 16, 1872.
75. S. P. Lee to Blair Lee, August 9, 1871.
76. S. P. Lee to Blair Lee, February 1, 1872.
77. In Francis Preston Blair's final will, he provided for the distribution of his property among his children. Although he had originally planned to leave Silver Spring to Frank, he changed the bequest at Frank's request. According to the terms of Blair's will, Elizabeth received Silver Spring and the Lees were to pay Frank $20,000. E. B. Smith, *Francis Preston Blair*, 438–39; Cornish and Laas, *Lincoln's Lee*, 176–77.
78. Elizabeth Blair Lee to Samuel Phillips Lee, January 8, 1879.
79. Log of Silver Spring Farm, Blair-Lee Papers (Princeton University).
80. Ibid., April 27, 1877, Blair-Lee Papers.
81. Elizabeth Blair Lee to Samuel Phillips Lee, August 1, 1894.
82. E. B. Lee to S. P. Lee, August 9, 1863, in Laas, *Wartime Washington*, 296.

AUTHORS' BIOGRAPHIES

Carol K. Bleser is the Kathryn and Calhoun Lemon Distinguished Professor of History Emeritus at Clemson University. A specialist in southern history, Professor Bleser has published *Tokens of Affection: The Letters of a Planter's Daughter in the Old South* (University of Georgia Press, 1996), *In Joy and in Sorrow: Women, Family, and Marriage in the Victorian South* (Oxford University Press, 1991), *Secret and Sacred: The Diaries of James Henry Hammond, a Southern Slaveholder* (Oxford University Press, 1988), *The Hammonds of Redcliffe* (Oxford University Press, 1981), and *The Promised Land: The History of the South Carolina Land Commission, 1869–1890* (University of South Carolina Press, 1969). She was president of the Southern Historical Association in 1998 and is currently the general editor of the University of South Carolina's series *Southern Women's Letters, Diaries, and Writings, 1700 to the Present*. Thus far, fourteen volumes have been published. Professor Bleser is presently at work on a study on southern women in the twenty-first century. Carol Bleser is both a contributor of an essay and the coeditor of this volume.

Peter S. Carmichael is assistant professor of history at the University of North Carolina at Greensboro. He is the author of *Lee's Young Artillerist: William R. J. Pegram* (University Press of Virginia, 1995). His forthcoming book focuses on a religious revival that changed ideas about masculinity among young Virginian slaveholders during the 1850s.

Sarah E. Gardner is assistant professor of history at Mercer University. She has received numerous awards for her work, including grants from Duke University, the American Historical Association, and the Mellon Foundation. She is currently working on a manuscript on white southern women's narratives of the Civil War, 1861–1937.

Lesley J. Gordon is associate professor of history at the University of Akron. She is author of *General George E. Pickett in Life and Legend* (University of North Carolina Press, 1998). Currently she is writing a book-length study of a northern Civil War regiment and their changing memory of war and captivity. Lesley Gordon is both a contributor of an essay and the coeditor of this volume.

Pamela Herr is an independent writer/historian living in Palo Alto, California. She is the author of *Jessie Benton Frémont* (Franklin Watts, 1987) and coeditor with Mary Lee Spence of *The Letters of Jessie Benton Frémont* (University of Illinois Press, 1993).

Virginia Jeans Laas is associate professor of history at Missouri Southern State College. She is coauthor of *Lincoln's Lee: The Life of Samuel Phillips Lee* (University Press of Kansas, 1986), editor of *Wartime Washington: The Civil War Letters of Elizabeth Blair Lee* (University of Illinois Press, 1991), and author of *Love and Power in the Nineteenth Century: Violet Blair's Marriage* (University of Arkansas Press, 1998). Her most recent publication is *Bridging Two Eras: The Autobiography of Emily Newell Blair, 1877–1951* (University of Missouri Press, 1999).

Shirley A. Leckie is professor of history at the University of Central Florida in Orlando, Florida. She is the coauthor of *Unlikely Warriors: General Benjamin Grierson and His Family* (University of Oklahoma Press, 1984); editor of *The Colonel's Lady on the Western Frontier: The Correspondence of Alice Kirk Grierson* (University of Nebraska Press, 1989); and author of *Elizabeth Bacon Custer and the Making of a Myth* (University of Oklahoma Press, 1993), winner of the 1993 Evans Biography Award and the 1993 Julian J. Rothbaum Prize. Her latest work, *Angie Debo, Pioneering Historian*, was published by the University of Oklahoma Press in 2000.

John F. Marszalek is William L. Giles Distinguished Professor of History, Mississippi State University. He has written or edited ten books and numerous articles, including two books on William T. Sherman and the *Diary of Miss Emma Holmes, 1861–1866*. His latest book is the *Petticoat Affair: Manners, Mutiny and Sex in Andrew Jackson's White House*. He is currently working on a biography of Union General Henry W. Halleck.

John Y. Simon is professor of history at Southern Illinois University and executive director of the Ulysses S. Grant Association. He has edited twenty-four volumes of *The Papers of Ulysses S. Grant* and also *The Personal Memoirs of Julia Dent Grant*.

Jennifer Lund Smith teaches at North Georgia College and State University in Dahlonega, Georgia. Her research, publications, and presentations have focused on the Civil War era, and the African American experience during Reconstruction.

Emory M. Thomas is Regents Professor of History at the University of Georgia. His many publications include *Robert E. Lee: A Biography* (W. W. Norton, 1995) and *Robert E. Lee: An Album* (W. W. Norton, 2000).

Sarah Woolfolk Wiggins taught at the University of Alabama, 1961–1995, and edited *The Alabama Review*, 1976–1996. She is the author of *The Scalawag in Alabama Politics, 1865–1881* (University of Alabama Press, 1977) and editor of *The Journals of Josiah Gorgas 1857–1878* (University of Alabama Press, 1995).